anarchism in
latin america

ÁNGEL J. CAPPELLETTI

Praise for *Anarchism in Latin America*

"The idea of 'utopia' was engendered by the European discovery of the Americas, and the continent has continued to be a site for alternative possibilities since then. Ángel Cappelletti's book is an informative and uniquely handy work of reference." —**Claudio Lomnitz, author of** *The Return of Comrade Flores Magón*

"Progressives have long looked to Latin America for models of resistance and alternative political structures. However, we tend to see these models in a Marxist light. *Anarchism in Latin America* provides an important corrective, recounting the anarchist historical roots of some of the most important movements of our time." —**Todd May, author of** *A Fragile Life: Accepting Our Vulnerability*

"For the first time, English-language audiences have access to Ángel Cappelletti's *Anarchism in Latin America*, one of the historiographical cornerstones of Latin American anarchism. While the study of anarchism has exploded since Cappelletti originally published his work in 1990, his book remains an invaluable introduction to the hemispheric history of anarchism in Latin America. Gabriel Palmer-Fernández's clear, skilled, and lucid translation includes an insightful introduction by modern scholar-activists that updates Cappelletti by expanding our understanding of how anarchists have dealt with feminist, environmental, and indigenous issues. This is a welcomed and timely book as anarchist ideas and movements once again surge throughout the Americas." —**Kirwin Shaffer, author of** *Black Flag Boricuas: Anarchism, Antiauthoritarianism, and the Left in Puerto Rico, 1897–1921*

"My feeling is that movements around the world and specifically in the United States require a melding, a synthesis of anarchism and Marxism. This necessary project has been richly explored in Latin America but little of that exploration has been reported in El Norte. This book will introduce American readers to the extraordinary history of anarchism among our southern neighbors." —**Staughton Lynd, co-author of** *Wobblies and Zapatistas: Conversations on Anarchism, Marxism, and Radical History*

anarchism in latin america

ÁNGEL J. CAPPELLETTI

TRANSLATED BY GABRIEL PALMER-FERNÁNDEZ

INTRODUCTION BY ROMINA AKEMI & JAVIER SETHNESS-CASTRO

Anarchism in Latin America, by Ángel Cappelletti
© 2017 Andrés Cappelletti
Translation © 2017 Gabriel Palmer-Fernández
Introduction © Akemi and Sethness-Castro
This edition © 2017 AK Press (Chico, Oakland, Edinburgh, Baltimore)

ISBN: 978-1-84935-282-6
E-ISBN: 978-1-84935-283-3
Library of Congress Control Number: 2017936242

AK Press   AK Press
370 Ryan Ave. #100   33 Tower St.
Chico, CA 95973   Edinburgh EH6 7BN
USA   Scotland
www.akpress.org   www.akuk.com
akpress@akpress.org   ak@akedin.demon.co.uk

The above addresses would be delighted to provide you with the latest AK Press distribution catalog, which features books, pamphlets, zines, and stylish apparel published and/or distributed by AK Press. Alternatively, visit our websites for the complete catalog, latest news, and secure ordering.

Cover illustration by Mazatl, www.justseeds.org
Printed in the USA on recycled paper

Table of Contents

Translator's Acknowledgments

The publication of this translation would not have been possible without the good and dedicated work of Zach Blue and AK Press. Zach showed a keen interest in this project from its beginning. When we encountered what seemed to be an insurmountable hurdle thrown in our path by the bureaucracy of a State, he found a way for us to overcome it. I am indebted to Romina Akemi and Javier Sethness-Castro for accepting Zach's invitation to write the Introduction to this volume. I am very grateful for the talented editorial hands first of Molly Toth, of Youngstown, Ohio, and then of Emma Young, of Bloomington, Indiana. My home institution, Youngstown State University, provided me with a Research Professorship to complete this project. I am most grateful—and grateful everyday—for the kindness, friendship, and love of my wife, Sarah V. Lown. These simple words of thanks to them leave much unsaid.

Ángel Cappelletti, Biographical Note

Ángel Cappelletti was born in 1927 and died in 1995 in Rosario, Argentina. This industrial port city was a major center of anarchist activities beginning in the late 19th century, when Italian immigrants formed a group called El Miserable. A little later, the anarcho-communist group Ciencia y Progreso was formed in Rosario, and the Italian anarchist paper *Demoliamo*, as well as the anarcho-feminist *La Voz de la Mujer*, edited by Virginia Bolten, were published there. In 1890 Bolten headed the first march ever held in Rosario to mark the 1st of May. She carried a red flag with this inscription in black: "First of May. Universal Brotherhood. We, the workers of Rosario, abide by the dispositions of the International Labour Committee in Paris." Other anarchist papers published in Rosario at this time were *La Verdad* (1896), *La Libre Iniciativa* (1895–1896), *La Federación Obrera* (1896), and *La Libera Parola*. There were also general strikes in 1901 and 1907, as well as repression, persecution, and execution of militants. Ernesto "Che" Guevara would be born in Rosario in 1928.

Cappelletti received a doctorate in philosophy from the University of Buenos Aires in 1954 and for the next twenty-seven years taught the history of philosophy, logic, sociology, Latin, Greek, and the history of political ideas at the Universidades de Cuyo y Litoral, Argentina, Universidad de Montevideo, Uruguay, and the Universidad Central y Simón Bolivar de Caracas, Venezuela. He is the author or editor of 40 books, including *Utopías antiguas y modernas* (Puebla, 1967), *Abelardo* (Buenos Aires, 1967), *El Socialismo utópico* (Rosario, 1968), *Marco Aurelio* (Buenos Aires 1968), *La filosofía de Heráclito de Efeso* (Caracas, 1969), *Introdución a Séneca* (Caracas, 1973), *Introdución a Condillac* (Maracaibo, 1974), *Cuatro filósofos de la Alta Edad Media* (Mérida, 1975), *Etapas del pensamiento socialista* (Madrid, 1978), *El pensamiento de Kropotkin* (Madrid, 1978), *Ensayos sobre los atomistas griegos* (Caracas, 1979), *La teoría de la propieded en Proudhon* (Madrid, 1980), *Ciencia jónica y pitagórica* (Caracas, 1980), *Prehistoria del Anarquismo* (Madrid, 1983), *La filosofía de Anaxágoras* (Caracas, 1984).

The present translation originally appeared as a Preface by Cappelletti to a volume of previously published anarchist writings by Latin American authors. The volume was conceived and begun by Carlos Manuel Rama. At the time of his death in 1982, Rama had completed an initial selection of the material. Cappelletti would conclude the project several years later.[1] The volume was scheduled to appear in 1990 through the Venezuelan publisher Biblioteca Ayacucho. But due to several complications it did not appear in print until 1993. Rama was a Uruguayan historian and sociologist. Among his publications are: *Historia del movimiento obrero y social latinoamericano contemporáneo* (1967), *Sociología de América Latina* (1970), *Las ideas socialistas en el siglo XIX* (1976), *Sociología de América Latina* (1977), and *La ideología fascista* (1979), among others.

—Gabriel Palmer-Fernández

---

[1]   See Appendix B for the entire selection.

Abbreviations

ACAT	*Asociación Continental Americana de Trabajadores*
AFL	American Federation of Labor
AIT	*Asociación Internacional de Trabajadores* (International Workers' Association, IWA)
ALU	*Acción Libertaria Uruguaya*
APRA	*Alianza Popular Revolucionaria Americana* (Peru)
CGS	*Centro Gremial Sindicalista* (Ecuador)
CGT	*Confederación General del Trabajo* (Argentina)
CGT	*Confederación General de Trabajadores* (Chile, also Mexico)
COA	*Confederación Obrera Argentina* (Workers Confederation of Argentina)
COB	*Confederación Obrera Brasileña*
CORA	*Confederación Obrera Regional Argentina*
CNT	*Confederación Nacional del Trabajo* (National Confederation of Labor)
CROM	*Confederación Regional Obrera Mexicana*
CRRA	*Comité Regional de Relaciones Anarquistas* (Regional Committee of Anarchist Relations)
CTCH	*Confederación de Trabajadores de Chile*

FACA	*Federación Anarco-Comunista Argentina* (Argentinean Anarcho-Communist Federation)
FAI	*Federación Anarquista Ibérica* (Iberian Anarchist Federation)
FAU	*Federación Anarquista Uruguaya*
FCPM	*Federación Comunista del Proletariado Mexicano*
FLA	*Federación Libertaria Argentina*
FOA	*Federación Obrera Argentina*
FOCH	*Federación Obrera Chilena*
FOH	*Federación Obrera de la Habana*
FOI	*Federación Obrera Internacional* (Bolivia)
FOL	*Federación Obrera Local de la Paz* (Bolivia)
FORA	*Federación Obrera Regional Argentina* (Argentine Regional Workers Federation)
FORP	*Federación Obrera Regional Paraguaya*
FORP	*Federación Obrera Regional Peruana*
FORU	*Federación Obrera Regional Uruguaya* (Uruguayan Regional Workers' Federation)
FOT	*Federación Obrera del Trabajo* (Bolivia)
IWA	International Workers' Association
IWW	Industrial Workers of the World
PRC	*Partido Revolucionario Cubano* (Cuba).
PIT-CNT	*Plenario Intersindical de Trabajadores* and *Convención Nacional Trabajadores*
UGT	*Unión General de Trabajadores* (General Union of Workers)
USA	*Unión Sindical Argentina* (Syndicalist Union of Argentina)
USU	*Unión Sindical Uruguaya* (Syndicalist Union of Uruguay)

Preface

Anarchism emerged in Europe as an ideology and social philosophy during the first half of the nineteenth century. One of several kinds of pre-Marxist socialist thought, it was essentially a French product and owed its name and first systematic formulation to Proudhon, although it had two powerful predecessors in England and Germany, Godwin and Stirner, respectively. Prior to 1850 in France, as a social movement of the productive classes (workers, artisans, peasants), it assumed a mutualist form. Under Bakunin after the 1860s it appeared in a collectivist form and joined its activities to the First International, gradually becoming the dominant position within the movement. During these decades the majority of organized workers in Italy, France, Spain, Portugal, Switzerland, Belgium, Holland, and elsewhere either were anarchist or professed a closely related revolutionary socialism. Even trade unionism in Great Britain, though of moderate tendencies, was closer to Proudhon than to Marx.

By the 1860s anarchism reached Latin America and took root in a number of activist groups. Sections of the First International formed in the French Antilles; the ideas of Proudhon and Bakunin were disseminated throughout Mexico; and the first organizations of workers, peasants, and students with a libertarian bent were established there. In the 1870s there was a clear presence of anarchist groups on both sides of the Río de la Plata. For the next half century, anarchism enjoyed a steady even if often irregular history in many Latin American countries. It absorbed the major part of the working classes through unions and resistance societies for several decades in Argentina and Uruguay. In other countries, like Mexico, it played an important role in their political history and armed struggles. In Chile and Peru it sparked the revolutionary dimension of the working class struggle. There is no doubt that even in some countries whose later history failed to produce an organized and significant labor movement—such as Ecuador, Panama, and Guatemala—there were early workers' organizations that went beyond simple mutual aid societies and carried forward the class struggle, and they were anarchist.

Thus anarchism in Latin America has an ample history rich in struggles peaceful and violent; in demonstrations of individual and collective heroism; in organizational efforts; in oral, written, and practical propaganda; in literary works; and in theatrical, pedagogical, cooperative, and communitarian experiments. That history has not been totally documented, although a few fine partial studies are available. Moreover, many writers of the social, political, cultural, literary, and philosophical history of the continent either ignore or downplay the important role of anarchism—the result of ignorance or bad faith. Some historians do not know the achievements of anarchism or consider anarchism a marginal philosophy or totally undesirable. Others are aware of the significant role anarchism has played in the history of socialist ideas and understand its position towards Marxism well, but precisely because of that forget or belittle its role: a sign of their revolutionary immaturity, abstract utopianism, pragmatic or petty bourgeois rebelliousness.

This work does not pretend to be a comprehensive history of Latin American anarchism but simply a sketch of it. But the range of the material and the dearth of impartial studies available do prompt a sustained treatment of that history. Hence this work examines the social achievements, the popular writings, and the anarchist literature of each Latin American country from Argentina to Mexico.

As with other ideas of European origin, anarchist ideology was a product imported to Latin America. But ideas are not simply products. They are also living organisms and, as such, ought to adapt themselves to new environments; in so doing, they evolve in lesser or greater ways. To say that European immigrants brought anarchism to these shores states only the obvious. And to take that as a kind of weakness is plain stupidity. Like the very ideas of nation and of a nationalistic ideology, anarchism comes to us from Europe.

Anarchism is not merely the ideology of the working and peasant masses who, arriving in the new continent, are robbed of their hopes for a better life and witness the exchange of oppression by the ancient monarchies for the no less brutal oppression of the new republican oligarchies. Soon some of the native and also indigenous masses adopt the anarchist view of the world and society, from Mexico to Argentina, and from Francisco Zalacosta in the Chalco to Facón Grande in Patagonia. It is seldom noted that the anarchist doctrine of self-managed collectivism has a close resemblance to the ancient ways of life and organizations of the indigenous peoples of Mexico and Peru, ways of life that were practiced prior to the imperialism of not only the Spanish, but also the Aztecs and Inca before them. To the extent that anarchists reached the indigenous, they did not have to inculcate exotic ideologies but only to make conscious the ancient peasant ideologies of the Matagalpan *calpulli* and the Andean *ayllu*.[1]

At the same time, a tendency towards liberty and indifference towards all forms of statist structure was already present in the Creole population. When that tendency was not usurped by the ways of the feudal *caudillos*, it proved fertile soil for a libertarian ideology. Few mention the existence of an anarchist *gauchaje* in

---

1   In the language of the Matagalpan Indians *calpulli* refers to a group consti-
     tuting the fundamental unit of Aztec society. *Ayllus* were the basic politi-
     cal and social units of pre-Inca life (*Trans*).

Argentina and Uruguay, or its literary expression in libertarian *payadores*.[2] But those matters aside—undoubtedly they will be looked upon as having little consequence by academic and Marxist historians—without hesitation we can say that anarchism took root much more deeply and extensively among indigenous workers than did Marxism, perhaps with the exception of Chile.

It is important to note that from a theoretical perspective, even if the Latin American movement did not make fundamental contributions to anarchist thought, it did produce forms of organization and praxis that were unknown in Europe. For example, the Federación Obrera Regional Argentina (FORA), a labor union that was majoritarian (becoming almost the only union), never conceded to syndical bureaucracy, and developed an organizational form as different from the Confederación National del Trabajo (CNT) and other European anarcho-syndicalist unions as it was from the North American Industrial Workers of the World (IWW). A second example, typically Latin American, is the Partido Liberal Mexicano (PLM). Primarily through the efforts of Ricardo Flores Magón, within a few years of its founding it adopted an ideology that was unquestionably anarchist, nonetheless keeping its name while continuing as a political party, and thereby earning sharp criticism from some European orthodox thinkers like Jean Grave.

With the exception of that singular case, anarchism in Latin America is nearly always anarcho-syndicalism and is essentially linked to workers' and peasants' organizations. To be sure, there were some anarcho-individualists in Argentina, Uruguay, Panama, and other places, as well as anarcho-communists, the latter foes of the syndical organization in Buenos Aires in the 1880s and 1890s. But the vast majority of Latin American anarchists were adherents of a revolutionary and anti-political syndicalism—not, as some say, a-political. That is an important difference between Latin and North American anarchism. An anarchist syndicalism was evident

---

2   In Argentina, Uruguay, southern regions of Brazil, as well as in parts of Paraguay and Chile, a musical form accompanied by guitar (*Trans*).

in the United States and its greatest witness was the sacrifice of the Chicago martyrs. It represented the continuation of the anti-slavery movement into the industrial context, and was promoted by Italians, Germans, and Slavic immigrants, with the German Johann Most as its revolutionary prototype. Later a revolutionary syndicalism emerged (anarchist or quasi-anarchist) among the working classes, organized through the IWW. There was also an earlier movement unrelated to the working classes, represented by important literary figures such as Thoreau and Emerson. Its predecessor is found in the liberal radicalism of Jefferson and other eighteenth century thinkers, and is perhaps represented today by what is known as "libertarianism." While it was not an anti-workers' ideology— although today there are Right-libertarians—it developed along lines quite alien to the struggles of the working classes, and its principal concerns include individual human rights, anti-militarism, and the abolition of bureaucracy and the State.

But anarchism developed in different ways in the various Latin American countries. In Argentina, FORA was sufficiently radical to be considered extremist by the Spanish CNT. In Uruguay it tended to be nonviolent, as Max Nettlau notes, perhaps because it was less persecuted, except during the last dictatorship. In Mexico it influenced government not only because of Magonist participation in the revolution against Porfirio Díaz, but also because La Casa del Obrero Mundial provided Venustiano Carranza his "red battalions" in the fight against Villa and Zapata, and because the leadership of the Confederación General del Trabajo (CGT) engaged President Obregón in public political debates. In Brazil, on the other hand, it was always at the margins of the state, and the military-oligarchic republic did nothing but persecute, ostracize, or assassinate its leaders. A phenomenon common in several Latin American countries between 1918 and 1923 was anarcho-Bolshevism. Following the Bolshevik revolution many anarchists in Argentina, Uruguay, Brazil, and especially Mexico supported Lenin and declared their unconditional support of the Soviet government, yet still considered themselves anarchists. With Lenin's death this trend disappeared.

Those who still chose to follow Stalin no longer dared to call themselves anarchists.

In addition to a vast newspaper propaganda and extensive bibliography, anarchism in all Latin American countries produced many poets and writers who were among the most prominent in their respective national literatures. They were not, however, equally numerous and important in all regions. It is safe to say that in Argentina and Uruguay most writers publishing between 1890 and 1920 were at one time or another anarchists. Likewise in Brazil and Chile, where during this time there were more than a few literary anarchist writers, though not as many as in the Río de la Plata region. In Columbia, Venezuela, and Puerto Rico, if a properly anarchist literature did not fully flourish, the influence of a libertarian ideology was greater among writers and poets than in the workers' movement. But even in those places where literature and anarchism were nearly synonymous, as in the Río de la Plata, anarchist intellectuals never played the role of elite or revolutionary vanguard, nor did they have any dealings with universities or official culture. In this respect anarchism's trajectory differs profoundly from that of Marxism.

The decline of the anarchist movement in Latin America (which does not imply its total disappearance) may be attributed to three causes. First is a series of *coups d'état*, mostly fascist, in the 1930s—Uriburu in Argentina, Vargas in Brazil, Terra in Uruguay. All are characterized by a general repression of the workers' movement, Left-leaning groups, and particularly of anarchists. In certain cases (e.g., Argentina) the state achieved the total dismantlement of the organizational and propagandistic structure of the workers' anarcho-syndicalist federations. A second factor is the founding of communist parties (Bolsheviks). The support of the Soviet Union and of affiliated European parties gave them a strength sorely lacking in anarchist organizations, which had no other resources than the dues paid by their own militants. Some anarchists chose to join the communist party, more in some countries (Brazil) and fewer in others (Argentina). Finally, the emergence of nationalist-populist sentiments more or less linked to the armed forces and, in a few cases, with the promoters of fascist *coups* completes the factors that caused anarchism's decline.

The unique situation of dependence in which Latin American countries found themselves with regard to European and, above all, North American imperialism caused the class struggle to be substituted by struggles for national liberation. Consequently, workers conceived of their exploitation as arising from foreign powers. The bourgeoisie, both domestic and foreign, together with various sectors of the military and the Catholic church, convinced them that the enemy was not Capital and State as such, but *foreign* Capital and State. Skillfully manipulated, this very conviction was the principal cause of the decline of anarchism. All else is secondary, even the intrinsic difficulties faced by anarchist organizations in the actual world, such as the need to make unions function without bureaucracy or the impossibility, real or apparent, of concrete proposals.

Introduction: Anarchism in Latin America

Romina Akemi & Javier Sethness-Castro

After authoring dozens of books on classical Greek and anarchist philosophy, Ángel Cappelletti dedicated his last monograph to a forgotten history of anarchism in the region. The publication of *Anarchism in Latin America* (*El Anarquismo en America Latina*) in 1990 coincided with important historical impasses such as the fall of the Soviet Union and the aggressive spread of neoliberalism. These events roused disillusionment about whether socialism was even still a viable option while, at the same time, frustration with austerity measures across the region catalyzed a revival of social movements after decades of military rule and civil wars. Cappelletti explains that his work is not intended to be "a comprehensive history of Latin American anarchism" but to fill a gap in labor and revolutionary literature dominated by Marxist historians who either glossed over or erased the contributions of anarchists. Cappelletti did not live long enough to see the revival of anarchism across the region, in which his work became an important fixture in the arsenal of ideas for a new generation seeking tenets to aid their struggles for liberation and the coming of socialist revolution.

Cappelletti's research covers the development of anarchism in the Americas, marking its origins in the mid-nineteenth century with the arrival of European migrants who brought with them ideas about socialist utopianism. The beginning of his chapters emphasize the role of the anarchist press in disseminating their ideas. The printed press is an obvious go-to in terms of archival research. But, at least in his description of Argentina, there is a sense that the press, literature, and popular poets were a prime force in spreading revolutionary prefigurative dreams among the popular classes. A combination of cultural and political language influenced the broader working class culture to embrace and familiarize themselves with the meaning of solidarity, mutualism, and *autogestión* (or self-management), even if they were not militants or partisans faithful to those ideas. He spotlights the role of workers' mutual aid societies in Venezuela and Mexico, some of which developed into prominent proto-syndicalist resistance societies, as well as numerous examples of anarchistic utopian experiments, such as the Cecilia colony (1890–1894), the Cosmos commune, and the potentially Tolstoyan Varpa community, all established in Brazil, to say nothing of the two utopian communities founded by Vasco de Quiroja in sixteenth-century Mexico, which strived to emulate Thomas More's *Utopia.* Though Cappelletti acknowledges Robert Owen's proposal (1828) to the Mexican government to establish a utopian-socialist colony in Texas, which remained merely abstract, he doesn't mention the Spiritual Franciscans's earlier attempts to construct Christian communism with Nahua people in Mexico.[1] He does focus attention on Plotino Rhodakanaty, the Greek anarcho-physician and missionary who founded several revolutionary collectivist organizations in Mexico after migrating there in the mid-nineteenth century with an eye to propagating Charles Fourier and Pierre-Joseph Proudhon's social prescriptions. In this way, the two strongest currents in Latin America soon became anarcho-syndicalism

---

1   John Leddy Phelan, *The Millennial Kingdom of the Franciscans in the New World* (Berkeley: University of California Press, 1970).

and anarchist-communism; while individualism developed into a regional anarchist tenet over time, it played a less significant role in comparison to Europe or the US. The relationship with Iberian anarchism remains particularly close up to this day, partly due to the colonial legacy, but mostly due to language that facilitated the easy exchange of ideas. This connection was most felt during the Spanish Civil War (1936–1939), when many Cuban anarchists joined the CNT-FAI in resisting fascism, but particularly in light of the thousands of refugees who arrived to the continent after their defeat by the combined forces of Franco, Mussolini, and Hitler.

Cappelletti correctly highlights the role of European migrants as central in bringing revolutionary traditions to the continent but misses the opportunity to connect anarchism with the region's prior revolutionary traditions. Latin America's regional characteristics, especially between 1860 and 1920, were more rooted in *transculturation*.[2] In other words, Latin American anarchism, with all its regional variants, was the product of a confluence of local and exogenous ideas, practices, and realities, the combination of economic and political pressures produced by the regional nation-states and imperialist forces and the modalities of struggle from below to resist hegemonic power.

Why is Cappelletti's Book Relevant for Anarchists in the United States?

National histories and languages influence how we think about political legacies and with whom we communicate. Residents of the US are bound to the Americas in terms of geography and migration, and due to the legacy of imperialism that rests heavily on its economic and military expansion over the region. US leftists tend to be influenced by European traditions thanks to the availability of

---

2   The term "transculturation" was coined by the Cuban anthropologist Fernando Ortiz.

English-language books and online resources, and the influence of a Western-centric education. However, with an ever-growing Latinx population, already a majority ethnic population in many US states, there is a growing group of bilingual speakers who also have regular communication with organizations south of the Río Grande. This heightens the need for US revolutionaries to become fluent in Spanish, and for the production and publication of more pamphlets and books either in Spanish or in bilingual form.

The power and violence relating to national borders and citizenship increases day by day. While heads-of-state expound nationalism and xenophobia in Latin America, the popular classes are bound together by colonial legacy and imperialist domination. It is not uncommon for a US citizen traveling in Latin America to refer to themselves as "American" and to be quickly corrected by a local that *we*, across the continent, are all Americans—yet only one country declares ownership. The reason for emphasizing this is to highlight two things: the need to challenge US exceptionalism in Left politics, and the reality that anarchist-communist revolution cannot succeed if only realized in one country.

The publishing of Cappelletti's monograph by AK Press feeds a growing hunger by Latinx anarchists who want to read more about their history, and for gringo anarchists to become further acquainted with a history to which they are historically bound. This connection ranges from the role of US Wobbly seafarers in forming the IWW in Chile in the early 1920s to the case of Magón and the revolutionary-anarchist Mexican Liberal Party (PLM), based importantly in Los Angeles, California.[3] The book is also a useful encyclopedic list of organizations and individuals to reference. It details some interesting political debates and challenges in organization-building. Too many books published about Latin America are geared toward a US audience, often emphasizing the continent's exotic revolutionary character, focusing less on political

---

3   Peter DeShazo, *The Industrial Workers of the World in Chile*, Ph.D. Dissertation in Latin American History at University of Wisconsin-Madison, 1977.

theory and analysis. For example, the many books and articles published in the 1990s—and, in fact, still being published[4]—highlighting the image and word of Subcomandante Insurgente Marcos, thus downplaying the organizational form of the Zapatista Army of National Liberation (EZLN). This was Marcos's precise point in announcing his "death" and subsequent resurrection as Subcomandante Insurgente Galeano, named after an EZLN support-base comrade who was murdered in a paramilitary attack on the *La Realidad caracol* in 2014: the media's emphasis on spectacle ensured that the focus would be on Marcos's style and appearance, based on his hegemonic and familiar European features, thus marginalizing the EZLN's base and the rest of its leadership, which is comprised of Tsotsil, Tseltal, Ch'ol, Zoque, Tojolabal, and Mam peoples.[5] Since this announcement, the indigenous Subcomandante Insurgente Moisés has taken over the role of EZLN spokesperson.

Thus, while US-based anarchists have more familiarity with the European historical tradition, Latin America is where we can learn more about cross-race solidarity and organizing in both its positive implementation and its disastrous effects due to racism and patriarchy. This includes indigenous *autogestión*, *quilombo* politics, and a regional common identity threatening the strength of national boundaries. Cappelletti does at times underscore the importance of certain figures such as Malatesta in Argentina or Fourier, Proudhon, and Mikhail Bakunin in Mexico, but their influence and ideas, while important guiding voices, were part of something larger than themselves during this time period. Also,

---

4   See e.g. J. M. Towle, "The Savvy Guerrilla: How the Literature of Subcomandante Marcos Funds the Zapatista Rebellion," *Confluencia: Revista Hispánica De Cultura Y Literatura*, 32, 2 (January 1, 2017), 7–90; Oswaldo Estrada, "The Masked Intellectual: Marcos and the Speech of the Rainforest," *Mexican Public Intellectuals*, eds. D. Castillo and S. Day (New York: Palgrave Macmillan, 2014), 197–216; Nick Henck, "Subcomandante Marcos: The Latest Reader." *The Latin Americanist*, 58.2 (2014): 49–73.

5   Subcomandante Insurgente Marcos/Galeano, "Entre La Luz y la Sombra," May 25, 2014. Available online: http://enlacezapatista.ezln.org .mx/2014/05/25/entre-la-luz-y-la-sombra.

rather than continually exoticizing Latin American figures, rang-
ing from Clotario Blest to Flores Magón, without knowing their
political opinions, we need to see these individuals too as participants in broader political movements.

Cuba, Mexico, Nicaragua: National Liberation, Anti-Militarism, Social Revolution

The extensive regional historical entries that Cappelletti shares in this
volume contain multitudes of lessons, which resonate through time.
Past anarchist efforts in Latin America continue to inform ongoing
struggles on the continent, holding great promise for the prospect
of global emancipation from capitalism, militarism, and authority.
Given the historical weight of colonialism and neo-colonialism hang-
ing over the continent, anarchism in Latin America has intersected
critically with national-liberation and anti-militarist movements to
present a social-revolutionary challenge to the oppression upheld
by imperialists in conjunction with local elites. This dynamic brings
to mind the luminous observation made by the Nicaraguan radical
Augusto Sandino, that *"only the workers and peasants will go all
the way, only their organized force will attain victory"* for the social
revolution.[6] As anarchists, we are critical of the nation-state as either
a stage or end goal for social liberation, but we nevertheless embrace
the spirit of autonomous organizing against colonial oppression and
the intersection of such proletarian-peasant unity with struggles for
libertarian communism. With that in mind, we'd like to highlight
important lessons for anarchists from the revolutionary national-
liberation movements in Cuba, Mexico, and Nicaragua during the
nineteenth and twentieth centuries, struggles that persist to this day.

Alongside Puerto Rico, Cuba was the last of the Spanish colonies in Latin America to gain formal independence, in 1902, four

---

6   Quoted in William I. Robinson, *Promoting Polyarchy: Globalization, US
     Intervention, and Hegemony* (Cambridge: Cambridge University Press,
     1996), 208 (emphasis in original).

years after the end of the Spanish-American War, which saw the former colonial power replaced by US military occupation. Cappelletti stresses that Cuban anarchists participated enthusiastically in the national-liberation movement, anticipating a future liberated from the "colonial authoritarian spirit and bureaucratic structure[s]." In this way, they echoed Bakunin and Alexander Herzen's agitation in favor of Polish emancipation from tsarist domination, and Rhodakanaty's participation in the 1848 Hungarian war of independence. In their struggle, the Cuban anarchists directly confronted racism in labor, opposed the neo-colonial stipulations of the Platt Amendment (1901), and organized numerous strikes among sugarcane workers and other proletarian sectors against the post-colonial State. Through the efforts of individuals such as Alfredo López and groups like the General Union of Industrial Fabric Workers and the Workers's Federation of La Havana (FOH), together with a vibrant libertarian press, anarcho-syndicalism became the predominant ideology among the Cuban working class. While Cuban anarchists continued to organize workers and the oppressed after independence from Spain and the US, conflict with the Communists undermined their effectiveness. The Communist's emphasis on the construction of parties led them, during the dictatorships of Gerardo Machado (1933) and Fulgencio Batista (1935), respectively, to actively disrupt strikes organized by anarcho-syndicalists. Such undermining of anarchist efforts, presaging the generalized repression after the 1959 Revolution, would prepare the way for its Stalinization, a development that echoed the fate of the Russian Revolution four decades prior. Indeed, throughout Latin America, the fate of the Russian Revolution considerably accentuated the differences between anarchists and authoritarian socialists, divergences that have resonated in the distinct tactics and strategies taken up by radicals on the continent since.

Shifting southwest, the Mexican Revolution (1910–1920) should be considered a national-liberation struggle of sorts, in light of the vast foreign control of land and resources that underpinned the *Porfiriato,* or Porfirio Díaz's dictatorship (1876–1911), perpetuating the titanic social discontent that would explode during the upheaval. Indeed, collectivist anarchism and anarcho-communism had melded with indigenous autonomy in Mexico to propel the specter of a libertarian-emancipatory revolution, summarized by the slogan "*¡Tierra y Libertad!*" ("Land and Freedom!") This very slogan, in fact, was developed by Herzen and Bakunin through their collaboration with the Polish opposition, taken up and propagated by Ricardo Flores Magón and the Liberal Mexican Party (PLM) in their renowned newspaper *Regeneración*, and ultimately emblazoned in the program and banners of the Zapatista *Ejército Libertador del Sur* during the Revolution.[7] Whereas the *PLMistas* organized via networks of *Clubes Liberales* on both sides of the U.S.-Mexico border and championed strikes and insurrections as the means to restore popular control over the fields, factories, and workshops, the revolutionary potential of the PLM's vision was inhibited by the targeted imprisonment and martyrdom of its leading figures, including Magón and Praxedis Guerrero.[8]

In contrast *La Casa del Obrero Mundial* (The House of the Global Worker), a syndicalist union founded in 1912 by some ex-comrades of Magón's in Mexico City, represented a more "successful" anarchist movement at the time. As La Casa faced immediate repression at the hands of the Huerta dictatorship that overthrew Madero in 1913, its membership anticipated Huerta's defeat by the combined forces of Zapata, Pancho Villa, and the Constitutionalists. Yet geographical and cultural differences between

---

7   Alexander Herzen, *My Past and Thoughts*, trans. Constance Garnett (Berkeley: University of California Press, 1973), 581–4.

8   Ricardo Flores Magón, "Manifesto, September 23, 1911," in *Dreams of Freedom*, eds. Chaz Bufe and Mitchell Cowen Verter (Oakland: AK Press, 2005), 138–44; Adolfo Gilly, *The Mexican Revolution: A New People's History* (New York: New Press, 2006); Claudio Lomnitz, *The Return of Comrade Ricardo Flores Magón* (Brooklyn: Zone Books, 2014); Ward S. Albro, *To Die On Your Feet: The Life, Times, and Writings of Praxedis Guerrero* (Fort Worth: Texas Christian University, 1996); Praxedis Guerrero, *I Am Action: Literary and Combat Articles, Thoughts, and Revolutionary Chronicles*, trans. Javier Sethness-Castro (Chico, California: AK Press, forthcoming 2018).

the more rationalist anarchist workers and the indigenous-*campesinx* Zapatistas led the former to find affinity with the Constitutionalists. In fact, in 1915 La Casa made a fatal deal to support the latter's counter-insurgent efforts by supplying troops for the *Batallones Rojos* that were used specifically against Zapata and Villa's armies. In exchange, La Casa was allowed to organize labor freely, resulting in the establishment of numerous sections throughout the country. La Casa sealed the fate of the Revolution with this move, serving to disrupt the potentially emancipatory unity of proletariat and peasantry, as recognized by the PLM and Sandino alike, thus greatly facilitating the nationalist integration of labor into the post-revolutionary State.[9] Nonetheless, perhaps preserving a future hope for a profound social revolution uniting proletariat and peasantry, Cappelletti auspiciously clarifies that his research on the *Batallones Rojos* suggests that *La Casa*'s rank-and-file membership disagreed with the leadership over this fateful decision.

Unfortunately, the 1979 Sandinista Revolution to depose General Somoza was similarly constrained by the insurgents' opting to seize state power rather than seeking its abolition. All this despite the fact that the FSLN (Sandinista Front for National Liberation) was named for the anarcho-syndicalist guerrilla Sandino, whose peasant army expelled the US Marines in 1933. Since that time, the nominally left-wing FSLN has struck deals with the far-right to prohibit abortion, advance free-trade agreements, and effectively become a brand that represents the interests of a small elite of families content with managing the "*hacienda* feudalism" that the revolution had sought to abolish.[10] Self-evidently, Sandino's emphasis on cooperative labor and his followers' historical anti-dictatorial orientation retain all their relevance today.

---

9   See Ricardo Flores Magón's caustic portrayal of the arrangement in Act IV of the play "Tierra y Libertad," in *Obra Literaria: Cuentos. Relatos. Teatro*, ed. Jacinto Barrera Bassols (Ciudad de México: Dirección General de Publicaciones, 2009), 179–189.

10 *Until the Rulers Obey: Voices from Latin American Social Movements*, eds. Clifton Ross and Marcy Rein (Oakland: PM Press, 2014), 115–47.

Taking a global view, we see that Cuba's national-liberation struggle shares some similarities with those of South Asia and Algeria, considering the militant and, sometimes, anarchist network known as the Ghadar movement that was central to the resistance against the British Raj, giving rise to India, Pakistan, and Bangladesh, and the widespread *autogestion* that arose in the fields and factories abandoned by French settlers in Algeria following its victory in the independence war. Whereas formal independence ultimately yielded despotic, centralized post-colonial power elites in Cuba and Algeria—Castro and the Communist Party and the Front de Libération Nationale (FLN), respectively—as well as repression of the Kabyle minority and a brutal civil war between Islamists and the Algerian State, India since independence has vacillated between domination by neo-liberal parliamentarism and neo-fascist communalism, both of which perpetuate vast human suffering.[11]

Visibilizing Gender Relations

While Cappelletti's book is groundbreaking, it nevertheless overlooks the contributions by women in the development of Latin American anarchism. He does mention some anarchist-feminists by name, including the Argentine Virginia Bolten who was editor of the Rosario-based *La Voz de la Mujer*—the only anarchist-communist newspaper dedicated to women's emancipation at the turn of the last century.[12] However, there are major omissions, such

---

11   David Porter, *Eyes to the South: French Anarchists and Algeria* (Oakland: AK Press, 2011); Maia Ramnath, *Decolonizing Anarchism: An Antiauthoritarian History of India's Liberation Struggle* (Oakland: AK Press and the Institute for Anarchist Studies, 2011) and Ramnath's *Haj to Utopia* (University of California Press, 2011).

12   Maxine Molyneux, "No God, No Boss, No Husband: Anarchist Feminism in Nineteenth-Century Argentina" (*Latin American Perspectives*, Vol. 13, No. 1, Latin America's Nineteenth-Century History, Winter, 1986); also see film about Bolten: Dir. Laura Mañá, *Ni Dios, ni patrón, ni marido* (Catalan Films, Barcelona, 2008).

as Luisa Capetillo, a central figure in the Puerto Rican labor movement, and Juana Belén Gutiérrez de Mendoza, an anarchist journalist who joined Madero temporarily after Magón had her expelled from the PLM for being a lesbian, only to unite with the Zapatistas, co-author the *Plan de Ayala,* and serve as *comandanta* in the *Ejército Libertador.*[13] Yet, beyond individual female mentions, the overall analysis fails to weave in how these women contributed, the issues they emphasized, the challenges they faced, and how patriarchy affected solidarity and movement building. These issues and experiences cannot be separated from the history of anarchism.

Beyond the purview of this book, we would like to use this opportunity to urge readers and future researchers to devote themselves to developing the history of anarchist-feminism and gender relations within the movement. In the period that this book covers, female anarchists were part of a larger current of revolutionary and militant women who defined themselves against the First Wave of middle-class and elite feminism that fought for suffrage. These women did not want political equality under capitalism, they sought revolution; they did not center their activism on charity and social uplift, but instead on autonomy and *autogestión*. Some of the best theoretical and organizational contributions by anarchist women during this time were critiques about the family, support for free love, and the creation of mutualism and labor unions by and for women. In reviewing many writings in which these women are mentioned or were written about, we see two elements emerging: First, that many of these revolutionary-minded women across the globe were in communication with each other; second, they

---

13   Jorell A. Meléndez Badillo, *Voces libertarias: los orígenes del anarquismo en Puerto Rico* (Bloomington, IN, Secret Sailor Books, 2013); Norma Valle-Ferrer, *Luisa Capetillo: Pioneer Puerto Rican Feminist* (New York, Peter Lang Publishing, 2006); Kirwin R. Shaffer, *Black Flag Boricuas: Anarchism, Antiauthoritarianism, and the Left in Puerto, 1897–1921* (Champaign, Il: University of Illinois Press, 2013); Lomnitz, *The Return of Comrade Ricardo Flores Magón*, 202–3; Vicki L. Ruiz and Virginia Sánchez Korrol, eds., *Latinas in the United States: A Historical Encyclopedia*, vol. 1 (Bloomington, IN: Indiana University Press, 2006), 463.

tended to suppress their gendered hardships for the good of the movement.[14] In the case of Virginia Bolten, she was in direct correspondence with Emma Goldman and Louise Michel.[15] The Chilean anarchist Flora Sanhueza owed a great deal of her political development to when she travelled to Spain in 1935 to subsume herself in the libertarian struggle.[16] There is also the story of the Argentine anarchist Mika Feldman de Etchebéhère, who was active in *Mujeres Libres* and a captain in a POUM squadron.[17] Even though there are many books that discuss the impact of the Spanish Civil War in Latin America, there are no studies on whether *Mujeres Libres* influenced the anarchist movement on the continent.[18] In the article "Breaking the Waves: Challenging the Liberal Tendency in Anarchist-Feminism," Bree Busk and Romina Akemi explain the difficulty in defining anarchist-feminism due to the lack of a historical narrative that describes its contributions within the movement rather than placing individuals on pedestals.[19] There are also examples in Latin American anarchism of innate challenges to gender politics and patriarchy, in which the most striking cases emerged during the Mexican Revolution; a moment at which social order and gender expectations were in question. This ranged from the role by the *soldaderas*, also known as *Adelitas*, who challenged the masculine assumption of soldiering that was tied to citizenship, and individuals such as the Zapatista Amelio Robles who, assigned female at birth, emerged a colonel and recognized veteran for his role

---

14   Angelica Balabanoff, *My Life as a Rebel* (Bloomington: University of Indiana Press, 1973 [1938]).

15   Anna LB, "Virginia Bolten: Ni Dios, ni patrón ni marido," *El Cosaco* (30 de abril 2017): http://www.elcosaco.org/virginia-bolten-dios-patron-marido/.

16   Gaspar Garcia M. and Leyla Morales M., "Historia de Vida: Flora Sanhueza Rebolledo. Su lucha social en Iquique (1942–1974)," *Centro de Estudio Miguel Enríquez* en ARCHIVO CHILE (2003–2007).

17   Mika Etchebéhère, *Mi Guerra en España* (Oviedo, Cambalache Memoria, 2003 [1976]).

18   Martha A. Ackelsberg, *Free Women of Spain: Anarchism and the Struggle for the Emancipation of Women* (Oakland, AK Press, 2005).

19   Romina Akemi and Bree Busk, "Breaking the Waves: Challenging the Liberal Tendency in Anarchist-Feminism," in *Perspectives on Anarchist Theory*, Issue 29 (Spring 2016): 104–119.

in the revolution.[20] These histories are often treated as side stories, and we still struggle today to discuss them as examples that molded, guided, and influenced the politics of anarchism.

In the 60s and 70s, Latin America experienced continental revolutionary upheaval inspired by the 1959 Cuban Revolution and in reaction to growing economic crises. The second wave feminist movement that swept through Western countries had little resonance in the Global South, which was embroiled in national liberation movements and US sponsored military dictatorships. Women and queer militants in these revolutionary movements had minimal space to engage or discuss their political struggles and incorporate them into their organizational programs and praxis. In countries that fell under dictatorial rule, many social gains, especially those made by the working class, as well as indigenous and women's rights, were severely rolled back. According to the Chilean feminist Julieta Kirkwood, the military dictatorship was the embodiment of patriarchy.[21] In the case of Chile, feminism grew from a social movement in the 1980s resisting Pinochet's dictatorship. Feminists used their position as women—perceived as the weaker and fragile sex—to create political space. Such scenes were repeated across the continent, especially by the mothers of the disappeared from Guatemala to Argentina who became symbols of political and feminist resistance. By the 1990s with the return of liberal democracies and the growing influence of anarchism, women began to openly discuss the pressures and labors of double-duty militancy—as members of their political or social organizations and, in addition, their feminist work. Issues that were once deemed "private matters" or "between couples" began to

---

20 Elena Poniatowska, *Las Soldaderas: Women of the Mexican Revolution* (El Paso, Cinco Puntos Press, 2006); Jocelyn Olcott, *Revolutionary Women in Postrevolutionary Mexico* (Durham, Duke University Press, 2005); Gabriela Cano, "Unconcealable Realities of Desires: Amelio Robles's (Transgender) Masculinity in Revolutionary Mexico" in *Sex and Revolution: Gender, Politics, and Power in Modern Mexico*, ed. Jocelyn Olcott et al (Durham, Duke University Press, 2007).

21 Julieta Kirkwood, *Ser política en Chile: las feministas y los partidos* (Santiago, FLASCO, 1986).

be discussed more openly. And by the mid-2000s a feminist movement was brewing that drew from women's past political experiences
yet was informed by the present, embracing demands for the legal-
ization of abortion and the end of femicide. Now it was up to *their*
political and social organizations taking up the banner of feminism
and sexual dissidence and supporting their demands as part of a prefigurative program. When a group of female members of the Chilean Federación de Estudiantes Libertarios (FEL), or the Libertarian
Student Federation, decided in 2012 to organize an informal meeting
to discuss patriarchal behavior within the student movement, rather
than receiving support from their comrades, they were bullied and
mocked. Such hostility motivated several of these women, along
with male accomplices, to form *La Alzada-Acción Feminista Libertario* in 2013.[22] This example marks a historical shift within anarchism and feminism, when for most of the twentieth century, the
formation of separate anarchist spaces by and for women was openly
criticized. Instead of accusing anarchist feminists, queers, and sexual
dissidents of dividing the movement, we should use the opportunity
to challenge our own presumptions. As Latin American revolutionary feminists exclaim: *"la revolución será feminista, ¡o no será!* ("the
revolution will be feminist or it will not be!").

Is Anarchism an Ideology that Transcends the European Experience?

The question of whether radical ideologies such as Marxism and
anarchism are European or white impositions that have no place in
anti-colonial struggles or resistance among people of color is raised

---

22   José Antonio Gutiérrez D., trans. Romina Akemi, "La Alzada: The rev-
      olution must include the feminist struggle, with and inside the libertari-
      an," *Ideas and Action* (October 2013): http://ideasandaction.info/2013/10/
      la-alzada-the-revolution-must-include-the-feminist-struggle-with-and-
      inside-the-libertarian/. This article was originally published in Spanish on
      Anarkismo.net in March 2013.

more in the US than in Latin America—but nonetheless, it warrants engagement. Initially, we can say that anarchism shares little of Marx and Engels's enthusiasm for British colonialism in India or US victory in the Mexican-American War of 1848, respectively, regardless of the degree to which the former rethought his stance later in life after studying anthropology and history more closely.[23] Though Bakunin doubtless was, like Proudhon, a vile anti-Semite, he consistently supported national-liberation struggles and stressed the importance of coordinated global revolution against all empires and despots: "But states do not topple of their own accord; they can only be toppled by a multi-national, multi-racial, world-wide social revolution."[24] Additionally, his critique of Marx's deterministic stages theory of history can be considered anti-racist in that it rejects the illogic that demands the full development of imperialism and capitalism—whether in India, Mexico, or elsewhere—as a precondition for the flowering of communism.

Yet in parallel to the anti-Semitic associations he would make between Jews and political centralism, Bakunin subscribed to some rather questionable racialism, particularly in *Statism and Anarchy* from 1873, where he expounds his views on the German nation and Pan-Germanism, both of which he considered great centralizing threats, no doubt due at least in part to Marx's expulsion of himself and his comrade James Guillaume from the First International. In this text, the anarcho-collectivist further expresses Sinophobia, worrying that China is "a threat by virtue of [its] numbers alone." Bakunin's caricatures about Germans being "intrinsically bourgeois and thereby statist" are hence nearly as absurd as Engels's celebration of California having been taken by the white-settler State from

---

23 See Karl Marx, *Ethnological Notebooks* (1881), trans. Lawrence Krader (available online at https://www.marxists.org/archive/marx/works/1881/ethnographical-notebooks/notebooks.pdf); Kevin B. Anderson, *Marx at the Margins* (Chicago: University of Chicago Press, 2010); and Teodor Shanin, *Late Marx and the Russian Road* (New York: Monthly Review Press, 1983).

24 Mikhail Bakunin, *Statism and Anarchy*, trans. Marshall Shatz (Cambridge: Cambridge University Press, 1990), 45.

the "lazy Mexicans [*sic*]."[25] Nevertheless, Bakunin's alarm over the "danger" supposedly "threatening us from the East" likely springs from a similar source as does Marx and Engels's chauvinism.[26] Still, whether ironically or not, both Marxism and anarchism have inspired revolt and revolution in Latin America and much of the rest of the Global South. Cappelletti clarifies, however, that among radical Cuban workers of the late nineteenth century, "[n]o one speaks about Marx or Engels," whereas Bakunin, Malatesta, Peter Kropotkin, Élisée Reclus, and Anselmo Lorenzo were "read and interpreted on a daily basis."[27]

Cappelletti premises his presentation by underlining the role of Spanish and Italian migrants in spreading socialist utopianism and anarchism in the mid- to late-nineteenth century. Anarchism has had a mass appeal in Latin America due to its ability to transcend and connect with material demands for autonomy and better living conditions, including those sought by indigenous peoples. More in passing, Cappelletti offers some examples in which indigenous communities viewed anarchism as either a useful tool for struggle or an ideology that complemented their own struggle for land and autonomy. For example, in his chapter on Peru he notes the attempt to organize the Federación Regional de Obreros Indios (Regional Federation of Indian Workers) in 1923. In Bolivia, he highlights the role of a *ch'ixi* mechanic, Luis Cusicanqui, in keeping anarcho-syndicalism alive at a moment when Marxism was gaining ground among the working classes.[28] In Brazil, the author

---

25   Ibid, 38; Friedrich Engels, "Democratic Pan-Slavism," in *Neue Rheinische Zeitung*, no. 222 (1849). Available online: http://marxists.anu.edu.au/archive /marx/works/1849/02/15.htm.

26   Bakunin, *Statism and Anarchy*, 99–100.

27   Anselmo Lorenzo (1841–1914) was a Spanish anarchist who participated as a delegate to the First International after befriending Giuseppe Fanelli, the revolutionary Italian emissary that Bakunin sent to Spain on a mission to propagate anarchism. Lorenzo was a co-founder of the Confederación Nacional del Trabajo (CNT), a comrade of Francisco Ferrer, and an advocate of rationalist education.

28   According to Silvia Rivera Cusicanqui, Luis Cusicanqui was a *ch'ixi*, which is an Aymara term that refers to a certain mestizo that is "Indian

identifies the *quilombos* established by former slaves as "indigenous precedents to the anarchist movement," and in Mexico, Cappelletti points out the commonalities between anarchism and Zapatismo, though he underplays the specifically indigenous dimension of the latter movement, portraying it as primarily rural and *campesino*.

There are at least three issues with Cappelletti's analysis that should be mentioned here. First, he begins his historical arch with Spanish, Italian, and Greek proselytizers of the faith as active subjects while indigenous and mestizo people are described as the objects who consume the faith. In various chapters, Cappelletti insists that anarchism was introduced throughout the region only through contact with Euro-American workers and migrants. For example, in the Brazil section, the author simply mentions how a Frenchman named P. Berthelot "made contact with some indigenous tribes and attempted to promote libertarian organization among them" in the early twentieth century. There is no explicit recognition of the neo-colonial dimensions of these or related relationships, including Owen's proposal to establish socialist colonies in Texas or Giovanni Rossi's acceptance of Emperor Pedro's granting of land to the Cecilia colony. Second, the author mentions the Aztec *calpulli* and the Andean *ayllu* systems as being important foundations for political commonality, but does not clarify why those pre-Columbian governing systems complemented socialist utopianism. We presume that this is due to a shared emphasis on the importance of the commons, as is reflected in the overlap between Zapatismo and the PLM's anarchism. Third, Cappelletti presents an over-idealization of the Aztec and Inka empires that does not take into account the oppressive role those empires played in colonizing and enslaving surrounding indigenous communities, though at times he does point out how the anarcho-agrarian revolts of the nineteenth and

---

spotted with white." For further analysis of Cusicanqui's ideas see Silvia Rivera Cusicanqui's "The Ch'ixi Identity of a Mestizo: Regarding an Anarchist Manifesto of 1929," in *No Gods, No Masters, No Peripheries: Global Anarchisms*, Raymond Craib and Barry Maxwell, eds. (Oakland: PM Press, 2015).

twentieth centuries echoed ancestral indigenous organizing practices against European and native imperialism alike. Although his points about endogenous and exogenous connections that defined Latin American anarchism were not fully developed in understanding indigenous and African influences, he nevertheless touches on a few historical threads and ideas about their confluence that need to be examined more closely by future researchers.

Many historians have glossed over indigenous identities, emphasizing their class relationships instead and encompassing them in the larger category of peasant or urban worker, ignoring the reasons *why* indigenous communities supported land reform and where those reasons contrasted those of mestizo or criollo peasants. Identifying those disparate reasons does not minimize the material conditions that brought them together; this form of alliance building needs to be replicated more and not less. The Peruvian anthropologist Marisol de la Cadena explains how the Quechua *paqo* leader, Mariano Turpo, described this legacy: "From him I learned that indigenous utilization of class rhetoric was a political option that did not represent the loss of indigenous culture, but was rather a strategy toward its empowerment."[29] She learned that at times indigenous communities minimized their ethnic identity in their political slogans to create alliances or have broader appeal that could be read by some as de-indianization. Other times their cultural or ethnic identities were emphasized to gain ground or make certain claims to the state. Such intentionality to the outside viewer has often been misinterpreted as a progressive loss of identity or a Foucaultian submission to the state and its economic system, rather than calculated decisions. What appears as a growth of indigenous identities in Latin America beginning in the 1990s is actually the consequence of greater visibility by which these communities have been able to assert themselves in the public arena and make political demands to reclaim stolen resources and land, as well as combat

---

29   Marisol de la Cadena, "Reconstructing Race: Racism, Culture and Mestizaje in Latin America," *NACLA* vol. XXXIV, No. 6 (May/June 2001): 21.

against imposed political and economic systems from European to nation-state colonialism. *Wingka* anarchists—to use the Mapuzungun term—rooted by their experiences with national-liberation, have learned the need to support indigenous demands and become accomplices in their struggles.[30] Liberation from capitalist oppression and imperialism will require alliances, trust-building, and respect for autonomy in many spheres.

Autonomy and Ecology in Latin America

The environmentalist and ecological movements in Latin America have produced their own martyrs, including Chico Mendes and Berta Cáceres, Mariano Abarca, and Bernardo Vásquez Sánchez—anti-mining organizers from Chiapas and Oaxaca, respectively—along with countless others. Indeed, ecologists and land defenders have been singled out for repression at the hands of the state and private interests in Latin America, with hundreds of organizers killed annually in the past few years.[31] The severity of such suppression reflects the fears of the ruling classes regarding the potential for autonomous indigenous, communalist, and anarchist movements engaging in radical ecological praxis: recovering and communizing the land, expropriating the expropriators, employing agroecology, abolishing or at least minimizing alienated labor, completely redistributing wealth and resources, redesigning the cities for collective living and sustainability, reducing pollution and productivism, halting economic growth, delineating biosphere reserves, and equilibrating the overall relationship between humanity and nature.

---

30 The term *"wingka"* means the "new Inca" in reference to the arrival of Spanish Conquistadors. The Mapuche had resisted Inca invasion for over a century prior to Spanish arrival. The term has evolved to refer to mestizos, Chileans, Argentinian, or non-Mapuche in general.

31 Oliver Holmes, "Environmental activist murders set record as 2015 became deadliest year," *The Guardian*, June 20, 2016.

Against such ends stand foreign and domestic capital and the state. Canadian capital, for example, owns between 50–70% of all mines in Latin America, and for this reason is responsible for vast environmental destruction and widespread human-rights abuses.[32] In many cases, Latin American states facilitate these extractive ventures, or themselves greatly accelerate domestic extractivist projects. We see this in the "Pink Tide" countries of Venezuela, Bolivia, Ecuador, Brazil, and Uruguay that are pursuing a "Twenty-First Century Socialism" that closely mimics neoliberalism.[33] Such productivism in turn belies these states' claims to be environmental champions: while Brazil commits itself to the goal of "zero illegal deforestation" by 2030, researchers project that the majority of Amazonian tree species will be extinct by mid-century at current rates of clearance.[34] The Brazilian Labor Party has also encouraged the construction of hundreds of dams in the Amazon, with the most notorious being the Belo Monte mega-dam on the Xingu River, a project that would flood vast expanses of the rainforest, forcibly displace tens of thousands, threaten the survival of indigenous peoples, and affect peasants both in Brazil and regionally.[35] The stipulation that nature or *Pacha Mama* has a right to be "comprehensively respected," as enshrined in the Ecuadorean Constitution since 2008, has not stopped petroleum extraction from the highly biodiverse Yasuní National Park.[36] For its

32   David Hill, "Canadian mining doing serious environmental harm, the IA-
      CHR is told," *The Guardian*, May 14, 2014.
33   Pablo Dávalos, "Latin America - Economic Socialism in the 21st Centu-
      ry: Neoliberalism Pure and Simple," trans. Danica Jorden. *Upside Down
      World*, April 15, 2014. Available online: http://upsidedownworld.org/
      archives/international/latin-america-economic-socialism-in-the-21st
      -century-neo-liberalism-pure-and-simple/.
34   Jonathan Watts, "Amazon deforestation report is a major setback for Bra-
      zil ahead of climate talks," *The Guardian*, November 27, 2015; Damian
      Carrington, "Half of tree species in Amazon at risk of extinction, say sci-
      entists," *The Guardian*, November 20, 2015.
35   Jonathan Watts, "Amazonian tribes unite to demand Brazil stop hydro-
      electric dams," *The Guardian*, April 30, 2015; "Brazil's Belo Monte Dam:
      Sacrificing the Amazon and its Peoples for Dirty Energy," *Amazon Watch*.
      Available online: http://amazonwatch.org/work/belo-monte-dam.
36   "La Constitución consagra los derechos de la naturaleza [*sic*]," Ministerio

part, the resistance of the US government to decriminalizing or legalizing drugs effectively perpetuates the power of the cartels, whose paramilitary-capitalist operations involve considerable environmental damage. Direct military support from the US for Mexican and Colombian counter-insurgency operations and its coordination of trade and investment throughout the hemisphere help maintain profits at the expense of the environment and society.[37]

Let us briefly consider revolutionary indigenous movements in Colombia and Mexico that represent dialectical inversions of the dominant, globally ecocidal, and thanotic trends. First, in southwestern Colombia, the *Consejo Regional Indígena del Cauca* (Regional Indigenous Council of the Cauca, or CRIC), is a collective organization of 120 indigenous council governments comprised of Coconuco, Nasa, Misak, Totoró, Ambalueño, Quizgüeño, Heperara, and Inga peoples. Founded in 1971, the CRIC is engaged in the recuperation of the commons, the expropriation of privately-owned lands, the furtherance of cooperatives, the maintenance and expansion of indigenous government, resistance to megamines, organizing in favor of political prisoners, and advocating a popular and reconstructive resolution to the country's civil war. Similar to the repression faced by the EZLN, the seizure of lands by CRIC communards for purposes of communal subsistence often meets with direct military and paramilitary repression, particularly during days of collective labor.[38] Paramilitary violence against organized indigenous-*campesinx* communities in Cauca seeks to clear the way for capitalist development, such that only the "the dedicated and sincere organization,

Coordinador de Conocimiento y Talento Humano de Ecuador (2008). Available online: http://www.conocimiento.gob.ec/la-constitucion-consagra-los-derechos-de-la-naturaleza/; John Vidal, "Ecuador drills for oil on edge of pristine rainforest in Yasuni," *The Guardian*, April 4, 2016.

37   Dawn Paley, *Drug War Capitalism* (Oakland: AK Press, 2014); Alexander Reid Ross, ed., *Grabbing Back: Essays Against the Global Land Grab* (Oakland: AK Press, 2014).

38   Centro de Educación y Comunicación Popular - Enraizando, "[Audio] Violento desalojo del ESMAD a proceso de liberación de la Madre Tierra." *Anarkismo*, February 14, 2017. Available online: https://www.anarkismo.net/article/29998?search_text=cauca.

actions in solidarity, and struggle of all the oppressed social classes and sectors" can do away with "the unhappy world of mineral and agro-industrial exploitation of the land and labor."[39]

In several states of southern Mexico, communal self-defense groups and *autogestive* processes have arisen in recent years to resist *caciques* (local bosses), the state, foreign extractive industries, and narco-traffickers alike. In Guerrero, the Regional Coordinator of Communal Authorities-Communal Police (CRAC-PC) has been defending indigenous communities from these forces for two decades, while in April 2011, women from the P'ur'hépecha community of Cherán K'eri, Michoacán, rose up to overthrow the hegemonic drug cartels engaged in mass-deforestation, establishing an emancipatory Commune in the process.[40] In 2013, *autodefensas* surged elsewhere in Michoacán to resist societal domination by the Knights Templar cartel, leading President Peña Nieto to send the Army in to quell and disarm the revolt. Though these *autodefensa* brigades, some of whom explicitly organized in the model of popular security, achieved a great deal in a short period of time, many of them ultimately integrated into the state or the Jalisco New Generation Cartel, rivals to the Knights Templar.[41] In contrast, in Ayutla de los Libres, Guerrero, home of several of the 43 students from Ayotzinapa who were forcibly disappeared in Iguala in September, 2014, the majority of neighborhoods and communities opted for *autogestión* via popular assemblies during a vote in June 2017, thus exercising their right to associate according to indigenous "uses and customs," rejecting electoralism.[42] This right, recognized by the International Labor Organization's Convention 169, is hardly binding

39 "Solidaridad y Defensa de las Comunidades Frente al Avance del Paramilitarismo en el Cauca," *Anarkismo*, February 13, 2017. Available online: https://www.anarkismo.net/article/29972.

40 María González et al., "Cherán: lo importante no es llegar sino mantenerse," *Agencia SubVersiones*, May 24, 2016. Available online: https://subversiones.org/archivos/123674.

41 José Gil Olmos, "La falsa paz de Michoacán," *Proceso*, September 14, 2016.

42 Fernando Camacho Servín, "Reconocen a Ayutla de los Libres derecho de elegir autoridades mediante usos y costumbres." *La Jornada*, June 17, 2017.

on states, being part of international law. Current events and the history of Latin America clearly reveal a systematic disregard from above for indigenous autonomy, human rights, collective liberation, and environmental balance. Within such a context, amidst the utter failure of capital and authority to address such radical demands, these hegemonic forces must be swept away so that the rest of us can get on with reorganizing society. Today, a hundred years since the Russian Revolution, the time is ripe for another global rebellion against capital and the state: another Mexican Revolution, a worldwide neo-Zapatista uprising.

The Re-Emergence of Anarchism as a Viable Current

This book follows on the heels of other books by AK Press concerned with the region, including the English translated editions of *Horizontalism* (edited by Marina Sitrin), Osvaldo Bayer's classic *Rebellion in Patagonia*, and Juan Suriano's *Paradoxes of Utopia*, among other publications. However, anarchist history and theory produced in Latin America, past and present, is extremely vast and difficult to detail. It should be noted that Cappelletti's book marks the beginning of a reengagement with libertarianism after decades of its being overshadowed by Marxism. The 90s anarchist revival was more than a social movement phenomenon, as more people sought to revisit their anarchist predecessors once deemed "ultra-leftists" or proto-communists, engendering new research by academics and worker-intellectuals alike.[43]

The worldwide rebirth of anarchism in the 90s was spurred on by the failures by authoritarian socialism, exemplified in the fall of the Soviet Union, the aggressive spread of neoliberal policies

---

43   There are numerous authors and some already listed in previous footnotes: Víctor Muñoz Cortés, *Sin Dios Ni Patrones: Historia, diversidad y conflictos del anarquismo en la región chilena, 1890–1990* (Valparaíso, Mar y Tierra Ediciones, 2013); Sergio Grez Toso, *Los anarquistas y el movimiento obrero: La alborada de "la Idea" en Chile, 1893–1915* (Santiago, LOM, 2007).

disguised as globalization, and the breaking down of class identities that asserted individual identities and activism, as well as support for specific causes. There is a tendency to assume that these patterns manifested in the same way across the world as in the US. However, the overly-individualistic modality seen in US anarchist circles is not universal across the Americas, where anarchism remains a political ideology and not an individual identity or lifestyle. This is not to say that squats and communal living did not spread across the continent—they did, especially in the early 2000s. Living together did not create de-facto prefigurative politics, but fighting together to demand housing and land rights was foundational. As Sitrin covers in *Horizontalism*, the deep economic crisis experienced in Argentina in the 90s impulsed many to organize and create new forms of social movement organizations that were rooted in *autogestión*, becoming the living embodiment of popular power.

Cappelletti's book ends around the middle of the twentieth century. For those unfamiliar with anarchist and autonomist organizing since then, we will offer some highlights. In his chapter on Uruguay, he notes the formation of the Federación Anarquista Uruguaya (FAU), founded in 1956. The FAU, after surviving state terrorism and dictatorship, proved influential in the development of organized anarchism across the southern region. FAU was founded by mostly Spanish anarchist refugees fleeing General Franco's fascist forces who realized the need for a specific anarchist organization that they termed *especifismo*. Their social insertion work has centered on constructing *autogestión* neighborhood centers and social insertion work in industrial unions constructing an independent militant class politic. For young libertarians seeking guidance on how to build an organized presence within their class, a pilgrimage to the FAU headquarters in Montevideo was imperative in the 90s and 00s. The FAU's steady work with young anarchists in the neighboring Brazilian province of Rio Grande do Sul led to the eventual formation of the Federação Anarquista Gaúcha (FAG) in 1996. The FAG militants eventually influenced the formation of especifista groupings in Brazil, including the Federação Anarquista do

Rio do Janeiro (FARJ). During the FARJ's 2008 congress, the document "Social Anarchism and Organization" emerged from their discussions about strategy, rooted in their current organizational and social movement experiences. They eventually joined efforts made by the Forum of Organized Anarchism (FAO) that evolved into the larger federative network—Coordenação Anarquista Brasileira (CAB)—that includes locals from 11 cities. In the realm of anarchist stratagem to organize for revolution, the FAU's main contributions were especifismo, while the FARJ, in discussion with other libertarian militants in Brazil, gave social insertion greater emphasis as a method of struggle to insert ourselves into the organizations and movements that are the best expressions of resistance by our class. Social insertion is both a commitment to those spaces to flourish into healthy organizations and, at the same time, a means to assert our core ideological principles as we fight for the hearts and minds of the working class.

The other region with an important organized libertarian network is Chile. The presence of anarchism within the labor movement from the 1950s to the 1990s is owed to syndicalists such as Clotario Blest, Celso Poblete, Ernesto Miranda, José Ego-Aguirre, and Hugo Cárter. Ego-Aguirre and Cárter, older anarcho-syndicalists, influenced a group of young people in the 1980s that led to the foundation of the *Hombre y Sociedad* (Man and Society) newspaper that ran from 1985 until 1988, with financial support from anarchists exiled in Europe, including Nestor Vega and Urbano Burgos.[44] From then on, other small publications emerged across the country, including *El Ácrata* and *Acción Directa*. The multi-generational formation associated with *Hombre y Sociedad* became an important confluence of experience and new ideas.

According to the Chilean anarchist José Antonio Gutiérrez Danton, the 1990s can be described as "a virtual 'boom' of anarchist ideas and practices" and a "rediscovery" of anarchism as a historical

---

44   "Platformism without illusions: Chile, Interview with José Antonio Gutiérrez Danton," *Common Struggle/Lucha Común*, North Eastern Federation of Anarchist Communists. Available online: http://nefac.net/node/424.

current in Chile. In 1998 the publication of George Fontenis's *El Manifiesto Comunista Libertario* sparked polemics among libertarian circles and helped consolidate those interested in forming an anarchist-communist organization, motivating a sector that were mostly punk rock anarchists to become serious political actors. The Congreso de Unificación Anarco Comunista (CUAC), founded in November 1999, was an important milestone for a new generation of libertarian revolutionaries attempting to expand their political work into various social sectors—bolstered by their unity around a set of agreed-upon principles, in a single organization. CUAC was formed in the construction workers union hall, FETRACO-MA, which also functioned as their headquarters. This proximity helped develop deeper bonds and integration with the labor movement. CUAC owes a greater deal of its political development to the Chilean Marxist organizations such as the Movimiento Izquierda Revolucionario (MIR) and the Frente Patriótico Manuel Rodríguez (FPMR). CUAC played a key role in initiating discussions about the need for organized presence within the burgeoning student movement that led to the formation of the Frente de Estudiantes Libertarios (FEL) in May 2003.[45] The CUAC split in 2003, leading to the formation of two currents: the Organización Comunista Libertaria (Communist Libertarian Organization—OCL) and the Corriente Revolucionaria Anarquista (Anarchist Revolutionary Current—CRA), while the FEL remained aligned with the OCL. The eventual explosion of a militant high school student movement in 2006, calling for free education, evolved into a well-strategized (yet very top-down) university student movement. The movement climaxed in 2011, and has assured anarchism's ideological viability in Chile today.

Another important turning point in organized anarchism in Chile occurred in 2013. A sector within OCL and FEL called Red Libertaria (Libertarian Network—RL) who "firmly and

---

45 "The Process of the Initial Construction of FEL," *Struggle/Lucha Común*, North Eastern Federation of Anarchist Communists, published January 14, 2012, http://nefac.net/node/2576.

enthusiastically joined the 'Todos a la Moneda' (Everyone to La Moneda) platform, whose candidate was Marcel Claude."[46] In an article penned by Gutiérrez Danton and Rafael Agacino, they underscore, "But it was not only the decision *itself* to participate in an election that produced this seismic reaction within the Chilean libertarian movement; it was the *manner* in which the decision was made," especially the secrecy by a sector within OCL and FEL that left many of their comrades dumbfounded and feeling betrayed. Those who questioned the creation of RL and a move toward electoralism were expelled, sparking resignations. The expelled grouping, along with other collectives and individuals not associated with OCL, organized the Communist Libertarian Congress over the course of two years that led to the founding of Solidaridad-Federación Comunista Libertaria (Solidarity—Communist Libertarian Federation) in January 2016.

This organizational split placed the FEL in a difficult position when anarchists gained the presidency of the Chilean University Student Federation (FECH) with their candidate Melissa Sepúlveda, a feat not accomplished since the 1920s. A decision was made to postpone the FEL split until the end of Sepúlveda's term. Sepúlveda, who ran on an explicit feminist and anarchist platform, was a political departure from Camila Vallejo, a Communist Party member and FECH president in 2011 who received international attention. Sepúlveda publically supported student-worker alliances and autonomous organizing amongst the working class. At the end of her term in April 2015, Sepúlveda, along with other FEL dissidents who opposed the electoralism move, founded Acción Libertaria (Libertarian Action—AL).

While authoritarian dictatorships claimed the lives of thousands in Brazil, Argentina, Chile, and Uruguay, Mexico's "Dirty War" of the 60s and 70s saw the full repressive power of the

---

46   José Antonio Gutiérrez D. and Rafael Agacino, "Some reflections on libertarians in Chile and electoral participation," Libcom, January 4, 2017, https://libcom.org/library/some-reflections-libertarians-chile-electoral -participation.

Institutional Revolutionary Party (PRI) directed against leftists, youth, organizers, and the landless peasantry in the wake of the Tlatelolco massacre of October 2, 1968. The State murdered hundreds of students in Mexico City that day, and the PRI forcibly disappeared and extrajudicially executed thousands more as part of its counter-insurgency strategy to suppress the generalized societal outrage provoked by the same.[47] The EZLN itself was founded in 1983 as a union between landless indigenous *Chiapanecxs* and urban-based mestizo and European-descended militants from the *Fuerzas de Liberación Nacional* (FLN), which had been created in 1969[48]—much as the ten-year Colombian civil war known as *La Violencia*, which claimed thousands of lives catalyzed the founding in 1964 of the FARC (Revolutionary Armed Forces of Colombia) and the ELN (National Liberation Army).[49] The neo-Zapatista insurrection on January 1, 1994, proclaimed a radical halt to the ceaseless ethnocide targeting indigenous peoples since the Spanish conquest. The rapid response of domestic and international civil society to the uprising limited the intensity of direct repression by the Mexican Army, resulting paradoxically in the PRI's resorting instead to employing paramilitary terror against Zapatista support-bases and Zapatista-sympathizing communities in Chiapas—a strategy that continues to this day. Following the inevitable breakdown of negotiations with a racist state failing to observe the San Andrés Accords (1996), the EZLN focused intensely on furthering communal autonomy by strengthening the participatory alternate institutions that comprise the movement. These insitutions, including cooperatives, autonomous education, the public health sector, and popular assemblies, exist alongside the military structures. This project of autonomy advanced importantly in 2003 with the announcement of

---

47   Elena Poniatowska, *La noche de Tlatelolco: testimonios de historia oral* (México, D.F.: Ediciones Era, 2012 [1971]).
48   Raúl Romero, "EZLN: 17 de noviembre de 1983," *Rebelión*, November 17, 2012.
49   Chris Kraul, "The battles began in 1964: Here's a look at Colombia's war with the FARC rebels," *Los Angeles Times*, August 30, 2016.

the Good-Government Councils (JBG's), comprised of delegates, sometimes as young as adolescents, who rotate in the administration of the five regions of Chiapas where the EZLN has a presence.

Hence, while it is true that the EZLN's initial uprising sought to inspire a regional or country-wide revolution to take over the state—with the Zapatistas hoping to march on Mexico City and liberate it once again—the neo-Zapatista movement has distinguished itself from other Latin American guerrilla struggles by the anti-electoralism and anti-statism that has defined the development of its autonomy. A decade ago, the EZLN launched *La Otra Campaña* as an effort to unite a nation-wide anti-authoritarian left alternative to political parties and the state amidst the ongoing battle for power between the right-wing National Action Party (PAN) and Andrés Manuel López Obrador, the social-democrat candidate, in the 2006 elections. In parallel, *la Sexta Declaración de la Selva Lacandona* (Sixth Declaration of the Lacandon Jungle [2005]) proudly declared the movement's autonomy in search of a new constitution that would meet its original thirteen demands.[50]

Yet now, after having championed autonomous social organization as a viable alternative for over a decade, the EZLN joins its comrade-representatives from the National Indigenous Congress (CNI) in endorsing the proposal for an Indigenous Government Council (CIG) and in presenting the Nahua traditional healer María de Jesús "Marichuy" Patricio Martínez as CIG spokesperson, councilor, and candidate for the 2018 presidential elections.[51] The CNI describes this move as "going on the offensive," and it paradoxically claims not to want to administer power but rather to

---

50   These are: shelter (or housing), land, food, health, education, information, culture, independence, democracy, justice, freedom, and peace. Comité Clandestino Revolucionario Indígena-Comandancia General del Ejército Zapatista de Liberación Nacional (CCRI-CG EZLN), "Sexta Declaración de la Selva Lacandona," June 2005. Available online: http://enlacezapatista .ezln.org.mx/sdsl-es/.

51   CNI y EZLN, "Llegó la hora," *Enlace Zapatista*, 28 May 2017. Available online: http://enlacezapatista.ezln.org.mx/2017/05/28/llego-la-hora-cni-ezln/.

dismantle it. Since the announcement, Marichuy and comrades have stressed that the focus is not on the ballot but rather "organization, life, and the defense of territory." Yet the conclusion of the Fifth CNI in early 2017 is clear: the CIG is meant to "govern this country."[52] It remains to be seen how this move will play out, and how it will affect the Zapatista movement and autonomous indigenous movements elsewhere in Mexico and Latin America. We imagine that this shift toward electoralism is being met with a degree of resistance within Zapatista ranks, particularly among the youth who have been raised with the JBG's and *la Sexta*.

Acknowledgments

We would like to thank by name several comrades across the Americas who contributed to this introduction: José Antonio Gutiérrez D. and Pablo Abufom S. for their useful input about the history of contemporary organizations in the Southern Cone; Lorena Mans and Bree Busk whose anarchist-feminist contributions make us all better militants and more accurate writers; Joshua Savala, whose historical analysis is informed by his everyday praxis, and who can be counted on for his historical knowledge and attention to detail; also Scott Nappalos, who will ensure that our platformism does not overshadow the contribution of anarcho-syndicalists; and finally, all those in Latin America who, past and present, make anarchism a viable option and this revolutionary dream not only possible, but necessary.

---

52   "Convocatoria a la Asamblea Constitutiva del Concejo Indígena de Gobierno," *Enlace Zapatista*, April 2, 2017. Available online: http://enlacezapatista.ezln.org.mx/2017/04/02/convocatoria-a-la-asamblea-constitutiva-del-concejo-indigena-de-gobierno-para-mexico.

1. Argentina

A. Utopian Socialism

Utopian socialism is a designation commonly carrying a pejorative meaning in Marxist literature and is considered a precursor to anarchism. But we must recognize that it is a precursor to Marxism as well. During the dictatorship of Juan Manuel de Rosas (1829–52), Eugenio Tandonnet, a Fourierist, visited Buenos Aires. He got along just as well with that bloodthirsty feudal ruler as with the liberal Domingo Sarmiento, future president, whom he met on board a ship en route to Europe.[1] Even though the latter seemed to have understood and appreciated the French journalist's politics, the dictator doubtless considered them insane, as De Angelis, his biographer, would later say.[2]

The ideas of Saint-Simon, Leroux, and other utopian socialists had already influenced the Generation of '37 and Esteban

---

1   Alfredo Cepeda, *Los utopistas* (Buenos Aires: Editorial Futuro, 1950), 50; A. Ardao, *Filosofía preuniversitaria en el Uruguay* (Montevideo: Claudio García Editores, 1945), 117–35. For Fourier, see Armand-Maublanc, *Fourier* (México: F.C.E., 1940); C. Gide, *Fourier* (Paris: Sirey, 1932).

2   Carlos Rama, *Utopismo socialista (1830–1893)* (Caracas: Biblioteca Ayacucho, 1977), xxxii; see also Domingo Sarmiento, *Viajes, I. Del Valparaíso a París* (Buenos Aires: Librería Hachette, 1955), 174.

Echevarría, who referred to them in his *Dogma socialista*.[3] Their ideas entered the pages of *La Moda*, the weekly publication run by Juan Bautista Alberdi and Juan María Gutiérrez. The term *socialismo* itself, meant to describe a "tendency towards sociability and humanitarianism," was used for the first time in the Río de la Plata region during the Rosas era.[4]

In all of Latin America, utopian socialism had no greater influence on the leading Romantic writers than in Argentina. But while it is important to note this, for obvious reasons we must put aside the examination of that ideological movement here.[5]

Between this early period and the organization of workers brought about by the First International, we should mention the little known figure of the Balearic printer Bartolomé Victory y Suárez, who "arrived in Argentina around 1860 already with a history of engagement in social struggles." He was associated with freemasonry; served as editor of *La República* (journal of the Bilbao brothers) and as director of *La Crónica del Progreso* and *Revista masónica americana*; and was the translator, as well as commentator, of Cabet's *El comunismo*, although he made clear that he was not partisan to the "monastic system." His humanistic socialism was influenced by Fernando Garrido, and the latter's exposition of Rochdale's experience greatly interested him.[6]

---

3   See José Ingenieros, *Las direcciones filosóficas de la cultura argentina* (Buenos Aires: Eudeba, 1963), 71 *et seq.*; A. Cedepa, *Los utopistas*, 44; A. Palcos, *Prólogo al Dogma Socialista* (Buenos Aires: n.p., 1944), xxii–iv. On Saint-Simon, see M. Dondo, *The French Faustus: Henri de Saint Simon* (New York: Philosophical Library, 1955).

4   Rama, *Utopismo socialista*, xxx. Also see, Carlos M. Lombardi, *Las ideas sociales en la argentina* (Buenos Aires: n.p. 1965), 56–58.

5   On utopian socialism in general, see M. Buber, *Caminos de utopia* (Mexico: F.C.E., 1978); G.D.H. Cole, *Historia del pensamiento socialista–I Los Precursores* (Mexico: F.C.E., 1957); Ángel Cappelletti, *El socialismo utópico* (Rosario: Grupo Editor de Estudios Sociales, 1968).

6   D. A. de Santillán, *El movimiento anarquista en la Argentina* (Buenos Aires: Argonauta, 1930), 12–13.

B. Beginnings of Anarchist Propaganda, 1871 to 1889

Refugees from the Paris Commune began to arrive in 1871. Some of them were anarchists, such as Gobley, who had been imprisoned in Quelern along with the illustrious geographer Élisée Reclus. After brief stays in Rio de Janeiro and Montevideo he settled in Buenos Aires in 1878.[7] Vladimir Muñoz recounts that in 1885 V. Mariani distributed *Le Revolté* in the Argentinean capital and notes that on July 15, 1887 that journal, founded in Switzerland by Kropotkin, published the following note: "The anarchist group of Buenos Aires meets every Wednesday at eight o'clock in the evening in the Café Turco on Serrito Street on the corner of Cuyo."[8] Before this, a public gathering in solidarity with the martyrs of Chicago had attracted some 350 persons. On March 18, 1888 anarchists celebrated the anniversary of the Paris Commune in the headquarters of the social democrats of Buenos Aires, with six of the event's organizers arrested by police.

In these early years anarchist books and pamphlets frequently arrived in Buenos Aires from Spain, Italy, France, and other places. For example, the Belgian Emile Piette received a parcel with a dozen copies of Kropotkin's *Words of a Rebel*. In 1889 Piette served as courier for a sum of money sent by a group of Chilean anarchists—Washington Marzoratti, Alfred Müller, Bernard Bouyre, Salamón y Prim—to assist the already famous libertarian champion *Le Revolté*.[9] Meanwhile, some early local groups were beginning their own written propaganda. And the Catalan carpenter Juan Vila in Buenos Aires was at work on his translation of Kropotkin's *The Conquest of Bread*.[10]

During this early period of anarchist propaganda in Argentina members of a few French and Italian groups stand out for the vigor

---

7   E. Reclus, *Correspondence II* (Paris: n.p., 1911), cited in V. Muñoz, *Notas* to Max Nettlau.

8   V. Muñoz, *Notas* to M. Nettlau, "Viaje libertario a través de América Latina," *Reconstruir*, 76; Santillán, *El movimiento anarquista*, 39.

9   Muñoz, *Notas*, 39; Santillán, *El movimiento anarquista*, 38.

10   Santillán, *El movimiento anarquista*, 54.

they brought from their home countries to the libertarian workers' movement. Several of them retained their militancy for many decades, such as A. Sadier, who died on March 8, 1936; others were active for shorter periods of time, such as F. Denambride, who after 1887 tried to spread anarchist ideology in the province of Santa Fe.[11] A few Italian anarchists from the same native town or region formed groups and then with missionary zeal reached deep into national territory settling in agricultural or manufacturing centers to spread the good news of libertarian socialism. Thus Italian militants originally from Isola Dovarese, where a group had formed under the name *I Ribelli*, set out to the industrial port city of Rosario and established a group called El Miserable. An anonymous French militant arrived in Azul, a city in the province of Buenos Aires, and was able to bring together anarchists and other similar groups into a single association.[12]

Coordinated action got a boost in the 1870s. An initiative by the Central Committee of the International Workingmen's Association to establish a section in Buenos Aires was warmly supported by a group of Spanish workers and promptly implemented by them. In September 1872, during the Hague Conference, news arrived of the existence of internationalist workers' groups in Australia, New Zealand, and Argentina. A letter dated March 23, 1873 reads:

> There are presently three sections of the International in Buenos Aires, based on the various languages: the French section, the Italian and Spanish sections that formed later; each section has its own central committee and matters of general interest are addressed by a federal committee of six members, two from each section.

The letter was signed by A. Aubert, then general secretary of the International in Buenos Aires, and reveals the enormous difficulties

---

11   On French anarchists who were active in Argentina, see D. A. de Santillán, "El anarquismo en la argentina," supplement to *La Protesta*, 260: 66–67.

12   V. Muñoz, *Notas*, 39. On Italian anarchists migrating to Argentina, see Enzo Santerelli, *Il Socialismo anarchico in Italia* (Milan: Feltrinelli, 1959), 76.

the project encountered in founding a section, specifically mentioning "the persistent attacks by the press."[13]

Soon enough ideological differences reflecting divisions in the international workers' movement emerged in the very heart of the Argentinean section.[14] In Buenos Aires disputes between "authoritarians" (Marxists) and "antiauthoritarians" or "federalists" (anarchists) were evident from the start.

We will soon see that in the French section the authoritarians dominated, rather puzzling when one bears in mind that Proudhonism was then the majority position in the metropolitan workers' movement; while Bakuninist ideas had always aroused the greatest following in the Italian and Spanish sections. Nonetheless, the authoritarian minority was able to impose the ideological tone of the Argentinean section, as we can surmise from a letter by F. C. Calcerán, secretary of the Uruguayan section, to his Mexican comrades on May 25, 1872: "We are preparing a newspaper that will be called *El obrero federalista* to fight the authoritarians who have set up camp in Buenos Aires." In a subsequent letter of January 1, 1873 addressed to the same group, Calcerán clarified who the "authoritarians" were: "We inform you and the section you represent that a group of French citizens in Buenos Aires has formed a section of the International representing the antidemocratic spirit of the Central Committee in London."[15] It thus appears that the members of the French section—undoubtedly the least numerous of the three—were in line with the politics of Marx and his allies. Perhaps they were Marxists. But given that Marxism was hardly present in France during this time, one can well suppose they were Blanquists, who had joined the Marxists in the Congresses of the International. In any event, after 1876 the "antiauthoritarian"

---

13   Santillán, *El movimiento anarquista*, 15–16.
14   See Victor García, *La Internacional obrera* (Madrid: Júcar, 1978), 90–124; B. Aladino, "La Associación Internacional de Trabajadores," in *Certamen internacional de "La Protesta"* (Buenos Aires: n.p., 1927), 142–57.
15   Santillán, *El movimiento anarquista*, 17–18; see also, Julio Godio, *Historia del movimiento obrero latinoamericano* (Caracas: Nueva Sociedad, 1985), 60–61.

Bakuninists dominated. In an article published in the *Almanaque Socialista de La Vanguardia* (1898), José Ingenieros wrote that "a Bakuninist Center of Workers' Propaganda has been established with the almost exclusive purpose of combating the Marxists."[16]

In early 1879 *El Descamisado* appeared in Buenos Aires, considered by some the "first anarchist newspaper" in Argentina.[17] We know from Max Nettlau that it was "very primitive in its conception of ideas," a "bit vague and confused." Perhaps on that account the title of that newspaper, and perhaps also its viewpoint, were echoed by the Peronist press seventy years later.[18]

The incipient anarchist movement in Argentina began to lose its vitality and by the 1880s seemed nearly extinguished. It did not take long, however, for it to regain full strength as a consequence of the enormous European immigration to Argentina and many regions of its interior.[19] Oved writes:

> From 1880 to 1914 massive waves of immigrants flowed into Argentina totaling 3,034,000 people, an important factor in the impressive growth of the population, from 2,492,00 inhabitants in 1880 to 7,855,000 in 1904. A direct result of this massive immigration was that in 1914 one third of the total population consisted of foreigners and the percentage of immigrants in the total population was the highest in the world.[20]

This very unusual demographic phenomenon proved decisive for the history of anarchism and the workers' movement in Argentina.

---

16   D. A. de Santillán, "*La Protesta*, Su historia, sus diversas fases, y su significación en el movimiento anarquista de América del Sur," in *Certamen internacional de "La Protesta*," 35.

17   Iaacov Oved, *El anarquismo y el movimiento obrero en Argentina* (México: Siglo Veintiuno Editores, 1978), 20.

18   Nettlau, "Contribución a la bibliografía anarquista de la América Latina desde 1914," in *Certamen Internacional de "La Protesta*," 9.

19   See G. Germani, *Política y sociedad en una época de transición* (Buenos Aires: Paídos, 1962), 181–82.

20   Oved, *El anarquismo*, 30–31.

As Santillán puts it, the main source of growth "came from the immigration of numerous internationalists persecuted in Europe who were able to make the most out of the harshness of the struggle for existence among the popular masses."[21]

It is important to remember the work of some of these internationalists. In 1880 Héctor Mattei arrived in Buenos Aires. An Italian militant, in 1887 he began to publish an anarchocommunist weekly along the ideological lines of Errico Malatesta, *El Socialista: Organo de los Trabajadores*. According to Mattei, a group of Italian workers—among whom he names Marino Garbaccio, baker; Washington Marzoratti, engraver; and Miguel Fazzi, cabinet-maker—founded an anarcho-communist group in June 1884 with the objective of engaging in public discussions on the "social question," and made available some of the anarchist papers from Europe free of charge. Several Spanish immigrants who were more inclined to the collectivism of Bakunin than the communism of Kropotkin and Malatesta, among them Francisco Morales and Feliciano Rey, also joined the propaganda efforts at this time.[22] The native anarchist press began to grow and to gain vigor. Between May 2 and September 28, 1884 *La Lucha Obrera* was published in Buenos Aires.[23]

In February (or March) 1885 to avoid another imprisonment the already famous revolutionary Ericco Malatesta, in an incredible episode, fled Italy inside a crate of sewing machines.[24] His destination was Buenos Aires. Mattei wrote the following in the September 1, 1909 issue of *La Protesta*:

---

21 Santillán, *El movimiento anarquista*, 31; See also, G. Gori, *Inmigración y colonization en la Argentina* (Buenos Aires: Eudeba, 1964).

22 Santillán, *El movimiento anarquista*, 32–34.

23 Nettlau, "Contribución a la bibliografía anarquista," 9.

24 On the life and thought of Malatesta, see A. Borghi, *Errico Malatesta* (Milan: Instituto Editoriale Italiano, 1947); Nettlau, *Errico Malatesta. El hombre, el revolucionario, el anarquista* (Barcelona: n.p., 1933); Tentro Tagliaferri, *Errico Malatesta, Armando Borghi e compagni davanto ai giurati di Milano* (Milan: n.p., n.d.); Vernon Richards, *Malatesta. Pensamiento y acción revolucionarios* (Buenos Aires: Proyección, 1974). For a complete bibliography, see Ugo Fedeli, *Errico Malatesta. Bibliografía* (Naples: n.p., 1951).

Communist and anarchist propaganda intensified when, after two or three months of the arrival in Buenos Aires of our comrade Malatesta, a Círculo de Estudio Sociales was formed with great enthusiasm, located in 1375 Bartolomé Mitre Street, where Malatesta and other comrades gave the first communist anarchist public speeches, later published in Italian in *La Questione Sociale*. In the following years other circles and clubs of "estudios sociales" were formed, some of them communist anarchist.... In 1887 Errico Malatesta cooperated with other anarchist comrades in the permanent organization of the Sociedad Cosmopolita de Obreros Panaderos, giving speeches at their meetings.[25]

In 1886 Malatesta set out on a journey worthy of being narrated by his compatriot Emilio Salgari: the search for gold in the vast Patagonian deserts captured from indigenous peoples several years earlier by the Argentinean army. His purpose was to gather funds to promote libertarian propaganda and to assist workers' organizations in their revolutionary activities. So, along with four comrades he settled in a cabin above Cabo Virgenes, preceded by a party with tools and other necessary supplies.

For a few weeks they lived on seafood, and then returned to Buenos Aires empty-handed. By mid–1889 Malatesta was en route back to Europe, returning not with the gold he had hoped to find but with the satisfaction of having organized the first workers' unions and planted the seeds of a great movement of anarchist workers in Argentina which, a few years later, the Valencian novelist Blasco Ibáñez would call the "people's land."

According to the German Marxist Augusto Kühn, between 1887 and 1888 a group known as Círculo socialista internacional, dominated by Spanish and Italian anarchists, would meet in Café Grutli (on Cerrito Street, between Bartolomé Mitre and Cangallo

---

25   Cited in J. N. Solomonoff, *Ideologías del movimiento obrero y conflicto social* (Buenos Aires: Proyección, 1971), 197.

streets). Once again libertarian ideology, particularly in its Kropot-kian and Malatestian visions, prevailed in the majority of groups within the Argentinean proletariat. But as the 1880s come to an end a new crisis emerged. As Kühn observed, the groups that had sprung up like mushrooms on the plains of the Pampas now split and recon-vened only "to wage an implacable war against the recent socialist organization (i.e., Marxist)." This constant battle between anarchists and Marxists culminated, Santillán says, "in oratories of epic pro-portions in the period of Pietro Gori." But polemics in Argentinean anarchism hardly rose to what was then common in Spain.[26]

C. 1890 to 1896

Marxists of the *Vorwärts* group sent Professor Alejo Peyret as a delegate to the 1889 International Socialist Congress in Paris, and convened a political rally in the Prado Español in Buenos Aires with the objective of founding a workers' federation and a Span-ish newspaper to articulate the ideas and aspirations of the work-ing class. Anarchists were also reorganizing their existing groups and starting new ones that will later show great determination, for example, Los desheredados. In the January 22, 1909 issue of *La Protesta*, M. Reguera recounted the prodigious propagandist activ-ity of Los desheredados:

> Let us summarize the first deeds of that handful of fight-ing enthusiasts: initiation of continuous and simultaneous speeches in three or four places distant from each other; un-interrupted publications of violent and provocative manifes-tations of combat and action... The speeches given by two or three orators would follow each other... It was not rare to an-nounce, for example, a speech at two o'clock in the afternoon in Almagro, another an hour later in Corrales, a third one at

---

26   Santillán, *El movimiento anarquista*, 40.

four o'clock in Barracas, and a fourth one in the city square
at night. For all of this two and sometimes one orator would
carry out the program with precision and punctuality. The
outstanding orator of that period was comrade Rafael Roca.

Roca, who died prematurely, had edited the initial "Manifesto" of *El Perseguido*, in which he articulated the meaning of
anarcho-communism. That manifesto led to severe political repression and the confiscation of a number of issues of the newspaper
that, precisely for that reason, was called *El Perseguido*.[27] In spite
of all the persecutions it published more than one hundred issues
and was available from May 18, 1890 until the last weeks of 1896.
The fruit of the enthusiastic and heroic labor of a small group of
militants, it can be considered the most representative libertarian
publication of the period. Its first page gave the following warning:
"Published when possible." Oved observes:

> The problems were abundant, the members of the group
> edited, printed, and distributed the paper; distribution was
> accomplished in clandestine conditions and with grave risks.
> It was delivered in the streets, in workers' neighborhoods, in
> gatherings, by mail, and sometimes surreptitiously placed in-
> side issues of *La Prensa*.[28]

Propaganda was not limited to the national capital. During
these same years the Italian anarchist paper *Demoliamo* and the
anarcho-feminist *La Voz de la Mujer*, edited by Virginia Bolten,
were published in Rosario.[29]

In addition to Roca and Mattei, active militants during this period also included the Belgian bookseller Emile Piette, the painter

---

27   Ibid., 44–45.
28   Oved, *El anarquismo*, 43; E. López Arango and D. A. de Santillán, *El
       anarquismo en el movimiento obrero* (Buenos Aires: Cosmos, 1925), 11.
29   Plácido Grela, "El movimiento obrero en Rosario," in *Todo es Historia*,
       No. 49, Buenos Aires, 1971.

Ragazzini, the Spanish worker Victoriano San José, the French journalist Pierre Quiroule, the Catalan Inglan LaFarga (later an editor of *La Protesta*), Manuel Reguera, Fortunato Serantoni, Juan Vila, F. Denambride, Espinosa, Lacour, Reaux, and the writer Orsini Bertani, who was the editor of Barrett's work, and in later years during his residency in Montevideo was a proponent of that current of thought then known as anarcho-Batllism. Also during this period two notable anarchist physicians began their popularizing work: Dr. Creaghe in Luján and Dr. Arana in Rosario, both magnificent and overlooked examples of the Latin American professional committed to the people. As Santillán notes, "The salient character of the movement in this period is the aggressive, enthusiastic, and proselytizing fever that did not back down from any sacrifice."[30]

The first important polemic within the Argentinean anarchist movement occurred during the 1890s. On the one hand, the anarcho-communists of *El Perseguido* showed themselves to be enemies of all organization that transcends affinity groups, and in particular opposed the creation of anarchist syndicates. On the other hand, those called "anarcho-socialists," whose organs were Serantoni's *La Questione Sociale* and Dr. Creaghe's *El Oprimido* and were in contact with Malatesta and the dominant tendency of the Italian movement, supported the creation of resistance societies and anarchist syndicates.[31] In the mid–1890s the latter group, which responded equally to the example of Malatesta from the previous decade and to the thought of Kropotkin, came to comprise an ample majority of the workers' movement.[32] The Kropotkian view of *La Révolté* was represented by Pierre Quiroule's newspaper *La*

---

30   Santillán, *El movimiento anarquista*, 46.

31   The polemic between organizers and anti-organizers developed at the level of strategy and did not coincide, as one might imagine, with the ideological struggle of anarchists partisan to communism or collectivism against those who are individualists, or followers of Stirner or, sometimes, Nietzsche.

32 .   The Kropotkian and Bakuninist trends favored by workers' organizations and revolutionary unionism dominated in Italy beginning in the 1880s, and a bit later in Spain. See J. Peirats, *La CNT en la revolución española* (Paris: Ruedo Ibérico, 1971), 28.

Liberté, for which the later celebrated Auguste Vaillant would write during his residence in Argentina.[33] Quiroule's *La Liberté*, though partisan to workers' organizations, favored propaganda by the deed and, like *El Perseguido*—from which it differed by a more theoretical and doctrinaire attitude—defended all anarchist *attentats*, then much in vogue, but more frequent in Europe than in Argentina. Yet in Rosario, the anarcho-communist group Ciencia y Progreso, apparently influenced by Dr. Arana, had since 1896 opposed terrorism as a tactic and even as a rhetorical trope.[34]

D. 1897 to 1910

An organizational tendency favorable to the syndicalist's struggle in Argentinean anarchism clearly asserted itself during this period. Anarcho-communist groups, which had predicted an immediate social revolution and rejected all forms of syndicalism as either an obstacle or a trap set by social democrats, by 1905 had waned to the point of near extinction.

Strikes and other workers' struggles were abundant in 1896, yet anarchist intervention was limited, according to the chief of police of Buenos Aires, Manuel Campos.[35] Things changed the following year, however. In 1897, both as effect and cause of the growing anarchist presence in the struggles of Argentinean workers, *La Protesta Humana* was founded, the most important and enduring anarchist newspaper in Latin America. Its pages reflected not only the turbulent trajectory of the libertarian movement, but also the

---

33   Upon his return to Paris in 1893, Vaillant threw a bomb in the Chamber of Deputies. No one was killed, but he was nonetheless sentenced to death. He climbed the scaffold with great courage, exclaiming: "Long live Anarchy! My death shall be avenged!" And it certainly was, not once but multiple times. Just one month later, Emile Henry detonated a bomb at the Saint Lazare station, leaving one dead and twenty injured (G. Woodcock, *El anarquismo* (Ariel: n.p., 1979) 288).

34   Santillán, *El movimiento anarquista*, 61–62.

35   Oved, *El anarquismo*, 63–64.

entire history of the Argentinean workers' syndicalism from a point of view that is at once revolutionary, ethical, socialist, and libertarian. According to Fernando Quesada:

> During its long life it survived all the alternatives; overcame all internal crises that destroyed a large part of the movement; absorbed all challenges and provocations. Neither state persecutions nor ideological disagreements between brothers were able to blunt its cutting edge. ... It was born to overcome all calamities."[36]

The inaugural issue hit the streets on June 13, 1897. Its first editor was the Catalan carpenter Gregorio Inglan Lafarga; its first administrator, the Italian baker Francisco Berri; and among its first collaborators were José Prat, Eduardo Gilimón, and Mariano Cortés, later joined by well-known literary figures of the time, for example, Florencio Sánchez, Pascual Guaglianone, Julio Camba, and Santiago Locascio.[37] After November 7, 1903 the journal's title was shortened to *La Protesta*. A group of collaborators and sympathizers headed by Dr. Creaghe were successful in obtaining a proper printing press, first used on March 5, 1904 for issue number 253 of the paper. A few weeks later, on April 1, it became a daily publication. Its first daily issue contained the following remark: "The importance of this publication to the world of laborers is so great that it is difficult to measure. It affirms the anarchist personality in Argentina." The editorship went first to Elam Ravel and then Alberto Ghiraldo, with whom prominent literary figures like Julio R. Barcos, Edmundo Biachi, and José de Maturana collaborated.

On March 7, 1910 Argentinean anarchists started a second daily paper, *La Batalla*, published in the evenings, with the dramatist Rodolfo González Pacheco and the journalist Teodoro

---

36   Fernando Quesada, "La Protesta. Una longeza voz libertaria," in *Todo es Historia*, No. 82, Buenos Aires, I, 76.

37   Quesada, "La Protesta," 80.

Antillí as principal editors.[38] Their accomplishment clearly shows the vitality of the movement at this time. Anarchist newspapers in Spanish, Italian, and French flourished everywhere, not only in Buenos Aires but also in the interior of the country. Nettlau gives us a list: in Buenos Aires, in Spanish *La Revolución Social* (1897), *Ni Dios ni amo* (1896), *Ciencia Social* (1897–1899), *Germinal* (1897–1898), *El Rebelde* (1899–1902), *Los Tiempos Nuevos* (1900), *Vida Nueva* (1903–1904); in Italian, *Lavoriamo* (1893), *La Nuova Civilitá* (1901), *Venti Settembre* (1895–1903); in French, *Le Cyclone* (1895). And in the interior of the republic: in Rosario, *La Verdad* (1896), *La Libre Iniciativa* (1895–1896), *La Federación Obrera* (1896), and *La Libera Parola*; in La Plata *La Anarquía* (1895), in Barracas, *El Revolucionario* (1895), and in Chilcoy, *La Fuerza de la Razón*.[39]

It is also worth noting publications by syndicates and diverse groups with anarchist leanings, as well as an increasing number of translations of well-known European anarchists. Kropotkin's *Conquest of Bread* appeared in 1895, followed in 1896 by Jean Grave's *The Future Society*. The group called Los Acratas published a series of books and pamphlets, such as Malatesta's *Among Peasants* and Kropotkin's *Anarchism: Its Philosophy and Ideal*, among others.[40]

With the objective of overcoming anti-organization tendencies, still present even if only in a minority, the Federación Libertaria de los Grupos Socialistas-anarquistas was founded, with Pietro Gori drafting its fundamental principles.[41] This celebrated Italian lawyer and criminologist, born in Messina in 1869, arrived in Buenos Aires on July 21, 1898 fleeing authorities that sought to arrest him for disseminating anarchist propaganda. Several months later he

---

38   Quesada, "La Protesta," 84–86.
39   Nettlau, "Contribución a la bibliografía," 13–14.
40   López Arango and Santillán, *El anarquismo*, 12–13.
41   Santillán, *El movimiento anarquista*, 62. See also, Jorge Larroca, "Pedro Gori, un anarquista en Buenos Aires," in *Todo es Historia*, No. 47 (Buenos Aires, 1971).

founded the journal *Criminología moderna*, later titled *Archivos de psiquiatría y criminología*. A brilliant group of young jurists and criminologists—José Ingenieros, Antonio Dellepiane, Luis Maria Drago, Rodolfo Rivarole, Juan Vucetich, and others—was attracted to his scientific teachings; another group, no less brilliant, of young writers and poets—Pascual Guaglianone, Félix Basterra, Alberto Ghilardo—was swayed by his socialist libertarian ideology. An orator of easy and fiery speech, and at the same time of firm and coherent ideas, always more attentive to scientific rigor than rhetorical effect, Gori travelled to all the principal cities of Argentina, receiving great acclaim not only from workers and anarchists but also from bourgeois and conservatives. He wrote several pamphlets such as *Las bases morales de la anarquía*, *Vuestro orden y nuestro desorden*, among others. In January 1902 he returned to his native land, but not without leaving a profound influence on the scientific, literary, and anarchist movements in Argentina.[42]

With the crisis of 1890 the economic situation worsened. As always, the working class suffered the most painful consequences. According to *La Prensa*, in Buenos Aires there were some forty thousand unemployed. Strikes proliferated in the capital as well as in various urban centers of the interior. The strikes were sometimes successful, but they did not lead to lasting results and in more than a few instances victories quickly were rendered meaningless or simply disregarded. Consequently, a workers' central came to be seen as an absolute necessity in the struggle.

The idea that began to take hold among workers and anarchist groups was to convene all resistance societies in Argentina with the objective of starting such a central. On June 25, 1901 a congress assembled with attendance "of some fifty delegates representing thirty to thirty-five workers' organizations both from the capital

---

42   See E. G. Gilimón, *Hechos y comentarios* (Buenos Aires-Montevideo: n.p., 1911), 32; Oved, *El anarquismo*, 88–93; Solomonoff, *Ideologías del movimiento*, 198; Santillán, "La Protesta: Su historia, sus diversas fases y su significación en el movimiento anarquista de América del Sur," in *Certamen internacional de "La Protesta,"* Buenos Aires, 1927, 38.

and the interior,"[43] but not without objections from various radical groups, always fearful of traps by the social democrats. There the Federación Obrera Argentina (FOA) was founded. Anarchists did "all possible to create an entity that included all workers without regard to their races or beliefs, based on a solid foundation of direct action and economic struggle."[44] Nonetheless, the Marxist socialists, obviously a minority position, soon broke away, unable to put the new organization to the service of the party or their political goals. Adrián Patroni, a delegate to the founding congress, and the Marxist group La organización began an "incessant and treacherous war against FOA," and promoted the idea that it is necessary to create a second workers' federation without anarchists—of course, controlled by the Socialist Party and as its mere mouthpiece—an act tantamount to excluding the vast majority of workers who were politically aware and ideologically defined.

The new federation had immediate occasion to commit itself in a struggle, as the period of 1901–1902 was one of great social and proletariat agitation. Strikes erupted in all trades and regions of the republic. The crisis produced a stern defense of higher salaries and better working conditions. At the time, the workday was usually no less than ten hours long and wages were at best subsistence pay. Many of the strikes were successful and brought a relative degree of relief to the condition of workers, demonstrating to the majority of anarchists the effectiveness of syndicalist organization. In December 1901 painters of the Mar del Plata achieved the eight-hour workday and a wage increase of fifty cents per day; in February 1902 dockworkers in Buenos Aires achieved a nine-hour workday and a wage increase of four dollars per day. "In this manner," Santillán notes, "step-by-step workers asserted their rights from the usurpers, and not without the occasional bloodshed."[45] The assas-

---

43 Santillán, *La FORA—Ideología y trajectoria* (Buenos Aires: Proyección, 1971) 67; J. Godio, *Historia del movimiento*, 188–89.

44 Santillán, *La FORA*, 75; Antonio López, *La FORA en el movimiento obrero* (Buenos Aires: CEAL, 1987), vol. 1, 12.

45 Santillán, *La FORA*, 80.

sination of the young Austrian worker Budislavic, killed by police during the general strike in Rosario at the end of 1901, was but one example of the cost.

Between June 19 and 21, 1902 FOA's Second Congress convened in the headquarters of Buenos Aires' *Vorwärts*, with seventy-six delegates in attendance representing forty-seven workers' organizations. The socialists, under the pretext that the assembly had not accepted the credentials of a delegate, withdrew and provoked a split. Several groups joined the socialists, with a total membership of some 1,780 workers, while those that stayed with the anarchists totaled some 7,630. In early 1903 the splinter groups formed the Union General de Trabajadores (UGT), an appendix to the Socialist Party, and began to put into place "a strategy of partial reforms, including moderation in struggle and legal maneuvers."[46] Those who remained in FOA radicalized their attitudes, gradually became anti-parliamentarians, more antilegalistic, and missed no occasion to identify themselves as anarcho-communists.

The constant strikes, the increasing number of resistance societies guided for the most part by anarchists, the proliferation of newspapers spreading libertarian ideas among urban and rural workers, and the indefatigable activities of anarchist orators in all regions of the country began to intimidate both the managerial class and the government.

FOA declared a general strike. The immediate result of the fear it provoked was the improvised and sudden promulgation of the Law of Residence, on November 22, 1902, granting the Executive power to deport, without trial, any immigrant "whose conduct threatens national security or disturbs public order" (Article 2 of the Law). That law, in effect for more than half a century and not revoked by any of the Peronist governments, left the fortunes of all immigrants, who then comprised a large segment of the country's population, in hands of the police. At the same time, a state of siege was declared and the hunt for anarchists and militant workers

---

46   Santillán, *La FORA*, 93; Godio, *Historia del movimiento*, 190.

began. Many foreign-born workers were deported; others, born in Argentina, imprisoned.[47] Miguel Cané, a fine novelist, humorist, and author of *Juvenilia*, one of the classics of Argentinean literature, had the dubious honor of drafting the Law of Residence (law No 4144).[48]

Between June 6 and 8, 1903 FOA's Third Congress assembled in Buenos Aires, with eighty delegates from the capital and the interior in attendance. Addressing the recent Law of Residence, Alberto Ghiraldo, delegate from the stevedores of Villa Constitución, pointed out that this law amounted to the government's acknowledgement of the power of the Argentinean proletariat.

Repression continued. On May 1, 1904 police confronted a workers' rally held in observance of the Chicago martyrs and, taking advantage of the situation, added one more name to the lists of martyrs when they killed the sailor Juan Ocampo. In spite, or perhaps on account, of this the organization of workers only continued to evolve, becoming more militant and hardened. FOA's report, addressed to members of its Fourth Congress, showed its fervor:

> Progress in the idea of emancipation that all societies proclaim has been most distinguished by the tenacity of its resistance; in that terrain we affirm today the very significant step taken by the Federation towards acquiring the legitimate rights of men, even when capital and government have redoubled the shackles by which they aim to subjugate the worker.... Anyone who thinks otherwise should look to the striking railworkers, stevedores, sailors and firefighters, welders, bricklayers, and others. In each of these solidarity has exceeded our hopes, leaving our common enemies perplexed....

---

47   Santillán, *La FORA*, 97–98. See also Sánchez Viamonte, *Biografía de una ley antiargentina, ley 4144* (Buenos Aires: Nuevas Ediciones Argentina, 1952); López, *La FORA*, 33–36.

48   Quesada, "La Protesta," 81. See also Raúl Castagnino, *Miguel Cané* (Buenos Aires, 1952); R. Sáenz Hayes, *Miguel Cané y su tiempo (1851–1905)* (Buenos Aires: Kraft, 1955).

Compared to the previous year, the number of new members is a promising sign.[49]

At mid-year 1903 forty-two unions with a total of 15,212 dues-paying members were affiliated with FOA; twelve months later the numbers had soared to sixty-six unions and 32,893 members.

FOA's Fourth Congress was held in the capital city from July 30 to August 2, 1904. It approved a new name for the central federation, Federación Obrera Regional Argentina (FORA), a change that had an ideological motivation: by adding the adjective "regional" it made plain that Argentina was not considered a state or political unit, but a region of the world in which workers struggle for their liberation.[50] A solidarity pact was also approved, articulating the doctrine, organization, and tactics of the workers' confederation. It proclaimed the establishment of a classless society with neither state nor private property as the ultimate aim of their struggle. Thus its anarchist inspiration was clear.[51]

Meanwhile, as previously noted, UGT had developed as an instrument of the Socialist Party. But at its Third Congress, held from August 12 to 18, 1905, a syndicalist tendency emerged within its very core that was more favorable to the association of workers than to a political party, and accepted the general strike as "an effective means to express the grievances of the working classes"—such was the strength of anarchist influence even among workers who did not share the ideology. This ideological rapprochement between UGT and FORA also involved some agreement on tactics and strategy. Ghiraldo put the point well when he wrote in *La Protesta*:

> If capitalism harms us all, if it affects us all, if it humiliates us all, how is it possible that we do not in each and

---

49 Santillán, *La FORA*, 109. E. G. Gilimón, *Hechos y comentarios* (Buenos Aires), 42–44.

50 Oved, *El anarquismo*, 356–63.

51 Santillán, *La FORA*, 115–120; López Arango and Santillán, *El anarquismo*, 18; López, *La FORA*, 1, 13.

every opportunity act in concert against it? If we achieve the agreement we seek and which we believe is possible in a short time, the power of the working class shall be impossible to overcome.[52]

In fact, UGT proposed a solidarity pact to FORA. But in one of the meetings of the Fifth Congress on August 26, 1905—with five local federations (fifty-three unions), one trade federation (four unions), and forty-one unions from the capital and interior in attendance—FORA, dominated by its most radical elements, declared the proposal "useless, ineffective, and counterproductive." This Congress is FORA's most important, the moment when its ideological orientation was explicitly and definitively defined.

Subsequent to a proposal by the Workers' Federation local from Rosario and in solidarity with the editorial position of *La Protesta* and other workers' newspapers, the following declaration expressing the sentiments of the majority affiliated with FORA was approved:

> The Fifth Congreso Obrero Regional Argentino consistent with the philosophical principles that have provided the *raison d'être* of the organization of workers' federations declares: We advise and recommend to all our followers the broadest possible study and propaganda with the aim of instilling in workers the economic and philosophical principles of anarchist communism. This education, not content with achieving the eight-hour day, will bring total emancipation and, consequently, the social evolution we pursue.[53]

The Congress thus endorsed as its official ideology an anti-authoritarian, self-managed, and federalist communism of which Kropotkin was the principal exponent. As Oved rightly notes,

---

52   Santillán, *La FORA*, 130. See also Ricardo Mella, *Sindicalismo y anarquismo* (La Coruña: n.p., 1910).
53   Ibid., 142; J. Godio, *Historia del movimiento obrero*, 1, 210.

this is easily explained by the deep influence of that ideology on Argentinean anarchism. By this time most individualists were gone, and with them some who, calling themselves "anarcho-communist," had been enemies of the workers' organization, as well as the "anarcho-socialists," proponents of Bakuninist collectivism. Gradually, partisans of anarchist communism had come to dominate. They looked on unions as an instrument not only to assert workers' claims, but also to foster social revolution, following Kropotkin. Indeed, the latter's articles appeared frequently in 1905, and his autobiography, *Memoirs of a Revolutionist*, was serially published in *La Protesta*.[54] After heated disagreements in preceding decades, the same ideology had prevailed in the Spanish anarchist movement as well as in other countries such as Italy, France, Mexico, and Bulgaria. But the most complete merger of anarcho-communism and syndicalist organization was, without doubt, the Fifth Congress of FORA.[55] *La Protesta* reported: "It has been clearly and eloquently shown that this declaration of principles was demanded by the people. ... Before concluding this report, we express our great satisfaction with the doctrinal orientation the Fifth Congress has given to the organization." We can say that at this moment the merger of anarcho-communism and the Argentinean workers' movement reached its zenith. Oved observes: "A climate of exaltation prevailed at the conclusion of the Congress; participants judged it a great moral triumph, as much for the resistance against police efforts to impede its celebration as for the nature of the resolutions approved."[56]

In 1906 and 1907 strikes were widespread, in great part initiated by anarchists from FORA. The reaction by police and government was unrelenting. At the head of Buenos Aires' police was a Colonel Falcón, who, according to Santillán, "swore that he would finish off the anarchists, anticipating the effects not only of continuous

---

54   Oved, *El anarquismo*, 417.
55   Solomonoff, *Ideologías del movimiento obrero*, 194.
56   Oved, *El anarquismo*, 422. See also, R. Ansejo del Río, *Influencia del anarquismo* (Buenos Aires, Elvira Fernández, 1908).

abuses to individual liberty and the freedom to associate but also of restrictive laws, dictatorial decrees, and exceptional procedures."[57]

FORA's Sixth Congress convened in Rosario—a city which had merited the name the "Argentinean Barcelona"—between September 19 and 23, 1906, opening with a significant homage to Russian revolutionaries, and with one hundred five resistance societies from throughout the country in attendance.

The pact between FORA and UGT was never realized because—despite the efforts of those called "syndicalist," and of several socialists and anarchists—the majority of FORA's militants mistrusted and feared parliamentary and legislative socialism. This did not, however, prevent a strong collaboration between both workers' federations: together they called a general strike in 1907 in solidarity with cart drivers in Rosario. Some one hundred fifty thousand workers from around the republic joined the strike. Their announcement, endorsed by FORA and UGT, concluded with the following words:

> Protest has imposed itself and we shall realize it. Public powers are greatly mistaken if they sought to restrict our rights one by one, our liberties one by one, with impunity. Our actions today will teach them to be more measured in the future, to respect us as adversaries, since they have failed to respect us as men. Workers: Defend our liberty, our rights, our dignity, and legitimate aspiration for a better life. Workers: Join the general strike! Workers: Act with solidarity. The bulwark of our defense and triumphant weapon! Long live the general strike![58]

The general strike lasted from January 25 till January 27 with a total victory for the organized workers. The long-awaited congress merging FORA, UGT, and autonomous societies was convened on April 1 at the Verdi Theater. But its purpose would not be achieved, as the

---

57   Santillán, *La FORA*, 143; Godio, *Historia del movimiento obrero*, 1, 202

58   Santillán, *La FORA*, 150–53; Godio, *Historia del movimiento obrero*, 1, 205.

majority insisted on giving the workers' federation a revolutionary character and proclaiming adherence to anarchist communism.[59]

Echoes of FORA's Fifth Congress could clearly be heard. For example, in September 1907 there was a general strike in Buenos Aires, directed not at producers but consumers: a tenants' strike promoted and inspired by anarchists, and later supported by socialists and radicals. Initiated as a community protest by members of a neighborhood, it soon spread to the entire city. Quesada writes:

> For several weeks—the strike lasted three months—squads of agents, firefighters, and police could be seen throughout the city; even Colonel Falcón, chief of police, took part. A period of severe raids and deportations followed; among those deported were Roberto D'Angió and Marciano Forcat, editors of *La Protesta*.[60]

FORA's Seventh Congress convened between December 15 and 19, 1907 in La Plata. A general strike against the Law of Residence was called and in less than a month the strike took place, on January 13 and 14, 1908. FORA's leadership explained the reasons thus: "The criminal and barbaric actions by the state and the bourgeoisie in enacting a law of extradition against free thinking men constitutes a denial of the rights of man and requires us to respond to this challenge by the despots ruling the Republic of Argentina."[61]

For FORA and the anarchist movement, 1909 was a year rich in accomplishments. On May 1 the transport workers of Buenos Aires called a general strike to protest a repressive municipal regulation. On the same May Day the annual anarchist demonstration was brutally attacked by police on orders from Colonel Falcón.

---

59   A. Zacagnini, *Desde la barra del congreso de fusión* (Buenos Aires: Biblioteca de Progreso de la Boca, 1907).

60   Quesada, "La Protesta. Una longeza voz libertaria," 87; López Arango and Santillán, *El anarquismo en el movimiento obrero*, 20–21; López, *La FORA*, 1, 17–19.

61   Santillán, *La FORA*, 172–73. See also E. Del Valle Iberlucea, *Las leyes de excepción* (Buenos Aires: La Vanguardia, 1914).

This so-called "valiant" man left eight dead and nearly one hundred of the unarmed protestors wounded. In the long run he would not go unpunished. In solid alliance with UGT, FORA called a general strike on the following day that proved successful. After a week of intense mobilization by workers, the government of Figueroa Alcorta was forced to capitulate: it rescinded the repressive municipal regulation against transport workers, allowed the reopening of workers' and anarchists' locals, and began the release of the eight hundred workers jailed during the strike.[62]

Once more, solidarity in the struggle led to renewed hopes of a merger between socialists and anarchists within the workers' organization. On September 25 and 26, 1909 a new congress was convened. However, no more than a dozen of FORA's societies attended. Socialists and syndicalists, headed by Sebastián Marotta, dominated. The formation of a new central workers' organization, called Confederación Obrera Regional Argentina (CORA) with its own publication titled *La Confederación*, was therefore no surprise. Although several groups and individuals who still considered themselves anarchists stayed alongside socialists and syndicalists in this new central organization, it was clear that FORA could not recognize the union. Yet CORA adopted not only FORA's structure, but also its solidarity pact. Hence after 1909 there were two workers' federations in Argentina: FORA, definitely anarcho-communist, and CORA, syndicalist, but not without ideological influences from anarchism.[63]

In July 1909 Francisco Ferrer, founder of the Escuela Moderna, was condemned to death, presumably for leading a popular insurrection in Barcelona, and executed by firing squad at Montjuich Castle on October 13.[64] Immediately, FORA convened a meeting

---

62 Santillán, *La FORA*, 176–79. See also E. Del Valle Iberlucea, *Las leyes de excepción* (Buenos Aires: La Vanguardia, 1914). See also C. M. Echagüe, *Las grandes huelgas* (Buenos Aires: Centro Editor, Serie Historia Popular, No 1, 1971). López, *La FORA*, 1, 36–40.

63 See Luigi Fabbri, *Sindicalism y anarquismo*, trans. J. Prat (Valencia: Sempere, n.d.); *Sindicalism y socialism*, (La Coruña); J. A. Arraga, *El sindicalismo* (Buenos Aires: n.p., n.d.).

64 Joan Conelly Ullman, *La semana trágica. Estudio sobre las causas del*

attended by some twenty thousand workers and declared a general strike between October 14 and 17 to protest this "brutal assassination."[65] It joined similar demonstrations against military-clerical barbarism held in the principal cities of Europe—Paris, Marseille, Liège, Brussels, Berlin, Lisbon, Oporto, Coimbra, Rome, Turin, Genoa, Venice, Naples, London, and others.[66]

Simón Radowitzky, a young Jewish anarchist, deeply outraged by the killings perpetrated by Buenos Aires police during the course of a workers' rally on May Day, including the murder of children and elderly, took it upon himself to avenge these crimes by the method then common among European anarchists. He fixed on the chief of police, Colonel Falcón, a most appropriate target, for above all others he had unleashed the greatest hatred against workers. On November 14 Radowitzky detonated a bomb killing Falcón. The reaction by the "democratic" state, the army, and bourgeoisie was swift. Jails were once again filled, a state of emergency was declared, anarchist and socialist newspapers were targeted, and workers' unions were shut down. In an underground edition, *La Protesta* advanced a moral justification for the killing; FORA, also in a clandestine manner and through the state of emergency, issued a special publication titled *Nuestra Defense* explaining the reasons for the execution and giving a spirited defense of Radowitzky.[67] González Pacheco would later write: "We must rise to the revolution in Argentina for liberty and the life of Anarchism's first groom. Long live Simón Radowitzky!"[68]

---

anticlericalismo en España (1898–1912) (Barcelona: n.p., 1972), 528. See also Romero Maura, "Terrorismo en Barcelona, 1904–1909," *Past and Present*, No. 4, 1968.

65   Santillán, *La FORA*, 185–86.

66   G. Lapouge and J. Bécarud, *Los anarquistas españoles* (Barcelona: n.p., 1977), 70.

67   Agustín Souchy, *Una vida por un ideal, Simón Radowitzky* (Mexico: Grupo "Amigos de Radowitzky," 1956); D. A. de Santillán, *Simón Radowitzky, el vegador y el mártir* (Buenos Aires: n.p., 1927). See also Policía de Buenos Aires, *Procesos y sus causas* (Buenos Aires: n.p., 1909).

68   R. González Pacheco, *Carteles* (Buenos Aires: Americalee, 1956) II, 114. See also Alberto del Sar, *Usuhaia! Tierra maldita* (Buenos Aires, 1925).

In 1910 Argentina celebrated the centenary of its first national government. It was a time when all considered the country prosperous and promising, a magnet for European immigrants, and a model for its sister nations in Latin America.[69] Hence the national government felt bound to spare no expense. Parades, receptions, and spectacles of all sorts were planned as part of the festivities. The celebration by the bourgeoisie completely lost sight of the day's original republican character and focused instead on welcoming foreign nobles and kings. Only one specter hovered over the anniversary of the nation, and that was the workers' and anarchist movement.[70] Neither prison, nor exile, nor police interrogation could contain their revolutionary zeal. Consequently the repression intensified, if only to show the "civilized" world that law and order prevailed in Argentina.[71]

Between April 23 and 29, 1910 FORA celebrated its Eighth Congress and invited the various groups that formed CORA to join it, given that CORA had accepted the latter's solidarity pact and programmatic ideas. It was also determined there that a South American workers' congress would be held in Montevideo in January of the following year.[72]

Workers were intent on calling a general strike to free political prisoners and to overturn the Law of Residence. On May 8 nearly seventy thousand people, a new record for Buenos Aires, gathered in front of the National Penitentiary, protesting the abuse of prisoners. The strike was called for the 18th of the same month. On the 14th, the government declared a state of internal war and arrested members of the Federal Council of FORA, along with many other anarchist militants. Nido wrote:

---

69   See C. M. Urien, E Colombo, *La República Argentina en 1910* (Buenos Aires, 1910).

70   Solomonoff, *Ideologías del movimiento obrero*, 228–29.

71   Quesada, "La Protesta. Una longeza voz libertaria," 94. See also, A. S. Pennington, *The Argentine Republic* (London: Stanley Paul, 1910).

72   Santillán, *La FORA*, 192–95.

The nationalist bourgeoisie, supported by police, organized several anti-worker rallies with students and employees. Offices of *La Protesta* were sacked and set ablaze, so too was *La Vanguardia*, the socialist daily newspaper; workers' locals were raided, their furniture destroyed, and libraries burnt.[73]

In June a bomb exploded in the Teatro Colón. No one is killed. Two anarchists who were initially suspected were later found innocent. On the day immediately following the event the Chamber of Deputies called an emergency session and (with uncharacteristic speed) enacted a new repressive law known as the Law of Social Defense, by which all liberties guaranteed by the national Constitution were effectively annulled: freedom to assemble, public expression of opinion, and freedom of the press. Its draconian sanctions included imprisonment for up to twenty years, and even for an indeterminate period of time. Many Argentinean militants were confined to Usuhaia, and just as many immigrants expelled. Quesada writes: "The Centennial festivities were celebrated under uncertainty and insecurity. Buenos Aires looked like a fortress. More than two thousand anarchists were arrested or deported, eliminating their political activities. Extreme measures were taken to secure their captivity."[74] In the eyes of the workers of the world, a "democratic" Argentina found itself likened to czarist Russia.

In the years immediately preceding the Centennial celebrations the anarchist press experienced an extraordinary growth. Nettlau provided a list of most publications during this time, and among them were: in Buenos Aires, *El Trabajo* (1906), *Rumbo Nuevo* (1906), *Fulgor* (1906), *Labor* (1907), *J'Accuse* (1906); in Córdoba, *El Proletario* (1907); in Chacabuco, *El Precursor* (1909); in Tucumán,

---

73 Enrique Nido, *Informe general sobre el movimiento anarquista en la Argentina* (Buenos Aires: La Protesta, 1923); Santillán, *La FORA*, 197–98; J. Godio, *Historia del movimiento obrero latinoamericano*, I, 206–07.

74 Quesada, "La Protesta. Una longeza voz libertaria," 95–96; López Arango and Santillán, *El anarquismo en el movimiento obrero*, 24–26; López, *La FORA*, 1, 40–44.

Germinal (1909); in Bahía Blanca, *L'Agitatore* (1906). He also mentioned a number of publications he considered to be influenced by libertarian ideas: *Libre Examen* (1905) and *Los Nuevos Caminos* (1907) in the federal capital; *Nuevas Brisas* (1905) in Rosario; *La Ráfaga* (1908) in Paraná; *Pensamiento Nuevo* (1909) in Mendoza; *Ideas* (1909) and *Vibraciones* (1909) in La Plata.

The trade union press attached to FORA during the first decade of the century was too numerous to attempt a complete inventory here. Suffice it to mention *La Organización Obrera*, the official publication of the Federation, which began to appear in Buenos Aires on August 1, 1901 under the editorship of Alberto Ghiraldo.[75]

E. 1911 to 1920

The years immediately following the Centennial were quite hard for anarchism and the workers' movement in Argentina. With many of its most active militants exiled, living as fugitives, or imprisoned, and its unions functioning underground, everything seemed destined to languish and to die in short order. Journalist and educator Enrique Nido recalled that in 1911 publication of *La Protesta* was attempted twice, but police sacked the offices and jailed its editors.[76] The movement did not waver, however. Anarchist ideas were already firmly held by a large number of manual laborers and intellectuals, and soon enough they led to new actions and demonstrations. Many vigorous initiatives were obvious in the journalistic realm. For example, in 1911 the following publications appeared: the newspaper *El Libertario*, the monthly journal *El Trabajo*, the biweekly *La Cultura*, and the journal of rationalist pedagogy *Francisco Ferrer*. In 1912 an underground newspaper appeared with the revealing title of *A prepararse!* along with another titled *El Manifiesto*. *La Escuela Popular*, a publication

---

75   Nettlau, "Contribución a la bibliografía," 23–25.
76   Nido, *Informe general del movimiento.*

of the Liga de Educación Racionalista, appeared, while *La Fioc-cola* was published in Italian. In 1913 the following appeared: *El Obrero* in Buenos Aires; *La Rebelión* in Rosario; *El Combate* in Chacabuco; *Prometeo* in Diamante (Entre Ríos), among others. At the same time, unions attached to FORA continued publication of *El Aserrador, La Unión del Marino, El Obrero Ferroviario, La Antorcha* (foodworkers' union), *El Obrero Carpintero, La Auro-ra,* and others.[77] Publication of *La Protesta* resumed in 1913 without interruption until it was again suspended on March 5, 1919.[78] Quesada observes: "By the second half of 1913 we can say that the terrible period of the Centennial had passed, but those who assumed positions of prominence were for the most part new."[79] In that same year FORA sent delegates to the First International Syndicalist Congress in London, which aimed to rebuild the International Workers' Association—formed in Berlin after the end of the First World War—and to the second congress of the Confederação Operária Brasileira, held in Rio de Janeiro between September 8 and 13. FORA also played a central role in a new series of strikes, the most famous of which was that of the glassware workers in Berazategui. It was a success for workers, but took a heavy toll in persons wounded, jailed, or killed.

A new unification congress, convened in September 1914, concluded with the majority of autonomous societies attached to CORA joining FORA.[80] The outbreak of the First World War occasioned, on the part of FORA's federal council, an energetic reaffirmation of the anarchist anti-war position with the aim of substituting the war between people and states with the class struggle. Santillán writes:

> The European war is nothing more than a commercial venture
> of the bourgeoisie, which has all to gain, while the working

---

77   Nettlau, "Contribución a la bibliografía," 23–25.
78   Quesada, "La Protesta. Una longeza voz libertaria," No. 83, 72.
79   Santillán, *La FORA,* 203.
80   Quesada, "La Protesta. Una longeza voz libertaria," 73.

class has all to lose, including its blood and life. ... Argentinean workers, without national or any other kind of distinc-
tions, know to launch a powerful criticism of all perpetrators
of the war. ... They do not want nations or flags. Workers of
the world have only one enemy: bourgeois society.[81]

This anti-war, anti-military, and anti-nationalist exhortation held
a special meaning in Argentina in 1914 where foreigners from all
European nations, and some from Asia, comprised 46.1 percent of
the economically active population,[82] of which only 1.4 percent had
become citizens.[83]

The massive enrollment of CORA's unions, effected in the unification congress of 1914—which, at first sight, may be seen as a
victory for the anarchist FORA over the partisans of a neutral and
economistic syndicalism—turned out to be a tactic by its enemies
and the lamentable start of a sharp division at the very heart of the
Argentinean workers' movement. The unions led by reformists and
legalist socialists, or by lukewarm and increasingly less doctrinaire
anarchists, soon enough became the majority. Consequently, when
FORA convened its Ninth Congress on April 1, 1915 they became
the dominant party simply on account of their numerical superiority
in delegates. They were able to impose the thesis of a neutral syndicalism, and to adopt a proposal nullifying the anarcho-communist
position of the Fifth Congress.[84] The minority that was partisan to
the latter position split away and, on May 2, two FORAs emerged,
one identified with the Fifth—anarcho-communist—and the other
with the Ninth Congress—neutral syndicalism.

---

81   Santillán, *La FORA*, 221–23.
82   Solomonoff, *Ideologías del movimiento obrero*, 125.
83   Ibid., 111.
84   López Arango and Santillán, *El anarquismo en el movimiento obrero*, 28–
    29. For the "unionist" version of this process, consult the very fine work
    by Sebastián Marotta, *El movimiento syndical argentino, su génesis y de-
    sarrollo* (Buenos Aires: Lacio, 1960–1961). The socialist version is given,
    though not without errors in interpretation and facts, in Jacinto Oddone,
    Gremialismo proletario argentino (Buenos Aires: La Vanguardia, 1949).

The refusal of anarchist delegates to comply with the resolution of the Ninth Congress is quite understandable. It was a clear maneuver to penetrate the Congress of 1914, rendering the workers' federation ideologically vague and leaving it to serve solely as a means to assert workers' rights. But it was a strategic error, as the anarcho-communists could soon have regained their central position at the core of a single federation. In no time, the two FORAs confronted each other and, in 1916 and 1917, frequently engaged in public disputes.

The Russian Revolution played a reinvigorating and catalyzing role for Argentinean anarchism. The reformism of FORA IX lost ground in light of the renewed prestige of revolutionary ideas, even if FORA V did not always take advantage of this favorable historical condition. In Argentina, as in many other countries, the Russian Revolution awakened not only the interest but also the enthusiasm of anarchists. In Spain, for example, during the Congreso de la Comedia (December 10 to 18, 1919), the CNT—even as it declared itself a "firm defender of those principles of the First International proposed by Bakunin"—adhered "to the Third International provisionally, on account of the revolutionary character that presided over it."[85] Angel Pestaña was commissioned to assist the Third International in Russia and to inform its leadership of CNT's resolution.[86] Nonetheless, in Spain and in other European countries the initial enthusiasm soon waned and a mood of suspense and critique emerged. Substantive debates followed. By 1920 the majority of Argentinean anarchists had distanced themselves from Leninism and were beginning to understand the authoritarian character of the Bolshevik revolution, as was evident from Kropotkin's own correspondence with Lenin.[87] Groups identifying themselves as "anarcho-Bolshevik"

---

85   Juan Gómez Casas, *Historia del anarco-sindicalism español* (Madrid: n.p., 1949), 128–30.

86   Daniel Guerin, *Ni Dios ni Amo II* (Madrid: Campo Abierto Ediciones, 1977), 24.

87   See Paul Avrich, "Una nueva bibliografía soviética de Kropotkin," in *Reconstruir*, 97, 1975; Emma Goldman, *Living My Life* (New York, 1934), 769–70.

were formed and active during the 1920s. They published various newspapers, some of which were widely read, like *Frente Proletario* (1920), *Frente Unico* (1920), *El Sol* (1921), *El Libertario* (1923), *La Plebe*, which became a daily, and, above all, *Bandera Roja*. But in its 1923 Congress FORA V roundly rejected "the so-called dictatorship of the proletariat."[88] As early as 1921 Lenin had ordered the confiscation of various works by Bakunin and Kropotkin, which with good reason he considered responsible for the Leftist opposition inside the Bolshevik party itself.[89]

January 1919 brought the Tragic Week to Buenos Aires. A strike in the Vanesa metalworks provoked a violent reaction by police. Several workers were killed and FORA V called for a general strike. All the workers in the capital responded, and production and services ceased. The city was left in the hands of workers, mostly under the direction of anarchists. *La Protesta*, reviewing the events, later observed: "All work came to a halt in the city and its suburbs. Not one single proletarian betrayed the suffering of comrades." Without a doubt, a revolutionary situation had emerged. Nonetheless, as Santillán notes, "the capacity to direct the people's energies and offer them an immediate revolutionary objective was missing." Lacking a well-defined objective fatigued the movement. The government, the armed forces, and the bourgeoisie transformed their fear into a thirst for vengeance. Consequently, some fifty-five thousand workers were arested, the island Martín García was filled with anarchists, and the typical xenophobic and anti-Semitic backlash arose. The hunt for Reds was on.[90] The first of the Argentinean fascist organizations was then formed: the Liga Patriótica, organized by sons of the well-healed, students, police, and thugs who, gathering at the Centro Naval, received the support of the armed forces. Nicolás Babini observes: "Rear Admiral Domecq García provided military instruction and Rear Admiral O'Connor urged them on,

---

88 Santillán, *La FORA*, 264–65; López Arango and Santillán, *El anarquismo en el movimiento obrero*, 31.

89 D. Avrich, *Los anarquistas rusos* (Madrid: Alianza, 1974), 230.

90 Santillán, *La FORA*, 243–44.

comparing Buenos Aires with Petrograd in 1917, and the next day incited them to assault 'Russians and Catalans' ... in their neighborhoods if they did not dare to confront them at the Centro."[91]

Well armed fascists attacked, insulted, humiliated, and murdered with impunity not only workers, but also many individuals who were not even involved in the strike. This band of criminals anticipated the famous Alianza Argentina Anticomunista of the 1970s. The conservative daily, *La Nación*, estimated some one hundred killed and four hundred wounded, but the report by the socialist paper *La Vanguardia* of seven hundred killed and two thousand wounded may be closer to the truth.[92] Fascist writer Arturo Cancela narrated the events with reactionary humor in a story titled "Una semana de jolgorio."[93] But the anarchist FORA stayed its course; *La Protesta* published as many as fifteen thousand copies, and quickly the popular daily *Bandera Roja* was launched. In March, a governmental decree prohibited all anarchist press, but in July a new daily, *Tribuna Proletaria*, appeared, promoted by FORA V.[94] In September 1920 FORA V convened an extraordinary congress attended by two hundred unions.

The anarchist press of the 1920s was ubiquitous, with publications both short- and long-lived; polyglot, as is fitting for a country of immigrants. Some of the publications had a literary character, like *Alas*, published by Cordón Avellán; others had an individualist orientation, such as the biweekly *Estudios*, first published on November 1, 1915 in Rosario by Enrique Nido, José Torralvo, and A. M. Dopico. There were newspapers in Italian, like *La Canaglia*, first published in May 1915 and continuing for several years, and

---

91 Nicolás Babini, "La Semana Trágica – Pesadilla de una fiesta de verano," in *Todo es Historia*, No. 5, 1967.

92 Quesada, "La Protesta. Una longeza voz libertaria," No. 83, 77.

93 The story forms part of a work titled *Tres relatos porteños* (Buenos Aires: n.p., 1922). His "apparent innocence in recounting the events without dramatization" is nothing but profound indifference to the shedding of workers' blood." A. Berenguer Carisomo, *Literatura argentina* (Barcelona: Labor, 1970), 77.

94 Santillán, *La FORA*, 245–246; López, *La FORA*, 1, 44–46.

La Rivolta, published in 1917 in opposition to the war that Italy had entered. Others were published with a specific objective, like *El Burro*, launched June 20, 1918 by Oreste Ristori, aimed at the struggle against clericalism; *El Soldado*, launched in 1919, combating militarism and mandatory military service; and *Socorro*, which in June 1915 denounced the horrors of Czarist prisons. Many cities in the interior had their own libertarian publications: in Laboulaye (Córdoba) *Libre Palabra* (1913) appeared; in Rosario, *Tierra Libre* (1913); in Tucumán, *Odios* (1913); in La Plata, *La Simiente* (1913); in Mendoza, *Nuevos Rumbos* (1913); in Punta Alta, *La Voz del Esclavo* (1913); in Córdoba, *El Proletario* (1914); in Campana (Buenos Aires), *Voces Proletarias* (1915); in Paraná, *Ideas* (1915); in Mar del Plata, *El Grito del Pueblo* (1916); in San Fernando (Buenos Aires), *El Amigo del Pueblo* (1915); in Santa Fe, *La Verdad* (1916); in San Juan, *Humanidad* (1917); in Bahía Blanca, *Brazo y Cerebro* (1916) and *Alba Roja* (1917); and in Junin, *Nubes Rojas* (1917). Perhaps the most important of them, after *La Protesta*, was the weekly *La Obra*, published between 1917 and 1919 by Rodolfo Pacheco and Teodoro Antillí.[95]

F. 1921 to 1930

In April and May 1921 dozens of workers at La Forestal (in the Chaco) were brutally murdered when they demanded better salaries and working conditions. Consequently, the anarchist FORA proposed a movement of solidarity with the Chaqueño victims and agricultural workers, but the unionists of FORA IX avoided the proposal and nothing came of it.[96] The same occurred when the Liga Patriótica murdered several workers in Gualeguaychú (Entre Ríos) on May 1, 1921. The non-anarchist syndicalism began to stray towards a myopic pragmatism lacking solidarity. But the most

---

95   Quesada, "La Protesta. Una longeza voz libertaria," No. 83, 79.
96   Angel Borda, "Los sucesos de la Forestal," in *Reconstruir*, 92, 24–28.

tragic events of that year were among the least known by the Argentinean people, for no newspaper but *La Protesta* and some other anarchist publications provided any coverage: in Patagonia the army indiscriminately murdered rural workers striking for minimal improvements in their working conditions.[97] The organizers of the strike and of the subsequent insurrection were anarchists of different nationalities, with Argentinean creoles certainly among them. On January 23, 1923 the young anarchist Kurt Wilckens executed the leader of this genocide, Lieutenant Colonel Varela.[98] González Pacheco wrote in one of his *Carteles*: "Why has he killed this man? Must we still say? Why is a bridge spanned over an abyss, a rocky cliff blown up, or a wolf killed?.... Explain this and you have explained the death of Varela."[99]

In March 1922 FORA IX convened a new unification congress and, together with several unions of FORA V, founded the Union Sindical Argentina (USA). A year later, FORA V convened its ordinary Congress, considered its Ninth, as the Congress of 1915 in which it had split into two was not acknowledged. In July, 1923 Wilckens was murdered by cowardly members of the Argentinean army, provoking a general strike by all sectors of the working class. *La Vanguardia*, publication of the Socialist Party, wrote, "this murder was condemnable and nefarious, and when brought against a defenseless and crippled victim while asleep is even more monstrous, repulsive, and incomprehensible."[100] In 1924 FORA anarchists became critical of groups associated with *La Aurora* and *Ideas y Pampa Libre*. Their argument was poorly defined and perhaps senseless, hardly relevant to disputes long held with syndicalists and those elements at the core of USA that supported them,

---

97   O. Bayer, *Los vengadores de la Patagonia Trágica* (Buenos Aires: Galerna, 1972–1974); "Los vengadores de la Patagonia Trágica," in *Todo es historia*, No. 15, 1968; Federación Obrera Local Bonaerense, *La Patagonia Trágica* (Buenos Aires, 1922).

98   "Causas y efecto. La Tragédia de la Patagonia y el gesto de Kurt Wilckens," in Supplement to *La Protesta*, 31, January 31, 1929.

99   R. González Pacheco, *Carteles* (Buenos Aires: Americalee, 1956) II, 116.

100   Quesada, "La Protesta. Una longeza voz libertaria," No. 83, 81.

and beyond the usual controversies with anarcho-Bolsheviks on the transitional dictatorship of the proletariat. The trial and sentence of Sacco and Vanzetti in the United States occasioned a prolonged newspaper campaign, numerous public acts and street demonstrations, and solidarity strikes among Argentinean anarchists.[101] On their execution of August 23, 1927, *La Protesta* wrote:

> These two rebels accused of theft and murder could not avoid the electric chair. Sacco and Vanzetti were not members of gangs engaged in [the] contraband of liquor, freely organized in the United States. They were not heads of any of the numerous criminal associations that have their headquarters in Chicago, in New York, or in Philadelphia. They were accused of a common crime, convicted by Judge Thayer, after tortuous interrogations by police, and condemned to death. To avoid the electric chair, to obtain one of the many exceptions to such a sentence available under Massachusetts law, Sacco and Vanzetti should have been Yankees. But they were Italian and anarchist. The world is unaware of the harshness and insensitivity of North American judges and governors. No one believed Yanqueelandia could reach such extreme contempt for the generous and altruistic sentiments that moved millions of people in an attempt to save the lives of Sacco and Vanzetti. We must, however, bow to the facts. The United States is beyond humanity.[102]

At the same time, Argentinean anarchists began a campaign to free Radowitzky, culminating in April 1930 with the radical government granting him amnesty. In 1925 FORA V launched a campaign for the six-hour day, as an immediate remedy for the high unemployment of workers.

---

101 Quesada, "Sacco y Vanzetti: Dos nombres para la protesta," (Buenos Aires: (Editorial Destelles, 1974), 77–80.

102 Ibid., 90; See also D. A. de Santillán, "La tragedia de Sacco y Vanzetti," Supplement to *La Protesta*, August 1928; López, *La FORA*, 1, 49–50.

In August 1928 FORA V convened its Tenth Congress, with the assistance of more than one hundred unions. Its ideological definition was reaffirmed and a recommendation very strongly approved that "propaganda of fundamental anarchist ideas" should be pursued. As if it could foretell the coming black plague in Argentina, FORA exhorted workers to "combat tirelessly the poison with which nationalism infects the anti-worker reaction, militarism, dictatorship, and war." In 1930 FORA V was comprised of more than one hundred thousand members, representing a clear majority of the conscious and militant proletariat of the country. According to Santillán, its growth was "one of the causes leading to Uriburu's *coup d'état*, which on September 6, 1930 inaugurated the era of fascist governments in Argentina."[103] This "revolution," supported by conservatives, by those so-called "independent socialists," by fascist groups,[104] and admirers of Mussolini, such as Captain Perón,[105] filled landowners, businessmen and bankers with euphoria and immediately inaugurated a systematic persecution of workers. It did not limit itself to shutting down anarchist newspapers and unions, to deporting or imprisoning the most active militants on the Left: it also murdered many of them, like the Correntino maritime worker Juan Antonio Morán—who had executed the torturer Rosasco—and the young Catalan worker Joaquín Penina, who without trial was sentenced to death by firing squad in Rosario for the mere suspicion of having distributed anti-government flyers.[106] The most celebrated of those murdered by Uriburu's dictatorship is Severino Di Giovanni, an Italian agitator who professed an anti-organizational and violent anarchism. Arriving in Buenos Aires in 1923, shortly after Mussolini's rise to power in Italy, he confronted the group supporting *La*

---

103 Santillán, *La FORA*, 277.

104 Alberto Ciria, "Crisis económica y restauración política (1930–1943)" in *Argentina: La democracia constitucional y sus crisis. Historia Argentina*, vol. 6 (Buenos Aires: Paidós, 1972), 162–64.

105 Carlos Ibarguren, *La historia que he vivido, 1877–1956* (Buenos Aires: Eudeba, 1969), 367–368.

106 Quesada, *Joaquín Penina, primer fusilado* (Rosario: Grupo Editor de Estudios Sociales, 1974).

Protesta, which opposed armed violence as a method in the struggle and instead looked to propaganda and syndicalist action. In 1929 the execution of Emilio López Arango, editor of *La Protesta*, was attributed to Di Giovanni. What is certain is that guided by the idea of expropriation he robbed several banks, leaving some people dead. Uriburu's government applied martial law and executed him by firing squad along with Paulino Scarfó.[107]

After the fascist takeover and consequent repression of anarchist and communist militants, unions of the Unión Sindical Argentina, in the hands of pure syndicalists but not without the participation of leaders who still defined themselves as anarchists, joined those of the Confederación Obrera Argentina (COA). The latter was dominated by reformist socialists and founded the Confederación General del Trabajo (CGT). Members of CGT were spared persecution. Its sole function was always to advocate and negotiate for workers as they awaited the emergence of Colonel Perón. CGT, a "representative body of the sane forces of the nation," petitioned Uriburu's government for clemency for those FORA drivers who had been sentenced to death, something FORA itself would never have been able to do.[108]

The libertarian press in Argentina continued to flourish during the 1920s. In addition to *La Protesta* and its valuable historical and ideological *Suplementos*, which continued under the vigorous editorship of López Arango and Abad de Santillán, there was the journal *Ideas*, edited by Jacobo Prince, José María Lunazzi, and Fernando de Intento in La Plata; *Brazo y Cerebro*, already mentioned above, published in Bahía Blanca with the collaboration of Mario Anderson Pacheco, Julio Díaz, and Antonio López Almada; *Pampa Libre* published in General Pico and edited by Prince, Lunazzi, Varone, and others; *Nuestra Tribuna*, by Juana Rouco Buela in Necochea; *Verbo Nuevo*, by Juan Pérez Maza, José María

---

107   O. Bayer, *Severino Di Giovanni. Idealista de la violencia* (Buenos Aires: Galerna, 1970); O. Bayer, *Los anarquistas expropiadores y otros ensayos* (Buenos Aires: n.p., 1986).
108   López, *La FORA*, 1, 51–53.

Acha, and others in San Juan; *El Libertario*—not to be confused with another paper of the same name, representing the tendency then towards anarcho-Bolshevism—by Antillí and González Pacheco; *La Verdad* by Tandil, a publication of the Agrupación Aurora Libertaria; *Orientación*, both a newspaper and a magazine, by Cruz Romero and Francisco Rivolta, published in Santa Fe; *Tierra Libre*, in Tucumán; *Renovación*, in Avellaneda; *Libre Acuerdo*, in Rosario; *Impulso*, in Punta Alta; *La Obra*, in Santa Fe; *Abierto Cancha*, in Colón; *Palote*, a publication by Colomá and Mazzola; *Elevación*, a monthly by Juan Raggio; *La Campana*, edited in Santa Fe by Abad de Santillán and López Arango; and standing out among all the anarchist press of the period for its vibrant style, more poetic than discursive, more ethical and lyrical than sociological and political, *La Antorcha*, by González Pacheco, Antillí, Badaracco, and Bianchi. There was also a variety of publications in foreign languages, for example *Bezviatie*, published in Hungarian in 1926.[109]

G. 1931 to 1955

When constitutional guarantees were reinstated in 1932, FORA renewed its publication activities and *La Protesta* came out as a daily. Four individuals comprised the editorial staff: Santillán, Villar, Cimazo, and Anderson Pacheco. Nonetheless, the numerous actions initiated by the government of General Justo against its editors and the cancellation of postal services made publication increasingly difficult. It ceased publication as a daily (precisely what the government wanted), but continued first as a weekly, then biweekly, and finally as a monthly.[110]

Persecution, covert or open, had not totally disappeared, as one would expect with the installation of an ostensibly elected

109   Quesada, "La Protesta," in *Todo es Historia*, No. 83, 92–93.
110   Ibid., 91.

government.[111] Nonetheless, a group of militants detained in the Villa Devoto prison in 1931 conceived the project of a national Anarchist Congress, to meet for the first time in September 1932 in Rosario, with delegates in attendance from all over the country. One of the most important accomplishments of this Congress was the creation of a Comité Regional de Relaciones Anarquistas (CRRA), with the objective to prepare the organization for a Federación de Grupos Libertarios Argentinos. Three years later, the Comité convened a Second Congress—this time underground—in La Plata. What the federation sought in Rosario was achieved there, the Federación Anarco-Comunista Argentina (FACA), including an organizational structure and a declaration of principles. During this period, various Argentinean anarchist groups were involved in an intense campaign to free three comrades—Vuotto, Mainini, and De Diago—who, after suffering barbarous torture, languished in the Bragado prison for eleven years until their pardon was finally granted in 1942.[112] The newspaper *Justicia* was published with the single aim of defending the cause of these political prisoners. In general, the anarchist press during this period maintained its vigor and combativeness, even while the number of papers diminished, particularly in the interior. Several publishing houses dedicated themselves to the publication of works by libertarian authors. The magazine *Nervio* appeared, and spawned a publishing house under the same name; several works fundamental to anarchist literature—for example, *Incitación al Socialismo* by Gustavo Landauer—were published thanks to *Nervio*. Publishers like Imán, Tupac, Americalle, Reconstruir, and, a bit later, Proyección issued a long list of anarchist authors and works related to anarchism. In September 1933, *Acción Libertaria* appeared, later

---

111   Alberto J. Pla, "La crisis social: de la restauración oligárca a la Argentina de masas," in Alberto Ciria, *et al.*, *La década infame* (Buenos Aires, 1969), 98 *et seq.*; see also E. Palacio, *Historia de la Argentina* (Buenos Aires, n.d.), 377 *et seq.*

112   Quesdada, *El proceso de Bragado* (Buenos Aires: Editorial Korrigan, 1974); Pascual Vuotto, *Vida de un proletario* (Buenos Aires: n.p, 1939); López, *La FORA*, 54–55.

becoming the voice of FACA and of the Federación Libertaria Argentina (FLA) until 1971.[113]

During the decade of the 1930s, the most important international event for anarchism in Argentina and the world occurred in Spain. The progress of the CNT and the Federación Anarquista Ibérica (FAI), their decisive sway gained as a result of the political situation, and their enormous influence on workers and peasants in most parts of the peninsula awakened in many Argentinean anarchists the idea that a social revolution—long desired and fostered, but just as long frustrated—could finally become a reality. The rise of fascism, the struggle of the people against armies of an international coalition, and the simultaneous collectivization of farms and industries promoted by the anarcho-syndicalist CNT, led FORA, FACA, and all like-minded groups to a deep commitment to Solidaridad Internacional Antifascista and Comisión Coordinadora de Ayuda del Pueblo Español. Active Argentinean anarchists traveled to Spain and offered their services to CNT; some took up arms in the various battalions. José Grunfeld rose to the position of Secretary of FAI.[114] FACA published a journal titled *Documentos Históricos de España*, as well as a series of books and pamphlets about the civil war and the social revolution in the peninsula.[115]

Various publications that first appeared prior to 1930 continued, but with irregularity. *La Protesta*, *La Antorcha*, and *Organización Obrera* are sporadically published by FORA. FACA, for its part, put out *Solidaridad Obrera* starting in 1941, edited by Juan Corral and Laureano Riera. The first *justicialista* government later shut down the paper. FORA also started a series of booklets, such as *Todos contra la guerra* (1935) by Jacobo Maguid, and *Lucha constructiva por la libertad y justicia* (1944), among others. On January 1940 *Hombre de América* appeared and continued to the end of

---

113 Jacinto Cimazo, *Una voz anarquista en la Argentina* (Buenos Aires: Editorial Reconstruir, 1984), 37–38.

114 Hugh Thomas, *La Guerra Civil Española* (Ruedo Ibérico, 1976), vol. 2, 954.

115 On the role of anarchists in the civil war and the Spanish revolution, see J. Peirats, *La C.N.T. en la revolución española* (Paris: n.p., 1971).

1945, thus lasting for nearly the entire period of the Second World War. It was a cultural journal with libertarian orientation, but sufficiently open to all anti-Nazi writers.[116]

FACA quickly and energetically made clear its position, shared by FORA, with respect to the international conflagration. Aware that Western nations represented corrupt democracies and concealed a brutal capitalist exploitation, and cognizant that the Soviet Union, far from being even an imperfect socialism or one in the process of invention, was in fact a gigantic bureaucratic capitalism, FACA considered National Socialism the worst evil and the greatest threat to humanity. No greater disaster could befall Europe or the world than the triumph of the Third Reich.

In a 1942 General Plenary, FACA issued a statement concerning war and totalitarianism declaring that "totalitarianism is the greatest danger in our time," and expressed its solidarity with all peoples subjected to Nazi barbarities, while recognizing the threat of Soviet expansionism and the false promises of peaceful reconstruction by plutocratic democracies.[117] Meanwhile, in the domestic scene, FACA and FORA found themselves confronting the corporative populism of the Perón government. Individuals and unions were soon seduced by the demagogic fascism; the complacent CGT grew at the expense of the revolutionary FORA, now somewhat diminished but still combative. Nonetheless, FORA drew from the frail social conscience of a great mass of laborers in the suburban agricultural sector, who were no longer peasants and not yet workers.[118]

---

116 Cimazo, *Una voz anarquista en la Argentina*, 41–42.
117 Ibid., 43–44.
118 See José Luis Romero, *Las ideas políticas en la Argentina* (México: F.C.E., 1956), 248 *et seq.*; Alfredo Galletti, *La política y los partidos* (Buenos Aires: n.p., 1961), 198–199. Other authors interpret Peronism as "Bonapartism": Enrique Rivera, *Peronismo y frondizismo* (Buenos Aires: Patria Grande, 1958), 19; Abelardo Ramos, *Revolución y contrarevolución en la argentina* (Buenos Aires: Plus Ultra, 1961), 456; Torcuato S. Di Tella, *El sistema político argentino y la clase obrera* (Buenos Aires: Editorial Eudeba, 1964), 57.

In June 1946 anarchists launched a new newspaper, *Reconstruir*, edited by Luis Danussi. In its first issue Jacobo Prince shed light on the Peronist phenomenon in an article titled "El totalitarismo falsea el principio de justicia social."[119]

After 1945 FORA began to lose its influence and anarcho-syndicalism was reduced to a very small role in the Argentinean workers' movement. However, the Sociedad de Resistencia de Obreros del Puerto, attached to FORA, proved its anarcho-syndicalist combativeness when in 1952 they, at the height of Perón's dictatorship, published a manifesto rejecting the compulsory tax on wages for building a monument to the deceased Eva Perón. For this act, various militants were imprisoned for six months.[120]

Perón contributed more to the weakening of free unionism than his predecessor Uriburu, but used different methods, appealing to corruption rather violence. For its part, after its First Congress of 1935 FACA held a Second Congress in 1938, a Third in July 1940, and the Fourth in December 1951. Several months prior to Perón's overthrow, it convened a Fifth Congress in February 1955 and changed its name to Federación Libertaria Argentina (FLA). Under its new name, FLA convened a Sixth Congress from December 8–10, 1961.[121] Its journal, *Reconstruir*, began to appear in August 1959 and continued until March 1976, a date that coincides with the beginning of the most bestial and bloodthirsty dictatorship in the history of Argentina.

H. Poets, Writers, Dramatists

Between 1890 and 1930 a significant number of Argentinean writers had some relationship with anarchism. For some of them the relationship was sporadic; others committed themselves to an active if

---

119 Cimazo, *Una voz anarquista en la Argentina*, 45–46.
120 López, *La FORA*, 55–56.
121 Cimazo, *Una voz anarquista en la Argentina,* 47–48; Rama, *Historia del movimiento obrero y social latinoamericano*, 82.

brief militancy; still others declared themselves anarchists and remained so for their entire lives. The two most celebrated figures of
the twentieth century serve as sufficient examples: Leopoldo Lugones and Jorge Luis Borges. Both began their political—or, if one
wishes, anti-political—formations within libertarian associations.
Later they evolved—perhaps better to say, devolved—towards conservative positions. The former did not hesitate to call for military
action, that is, the "hour of the sword," or to declare his sympathies
for fascism.[122] The latter continually called himself an anarchist,
even after referring to Pinochet as "salt of the earth." Who knows
why he did so, perhaps it was aesthetic-literary calculus, perhaps
historico-philosophical confusion.

Setting aside Florencio Sánchez, who will be referred to in the
chapter on Uruguay (even though his militancy, literary, and journalistic work developed more in Argentina than in Uruguay), first
place in Argentinean literary anarchism belongs, Santillán writes,
to "Alberto Ghiraldo, rebel poet, fighter with distinct personality,
who embodied a special kind of propaganda, unequalled by anyone in any land, and despite voluminous writings." The journals
he published were unique "for their popular character, breadth of
view, and for the freedom they gave to sympathetic ideas without
ever losing the libertarian view."[123] He was born in Mercedes (a district of Buenos Aires) in 1875 and died in Santiago de Chile in 1946.
At first an enthusiast of the radicalism of Leandro Alem, he soon
turned to anarchism under Pietro Gori's influence. More than once,

---

122 Lugones traveled to Europe in 1921 and the then recent rise of fascism
impressed him. Upon his return to Buenos Aires he delivered a series of
lectures on this movement in the Teatro Coliseo, sponsored by the Liga
Patriótica Argentina. In those lectures he exalted patriotism and militarism, and argued that both were threatened by Leftists and by foreign sub-
version. "If during his time as an anarchist he had condemned the 'peace
with arms,' now, after his conversion to fascism, he sought an efficient
military prepared for war; and if at some time he had dreams of disarma-
ment and pacifism, events had turned them into the 'tragic end of a grand
illusion.'" Leopoldo Allub, *Orígenes del autoritarismo en América Latina*
(México: Katún, 1983), 152–53.
123 Santillán, *El movimiento anarquista*, 122.

and always under difficult circumstances, he edited *La Protesta*. Between 1898 and 1902, he published *El Sol*; between 1904 and 1905 *Martín Ferro*, with the collaboration of Augustín Alvarez and Roberto Payró; and from 1909 to 1916, *Ideas y Figuras*. A prolific poet and successful dramatist, his most acclaimed theatrical pieces are *Alma gaucha* (1909), *La Columna de Fuego* (1913), and *Los Salvajes* (1920). Among his collections of poetry, we should mention *Fibras* (1895), *Música prohibida* (1904), *Tiempos nuevos* (1911–1912), *La canción del peregrino* (1922), *Cancionero libertario* (1938), and *Canto a Buenos Aires* (1946). Examples of his combative prose are: *La tiranía del frac* (1905), *Crónicas argentina* (1912), *La Ley Baldón* (1915), *El peregrino curioso* (1917), and *La argentina: estado social de un pueblo* (1922). In 1928 he published an autobiographical novel, *Humano ardor*, recounting the struggles of workers and anarchists during the heroic years. In all his poetry no other better captures the libertarian lyrical character than "Madre Anarquía," published during "a period of political terror when the spirit found itself oppressed by reactionary mobs."[124]

During the last twenty years of his life, though at the margins of the syndicalist struggle and anarchist organizations, Ghiraldo never abandoned his libertarian ideology, publishing *Yanquilanda bárbara* (1929), *Cuentos argentinos* (1935), and *El pensamiento argentino* (1937). The libertarian friendship that had brought him close to Rubén Darío since 1912 led him to publish a collection of Darío's works in 1943.[125] Nonetheless, his poetry is quite different in both subject and structure from Darío's. Héctor Adolfo Cordero writes:

> It has been said that his artistic resources are simple in both verse and prose. That is an accurate appraisal if one means that his verse and prose have great clarity. Ghiraldo wrote so that those who are in most need of guiding words can understand.

---

124 Santillán, *El movimiento anarquista*, 123.
125 Alberto Fernández Leys, "Ghiraldo: su primer aniversario y la inmortalidad," in *Reconstruir*, 98.

His verse is put to the service of his cause and it resonates with the people. During his life no other poet was as popular as he, with the exception of Almafuerte. His books were frequently reprinted and just as quickly sold out, and Folco Testena translated several of his poems into Italian. They were sold in newsstands, mailed to the interior of the country, and requested more frequently than those of any other author. In verse as in his other works, Ghiraldo's personality is there without pretense. To be sure, his poetry has the tone of a harangue, but as an agitator of ideas and sentiments he expresses in it the fervor of his profound humanism. His pen is always a weapon of combat.[126]

In "Música prohibida" he addressed the suffering people directly, saying, "I am the minstrel of your misery":

> *¡Conmigo los hambrientos y los tristes!*
> *¡Conmigo los malditos y desnudos!*
> *¡Conmigo madres locas porque vieron*
> *padecer a los hijos, infortunios!*
> *¡Conmigo niños pálidos y enclenques*
> *cuya sangre absorbieron los ventrudos!*
> *¡Conmigo la canalla macilenta*
> *que ruge en la caverna del suburbio!*
> *¡Conmigo prostitutas y ladrones!*
> *¡Conmigo los leprosos y los sucios!*
> *¡Conmigo los que oran y se arrastran*
> *¡Todos los alejados del mendrugos!*

With me are the hungry and sad!
With me are the damned and naked!
With me are the mothers crazed with seeing

---

126   Héctor Adolfo Cordero, *Alberto Ghilardo, precursor the nuevos tiempos* (Buenos Aires: Claridad, 1962), 123. See also Max Henriquez Ureña, *Breve historia del modernismo* (México: F.C.E., 1978), 206.

Their unfortunate children perish!
With me are the pale and feeble children
Whose blood the fat cats sucked dry!
With me is the haggard mob
That roars in the caves of the suburb!
With me are the whores and thieves!
With me are the lepers and unbathed!
With me are those who pray and crawl
All who are alienated from bread!

Whatever distance postmodernism and pure poetry place between Ghiraldo's work and contemporary surrealistic sensibility, it is impossible to miss its vigor and sincerity, a generosity and vital commitment we so yearn for today. His poetry, Roberto J. Payró wrote in *La Nación*, "is the exact and artistic impact of the cry of the people on a written page; a symphony of a thousand cries of that people gathered and wisely balanced together."[127]

The poetry of Evaristo Carriego is far from a speech in a FORA meeting. It is much more like a *milonga* in a suburban setting. Carriego was born in 1883 in Entre Ríos and died prematurely in 1912 in Buenos Aires. He is the author of *Misas herejes* (1908) and *Alma del suburbio* (1908); he was a romantic with modernist influences. More sentimental than combative, he never declared his anarchism, but it is easily surmised from the following:

la viejita, la que se siente
un sedimento de material,
desecho inútil, salmo doliente
del Evangelio de la Miseria,

The old woman, the one who feels herself
a mere residue of matter,

---

127 Cordero, *Alberto Ghilardo*, 131. See also Juan Más y Pi, *Alberto Ghiraldo* (Buenos Aires: n.p., 1910); Juan Echagüe, *Una época del teatro argentino (1904–1918)* (Buenos Aires: n.p., 1926).

pointless undoing, suffering psalm
from the Gospel of Misery

or:

*que por el buen nombre de candidatos
en los peores trances expone el pellejo.*

who through the good name of candidates
in the worst difficulties risks his own skin.

finally:

*la costurerita que dio aquel mal paso
—y lo peor de todo, sin necesidad—*

the seamstress who took that wrong step
—and worst of all, without necessity—

Jorge Luis Borges wrote that while Evaristo Carriego was part of the *ecclesia visibilis* of Argentinean letters, he may more accurately be defined as belonging "to the true *ecclesia invisibilis*, to the community of the just," because of his position as an anarchist poet.[128] It is not hard to see in the verses of Carriego that deep sympathy for the poor and oppressed common to all libertarian poets of the period. Much like Ghiraldo, he "becomes popular with extraordinary speed," and his poetry "published in *Caras y Caretas* was quickly memorized and recited in hushed voices by romantic young women in tenement houses."[129] A poem dedicated to Juan Más y Pi, editor of *La Protesta* and later included in *Misas herejes*, reaches beyond narrative and shows its commitment to

---

128 Jorge Luis Borges, "Evaristo Carriego," in *Obras Completas* (Buenos Aires: Emecé, 1974), 101.
129 B. González Arrilí, "Carriegito," Prólogo a Evaristo Carriego, *Misas herejes* (Buenos Aires: Tor, 1946), 9.

the revolutionary enterprise of anarchist comrades:

> *En procession inmensa va el macilento enjambre:*
> *mordidas las entrañadas por los lobos del hambre*

> The pale swarm moves in large procession:
> its entrails devoured by the wolves of hunger

....

> *Lidiemos en la justa de todos los rencores...*
> *¡insignias de los bravos modernos luchadores!*

> Let us struggle in the justice of all resentments...
> badges of brave modern fighters!

José de Maturana, poet, active militant, and editor of *La Protesta*, was born in 1884 and died in 1917 in Córdoba. He edited the literary journal *Los Nuevos Caminos* between 1906 and 1907, and wrote two dramatic poems in the style of Villaespesa, *La flor del trigo* (1909) and *Canción de primavera* (1912). Ricardo Rojas says of Maturana that he "had picked up the torch of poetic drama that was slowly dying in Coronado." And Luis Ordaz rightly notes, Maturana breathed into romanticism "a determined attitude against abuse and injustice." Earlier he had published a collection of sonnets, *Cromos* (1901), and other works in verse: *Lucila* (1902) and *Poemas de color* (1903), as well as a series of stories, *Gentes honradas* (1907). On the occasion of the execution in Barcelona of the libertarian pedagogue Francisco Ferrer, Marturana edited a pamphlet titled, *Francisco Ferrer, la voz del siglo*.[130]

Another writer associated with *La Protesta* is Santiago Locascio, author of *Rasgos sociales* (1899), *Los mártires de Chicago*

---

130 Luis Ordaz, in Pedro Orgambide and Roberto Yahni, *Enciclopedia de la literatura argentina* (Buenos Aires: n.p., 1970), 448–49.

(1904), *Orientaciones* (1911), *Juan Bautista Alberdi* (1916), and several theatrical pieces. Pedro J. Calou is also notable. He was a poet much admired by later literary generations and, according to Santillán, briefly took part in the anarchist movement and in the editorial work of *La Protesta*. In the end he turned to theosophy. To his former anarchist comrades this undoubtedly was much less reputable than ending up a fervent anarcho-communist in the swamps of fascism, as did Juan Emiliano Carulla, physician and writer from Entre Ríos. Carulla collaborated in *Bandera Argentina* and in *La Fronda*, after his service for *La Protesta*—for which he suffered imprisonment and political persecution. He turned to the works of De Maitre and Maurras after Proudhon and Bakunin, and worked tirelessly for the fascist *coup* by Uriburu. The brilliant finale to his literary career is the book *Valor poético de la revolución de setiembre* (1930).[131]

A different case is that of the writer and pedagogue Julio R. Barcos. Barcos was born in Coronda (Santa Fe) in 1883 and died in Buenos Aires, 1960. In spite of his move from anarchism to Irigoyenist radicalism, paralleling Orsini Bertani's shift to Batllism in Uruguay, he continued to express a basically libertarian position until his death. As an educator, he helped to disseminate an innovative pedagogy, contributed both textbooks and methodological essays to Argentinean education, and worked for the teachers' union. He was president of the Liga Nacional de Maestros (1911), later helped to start the Internacional del Magisterio Americano, and edited the classics of Argentinean political thought—Echevarría, Alberdi, and Sarmiento. Among his books, *La libertad sexual de las mujeres* was widely read and then translated into various languages, which merits his status, along with Lazarte, as one of the anarchist pillars of modern feminism.[132]

It is important to mention here two anarchist writers who also presented a feminism that was quite radical for its time: Salvadora

---

131 Ibarguren, *La historia que he vivido*, 364–65. See also Federico Ibarguren, *Los origins del nacionalismo argentino* (Buenos Aires: Celcius, 1969).

132 Quesada, *La Protesta*, 2, 73.

Medina Onrubia and Juana Rouco Buela. The former, born in La Plata in 1895, was a teacher in rural Entre Ríos. She collaborated in *La Protesta* and the journal *Fray Mocho*, translated theatrical works and children's books, wrote several plays performed in Buenos Aires, such as *Alma fuerte*, and founded the group América nueva, which aimed to defend the civil and political rights of women.[133] Rouco Buela, born in Madrid in 1889, was very active in the workers' struggles in Argentina almost from the time of her arrival in Buenos Aires in 1900. She represented the Refinería Argentina de Rosario in FORA's Fifth Congress. In 1907 she was deported to her native country for militant participation in the tenant's strike. In 1909, she founded the newspaper *Nueva Senda* in Montevideo, and in 1910 was again arrested in Buenos Aires during the violent raids of the Centenary. She collaborated with several newspapers and journals in Rio de Janeiro, where she resided for several years, and upon her return to Buenos Aires wrote for *El Mundo* and the journal *Mundo Argentino*. In 1922 in Necochea, she founded a feminist biweekly, *Nuestra Tribuna*. Shortly before her death in 1970 she published a lively autobiographical story titled *Historia de un ideal vivido por una mujer*.[134] To these writers we need to add the name of the essayist Herminia Brumana, always close to libertarian circles and the *La Protesta* group.[135]

Alejandro Sux, pseudonym of Alejandro Daudet, son of a colonel by the same name, born in Buenos Aires in 1888, also collaborated in *La Protesta*, writing the column titled *Mis domingos*. He wrote for *Mundial*, Rubén Darío's journal, and during the First World War was a foreign correspondent in France for the Buenos Aires daily *La Prensa*. He travelled widely through Europe and the Americas, but late in life had little interest in anarchism or proletarian struggles. In his years of libertarian militancy he wrote the following works: *Seis días en la cárcel de Mendoza* (1908), a chronicle

133   Ibid.
134   Ibid., 88.
135   Marta Elena Samatán, "Herminia C. Brumana," in *Reconstruir*, 89, 21–24 and *Herminia Brumana, la rebelde* (Buenos Aires: Plus Ultra, 1974).

denouncing the lamentable conditions at the Mendoza penitentiary, as well as several novels, such as *Amor y Libertad* and *Bohemia revolucionaria*, both reflecting the sentiments of Argentinean anarchists in the early twentieth century. Other works by him are *Cantos de rebelión* and *Cuentos de América*.[136] In 1918 he wrote for *La Novela Semanal* published in Buenos Aires in the style of *La Novela Corta*.[137]

Julio Molina y Vedia, translator of the libertarian writer Edward Carpenter, also wrote for *La Protesta* and later published a semi-philosophical essay, *Hacia la vida intensa* (1904), which Santillán considers "well thought out."[138] Fernando Intento was born in Buenos Aires in 1886 and lived most of his life in La Plata. He was on the editorial staff of *La Protesta*, wrote for the journal *Germen*, edited by Sux, was himself editor of the biweekly *La Mancha* and, between 1919 and 1925, of *Ideas*. Among his books, the following stand out: *Salud ¡oh tiempos!* (1919), *Ideas* (1920), and *Libro del hombre* (1927).

Other libertarian authors prior to the First World War were: Mario Villa, Alfonso Grijalvo, and T. Ros; Ricardo Carrencá, author of a collection of poems titled *Desde mi selva* (1911); Pedro Maino, author of the novel *El crimen de muchos* (1907); Leoncio Lasso de la Vega, famous bohemian and editor of the newspaper *El Día* in Montevideo, who left us a miscellany of ingenious verse and prose titled *El moral de un bohemio* (1913); and Mario Chilopegui, a journalist and poet. Teodoro Antillí, wrote for well-known publications in Buenos Aires such as *Mundo Argentino* and *Fray Mocho*. Along with his close friend González Pacheco in 1908 he founded *Germinal* and later *Campana Nueva*. Both worked on *La Protesta*, *La Obra*, and *La Antorcha*, and in 1910 Antillí edited *La Batalla*, an evening paper. Several of his articles and essays appeared in a collection by *La Antorcha* under the title *¡Salud a la anarquía!* González Pacheco said of Antillí, "he was a clear and exemplary anarchist."

---

136 Santillán, *El movimiento anarquista*, 131; Quesada, *La Protesta*, 2, 70.
137 Berenguer Carisomo, *Literatura argentina*, 78, n. 15.
138 Santillán, *El movimiento anarquista*, 131.

González Pacheco, a brilliant prose writer and prolific dramatist, was himself one of the greatest literary figures of Argentinean anarchism. He was born in Tandil in 1881 and died in Buenos Aires in 1949. Along with Federico A. Gutiérrez, a former police officer who crossed over to anarchism, he founded a satirical newspaper in 1906, *La Mentira*, with the ironic subtitle of *Organo de la patria, la religion, y el Estado*. In the following year he published his first book, *Rasgos*, alternating prose and verse. As already noted, with Antillí he started the journal *Germinal* and in 1910 was editor of *La Batalla*. Then in 1911, while editing the anarchist newspaper *Alberdi* along with Apolinario Barrera, he was arrested and imprisoned in the remote penitentiary of Usuahia. Upon his return he started another newspaper titled *Libre Palabra*, co-edited with Tito Livio Foppa. A bit later he teamed up once again with Antillí to publish *El Manifiesto*. Argentinean by birth and sentiment, imbued with the landscape of the pampas, identifying with the gaucho and Creole, González Pacheco was, above all, an internationalist deeply interested in the destiny of the people of the world and the ultimate triumph of the socialist and libertarian revolution. Not surprisingly, he ventured to Mexico in 1911 to join the ranks of the Magonists.[139] He was back in Argentina by the onset of the First World War. In 1916 he opened his short play *Las víboras* in the Teatro Nuevo de Buenos Aires, and the following year Pablo Podestá directed *La inundiación*, his three-act play, in the same venue. In 1917 he founded a libertarian group called La Obra, publishing a newspaper by the same name. In 1919 he published *Carteles*, a collection of combative and lyrical essays that expressed, perhaps better than any of his other writings, his political and literary personality. In *El Hombre* (Number 131) published in Montevideo, a critic wrote: "Any reader of *Carteles* can certainly affirm that he knows the character of González Pacheco."[140]

---

139   See Salvador Hernández Padilla, *El magonismo: historia de una pasión libertaria* (México: Era, 1984), 136–37.

140   Vladimir Muñoz, "Una cronología de Rodolfo González Pacheco," *Reconstruir*, 90, 57.

In 1920 he started another newspaper, *El Libertario*, and the theatrical company Muiño-Alippi produced his play *Magdalena*. In 1921, along with a group of comrades, he published *La Antorcha*—the paper that for a while was the main rival to *La Protesta* within the wide spectrum of the Argentinean libertarian press—and opened his play *Hijos del Pueblo* in the Teatro Bodeo. The following year, Predo Zanetta's company performed *El Sembrador*, and after a trip to Chile to promote anarchism, his three-act play, *Hermano Lobo*, was performed on December 24, 1924. In 1926 González Pacheco was sentenced to six months in prison for his article defending Kurt Wilckens, the anarchist who assassinated Colonel Varela. He was then forced into exile. Nonetheless, on July 31, 1926 his play *Natividad* was performed in the Teatro Marconi. Later, on July 3, 1927, Enrique Muños directed his play *A contramano,* and the following year *El hombre de la plaza pública.* On April 1, 1929 *El grillo* was performed in the Teatro La Comedia in Rosario. The fascist coup of 1930 found Pacheco, along with thousands of anarchists and socialists, in prison in Villa Devoto, where he was held for eight months and wrote the play *Juana y Juan*, later performed by the Muiño-Alippi company on June 4, 1931 in the Teatro Buenos Aires.

While intensely involved with his dramatic compositions, González Pacheco continued writing his already famous *Carteles*, with the second series published in 1936, the same year in which his play in four acts, *Compañeros*, was brought to life in Montevideo. Meanwhile, fascism appeared in Spain, and CNT-FAI began a social revolution in the cities and countryside. González Pacheco, above all else an anarchist, simply had to be there. In 1937 he directed his play *Teatro Social* in Barcelona and, with Guillermo Bosquets, founded the Compañia de teatro del pueblo.[141] His *Carteles de España* appeared in 1938. A political commentator cited by Vladimir Muñoz writes: "Rodolfo González Pacheco, Argentinean anarchist, is universally recognized not only for his numerous theatrical works, but also for his *Carteles*, each of them a synthesis of idealism

---

141   Ibid., 58–59.

and rebelliousness."[142] What most impresses his readers is the power and insight of his analyses, and his synthesis of the lyrical and the polemical, of metaphor and agony. He feels nature but interprets it in terms of humanity and particularly of social struggle. For him, mountaintops are protests leveled against the sky; landscape is a product of society and its dominant classes.

González Pacheco returned home after the triumph of fascism in Spain and the defeat of revolutionary expectations, but he never ceased his work, which was always equally literary and libertarian. In 1940 Blanca Podestá premiered the drama *Manos de luz* in the Teatro Smart. The Cordoban anarchist Forti later published that work in *Cuadernillos Inquietud* in Tupiza, Bolivia. Muñoz remembers González Pacheco's visit in 1945 to Uruguay, and the painter Juan Pardo, who under the pseudonym El jinete l'azuleto wrote the following in an article titled "Ha pasado un gaucho" for the libertarian paper *Inquietud*: "Oh, old man Pacheco, anarchist brother, libertarian gaucho from La Plata! ... you're three times a gaucho: anarchist, singer, and Creole." And he certainly was, but in a manner that never overshadowed his broad internationalism, a universalism that truly embraced the whole world. No surprise that the last play by this prolific gaucho writer is titled *Cuando aquí había reyes*. It premiered in 1947 in the Buenos Aires theater Unione e benevolenza in Yiddish, and the following year was presented in Spanish in the Teatro Solís in Montevideo.[143] He left an unfinished work titled *El cura*, written as clericalism was becoming prominent in Argentina after the Peronist triumph. In collaboration with another Argentinean dramatist, Pedro E. Picco, he wrote several pieces that were as well received as his own individual works: *Nace un pueblo*; *Juan de Dios, milico y paisona*; *Campo de hoy*; *Amor de nunca*; and *Que la agarre quien la quiera*.

González Pacheco may also be considered one of the pioneers of Argentinean cinema, co-authoring a script with MacDougall on

---

142 Ibid., 60.
143 Ibid., 60–61.

the exotic writer from Buenos Aires Eliseo Montaine. He died on June 5, 1949 in Buenos Aires.[144] In 1953 his theatrical works were collected in a volume titled *Teatro Completo* by Alberto S. Biachi.[145]

Pascual Guaglianone, a collaborator in *La Protesta* and one of the most brilliant anarchist orators of the early twentieth century—sometimes called "the Argentinean Sébastien Faure"—edited the journal *Vida Nueva* (1903). He later showed great interest in the history of religions, employing a positivist methodology. Félix B. Basterra was, above all, a combative journalist who not only wrote for *La Protesta*, but also founded several libertarian publications, like the journal *Los Tiempos Nuevos* (1900) and the satirical newspaper *El Cuento del Tío* (1902). He wrote *Sobre Ciencia Social*, published in 1901 by *La Protesta*, *El crepúsculo de los gauchos* (1903), and *Leyendas de humanidad* (1904). He eventually abandoned libertarian ideology, and after publishing *Asuntos Contemporáneos* (1908) a few years later "was already on the other side of the barricade."[146]

Several forgotten authors who collaborated with the Argentinean anarchist press in the early twentieth century must be mentioned: M. R. Zuñiga, Francisco Sarache, O. Fernández Ríos, Segundo Nachón, Alfredo Piuma Schmid, and Pérez y Curis.[147] The educator Arturo Montesano was a popular and brilliant orator who "earned the praise of the full spectrum of the anarchist press."[148] Various well-known Spanish writers, like the humorist Julio Camba, exiled in Buenos Aires in 1902, and the novelist and dramatist Vicente A. Salaverri, at least during their residence in Argentina identified themselves with anarchist thought and the ideological struggles of native libertarians. Julio Camba, born in Villanova de Arosa (Pontevera) in 1882, resided in Buenos Aires for several years

---

144   Quesada, *La Protesta*, 75.
145   On the works of González Pacheco and especially on his drama, see Alfredo de la Guardia, *González Pacheco* (Buenos Aires: Ediciones Culturales Argentinas, 1963).
146   Santillán, *El movimiento anarquista*, 130.
147   Ibid., 131.
148   Oved, *El anarquismo*, 140.

and collaborated with the anarchist press. His writing shows great creativity, and contributed much popular literature to Argentina, along with his journalistic writings for *España Nueva*, *El País*, *El Mundo*, and for *La Correspondencia de España* as a foreign correspondent in Turkey. Vicente A. Salaverri, born in Viniegra de Abajo (Rioja) in 1887, was like Rafael Barrett editor of *El Diario Español* of Buenos Aires. In 1909 he moved to Montevideo and edited *La Razón*, later managing his father-in-law's farms. In addition to his articles in *Caras y Caretas*, *Fray Mocho*, and *Nosotros*, he left behind comedies, dramas, and skits, including *La mala vida*, *Resurrexit* and *Del picadero al proscenio*; novels, such as *Los niños bien*, *Deformarse es vivir*, and *El corazón de Maria*; and essays, notably *La vida humilde*, *Hombres del Uruguay*, *El teatro de Florencio Sánchez*, and *Animales con pluma: el periodismo por dentro*.[149]

A unique literary phenomenon that has so far been neglected in scholarly study is the gaucho tradition on both sides of the Río de la Plata, particularly as manifested in the songs of the libertarian *payadores*. A late example is found in *Carta Gaucha* by Luis Woolands, under the pseudonym Juan Crusao. An anarchist of Dutch descent, Woolands nonetheless integrated and identified with the Argentinean *pampas* and called its farm laborers, despoiled and exploited by the landed oligarchy, to an anarchist revolution, all the while remaining an internationalist. He wrote:

Gauchos! My countrymen, partners in misery: prepare the knives because war is about to break out! No one stays behind. Have courage unless you wish to be treated as mules and have your ears cut off. Start the revolution, even if all you have is a spear. Forward! The gringos will provide a helping hand. Long live the revolution! Long live the anarchist revolution and the freedom of the gauchos!

---

149 Santillán, *El anarquismo*, 127. See also W. Pi, *Semblanza literaria de V. A. Salaverri* (n.p., n.p., 1918).

La Carta Gaucha was widely distributed in the Argentinean interior and among urban workers. It is the expression of a native rebelliousness that was never fully captured in Hernández's *Martín Fierro* and indeed is suppressed in the meek if not fawning *Don Segundo Sombra*. As Luis Franco put it, *La Carta Gaucha* connects with "the rebelliousness of the earlier work *Martín Fierro* and reaches the inevitable and ultimate conclusion: The war of expropriation against the expropriators, the modern proletariat revolution."[150] Among the libertarian *payadores* we must mention Martín Castro, "the red *payador*"; Luis Acosta García, honored with a street named after him in Dorrego; and the Uruguayan Carlos Molina.

The years immediately following the First World War saw a flowering of Argentinean poets and writers who, at some point in their lives, were close to anarchism and joined one of its many organizations; or they were at least sympathetic to its ideals, even when later in life many of them adopted different political and ideological positions. Suffice it to mention the names of Alvaro Yunque, Elías Castelnuovo, and José Portogallo, all were later active in the Communist Party but not without exhibiting in their work the originating marks of libertarian thought and sentiment. Indeed, the group Boedo, frequently opposed to the group Florida, consisted of young writers ideologically formed by the anarchist press.

Alvaro Yunque, a prolific author, contributed poems, stories, essays, biographies, dramas, and comedies to his national literature. His collections of poetry include, among others: *Versos de la calle*, *Nudo corredizo*, *Cobres de 2 centavos*, *Poemas gringos*, *Descubrimiento de hijo*, *La o es redonda*, and *España 1936*. His children's literature, built on ideological and sentimental themes of the lukewarm socialism of D'Amicis, consists of titles like *Barcos de papel*, *Espantajos*, *Tatetí*, *Jauja*, *Bichofeo*, *Poncha*, *13 años*, *Muchachos pobres*, *Muchachos del Sur*, *La barra de 7 Ombúes*, and *El amor sigue*

---

150 Luis Franco, "Cómo conocí a Juan Crusao," prólogo a Luis Woolands (Juan Crusao), *Carta Gaucha y La descendencia del Viejo Vizcacha* (Mar del Plata: Agrupación Libertaria, 1960), 12.

siendo niño. Of his theatrical works we should mention *Violín y violón*, *Náufragos*, *Somos hermanos*, *Sonreír*, and *Comedieta*. The poems, stories, and drama of Alvaro Yunque all have the poor, humble, and meek of the world as main characters. His great sympathy for children and the people, for workers and the marginalized, has the mark of that strain of libertarian literature whose masters are not only Ghiraldo and Florencio Sánchez, but also Gorki and ultimately Tolstoy. Elías Castelnuovo was, as Francisco Herrera put it, the archetypical writer of the Boedo group. He collaborated in the journal *Los Pensadores* and later in *Claridad*. In 1920 he edited the supplement to *La Protesta*. Then in 1931 he traveled with G. F. Nicolai and Lelio Zeno to the USSR. His best know books are *Larvas* (1931), *Vidas proletarias* (1934), and the novel *Calvario* (1956). Other works include *Malditos* (1924), *Entre los muertos* (1925), the plays *Almas benditas* (1926) and *En nombre de Cristo* (1928)—premiered in the Teatro Experimental Argentino—and the novel *Carne de cañon* (1930). Herrera writes:

> The selection of characters, context, and conflict—consisting of marginal zones, of people dispossessed more than proletarians, and an underworld of deformed beings lost in a darkness from which they cannot escape—comprises the lexicon of Boedean options. That humbleness or pietism appeals to the best of anarchist thought. It is the ideological spring of the Boedo group, being the first national Leftist literature.[151]

But as we have already seen, Leftist literature in Argentina first emerged two if not three decades earlier, with Ghiraldo, Florencio Sánchez, and many other writers and poets who were already identified with libertarian communism from the closing years of the nineteenth century. We should instead doubt an Argentinean Leftist literature *after* the Boedo group and its immediate successors. A

---

151   Francisco Herrera in Orgambide and Yahni, *Enciclopedia de la literatura argentina*, 129–131.

youthful libertarian élan infuses all of these writers, with the exception of some sympathizers of Leninism and the USSR in the 1930s and 1940s.

Putting Roberto Arlt and a few others aside, José Portogallo, Herrera writes, "in some respects continues the testimonial character of the Boedo group," and from his very first book, *Tregua* (1935), "shows a determined militant attitude and a profound mastery of the expressive instrument."[152] Finally, Ernesto Sábato consistently preserved in his work the critical spirit and the affirmation of ethical values inherent in anarchist literature. His simultaneous aversion to Western capitalism and to Soviet bureaucratism may be regarded as an inheritance from his youthful libertarian militancy, even if he was not totally conscious of it. In any event, this interpretation is much closer to the truth than one that sees in him only a centrist position.

I. Ideologists, Propagandists, Polemicists

In this section we treat those writers and journalists whose work was totally dedicated to revolutionary action and the workers' movement, and did so as ideologists and propagandists of anarchism. For them aesthetic or literary preoccupations were secondary, though much of the work has considerable literary value. These authors produced a series of studies on a number of important topics: on anarchist doctrine, its philosophical and ethical foundations, the socioeconomic reality of the country and the world, and the history of the workers' movement and of anarchist organizations. Some of the writings were occasional pieces and tended towards commentary on topics such as the anarchist standpoint in relation to recent political, economic, and social events, as well as toward the promotion of syndicalist and popular action. Others had a

---

152   Herrera, in Orgambide and Yahni, *Enciclopedia de la literatura argentina*, 516. See also Carlos B. Giordano, *Capitulo. La historia de la literature argentina* (Buenos Aires: n.p., 1980,) iv.

polemical character and were aimed not only against apologists of the regime, but also against figures and institutions of the Left and even against the libertarian movement itself. In general, they adopted a tone of denunciation and radical critique of the system while remaining attentive to scientific and sociological principles. The arguments tended to follow statistical realities.

Antonio Pellicer Paraire was among the most prominent Argentinean ideologists and propagandists. Born in Barcelona in 1851, he died in Buenos Aires in 1916. His articles on workers' organization, collected in *Conferencias populares de sociología* (1905), were decisive in nourishing the attitudes that led to the founding of FORA.[153] His slightly older contemporary, the Irish physician Juan Creaghe was born in 1841 and died in Washington, 1920. After completing his studies at the University of Dublin and then serving as editor of the newspaper *The Sheffield Anarchist* in England, Creaghe arrived in Argentina. While practicing medicine in Luján between 1894 and 1896, he published *El Oprimido*; was part of the founding group of *La Protesta*, devoting much financial and intellectual support; and in 1911 traveled to Mexico because he was impressed by the revolutionary actions of Zapata and Flores Magón.[154]

Emilio Z. Arana was another physician and anarchist writer of this period. He collaborated in *La Protesta* and in *Ciencia Social*, launched the journal *Humanidad Nueva* and the anarcho-communist group Ciencia y Progreso of Rosario, convened several conferences, and later edited and published pamphlets, such as *La sociedad, su presente, su pasado, su porvenir* (1896), *La mujer y la familia* (1897), *La esclavitud antigua y moderna* (1898), *La medicina y el proletariado* (1899), and *Los males sociales-Su único remedio* (1900). Santillán writes: "Dr. Arana was never a partisan anarchist, but a man profoundly convinced of the goodness of anarchist communism and he remained faithful to that view until his death."[155]

---

153 Santillán, *La FORA*, 51–51; Godio, *Historia del movimiento*, 1, 134.
154 See E. Carulla, S. Locascio, and E. G. Gilimón, *Vía libre* (September 1920).
155 Santillán, *El movimiento anarquista*, 62.

As we noted before, among the first editors of *La Protesta* were Inglan Lafarga, the Catalan carpenter; Francisco Berri, an Italian baker; Mariano Cortés; and José Prat. The latter seems to have arrived in Buenos Aires fleeing the repression in Montjuich after the bombing at Cambios Nuevos in Barcelona in 1896. In Argentina he translated from French several pamphlets and the work of Agustín Hamon, *Psicología del socialista anarquista* (1898). Mario Cortéz left behind a manuscript of highly original content: *Fundamentos y lenguaje de la doctrina anarquista* (1900). The French journalist Pierre Quiroule wrote, in addition to a long series of articles, a utopian story titled *La ciudad anarquista Americana* (1914), a play in two acts titled *El fusilamineto de Francisco Herrera, o sea, la Infamia Negra* (1910), and a novel of anarchist propaganda, *Sobre la ruta de la Anarquía* (1912). Eduardo Gilimón, also a collaborator in *La Protesta*, was the author of a popular memoir, *Hechos y comentarios* (1911), and of several pamphlets, such as *Para los que no son anarquistas* (1913).

Ericco Malatesta and Pietro Gori are two great figures of Italian anarchism that lived and worked in Argentina for several years and are worth mentioning a second time. One of the key figures in the history of anarchism and the libertarian movement is Diego Abad de Santillán. His organizational, theoretical, and historical work makes him one of the most important libertarian ideologists in Argentina and Latin America. His true name was Sinesio Baudillo García Fernández. He was born in the mountains of León, Spain in 1897, and as a young boy arrived with his parents in Argentina, residing in Santa Fe from age eight. He returned to Madrid to pursue university studies, enrolling in the Faculty of Philosophy and Letters and studying under Ortega y Gasset and Cejador y Frauca. His interest in psychology and philology did not keep him from active participation in the turbulent political life of the city, and his ideas led to his first imprisonment in 1917. In jail he became acquainted with two illustrious Spanish anarchists, Julián Besteiro and Francisco Largo Caballero. He returned to Argentina in 1919 without completing his university studies, but one can certainly say that he returned having graduated in anarchism. That same year he began editing *La Protesta* and immediately found himself confronting the very harsh reality that exploded during the Tragic Week.

In 1922 he traveled to Berlin as a foreign correspondent for *La Protesta* and began medical studies. In the German capital he associated with the most prominent figures of international anarchism and many other intellectuals of the European Left. He participated in the founding of the Asociación Internacional de Trabajadores (AIT), began his tremendous work of translating the works of Bakunin, Rocker, and Nettlau into Spanish, and, with Emilio López Arango, wrote *El anarquismo en el movimiento obrero*, published in Barcelona in 1925.

Urged by his own militancy and without completing medical studies, he returned to Buenos Aires in 1927 to take charge of *La Protesta*, paving the way for a brilliant period in the paper's history. Under his editorship, *La Protesta* spawned a publishing house, changed the weekly *Suplemento* into a biweekly *Revista*, and published a series of classical works in anarchism, putting them within reach of working people. In 1930 he published his important book, *El movimiento anarquista en la Argentina desde su comienzo hasta 1910*, which we have quoted numerous times in these pages. As editor of *La Protesta* he was in a position to understand better than anyone else on the Argentinean Left the direction of the anti-Yrigoyenist conspiracy—undoubtedly an attempt to destroy the workers' movement, stop the social revolution (presumably close at hand), and establish the foundation of a corporatist State with the support of the armed forces, large landowners, and the clergy.

When the coup was carried out on September 6, Santillán used *La Protesta* to call for a general strike. FORA ignored the call. Its militants stuck to an apparently orthodox viewpoint, refusing to interfere in bourgeois party politics, treating this matter as if it were a mere dispute between conservatives and radicals, or between personalists and anti-personalists. Some of the inflexible and doctrinaire militants declared that for the anarchist and the proletariat there was no difference between the populism of Irigoyen and the fascism of Uriburu. But this error in judgment cost FORA many deaths and exiles, and one might even say that it cost FORA its very own life. When *La Protesta* closed and FORA was outlawed, Santillán took advantage of the pause to write two books, both quite important to the anarchist movement in Argentina: *Reconstrucción social—Bases para una nueva edificación económica argentina* (1932) (in collaboration with the physician Dr. Juan Lazarte), and *La FORA—Ideología y trajectoria del movimiento obrero revolucionario en la Argentina* (1933), with a prologue by Lazarte on the economic, social, and political conditions in which the movement developed. Anticipating the social revolution, he returned to Spain in 1933. He went on to edit the weekly paper *Tierra y Libertad* in Barcelona, was an activist in both CNT and FAI, had significant intellectual influence over important popular leaders such as Durruti, founded the journal *Tiempos nuevos* and the publishing house Tierra y Libertad, and wrote two works fundamental for the socioeconomic orientation of the Spanish revolution: *El organismo económico de la revolución* (1936) and *Cómo vivimos y cómo podríamos vivir* (1936).

At the initiation of the civil war, under orders of the Comité de Milicias Antifascistas, Santillán organized popular militias and later served as Consejero de Economía on behalf of CNT in the Generalitat of Cataloña. In 1938 he started the journal *Timón* and, on the fall of Barcelona to the fascists on January 26, 1939, fled to France and traveled to the United States in an attempt to gain asylum for the numerous libertarian exiles that were discriminated against by ad hoc committees controlled by the Communist Party. In 1940 he returned to Buenos Aires and published his reflections on the civil war and revolution in his book *Por qué perdimos la Guerra* (which served as the basis for the 1978 film with the same title).

In the last four decades of his life, removed from the workers' movement and syndicalist struggles, his literary production was significant. He continued to collaborate with the libertarian press of the country (*Reconstruir, Acción Libertaria*, as well as others) and abroad (*Comunidad Ibérica*); wrote substantial works on the contemporary history of Spain, like *De Alfonso XIII a Franco* (1974) and *Historia del movimiento obrero español*, as well as a history of Argentina titled *Historia Argentina* in five volumes, a *Gran Enciclopedia Argentina* in nine volumes, and the *Enciclopedia de la provincia de Santa Fe* in two volumes; he edited and gave commentary on various classics of the national literature of Argentina, like *Martín Fierro*; and near the end of his life published his *Memorias* (1977). His work as translator (from French, German, and Italian) was enormous. Among the thinkers he introduced to the Spanish-speaking world were Bakunin, Rocker, Landeaur, Nettlau, and Fabri, and other classics of anarchist literature, the work of jurists, sociologists, and philosophers such as von Ihering, von Wiese, Jaspers, and more. Surrounded by a small group of loyal friends, even if forgotten by many of his comrades, he died in Barcelona in 1983.

Santillán conceived of anarchism as a radical humanism and an ethical movement, the goals of which are justice and liberty. Even if, like Malatesta, he believed that the ideal form of economic organization is communism, he never blindly or dogmatically adhered to that view, and in the last decades of his life came to believe that economic systems (mutualism, collectivism, communism) are secondary to an anarchism without adjectives. As he aged his anti-dogmatism grew. Unlike other anarchists and socialists of the early twentieth century, Santillán did not attribute a palingenetic character of universal and sudden regeneration to revolution. On the contrary, he held that revolution has neither terms nor timelines, but has instead propositions and ideals. Much like Gustav Landauer, he held it to be a permanent and daily phenomenon. And nothing could be further from his thought than violence for the mere sake of violence. He wrote in his *Memorias*:

> Over a good number of years I filled thousands and thousands of pages in newspapers, journals, and books. You will not find anywhere in that mountain of paper one single line that applauds a surrender to injustice, but neither will you find a single line that exalts violence for violence's sake. I have been

as distant from obsequious meekness as from brutal homicidal protest and the law of the jungle. And I have known, have worked and lived with many friends and comrades who entered history as symbols of heroic anarchism—the heroism sung by those who lack the nature of a hero—and who avenged horrible antisocial crimes, though by their formation and character they were essentially anti-violent, perhaps even Tolstoyan and Christian.

Diego Abad de Santillán was the archetype of the hard-working militant, a model of ethical idealism, and of libertarian self-denial. Gúzman writes:

> Santillán dedicates long and intense work on behalf of others, and despite the effect of such work upon his health he never thinks of himself. Much like the cicada, but for entirely different motives, he lets spring, summer, and fall pass without even dreaming of gathering what will support him through winter. And when old age arrives he spends more years laboring until death, with a stack of papers in his hands and his thought brimming with new projects.[156]

Along with Santillán we must mention two of his closest collaborators, both born in Spain, but by their actions and militancy clearly Argentinean: Emilio López Arango and Manuel Villar. López Arango was born in Oviedo, 1894 and emigrated to Cuba as an adolescent and then to Buenos Aires, where he became an active militant of the bakers' union and served as editor of its journal, *El Obrero Panadero*. In 1926 he began to collaborate with *La Protesta* and then served as its editor for several years. On October 25, 1929 he was assassinated at the front door of his home, apparently by Severino Di Giovanni:

---

156   Eduardo de Gúzman, *Una lección de austeridad y sacrificio, Polémica*, 10, 41.

> Criminal hands moved by the foolish purpose of silencing a
> courageous journalistic campaign against the deviance of cer-
> tain men were determined to turn a revolutionary delinquen-
> cy into a theory justifying deeds that the morality of anarchist
> ideas categorically rejects, forever shortened with three bul-
> lets the life of Arango.[157]

Manuel Villar, born in Burgos in 1904, emigrated as a young boy to
Argentina, became an electrician, and joined *La Protesta* in 1925.
Four years later he was named Secretary of the Asociación Continental Americana de Trabajadores (ACTA) and editor of its journal *La Continental Obrera*. Deported from Argentina in 1932, he
edited various papers in Spain: in Barcelona *Solidaridad Obrera*,
CNT's daily in Madrid, and finally, in Valencia, *Fragua Social*. After the fall of the Republic, he was imprisoned for a year at the Cárcel Modelo in Madrid and shortly after his release attempted along
with several comrades the underground reorganization of CNT
and, again detained, languished in Franco's prisons for eighteen
years. He wrote *España en la ruta de la libertad* (1962) in prison,
and died there in 1972.[158]

The physician Dr. Juan Lazarte represents the Argentinean
anarchist from the interior of the country better than anyone else.
Born in Rosario in 1891 and in his youth a student of Julio R. Barcos, he majored in biology at the Instituto del Profesorado Secund-
ario de Buenos Aires, studied at Universidad de La Plata, Columbia
University in New York City, and finally graduated from the medical school at the Universidad de Córdoba. His years of study in this
"holy and learned" city coincided with the rise of national university reforms. Lazarte was, as Santillán puts it,

> the most prominent orator of the student movement of those
> years of passion. ... He acquired the reputation and popularity

---

157 ACAT, Prólogo a Emilio López Arango, *Ideario* (Buenos Aires: Edi-
     ciones ACAT, 1942), 10.
158 Quesada, *La Protesta*, 2, 91–92.

of a genuine leader. From the start he was considered a volunteer of pure conviction—fair, self-sacrificing, tireless, always ready to give, to offer his inexhaustible spiritual and moral resources without expecting anything in return.[159]

During a very long life he was able to bring his exemplary practice of the profession of medicine together with his prolific literary and journalistic activity, and his incessant work as a lecturer and popular speaker, commentator on science, and libertarian propagandist. He wrote thousands of articles published in Argentina, other Latin American countries, and Europe. In addition to the already mentioned work *Reconstrucción social*, written with Santillán, a biography of the social reformer Lisandro de la Torre, and many other books and pamphlets, the following titles show the breadth of interest this hard-working libertarian physician had: *La locura de la guerra en América, Psicosociología de los celos, Sociología de la prostitución, La crisis del capitalismo, La solución federalista en la crisis histórica argentina, Problemas de medicina social,* and *La socialización de la medicina.* Again, Santillán: "the problem of war, that monstrous anachronism, was one of his constant themes after the First World War. He was preoccupied with militarism, increasing defense budgets, and their pressure on social and political life."[160] From his years as a university student, Lazarte was also interested in issues particular to higher education, and was among the first who sought to bring the student and labor movements together. He retained such preoccupations and interests well into the last years of his life as a university professor in the Facultad de Ciencias Económicas, Comerciales y Políticas de Rosario. In addition, his research interests turned to eugenics and birth control and, at a time when such topics were ignored or prohibited, initiated the study of the psychology and sociology of sex.

---

159 Santillán, "Lazarte y su militancia social," in *Juan Lazarte, militante social, medico, humanista* (Rosario: Grupo Editor de Estudios Sociales, 1964), 5.
160 Ibid., 7.

His passion for libertarian federalism led him to study the thought of Lisandro de la Torre, whom he considered an anti-imperialist. We should also recognize Lazarte as one of the first to pursue the unionization of physicians at the regional, national, and continental levels. Angel Invaldi writes: "He was a representative to all medical union congresses in the country, presiding over a few of them. He was the soul of such congresses."[161] He died in June 1963 while caring for a patient in his office. The following epitaph was proposed for him:

> *Amó los versos, la tierra, la libertad*
> *fue amigo de las bestias y los libros,*
> *supo andar y reír,*
> *lucho por la justicia.*[162]

> He loved verses, the land, and liberty,
> was a friend of animals and books,
> knew how to relax and laugh,
> and fought for justice.

Many other libertarian writers and journalists could be mentioned whose publications appeared after the overthrow of the government in 1930, which, as we have indicated, represents the beginning of the decline of Argentinean anarchism. Among them, one should include Luis Di Filippo, Horacio E. Roqué, Fernando Quesada, and Jacobo Prince, all of them active into recent times.

Of the victims of the last military dictatorship we should remember Guillermo Savloff, collaborator in *La Protesta*, director of Extensión Universitaria, and founder of the Asociación de Educación Libre.[163]

There are, of course, other writers who migrated to this once open land of universalist calling, and who collaborated with the

---

161   Invaldi, "Lazarte y el gremialismo medico," in *Juan Lazarte*, 24.
162   Ángel J. Cappelletti, "Juan Lazarte, un humanista," in *Juan Lazarte*, 41
163   López, *La FORA*, 1, 20.

anarchist press and organizations. We mention two more. Gastón Leval from France was an active propagandist, a professor of secondary education in Rosario, and author of several works, including *Social Reconstruction in Spain* (1938), and *La falacia del marxismo* (1967). Finally, the famous German physiologist Georg F. Nicolai was one of the originators of the electrocardiogram and sports medicine. Along with Albert Einstein, he signed the letter by German intellectuals opposing war in 1916. He was the author of *Miseria de la dialéctica* and *Biología de la guerra*, and a professor at the universities of Rosario, Córdoba, and Santiago de Chile. Even if he was not an anarchist, he had sustained collaborations with Argentinean libertarians and a profound influence on many of them.[164]

---

164   Eugen Relgis, *Georg F. Nicolai, un sabio y un hombre del porvenir* (Buenos Aires, 1965); Cappelletti, "Georg F. Nicolai y el humanism positivista," *Reconstruir*, Nos. 85–86.

2. Uruguay

A. Groups, Syndicates, Propaganda

Utopian socialism entered Uruguay with Tandonnet's arrival in Montevideo in 1844. There he edited a Fourierist periodical.[1] A few years earlier, between June 3 and 8, 1841, Marcelino Pareja, a relatively unknown author possibly of Argentinean origin, published an article titled "De las ganancias del Capital," in the daily paper *El Nacional* of Montevideo. He cited Godwin and presented a pre-Marxist theory of surplus value that seems to be influenced by Owen or Saint-Simonians and Fourierists, but in any case prior to Victor Considerant's *Le Manifeste de la démocratie au XIXe siècle*, published the year before Marx's *Communist Manifesto*.[2]

Many Italians who fought alongside Guiseppe Garibaldi in the siege of Montevideo and Uruguay's Great War (1843–1852) were steeped in the republicanism of the *Risorgimento* and embraced socialist ideas. Garibaldi himself referred to socialism as

---

1   Rama, *Utopismo socialista*, xxxiv–xxxv.
2   Pareja's article was initially discovered by Arturo Ardao, it was then published in *Cuadernos Uruguayos de Filosofía* (1968) V, 149–61.

the "sun of the future."[3] Miguel Cané and Andrés Lamas promoted the ideas of Saint-Simon and his school in *El Iniciador*.[4] In the 1870s a mutualist movement began among artisans and workers of Uruguay, and several mutual aid societies formed. According to Yamandú González, "labor organizations emerged from an initial situation characterized by profound scarcity of welfare services and a deeply felt need to come together to achieve communal aspirations." Resistance societies and other groups striving to protect the working class soon enough appeared in the wake of these initial societies of mutual aid. González writes:

> The first associations formed by workers in the 1870s and 1880s were unions, organizations, or other groupings that sought to secure specific workplace demands—for example, on termination and salaries—as well as internationalist associations based on the principles of struggle against exploitation and the advancement of socialism.[5]

An Uruguayan section of the Asociación Internacional de Trabajadores (AIT) was established in 1872; its incipient activities alarmed the bourgeois press. Francisco Galcerán headed the section, located at 216 Florinda Street—today called Florida—in Montevideo. Ideologically, it was federalist and anti-authoritarian, in line with the thinking from Chaux-de-Fonds near the Jura Mountains in Switzerland, and it had close ties not only with the Argentinean section, but also, between 1872 and 1878, with Mexican internationalists. Its first public act was organized in June of 1875 and attended by some 2,000 individuals. A month later, a group affiliated

---

3   Rama, *Historia social del pueblo uruguayo* (Montevideo: Comunidad del Sur, 1972), 61.
4   Cepeda, *Los utopistas,* 50; A. Ardao, *Filosofía preuniversitaria en el Uruguay* (Montevideo: Claudio García Editores, 1945), 85, 114.
5   Yamadú González, "Génesis del sindicalismo uruguayo (1870–1890)," Primeras asociaciones: Rebeldías y esperanzas (II) in *La Lupa,* suplemento de *Brecha,* 13 February 1987. See also José Ingenieros, *Almanaque socialista de "La Vanguardia" para 1899* (Buenos Aires: n. p., 1898).

with the Uruguayan Section of AIT—whose members included Colombé Abbas, Domingo Marañón, Pedro Sabater, Esteban Andueza, Juan Zavala, Modesto Gómez, José Vilavoa, and Francisco Galcerán—published a manifesto that clearly declared anarchist ideas that were inspired by Bakunin, and called upon the workers of the country to unite under a single organization in preparation for the coming struggle:

> The present circumstances of the working class, always the victim of hateful privilege, force us to say that it is imperative that as soon as is possible all workers in the country unite and form a single common organization for the defense of their just interests. ... Listen! We should note that anyone who seeks his own advantage and explains through lovely and well-turned phrases that he holds the key to our emancipation, when the terrible reality of our condition drives us to finally end the many sufferings that oppress us, we recommend the instrument of self-redemption. Why should we deliver ourselves hands and feet tied by the indestructible bond of a blind faith? Who better and of greater faith than ourselves can destroy the criminal exploitation to which we are condemned? So, we ourselves should watch over our interests and our redemption should be our own work. ... Capital is entrenched. It is the yoke of the daily oppression of the disinherited classes, the scandalous abuse of the sweat of the working poor. They suffer the consequences of the monopoly of money by those who enrich themselves even at the cost of impoverishing the entire country. In hopes of increasing our strength—and keeping informed about all those matters of interest to us as workers, such as the workers' movement throughout the world and what affects the progress we are able to achieve—with these aims we pledge assistance to the local Association, located at 216 Florinda Street, where we can share those ideas that circumstances present to us and tirelessly promote our aspirations. Workers should expect

everything from workers. ... We should not complete this manifesto without shouting from our hearts a great Hurrah! Health, Work, and Justice.[6]

On May 5, 1878 the Uruguayan Section began publication of the newspaper *El Internacional*. The Federación Regional de la República Oriental del Uruguay, later called the Federación Obrera Regional Uruguaya (FORU), had formed two years earlier in 1876. In 1882 it published *La Revolución Social*, in 1884 *La Lucha Obrera*, and in 1885 *La Federación de Trabajadores*. Later it published *La Emancipación*, beginning May 1, 1907, and *Solidaridad*, from July 15, 1912 until May 1, 1970.

Vladimir Muñoz, a meticulous bibliographer and historian of Uruguayan anarchism, gives us the following facts in annotating an essay by Nettlau (who, though the Herodotus of anarchism, had neglected to mention them). The weekly *La Revolución Social* began to appear in Montevideo in 1882; in 1883 a group of "anarchists of both sexes" celebrated the anniversary of the Paris Commune on March 18 and collected forty pesos on behalf of libertarian prisoners in Lyon; during that time, the following anarchist militants were active in Uruguay—Louis Lambert, Jean Pedrotta, José Cerrutti, Séraphin Icaro, Jean Mahy, Pierre Figué, José Doldan, Pierre Bernard, Jorie J. Bernard, Luis Moglia, E. Ghiosti, Hélene Pedrotta, Rafaele Bandini, Carlos Rossi, Renna Felice, Lorenzo Conti, Pietro Peruca, Giovanni Bonetti, and Jean Larré; and in 1884 *La Lucha Obrera*, journal of the Federación Internacional de Trabajadores del Uruguay, began to appear; in 1885, Pierre Bernard collected a sum of 120 pesos to aid the already famous libertarian paper *Le Révolté*; that same year the anarcho-collectivist weekly *La Federación de Trabajadores* appeared in Montevideo.

Muñoz also mentions the following libertarians active in Montevideo in 1887: E. Introzzi, V. Costemmalle, D. Ceccarelli, C.

---

6   V. Muñoz, "El anarquismo en el Uruguay hasta 1900," *Solidaridad*, Montevideo, May 1956, 23–25.

Duchini, V. Febo, P. Lombardi, B. Gallo, M. Fautoux, C. Loncq, and, above all, the already mentioned Pierre Bernard. At the Sunday fair held at the corner of Arapey Street and 18 de Julio, Cleverie owned a bookstore in which he sold *La Revolté,* and Bernard and Moglia provided home delivery. Among the new libertarians who were active in 1888, Muñoz mentions the following: C. Lomoy, Washington Marzoratti—who would later work on behalf of anarchist ideas in Chile—J. Gariga, J. Arnaud, E. Lavandera, J. P. Arnaudie, J. Le Cabos, E. Spietz, J. Courtade, E. Barriere, H. Ferry, J. M. Pecantet, P. Antonion, and J. M. Fortasini. In that same year 150 pesos were collected to aid propaganda in France, and a group called Grupo anarquista compuesto de obreros de diferentes idiomas formed in Montevideo, issued a declaration addressed to "anarchist groups in the five regions of the world."

According to Muñoz, from 1889 on the militancy of new anarchists is noteworthy. It includes the activities of Bruschetti, J. Dumas, Théodore Fournes, I. Etchegoyen, Celestín, and Z. Vigliano. In 1890 P. Amilcare edited the libertarian journal *La Voz del Trabajador.* In 1891 Pierre Bernard died. On February 13 *Le Revolté* said of his funeral: "Last month, one of our oldest comrades, Pierre Bernard, was buried in Montevideo. More than two hundred people attended the burial. Police prohibited funeral prayers. A black-and-red flag preceded the procession. It was a major event for Montevideo."

Between 1890 and 1904, a number of publications came to light: *El derecho a la vida* (1893–1900), *La Aurora Anarquista* (1899–1901), *La Verdad* (1897–1898), *El Amigo del Pueblo* (1899–1900), *Tribuna libertaria, La Rebelión, Futuro, Primero de Mayo, La Idea Libre, El Obrero,* and others. *Il Socialista* was published in Italian.[7] Also published during this period were doctrinal pamphlets and propaganda, such as *A los jóvenes* by Kropotkin and *La mujer en la lucha ante la naturaleza* by R. Carreira and P. Taboada.[8]

---

7   Nettlau, "Contribución a la bibliografía anarquista," 15.
8   Ibid., 22.

In the years following 1904 newspaper publications were equally abundant, though short-lived. Among them were: *El libertario*, *En Marcha*, *La Acción Obrera*, *Adelante*, *El Surco*, *La Nueva Senda*, *Ideas*, *Tiempos Nuevos*, *Guerra Social*, *Crónica subversivas y Germinal*, edited in Salto. *La Giustizia* was published in Italian. FORU also published its own newspapers, *La Emancipación* and *La Federación y Solidaridad*.[9] The number of pamphlets edited by anarchist groups or by anarchist authors kept growing. Among them were: *Eliseo Reclus* published by the Circulo Internacional de Estudios Sociales (1905), *El asesinato de Ferrer: La Protesta del Uruguay* (1909), *El Problema urgente: La imposibilidad de las mejoras económicas* (1909), *Catecismo de la doctrina anarquista escrito por un grupo anarquista* (1909), *La Comuna de Paris: Lo que fue, lo que debio ser y lo que será* (1912), *1° de mayo: Su origen y significado* (1912), *Los Males de la Guerra* (1912), *Los estragos del alcohol* (1912), *Cómo pensaba Francisco Ferre* (1912), and *La religion y la cuestión social* (1912).[10]

A series of historical circumstances made Uruguay very receptive of anarchist ideas—for example, the belated Spanish colonization, absence of the typical institutions of the Counter-Reformation (Inquisition, pontifical universities, Jesuit colleges), secularism, and the great number of immigrants. Anarchist ideas had been known in Uruguay since the nineteenth century through the works of Proudhon and Reclus, whose names along with others are engraved on the façade of the Universidad de la República.[11] And it is fair to say that in no other Latin American country were anarchist ideas more familiar to the man on the street, the educated public, politicians, and intellectuals than in Uruguay.

According to official statistics, in 1911 there were 117,000 industrial workers in Uruguay. Of those, 90,000 were affiliated with FORU. They were members of the Federación de Obreros del Puerto de Montevideo (consisting of crewmembers, dockworkers,

---

9   Ibid., 25.
10   Ibid., 29.
11   Muñoz, "El anarquismo en el Uruguay," 21.

bargemen, and others), the Federación de Obreros de la Construcción, the Federación de Picaderos (with a national membership), the Sociedad de Obreros del Cerro, the Federación Metalúrgica, the Federación de Ferroviarios (which, according to Riera Díaz, was "well-known for its combativeness"), the Federación local de Salto, and many other resistance societies. At the time, FORU was a "true central union of workers," not by government decree or fascistic collusion, but by the will of the working class.[12]

After the Russian Revolution interference by Bolsheviks among workers, encouraged by the apparatus of the recently founded Communist Party, tended to divide the workers' movement and decreased the strength of FORU. But FORU remained the dominant organization among the Uruguayan proletariat well into the 1920s and early 1930s. According to Carlos Rama's *Historia ilustrada de la civilización uruguaya*, as cited by Riera Díaz, in 1919 there were thirty-eight unions and federations in Montevideo and eleven in the interior of the country. Ten years later, however, there was only one truly active and well-organized union, the Sindicato Unico del Automóvil. The old militants had gone over to the Unión Sindical Uruguaya (USU); the equivalent to the Unión Sindical de Argentina (USA) or the Bloque de Unidad Obrera, which was used by the Bolsheviks to cripple workers' unity in Uruguay. In spite of this, libertarian groups and newspapers were still numerous and active into the 1930s.

The number of newspapers in this period kept increasing and subscriptions were renewed year after year, giving rise to new titles and frequently to new themes and tendencies. Between 1916 and 1926 *El Hombre*, a newspaper with strong individualistic tendencies, was published in Montevideo; between 1921 and 1925, *La Tierra*, directed specifically at workers in the interior, was published in El Salto; from 1915 to 1927, *La Batalla*, for a while a proponent of anarcho-Bolshevism, was available in Montevideo. That city was

---

12   Laureano Riera Díaz, *Memorias de un luchador social* (n.p., 1982), 2, 50–51.

home to several papers: *Trabajo* was first published from August 1921 to July 1922 and later from November 1922 to the end of 1923. *El Hacha* appeared between December 1923 and early 1924. *Ideas y Estudios* published eight issues in 1921; *La Ruta* and *Tribuna Libertaria* were also published the same year; *El Sembrador* in 1924; *El Esfuerzo* in 1926; and the journal *Ahora* premiered in Montevideo in 1924. In Cerro, *Luz y Vida* appeared in 1927. A number of unions oriented towards anarcho-syndicalism published their own newspapers. For example, blacksmiths published *La Fragua* beginning in 1927, and three years earlier drivers had begun publication of *Hacia la libertad*. Five issues of the bilingual *Voluntad-Volontá* appeared in 1927. But the anarchist press in Uruguay lacked a daily publication like Argentina's *La Protesta*, and the movement was not able to "crystallize propaganda in regular publications of long duration."[13]

During the 1930s and 1940s the activities of anarchist groups in Uruguay did not significantly diminish, even though they had to compete among workers and students with a small but highly disciplined communist party that had appeared in the 1920s with the ambiguous slogan, "all power to the Soviets."

An important achievement in the history of the movement in the Oriental Republic was the founding of the Federación Anarquista Uruguaya (FAU) in 1956. Its journal *Lucha libertaria* took the place of *Voluntad*.[14] FAU had a relatively important influence in a number of workers' unions that were at the margins of FORU, and came to dominate ideologically various university student groups. In the 1960s uncritical support of the Cuban revolution by the majority of FAU's members led to a split, from which the Acción Libertaria Uruguaya (ALU) emerged with the participation of several of the most prestigious local anarchists. FAU was declared an illegal organization in 1968 and later, after 1972, was fiercely persecuted by a military dictatorship that imprisoned, tortured, and murdered

---

13   Santillán, *Certamen internacional de "La Protesta,"* 1927.
14   Rama, *Historia del movimiento obrero y social latinoamericano*, 82.

many of its militants. Rebuilt in 1986, it put forth a Declaration of Principles and a program of action for the period of transition to representative democracy. At the same time, FORU ceased to exist as a workers' federation. The syndicalist struggle, picked up by two unions acting in concert, Plenario Intersindical de Trabajadores and Convención Nacional Trabajadores (PIT-CNT) is not, however, alien to today's Uruguayan anarchists, many of which promote their ideas in various unions and sometimes achieve prominent roles in them.

B. Writers, Journalists, Activists

The most important literary figure in Uruguayan anarchism is Florencio Sánchez, whose *oeuvre* is also the best example of the dramaturgical work from the Río de la Plata region in the late nineteenth and early twentieth centuries. He was born in Montevideo in 1875, the same year that *El Internacional*, the first anarchist newspaper in Uruguay, appeared. Sánchez began to write in 1890 for the "white" newspaper *La Voz del Pueblo* in Minas, and the following year published his first play, *Los soplados*. On the suggestion of Juan Vucetich, inventor of the system of dactyloscopy that takes his name, Sánchez migrated to Argentina and worked in the newly established city of La Plata in 1892. After his return to Montevideo in 1893 he collaborated in *El Siglo* and *La Razón*, and published several stories under the pseudonym of Ovidio Paredes. The year 1897 proved decisive for Florencio Sánchez's ideological evolution. The legendary nationalist *caudillo* Aparicio Saravia once again took arms against the government, and Florencio, "white" by pedigree more than by political conviction, joined the militia. The direct contact with rebel leaders came to disillusion him in the cause. He fled to Brazil where he had occasion to meet Francisco Pereyra, the bloodthirsty *caudillo* from the Rio Grande do Sul region. Once back in Montevideo he wished to forget all traditional political parties and drew close to the anarchists of the recently founded Centro Internaciónal de

Estudios Sociales. There he premiered *Puertas adentro*, a dramatic skit in one act.[15] Although to earn a livelihood he edited the "white" newspaper *El Teléfono* in Mercedes, Uruguay and later worked for *La República* in Rosario, Argentina as assistant editor, it is fair to say that in the last years of the nineteenth century he was already firmly convinced of the libertarian cause. According to Anderson Imbert, by then Sánchez was organizing unions in Rosario, frequenting the Casa del Pueblo, and assisting in meetings of anarchist resistance societies.[16] He began to collaborate with Alberto Ghiraldo's *El Sol*, gave lectures at the Centro Internacional de Montevideo, and in a contest organized by that Centro presented a dramatic skit titled *¡Ladrones!* which served as the basis for his famous piece, *Canillita*.

In addition to his dramatic works, in 1899 he was a drama critic for *El País* of Buenos Aires and the following year published in *El Sol* his *Cartas de un flojo*, later collected in a single volume. For a brief period of time he collaborated in the recently founded anarchist daily *El Trabajo* in Montevideo. Later, in Rosario, while again editing *La República* to make ends meet, he actively participated in workers' gatherings and meetings, particularly those at the Casa del Pueblo in Santa Fe.[17] In Rosario he founded the newspaper *La Epoca*, in which he published *La gente honesta*, under the pseudonym Luciano Stein, a farce of local customs censored by the regional authorities. Sánchez's play in three acts, *M' hijo el doctor*, was premiered in the Teatro de la Comedia de Buenos Aires on August 13, 1903. It was one of the greatest triumphs of his career, and a few months later it was performed in Italian, translated by V. Di Napoli-Vita. The following year was one of the most productive periods of his dramatic work. Four of his most famous pieces were staged in Buenos Aires: *Canillita*, *Las cédulas de San Juan*, *La*

---

15   Muñoz, "Una cronología de Florencio Sánchez," in *Reconstruir*, 65, 59–61. His experience in the militia would later be the basis for a social psychological work, *El caudillaje criminal en Sud América* (1903).

16   E. Anderson Imbert, *Florencio Sánchez, vida y creación* (Buenos Aires: n.p., 1967).

17   R. González Pacheco, *Un proletario: Florencio Sánchez, periodista, dramaturgo y trabajador manual* (Buenos Aires: n.p., 1935).

gente pobre, and *La gringa*. In 1905 the plays *Barranca abajo* and *Los muertos*, the farce *Mano Santa*, and the dramatic comedy *En familia* premiered in Buenos Aires. Other works premiered in that city were: in 1906, his zarzuela (light opera) *El conventillo*, the farce *El desalojo*, and the comedy *El pasado*; in 1907 the farce *Los curdas*, and then an arrangement of three skits, *Gente honesta*, *La tigra*, and *Moneda falsa*, as well as the zarzuela, *El cacique Pichuleo*; finally the dramatic comedy *Nuestros hijos*. In that same year he premiered *Los derechos de la salud* in Montevideo, then in 1908, *Marta Gruni*, and in 1909 *Un buen negocio*.[18] While he developed this impressive dramaturgical work, Sánchez became a tireless collaborator in, and at times the only editor, of the great anarchist newspaper from Buenos Aires, *La Protesta*.[19] Ill with tuberculosis, he sailed for Italy in 1909 and died in Milan on November 7 of the following year.[20]

No critic or scholar who has taken a close look at Florencio Sánchez's work has failed to remark on the deep sympathy he shows for the people, and especially for the dispossessed. But as Muñoz rightly observes, most of them "treat Sánchez's libertarian ideas at best only marginally and hardly seriously; they are determined to turn him into an authoritarian."[21] W. Regla, an Uruguayan critic, writes: "his activity and behavior with the so-called active militancy was always vague and we dare to say that it was of a sentimental rather than doctrinaire nature."[22] Claims like that ignore his committed, rigorous participation in anarchist and workers' meetings, his energetic labor as editor of *La Protesta* in some of its most difficult moments, and the many articles he wrote for other anarchist publications, like Ghiraldo's *El Sol* and *El Trabajo*. That Sánchez also collaborated in the bourgeois press means only that he had to earn a living, just as Marx had done in writing for the North

---

18   Muñoz, "Una cronología," 61–64.

19   Quesada, *La Protesta*, 1, 82.

20   Muñoz, "Una cronología," 64.

21   Ibid., 65.

22   W. Regla, *Historia del teatro uruguayo, 1808–1968* (Montevideo: Ediciones de la Banda Oriental, 1969), 78.

American press. Admittedly, he was less than steadfast. However, his decision to let the Uruguayan government pay his fare to Italy when tuberculosis had almost totally consumed him is comparable to Roberto de las Carreras completing his career as consul in Curibita. It is a real misunderstanding to say that Sánchez is a "noble soul that becomes an honest bourgeois." "Anarchism and liberalism [were] the ideological pillars of his work," Lafforgue correctly declares, but to further say that "as one or the other of these prevails he compromises reality and invites the refutation of abstraction, the greater or lesser will be the value of his work" misses important aspects of Sánchez's efforts and the historical significance of anarchism.[23] Far from being an "abstract humanism," anarchism is the concrete synthesis of the two great political movements of the twentieth century: liberalism and socialism. When either one is taken to its logical conclusion, they coincide and become one under the name of libertarian socialism. The claim that anarchism has nothing to offer is incomprehensible, as what it does offer is precisely a social revolution. At the opening of the twentieth century this was such a concrete reality for anarchists that many of them gave away all that was not of basic necessity, confident in the imminent rebirth that would bring a society without classes or the State. Nonetheless, the synthesis could not be perfect in all anarchist writers. And just as the Marxism of this period in the region of Río de la Plata showed numerous remnants of both positivism and liberalism, the same may be said of anarchism. This is arguably the case with Florencio Sánchez in several of his writings, and particularly in the frequently mentioned letters to his fiancée.

Uruguay produced a phenomenon almost unique in the worldwide anarchist movement, the approach called "anarcho-Batllism," which brought a number of anarchist militants to follow, in principle, the radical liberalism of José Batlle y Ordóñez. For some moderate elements, like Orsini Bertani, A. Zamboni, E. Clérici, F.

---

23   J. Lafforgue, *Florencio Sánchez* (Buenos Aires: Centro Editor de América Latina, 1967), 48–49.

Berri, Virginia Bolten, and others from the newspaper *Idea Libre*, the respect for civil liberties, the secularism, and the politics of solidarity and cooperation of Batllism took the place of anarcho-communism and a classless society. But it would be mistaken to include Sánchez among these moderates. It is understandable that lovers of nationalist populism were pained by the fact that the most important figure of social drama in Latin America was a follower of Bakunin rather than a soldier of Aparicio Saravia. Sánchez's theatrical work is essentially social. It reflects intergenerational tensions, the conflicts between creoles and immigrants, the contradictions between urban and rural culture, and class struggle. It displays the conflicts of the rural peasant, the worker, the marginal suburbanite, and the petit bourgeoisie. The influence on Sánchez by Zola and French naturalistic theater is obvious and has some cathartic qualities, insofar as it seeks to remove the old rhetoric of *gauchesco* romanticism. But as an anarchist, Florencio Sánchez could not be content with Zola, just as he could not be content with Kropotkin. His work was a matter not only of revealing social reality with photographic harshness, but also of interpreting it in light of revolutionary ideals and of radically changing it. Even when his plays were not meant as propaganda or did not directly appeal to social revolution, there was in each and every one of them a way of presenting situations, characters, and trauma that has no resolution other than a revolutionary change. In no case was there taking pleasure in others' misery, or an eagerness for a picturesque style, or psychological analysis of selfish motives.

For Florencio Sánchez journalism and drama were indistinguishable. The kind of journalism he loved and practiced as often as he could was not merely informative, was not satisfied with detailed narration of facts or reporting on popular sentiments; it was a journalism that aspired to interpret social reality—even if sometimes only implicitly and impartially—and particularly the situation of peasants, workers, and others at the margins in a way that provided them with a radical solution, that is, a revolutionary solution. His dramatic work was never an improvisation; it was a sustained meditation, and even if not a synthesis of anarchist ideology it was certainly a concrete and dramatic prolegomenon to it.[24]

Canillita is not just the story of a popular character of urban Argentina, but an angry protest against child labor. In *M' hijo el doctor*, alongside an intergenerational conflict and a confrontation between the rigid norms of peasant and traditional morality and the new ideas of the modern city, we have the character of a rich young man subjected to public scorn for deceiving a young woman from the country. In *La gringa* the chauvinism of creoles and colonial pride are elevated to their only possible synthesis: the union of races in love, and shared work. *Moneda falsa* is a tragic portrait of the dispossessed that does not need any thesis or moral to issue an indictment against Argentinean society. The same could be said of *El desalojo* and of the zarzuela *El Conventillo*. In *Nuestros hijos*, an Ibsenian drama placed in a middle-class context, Sánchez presents a struggle against the hypocrisy and social taboos that control the sexual and family life of bourgeois society. It is no surprise that bourgeois and do-gooders looked on him as a dangerous subversive and attended his performances with a ghoulish curiosity, the way one might go to a pornographic spectacle or visit a prohibited place. Agustín del Saz writes:

> Sánchez was an anarchist who sought to destroy law and social order in his theatrical work. One approached it with morbid curiosity, as if one went to see the social bowels of the world. All would censor him, giving proof of their good

---

24   In addition to works on Florencio Sánchez already cited, there are the following: Ricard Rojas, "El teatro de Florencio Sánchez," in *Nosotros*, Año V, No. 27, Buenos Aires, April 1911; Roberto F. Guisti, *Florencio Sánchez, su vida y su obra* (Buenos Aires: n.p., 1920); Arturo Vázquez Cey, *Florencio Sánchez y el teatro argentino* (Buenos Aires: n.p., 1929); R. Richardson, *Florencio Sánchez and the Argentine Theater* (New York: n.p., 1933); Dora Corti, *Florencio Sánchez* (Buenos Aires: Instituto de Literatura Argentina, 1957); Tabaré J. Freire, *Ubicación de Florencio Sánchez en la literature teatral* (Montevideo: n.p., 1961); Jorge Cruz, *Genio y figura de Florencio Sánchez* (Buenos Aires: n.p., 1966).

judgment before others, but they would also desire to hear the madness produced by the talented theatrical hand of Florencio Sánchez. And to that unhealthy curiosity we must add the attitude of snobs, who are always wishing to be included in whatever is considered most sophisticated.

It is evident that the theatrical work of Florencio Sánchez articulated a relentless critique of society in the Río de la Plata region. And it is equally evident that he assaulted the bourgeois State and enabled the class struggle. But is it false to say that his obstinate bitterness leads to pessimism "without possible solutions."[25] That judgment can only come from someone ignorant of the opinions Sánchez expressed in his journalistic work, or oblivious to the fact that anarchism is, like Marxism, a fundamentally optimistic ideology.

There were on this side of the Río de la Plata as many poets and dramatists who at one time or another declared themselves anarchists, or were sympathetic to libertarian ideas, as on the other side. A number of them were major figures in their respective genres. In addition to Florencio Sánchez, the leading dramatist, we must include Julio Herrera y Reissig, the leading poet, and Horacio Quiroga, a prominent novelist.

Julio Herrera y Reissig (1875–1910), whose brief life was a constant search for poetic beauty through the roads of romanticism, modernism, and decadentism, was the author of three collections of sonnets, *Los Extasis de la Montaña*, *Los Parques Abandonados*, and *Sonetos Vascos*. He also published three collections of poems, *Las Pascuas del Tiempo* (1900), *Tertulia Lunática* (1903), and *Las Clepsidras* (1909), that established him as a brilliant and original author, but despite his vast merit he did not gain the same level of recognition on the continent as Leopoldo Lugones. He also left us three novels, *Aguas del Aqueronte*, *El Traje Lila*, and *Mademoiselle Jacqueline*, and three travel narratives, *Viaje a Buenos Aires*, *Viaje a*

---

25   Agustín del Saz, *Teatro social hispanoamericano* (Barcelona: n.p., 1967), 44–47.

Salto, and *Viaje a Minas*, in lieu of the European travel narrative he never wrote, unable to cross the Atlantic.

In 1899 he published a book of literary criticism, *Conceptos de Crítica*, and in 1902 a political critique, *Epílogo Wagneriano a la Política de Fusión*. Arturo Zum Felde writes:

> In Julio Herrerra y Reissig Uruguay has given us one of the greatest lyrical poets of the Spanish language. He is to be considered such for the intrinsic value of the work, apart from all limitations of nation or school. The quality of his work is one of the greatest representations of modernism in Latin American poetry. In this respect, only Rubén Darío and Leopoldo Lugones, among the prominent lyricists of the first quarter of the twentieth century, compete with him in the judgment of posterity.[26]

But unlike Rubén Darío, friend to many anarchists yet constant in his aesthetic apoliticalism, and Leopoldo Lugones, anarchist in his youth but later a socialist and finally a fascist, Herrera y Reissig, though never a militant did take great interest in the social problems of his time, read the anarchist classics, and always declared his agreement with them, overcoming his Jesuit education and aristocratic lineage. According to Zum Felde:

> He read avidly philosophers of individualism and theorists of scientific materialism. The seraphic student of the Catholic school, a congregant of Saint Louis, converted to the most nefarious materialistic heresies: the young man of patrician roots—renegade from sacred patriotic and dogmatic traditions—became an anarchist.[27]

Horacio Quiroga (1879–1937) was born in Salto, Uruguay, studied in Montevideo and spent many years in Buenos Aires. But

---

26 Alberto Zum Felde, *Proceso intellectual del Uruguay* (Montevideo: Editorial Claridad, 1941), 251.
27 Ibid., 267–68.

his true literary home was San Ignacio, Misiones, "which gave him the material for his best narrations and gave his personality as a writer a sylvatic character."[28] M. Benedetti says that his narrative, possessing "imprints of Poe and Maupassant," can be characterized as a magico-tragic realism that leaves little place for the social.[29] In his *Cuentos de amor, de locura y de muerte* (1917), *Cuentos de la selva* (1918), and *Anaconda* (1921) there is a hint of rebelliousness and nonconformity that sometimes makes us think about the stories of another brilliant sympathizer of anarchism, Joseph Conrad. In his youth, Quiroga was in contact with anarchist groups in Montevideo, and had a fleeting militant period with them. He lost interest in libertarian ideology before reaching adulthood, without ever repudiating it.

A striking figure in literary bohemia, more famous perhaps for the scandalous adventures of his life than for the brilliance of his verses, was Roberto de las Carreras (1873–1964), author of *Sueño de Oriente* (1900), *Oración Pagana* (1904), *Salmo a Venus Cavalieri* (1905), *En Onda Azul* (1905), *Diadema Fúnebre* (1906), *La Visión del Arcángel* (1908), *La Venus Celeste* (1909), and *Suspiro de Palmera* (1914).[30] Zum Felde says about him:

> At once dandy and anarchist, sometimes a ladies' man and aesthete, his life was a constant source of scandal in the Catholic and bourgeois environment of the city. His literature was a reflection of his life, consisting primarily of occasional writings and polemical pamphlets, advocating his revolutionary ideas or defending his sexual ones, and beneath the refined and lavish style they were genuine pleadings. Free love was one of the individualistic principles proclaimed by scientific

---

28 Arturo S. Visca, *Antología del cuento uruguayo, II Los del Novecientos* (Montevideo: Ediciones de la Banda Oriental, 1968), 69.

29 Mario Benedetti, *Literatura uruguaya. Siglo XX* (Montevideo: Editorial Alfa, 1963), 29.

30 Sarah Bollo, *Literatura uruguaya, 1807–1975* (Montevideo: Universidad de la República, 1976), 134–35.

anarchism. Availing himself of anarchist theories and mixing them with his Don Juan dandyism, he declared himself a preacher and champion of free love.[31]

One of his pamphlets, titled *Free Love*, has the suggestive subtitle, *Interviews voluptuosas con Roberto de las Carreras*.

The personality and style of Angel Falco (1885–1971) are quite different from Carrerra's. He is the author of *Ave Francia*, *A Garibaldi*, and *Cantos Rojos* (1906), a powerful articulation of anarchist and revolutionary sentiments. Some years after *Cantos* his writings turned to patriotic themes in *El Alma de la Raza* (1910) and *La Leyenda del Patriarca* (1911), and to aeronautical achievements in *El Hombre de Quimera* (1911) and *La Tragedia de las Alas* (1914).[32] Zum Felde writes:

Angel Falco had been an officer in the Uruguayan army and fought in the 1904 war. Later he was attracted to anarchist ideology. On account of it, he put his sword away and resigned from his military career, in which, because of his intelligence and character, he would doubtless have been promoted to high rank. He was twenty-five years old when he changed from a valiant infantry lieutenant to a leader of the social revolution.[33]

Ernesto Herrera (1887–1917), affectionately known as "Herrerita," was a successful dramatist and active libertarian journalist, much like Florencio Sánchez. His publications before 1911 include several one-act plays, such as *De mala laya*, *El pan nuestro*, and the celebrated farce *El caballero del comisario*. In 1910 he premiered his play *El estanque* in the Teatro Coliseo in Florida Street, and in 1911 *La moral de misia Paca* in Melo. But the work that brought him the greatest fame was *El león ciego*, concerned with the conflict

---

31   Zum Felde, *Proceso intellectual del Uruguay*, 411.
32   Bollo, *Literatura uruguaya*, 142–43.
33   Zum Felde, *Proceso intellectual del Uruguay*, 427.

between rural and urban life, which premiered in 1911 in the Teatro Cibils in Montevideo.[34] "Whoever sees or reads this play will know Uruguay better than from any map," González Pacheco wrote of it.[35] Herrera also collaborated in the anarchist press in Uruguay and Brazil, particularly in *A Lanterna* in São Paulo and *A Folha do Povo* in Santos, and with *Su Majestad el hambre* he helped to develop the social novel.

Edmundo Bianchi (1880–1965) was another dramatist and journalist who in his youth joined the libertarian cause. In 1910 he premiered his work *La quiebra*, dealing with social conflict, at the Teatro Solis in Montevideo. His second work, *Orgullo de pobre*, "is a faithful expression of the revolutionary ideas endorsed by the youth of Montevideo in the 1910s."[36] In 1913 he presented in the Teatro Nuevo of Buenos Aires another work with a social theme, *Perdidos en la luz*. According to Zum Felde:

> Edmundo Bianchi was poet and valiant anarchist in his youth; editor of *Futuro*, a journal of revolutionary ideology; and distinguished speaker from Polo Bamba. Later in life he turned almost exclusively to theater, producing excellent drama ranging from very serious topics to light humanism taken from everyday life.[37]

The following personal memory by Juana Ruoco Buela illustrates the cultural setting of anarchism in Montevideo in the early 1900s:

> After meetings and lectures we would gather in a well-known café at the Plaza Independencia called El Polo Bamba. A great number of comrades would take seats and around the tables were individuals of great intellectual and ideological power,

---

34   Carmelo Bonet, *El teatro de Ernesto Herrera* (Buenos Aires: Instituto de Literatura Argentina, 1925).

35   R. González Pacheco, *Carteles II* (Buenos Aires: n.p., 1956), 220.

36   Rela, *Historia del teatro uruguayo*, 91.

37   Zum Felde, *Proceso intellectual del Uruguay*, 161.

such as Leoncio Lasso de la Vega, Florencio Sánchez, Herrerita, Acha, and many others. There ideas developed that would
find their way into publications and manifestos. As social
problems were discussed our concepts became clearer. And
there were also genuine moments of camaraderie and affection. Almost on a daily basis, new strategies were developed
in the Centro Internacional, which was a very large venue
with more than adequate space and private meeting rooms.
Sometimes called the Casa de los Anarquistas, it was located
at the very heart of the city, at the juncture of Río Negro and
Maldonado streets. Many important figures in the anarchist
movement in Argentina and Uruguay would sooner or later
meet there. The Federación Obrera Regional Uruguaya, by
1909 already well organized, would hold its meetings in the
Centro Internacional, and in that same place we would meet
workers, anarchists, and intellectuals.[38]

We cannot fail to mention several other Uruguayan militants
who gave life and prestige to anarchist ideas: Alberto Marino Gahn,
a sculptor and the recipient of the Gran Premio Salón Nacional in
1952; José B. Gomensoro, neurologist, researcher, and educator, Vice
President of the Confederación Médica Panamericana; Pedro Tufró,
executed by communists during the Spanish Civil War for his membership in the Confederación Nacional del Trabajo; Juan Diego Sanz,
chairman of the Sindicato de Artes Gráficas; Roberto E. Franano,
graphic artist and journalist; Roberto Cotelo (1867–1970), founder of the journal *Esfuerzo*, and in Spain the editor of the publishing house Tierra y Libertad; Salvador Fernández Correa, educator
and poet; Mario Rodríguez, selfless physician in rural areas; Carlos
María Fosalba, physician, university professor, editor of *El estudiante libre* and of *Acción syndical*, journal of the Sindicato Médico,
and active collaborator in the libertarian press; Enrique Viavaca of

---

38   Juana Rouco Buela, *Historia de un ideal vivido por una mujer*, Buenos
      Aires, *Recontruir*, 27–28.

Paysandú; Aquiles Tettamanti of Salto; Elba Leite, translator of English and Italian works; Rubens Barcos, founding member of FAU and secretary general of the *canillitas* union (newspaper vendors); Jorge Errandonea, ceramicist, director of the Escuela de Bellas Artes, and FAU militant; and Alfredo Errandonea, sociologist, university professor in Montevideo, and editor of the journal *Utopía*.

Finally, we must mention Carlos Rama, historian and sociologist, university professor in Montevideo, Santiago de Chile, and Barcelona. Among his publications are the following books: *Historia social del pueblo uruguayo*, *La ideología fascista*, *Las ideas y movimientos socialistas en el siglo XIX*, and *Las relaciones culturales de España y América*. Rama died in 1982 while exiled in Spain.

Although Rama was open to all ideas from the Uruguayan Left and was at one time a candidate for Senator representing a coalition of Leftist parties and groups, he was fundamentally a libertarian socialist and maintained an affiliation with FAU and other anarchist associations. In all of his sociological and historical writings a libertarian conception of Uruguayan and Latin American reality is clearly present. Like many of his generation, Rama was deeply influenced by the Spanish Civil War. His brother, Angel, writes:

> I know that much of the hostility Carlos felt towards a few intellectuals of his generation was due to their siding at that historic moment with the fascists. The Spanish Civil War was *his* war, *his* hope, *his* political and social dream. I do not know whether he discovered anarchism then or at some earlier time. But it was the colors of FAI and the Durruti battalions that came to our home, to the great surprise of our parents, particularly my mother, who was a devout Catholic.[39]

One of the most important communitarian experiments in the history of anarchism in Latin America was founded in the 1950s

---

39 Angel Rama, "Carlos, mi hermano mayor," in *Cuadernos de Marcha*, Sept–Oct 1982, 81.

in Montevideo: the Comunidad del Sur. The community was self-managed and consisted of couples living, working, eating, and educating the children together. After some twenty years in Montevideo the military dictatorship forced its dissolution. In exile its members tried several times to reorganize, first in Peru and later in Spain, finally succeeding in Sweden. There it continues to this day and publishes a highly prestigious journal with an international circulation appropriately titled *Comunidad*.

It was in the 1850s that European anarchist writers first began to arrive in Uruguay. In 1851 the French botanist José Ernesto Gibert, a friend and collaborator of Proudhon, arrived in Montevideo. Exiled due to the failure of the Revolution of 1848, he dedicated his life to scientific investigations of the Uruguayan flora. His pioneering work was published in the volume titled *Ennumeratio plantarum sponte nascentium agro montevidensi* (1873).

The Italian Luigi Fabbri, born in 1877, a friend and biographer of Malatesta, educator and active promoter of anarchist ideas, fleeing fascism relocated to Montevideo on May 18, 1929. The next year he founded the journal *Studi Sociali*, one of the strongest libertarian publications in Uruguay and Latin America. He died on June 25, 1935. His daughter, Luce Fabbri, continued his work and edited the journal until 1946. In 1956, she took part in the founding of FAU; she also taught history and literature in middle schools and in the Universidad de la República, and participated in the local and international anarchist press, including *Voluntad* and *Luche Libre*. In addition to her works on Italian literature, among which we can mention *La poesía de Leopardi*, she published many books: *Los anarquistas y la revolución española, El anticommunismo, el imperialism y la paz, Camisas negras, Bajo la amenaza totalitaria, Problemas de hoy, El totalitarismo entre dos guerras, La libertad entre la historia y la utopía*, and *El anarquismo más allá de la democracia*, and others.

In 1947 the Romanian writer Eugen Relgis (Siegler) arrived in Uruguay, having been persecuted first by the Nazis and then by the Bolsheviks. Relgis was a defender of humanitarianism, an active promoter of pacifism in Europe, a friend of Romain Roland, Albert Einstein, and Georg F. Nicolai, and the author of many essays, novels, biographies, poems, and travel chronicles, among which we list the following: *Corazones y motores*; *Locura y siete antifábulas*; *El triunfo del No Ser*; *Mirón el sordo* (preface by Stefan Zweig); *Doce capitals: Peregrinaciones europeas* (preface by Han Ryner); *Diario de Otoño*; *La columna entre ruinas*; *Stefan Zweig, cazador de almas*; *Perspectivas culturales de América Latina*; *Albores de libertad* (preface by Rudolph Rocker); *El hombre libre frente a la barbarie totalitaria*; *La paz del hombre*; *El humanitarismo* (preface by Georg F. Nicolai); *¿Qué es el humanitarismo?* (prologue by Albert Einstein); *Historia sexual de la humanidad*; and *Profetas y poetas*.[40] Relgis was no militant anarchist, but he was close to libertarian positions on many issues. He died on March 22, 1987.

Other foreign anarchists, among them writers, journalists, and active propagandists less known than those named above, lived and worked in Uruguay. Some of them were: Antonio Marzavillo, an Italian and lifelong enthusiastic militant, born in 1880 and died in 1959 in Montevideo; Cristóbal D. Otero, Galician, born in 1892 and died in the Uruguayan capital in 1966, tireless propagandist and author of an autobiographical novel, *Ciempiés*; María Collaza (1885–1942), Argentinean, orator and indefatigable activist, of whom Arturo Carril in his book *Crónica de una cuidad y su musa* wrote, "when she rises to the platform she does so surrounded by her partner and sons, all of them with mythological names: Aurora, Themis, Venus, Hebe, Spartacus"; Ricardo Carril (1900–1923), Galician, whose brief and passionate life is recounted by Armonía Somers in *Las máscaras de la mandrágora* and J. C. Welker Bugallo in *Máquinas*; Manuél Domínguez Santamaria, also Galician, director of the Teatro del Pueblo in Montevideo; and Laureano Riera Díaz, founding member of FAU, one of the

---

40 Norma Siuffet, *Eugen Relgis, el escritor, el humanista, el maestro* (Montevideo: Communidad del Sur, 1970); Félix Alvarez Ferrera, "El gran humanitarista," *Reconstruir*, 74, 54–59.

promoters of the manufacturing cooperative EFCSA (Empresa Frigorífica de Cerro, Sociedad Anónima), and author of *Memorias de un luchador social.*

3. Paraguay

Anarchist activity first appeared in this most remote and isolated of all Latin American countries in the last decade of the nineteenth century. In 1892 a group called Los hijos del Chaco published a manifesto that quickly attracted the repressive vigilance of the government and, according to Nettlau, "appears to be the first libertarian document in that country."[1] In that same year several unions were organized, among them the carpenters' union, which would become "the backbone of the anarcho-syndicalist movement there."[2]

Pietro Gori drafted the constitution for the masons' union in 1900. And in 1906 in Asúncion, *El Despertar* appeared, the official publication of the Federación Obrera Regional Paraguaya (FORP), an anarcho-syndicalist federation formed with FORA's moral support. In subsequent years several libertarian newspapers appeared, such as *La Rebelión*, *La Tribuna*, and *Hacia el Futuro*. Publication of *Renovación* began in 1920 and ceased in 1926. A number of doctrinal and propaganda pamphlets were published by the group El Combate, and FORP published Rafael Barrett's *La huelga*.

---

1   Nettlau, "Viaje libertario a través de América Latina," *Reconstruir*, 77, 37.
2   Francisco Gaona, *Introdución a la historia social y germinal del Paraguay*, I, 42.

Anarchist activity continued throughout 1930s. An important and little-known event in the history of Paraguay is the proclamation of the commune in Encarnación by an anarchist group in 1931. On February 20 of that year a group of workers and students led by Obdulio Barthe took control of the city of Encarnación with the goal of establishing a libertarian commune, part of a plan to spark a socialist and libertarian revolution in Paraguay.[3] Among the libertarian militants participating in the takeover were Cantalicio Aracuyú, Ramón Durán, Ciriaco Duarte, Juan Verdi, J. P. Cuéllar, L. Naboulet, M. Kaner, and V. Canavesse. Gabriel Casaccia, the Paraguayan writer, alludes to this event in his novel *Los herederos*.

The struggle for the eight-hour day began in the 1890s, with anarchists active in various unions. Salinas writes:

> The first strikes occurred in 1889. On March 1 of that year railroad workers called a strike that foreshadowed important events. Other trade unions followed, like the carpenters', which had already distinguished itself as one of the principal advocates of anarchist ideology and which in September 1901, after a week-long strike, achieved the eight-hour workday. On the basis of these events, the emergence of anarcho-syndicalism shook the entire country.[4]

In the manifesto by Los hijos del Chaco referred to above and published in the May 21, 1892 issue of *La Democracia*, Paraguayan anarchists defined their ideology and goals thus:

> We are communist-anarchists and as such we seek the complete emancipation of the proletariat; as we fight to abolish the unjust exploitation of man by man we dedicate all of our

---

3   Fernando Quesada, *1931: La toma de Encarnación* (Asunción, 1985).
4   Darío Salinas, "Movimiento obrero y procesos politicos en Paraguay," in Pablo González Casanova, *Historia del movimiento obrero en América Latina* (México: F. C. E., 1984), 389.

moral and physical strength to overturn all tyrannies, to establish genuine liberty, equality, and fraternity in the human family. ... [W]e seek to transform private property into a common good. We seek to do so because individual property is the basic cause of all the evils that afflict us. It is on that basis that the dregs of humanity—government, clerics, lawyers, militaries, entrepreneurs—maintain themselves in power, live as parasites, and the continued enjoyment of their plunder finances large armies with the products of our labor.

As is evident from the above, anarchist ideas that were first planted by Spanish and Argentinean immigrants had blossomed by the end of the nineteenth century. Then "a very important step forward was taken when, under the influence of anarcho-syndicalism, the first workers' federation was formed. That took place on April 22, 1906 with the formation of FORP."[5] At first, it was joined by only three unions—illustrators, carpenters, and drivers—but later the numbers increased. Among its founders were M. Amarilla, J. Serrano, J. Cazzulo, G. Recalde, and L. Castellani.[6] Its programmatic ideas were similar to FORA's.

Rafael Barrett's arrival was the major ideological and cultural event for Paraguayan anarchism. His journal *Germinal*, along with *El Despertar*, was the most important expression of the libertarian and workers' movement at the time. For the Paraguayan proletarian and peasant, his work had an unequaled significance. Hence we offer some brief remarks on the work and life of this great Spanish writer, who was bound to this region of Latin America by his generosity of spirit and libertarian passion. As Roa Bastos writes, Barrett was the "discoverer of Paraguayan social reality."[7]

---

5   Ibid., 374. R. P. Ediciones of Asunción, Paraguay recently collected in a single volume all issues from 1906 to 1907 of FORP's journal *El Despertar*.

6   Ciriano Duarte, *El syndicalismo libre en Paraguay* (Asunción, 1978), 89 *et seq.*

7   Augusto Roa Bastos, "Rafael Barrett, descrubridor de la realidad social del Paraguay," Prologue to Rafael Barrett, *El dolor paraguayo* (Caracas: Biblioteca Ayacucho, 1978).

Barrett was born in Torrelavega, Santander on January 7, 1876, as Vladimiro Muñoz has established after careful review of various biographies,[8] including those by Armando Donoso and Norma Suiffet, who mistakenly identified Barrett's birthplace as Algeciras.[9] His father, Jorge Barrett, was Scottish, and his mother, Carmen Alvarez de Toledo, seems to have been related to the Dukes of Alba. We have no details of Rafael's youth other than he studied piano and languages, and took a degree in surveying engineering in Madrid. For a time he lived the life of a young, semi-intellectual gentleman and, as Hierro Gambardella speculated, published his first writings there, although they are unknown to us. At age twenty-six Barrett embarked for America, motivated perhaps by a desire for adventure, or by the wish to break with a frivolous past and "orient his life, already driven by ideals of renewal and justice, towards human solidarity and assistance to those who struggle for the same ideals."[10] He arrived in Buenos Aires in 1903, and not 1907 or 1908, as Jorge A. Warley has inexplicably claimed.[11] There he first earned his livelihood as a journalist for *El Tiempo* and *El Diario Español*. In the latter he published an article titled "Buenos Aires," in which he views with disbelief and anger the disparity between opulence and misery in that city teeming with European immigrants. He wrote:

So, too, in America! I felt the infamy of the species in my guts. I felt an unrelenting wrath rise to my temples and chew my arms. I felt that the only way to be good is to be ferocious, that only fire and killing are true, that we have to change the blood of rotten hatreds. At that moment I understood the

---

8   Muñoz, "Barrett," in *Reconstruir*, 98, 39.
9   A. Donoso, "Un hombre libre," Prologue to Barrett, *Páginas dispersas* (Montevideo: n.p., 1923), 13; N Suiffet, *Rafael Barrett* (Montevideo: n.p., 1958), 15. Rufino Blanco Fombona is not convinced by either position, although he inclines to Suiffet's.
10   J. A. Solari, "Rafael Barrett, misionero de la justicia y de la belleza," *Reconstruir*, 101, 11.
11   Jorge A. Warley, *Rafael Barrett, anarquismo y denuncia* (Buenos Aires: n.p., 1978), 7.

greatness of the anarchist's cause, and came to admire the magnificent joy with which dynamite thunders and cracks the vile human anthill.[12]

Obviously, the article angered the paper's editor, a man intent on pleasing both government and bourgeoisie. He fired the discourteous young author who, after being embraced by this hospitable country, dared to criticize its institutions and curse its social customs.

Surprisingly, this journalist of brilliant libertarian verse also had serious scientific interests. In that same year of 1903, he joined a group of engineers and university professors in forming the Unión Matemática Argentina.[13] On October 6 he wrote to Henri Poincaré, sending him several mathematical formulas that, according to the engineer E. García de Zúñiga, show the "disciplined study and patient tenacity" of their author.[14] Barrett left for Paraguay in 1904, as a correspondent for Dr. Vega Belgrano's daily *El Tiempo*. He had no idea that Paraguay would be his defining land, the setting for his most difficult fights, and the principal theme of his passionate writings. In that same year liberals replaced conservatives in government. Barrett, friend of Benigno Ferreira, who led the liberal revolution of 1904, took part in it and later was appointed director of the Department of Engineers of the Republic and secretary of the national agency for the management of railroads. At the same time, he collaborated with the Asunción newspapers *La Tarde* and *Los Sucesos*.[15] However, his growing awareness of the social reality

---

12   Barrett, "Buenos Aires," in *Obras completas*, I (Buenos Aires: n.p., 1943), 22.

13   V. Muñoz says that among the founders of the Unión Matemática Argentina was the well-known Spanish academic Julio Rey Pastor. But at that time Pastor, born in 1888, was only fifteen years old and not until 1917 did he arrive in Argentina. See José Babini, *La evolución del pensamiento científico en la Argentina* (Buenos Aires: La Fragua, 1954), 196.

14   E. García de Zúñiga, "Rafael Barrett, matemático," *Boletín de la Facultad de Ingeniería*, Montevideo, December 1, 1935, 30. See also Láxaro Flury, "Rafael Barrett, científico intuitivo," *Reconstruir*, 101, 35–36.

15   The liberal revolution of 1904 "confronted ideals of intellectual improvement and represented the frustrated rebellion of urban masses against the

of the country, his direct personal experience of the exploitation of workers and peasants, and his witness of bureaucratic corruption forced him to resign from all government employment and convinced him that removing conservatives and substituting them with liberals was not enough to bring change to Paraguay or the world.

In 1906 Rafael Barrett married Francisca López Maíz, who came from a very traditional Paraguayan family and was a relative of Father Maíz and Marshall Solano López. With an anarchist from Buenos Aires named José Guillermo Bertotto he published the newspaper *Germinal* between August 2 and October 11, 1908, when he was forced to leave the country by order, as Frugoni puts it, "of Jara, the petty brutal tyrant" who had taken control of the government. He arrived in Corumba, Brazil and a few days later, on November 5, headed for Montevideo, where literary friends and libertarian comrades warmly received him. He wrote frequently for Samuel Blixen's *La Razón*. His articles for that paper were later compiled into a volume titled *Moralidades actuales*, the only book he published during his lifetime. He also contributed to *El Siglo* and *El Diario* from Montevideo, and to *Caras y Caretas* from Buenos Aires. He enjoyed the affection and admiration of the most prominent figures of Urguayan intellectual life, such as Vaz Ferreira, Emilio Frugoni, Angel Falco, and José E. Rodó, who devoted an essay to *Las Moralidades de Barrett*, later included in *El mirador de Próspero*. But his health worsened as the tuberculosis advanced in the cold and humid climate of the Uruguayan capital. He left in early 1909 for the subtropical climate of Corrientes, and then again for Paraguay, without improvement, and by September of 1910, at about the same time that Florencio Sánchez departed for Europe, Barrett left for Paris seeking his last hope for a cure in science. On December 17, almost a month after Sánchez's death Barrett passed away, a victim of the same disease, in Arcachon, Gironde.

---

arbitrary and wicked decree of the sword," writes Carlos R. Centurión, *Historia de la cultura paraguaya I* (Asunción: Biblioteca Ortiz Guerrero, 1961), 567.

Barrett's writings, scattered through Argentinean, Paraguayan, and Uruguayan newspapers, were collected in several volumes. Orsini Bertani edited and published *Moralidades actuales* in a small volume titled *Lo que son los yerbales* in 1910, and the next year published *El dolor paraguayo* and *Cuentos breve*.[16] In 1912 four additional volumes of articles, notes, and essays by Barrett were published under the titles *Mirando vivir, Al margen, Ideas y crítica*, and *Diálogos, conversaciones y otros escritos*. In 1923 the Montevidean editor Claudio García published a volume titled *Páginas dispersas* by Barrett. The publisher Proyección of Buenos Aires released *El terror argentino* and the essay "Lo que son los yerbales." Juan Guijarro (Gandolfi Herrero's pseudonym) published an anthology titled *Barrett sintético* through Editorial Claridad of Buenos Aires.

The publisher La Protesta proposed to publish Barrett's *Obras completas* between 1931 and 1933, but the project only finally realized in 1943 with the assistance of Editorial Americalee of Buenos Aires. In 1959, the latter published another edition in three volumes, along with several additions.[17] A planned collection of a number of Barrett's unpublished writings by the Comisión de Homenaje a Rafael Barrett never went to press.[18]

---

16   *El dolor paraguayo*, though it contains a few brief pieces, is not a "series of short stories in the style of realism," as Rafael E. Velásquez asserts in his *Breve historia de la cultura en Paraguay* (1978), 240. It was reissued in Montevideo in 1926, with commentaries by Emilio Frugoni, José E. Rodó, Ramiro de Maeztu, longtime friend of Barrett's, and José G. Bertotto, who, according to V. Muñoz, is the author of a biographical and autobiographical work titled *Mi amigo Rafael Barrett*, to date unpublished. Bautista Fueyo later reissued in Buenos Aires *El dolor paraguayo* with the important essay "Lo que son los yerbales."

17   Also in 1943, the association Amigos de Rafael Barrett of Montevideo published *Obras completas*, although in the opinion of specialists like Miguel A. Fernández neither publication was really complete. In 1967 Barrett's *Cartas íntimas* was published in Montevideo with introduction and notes by Barrett's wife, and a preface by L. Hierro Gambardella. It is volume 119 of the series *Colección de Clásicos Uruguayos*.

18   Biblioteca Ayacucho of Caracas published in 1978 *El dolor paraguayo*, along with "Lo que son los yerbales," *El terror argentino, La cuestión social*, and other titles not contained in other publications of Barrett's work. It contains a preface by Augusto Roa Bastos and notes by Miguel A. Fernández.

Barrett was a man of fine aesthetic sensibilities and broad culture, equally versed in the physical and mathematical sciences as
well as in economics and politics. He was a close friend of Valle
Inclán, Ramiro de Maeztu, and García Lorca, and he seemed destined to achieve a prominent place in Spanish letters. Historical
and biographical fate prevented him from fully developing his tal-
ent and denied him the illustriousness in life that was achieved by
his comrades and friends. But what he did leave us is sufficient to
secure him a prominent place among the great prose writers of
Latin American during this period, alongside Rodó, who admired
him, and González Prada, his colleague. In a letter to Barrett,
Rodó wrote:

> You have exalted the chronicle without excising its inherent
> interest and simplicity. You have dignified it with thought,
> sensibility, and style.... Your critical work is accurate and
> forceful; your skepticism is effective, getting at the foundation
> of things; and nonetheless, the reading of those pages comforts
> and ennobles, and in their irony there is a deep affirmation, a
> nostalgic idealism, a yearning dream of love, justice, and piety
> that is more effective in its simple and ironic melancholy than
> are emphases of enthusiasm or tragic protest. Your stance as
> detached observer in the theater of life has all the nobility of
> stoicism, but it also carries with it a profound sense of charity.

On Barrett's life, thought, and work see, in addition to those works already
mentioned, the following: Manuel Domínguez, *Rafael Barrett* (Asunción:
n.p., 1910); J. R. Forteza, *Rafael Barrett. Su obra, su prédica, su moral* (Buenos Aires: Ediciones Atlas, 1927); Victor Massuh, *En torno a Rafael Barrett,
una conciencia libre* (Tucuman: Editorial La Raza, 1943); Noel de Lara, *La
obra de Rafael Barrett* (Buenos Aires: Ediciones Sol, 1921); Alvaro Yunque,
Rafael Barrett, su vida y su obra (Buenos Aires: Claridad, 1929). On the occasion of Barrett's centenary, *Reconstuir* published several articles about him
(No. 101, 1976). A new and more comprehensive edition of Barrett's *Obras
completas* was published in 1990 by R. P. Ediciones of Asunción, Paraguay,
under the editorship of Miguel Angel Fernández and Francisco Corral. Volume V contains previously unpublished material.

3. Paraguay

In his *Lecciones de pedagogía y cuestiones de enseñaza*, the Uruguayan philosopher Vaz Ferreira wrote:

> Rafael Barrett has been one of our most sympathetic and noble literary figures. A good, honorable, and heroic man; as a guest in a foreign country, he adopted its suffering and protest; and he recognized that at the time he could not offer hopes or expectations of glory. He was a man of reflection, of feeling, and of action. He is proof that it is possible to avoid dogmatism, to entertain doubt, to be skeptical and, at the same time, to be a man of action—noble and valuable action—quite likely more effective than those who are dogmatic. And as a writer, working in the saddest and most implausible conditions, in the whirlwind of journalism, without sufficient time or adequate health, he was able to produce work of great intellectual rigor and humanity, bringing together intelligence and sentiment.

In his book *La literatura en la Argentina*, Alvaro Yunque considered Barrett the most illustrious representative of anarchist literature in this region of South America.

Barrett was not a militant anarchist during his youth, although he did sympathize with libertarian ideas that were widespread at the time in the Iberian peninsula. When he arrived in Buenos Aires he expressed his admiration for direct action against intolerable injustice. But it was in Paraguay that he truly became a militant. There he not only published *Germinal*, but also participated in the First Conference of Paraguayan Workers, organized by FORP. At that conference he "developed the initial guidelines for the problem of land and addressed one of the central points of the national economic process: the agrarian question."[19] His anarchism was never dogmatic. Extremely acute and incisive in his critique of capitalist and bourgeois society, Barrett was always flexible in those socialist

---

19   Salinas, "Movimiento obrero y procesos politicos en Paraguay," 375.

formulas and programs he thought should be adopted. He was not concerned with the disputes internal to the anarchism of the time. And unlike other libertarian writers, he did not show an excessive aggression against Marxists. Instead, he thought that an agreement between the two great schools of international socialism could assist the overthrow of the capitalist system. At the same time, he was not an unqualified believer in science, as were many of his libertarian comrades, nor did he seek the philosophical foundation of anarchism in a mechanistic and deterministic materialism in the manner of Kropotkin. Like Malatesta, he admitted a degree of freedom of will. And on more than one occasion he appeared to express an acceptance of a vitalist conception of the world, perhaps analogous to Bergsonian philosophy, then influential in European thought. There is in Barrett a high doctrine of free will that is close to the idealism of Baroja, one of his contemporaries. He shares with Baroja a critical approach, a bitter irony, and a vision of reality as opaque. Unlike Baroja, however, that opacity does not lead to hopeless resignation but to an act of faith in an imminent revolution. In matters of style, on the other hand, he is much closer to Valle Inclán than to Baroja.

The Paraguayan Leopoldo Ramos Giménez also deserves mention. A libertarian poet with a "violent social tone," he was born in 1896 and authored a collection of poems titled *Piras sagradas*. As happened with a number of Argentinean poets, his muse later took a less combative and more aesthetic tone in *Eros* and in *Alas y Sombras*.[20]

---

20   E. Anderson Imbert, *Historial de la literatura hispano-americana* II (México: F. E. C., 1966), 66.

4. Chile

Anarchism played a less important role in Chile than in Argentina, Uruguay, or Mexico. But the role it did play has been minimized or simply neglected by academic and Marxist historiography, when not misinterpreted and distorted. Anarchist propaganda began in this Andean country in the 1880s, thanks to literature that arrived from Spain and, very likely, Argentina as well.

With good reason, then, Nettlau supposes that prior to the 1880s propaganda activities were weak and sporadic. He mentions *El Oprimido*, published in Santiago in 1893, as the first anarchist newspaper in Chile known to him. We also know from several sources that at the heart of the Partido Democrático, founded in 1887, there was a group of militants who ideologically identified themselves as anarchist.[1] A number of small and sometimes short-lived newspapers were published between 1890 and the start of the First World War: *El Acrata*, *La Rebelión*, *La Luz*, *La Revuelta*, and *La Protesta*, among others. Nettlau names *El Siglo XX* as a publication of Chilean resistance societies, and *La Imprenta* and *El Marítimo* by typographers and sailors in Antofagasta, respectively.[2]

---

1   Victor Alba, *Historia del movimiento obrero en América Latina* (México: Libreros Mexicanos, 1964), 99.

2   Nettlau, "Contribución a la bibliografía anarquista," 15.

La Batalla was published between 1912 and 1926.[3] We should also add the activity of the publisher Editorial Lux, "led by the libertarian Luisa Soto," which published the works of European and Chilean anarchists, like Ricardo Mella's *Organización, agitación y revolución*, Manuel Márquez's *Mi palabra anarquista*, and José Domingo Gómez Rojas' *Rebeldías líricas*. Muñoz notes that beginning on April 6, 1918 the newspaper *El Hombre*, published in Montevideo, included a work by Juan F. Barrera, from San Felipe, Aconcagua, titled *Desde Chile: La propaganda anarquista y el movimiento obrero*, outlining the history of Chilean anarchism in the first decades of the twentieth century. The group Libertad from La Calera published a pamphlet titled *Presencia anarquista*, containing biographies of two active Chilean militants, José Domingo Gómez Rojas and Celedonio Arenas Robles.[4] Also active during this early period were Magno Espinoza, Luis Olea, and Alejandro Escobar y Carvallo, all of them founders of multiple resistance societies. González Pacheco mentioned the typographer Enrique Arenas, from Iquique, dubbing him the proletarian, the plow, and the planter. "He was the anarchist press: They were one and the same."[5]

A group quite discontent with the authoritarianism and centralism of the Partido Socialista split from it and founded the libertarian socialist newspaper *La Campaña*.[6] There were also a number of anarchist communes, some of which were definitely Tolstoyan. One of them consisted of artists, writers (among them editors of *La protesta humana*), French merchants, and even a millionaire.[7] Viñas writes:

> In addition to intense syndicalist work undertaken by anarchists, there were diverse groups of intellectuals who not only

---

3   Nettlau, "Viaje libertario a través de la América Latina," *Reconstruir*, 77, 37.
4   V. Muñoz, Notas a Nettlau, Nettlau, "Viaje libertario a través de la América Latina," 43–44.
5   R. González Pacheco, *Carteles*, II (Buenos Aires: n.p., 1956), 134.
6   Ramírez Necochea, *Historia del movimiento obrero en Chile* (Santiago: n.p., n.d.), 239–41.
7   Alba, *Historia del movimiento obrero*, 99.

expressed libertarian sympathies in their work, but also sought to organize groups and communes modeled on Tolstoy's communitarian experiments. Fernando Santiván provides a detail review of this in his *Memorias de un tolstoyano*.[8]

Propaganda activity was not limited to the capital. All regions of the country, from the frozen south to the burning north, sprouted centers for propaganda and debates, and publications for the diffusion of ideas. In 1911 the following libertarian newspapers appeared: in Valparaiso, *Luz al Obrero*; in Punta Arenas, *Adelante*; at the other end of the country, in Antofagasta, *Luz y Vida*; and in Estación Dolores (Tarapacá), *La Agitación*.

Anarchist groups seemed to have played an important role in the great boaters' strike in Iquique, which later spread to Antofagasta, Valparaiso, Concepcion, and other places. The strike concluded in June of 1890 with a mass slaughter at Iquique. In early 1900 in Santiago, a Centro de Estudios Sociales Obrero was formed; university students there founded the group La Revuelta with the aim of promoting anarchist ideals; and in Valparaiso the group La Libertad first met.[9] Around the same time, while living in Argentina, the famous Italian libertarian writer Pietro Gori visited Chile with the purpose of spreading propaganda and agitating. According to Heredia, a Casa del Pueblo formed and "became the center of activities of the already militant proletarian and a home for both socialists and anarchists, without hostilities arising between them."[10]

In 1901 and 1902 Chilean and Argentinean militaries, each in control of their respective countries, began to raise questions about shared borders and frontier lands that quickly moved to provoking the stupid patriotism of the masses and to preparing for a fratricidal war. The anarchist's position on this imminent conflict was clearly presented in the January 1, 1902 issue of *La Agitación*:

---

8   David Viñas, *Anarquistas en América Latina* (México: Katan, 1983), 165.
9   Luis Heredia, *El anarquismo en Chile* (México: Ediciones Antorcha, 1981), 13–14.
10   Ibid., 15.

Rulers, those eternal exploiters of misery, are beginning to stir us to the killing of our brothers, the workers of the Republic of Argentina. ... Listen: Beyond the Andes there are workers who suffer the same miseries and tyrannies that we do and who, like ourselves, have nothing to defend. They cannot be our enemies because they are our brothers in slavery. ... Chilean workers: throw down those rifles our rulers wish us to use against our brothers. Let the proprietor defend his property and let the ruler defend his political institutions.[11]

La Protesta issued the same message with almost identical wording to Argentinean workers, who were being called by their government to kill their Chilean brothers. Fifteen years later, Flores Magón would give a similar message to North American workers recruited to fight in Europe against Germany.

In 1903 workers at the steam plant Compañia Sud América struck for better wages. The arrogant attitude of management prolonged the strike and turned it violent. Bloodily repressed, workers set the main offices of the Compañia ablaze and tried to do the same to the newspaper *El Mercurio*, already an ardent champion of employers and enemy of proletarians. The role of anarchists in this strike was decisive.

In 1905 the Semana Roja erupted in Santiago, a spontaneous movement of the masses stimulated by anarchists. A meeting called to address the repeal of a tax on imported meat was violently repressed by police, a confrontation ensued, and some two hundred workers were killed. The indignation of workers was such that railroad and other unions called for a general strike. The government prepared to defend itself, called a state of emergency, and appealed to the armed forces. Led by anarchists, workers nonetheless attempted to occupy the government palace, and the city briefly came under their control. But the State was not slow to respond. Confronted by a proletariat that is enthusiastic and heroic but totally

---

11   Ibid., 16–18.

lacking weapons and tactical skills, the State was soon able to impose bourgeois order. According to Heredia:

> This strike was the general revolutionary strike recommended by anarchists and revolutionary syndicalists; it met all the conditions necessary to overthrow governmental powers, but the lack of experience and knowledge of subversive doctrines helped the government triumph over popular aspirations.[12]

In spite of this bloody repression and subsequent persecutions, the workers' and anarchist movement maintained its combativeness in all regions of the country. In February 1906, in response to a relatively minor demand by railroad workers, a general strike was called in Antofagasta. In December 1907 another strike demanding better wages was called among mine workers in Iquique. Anarchists were at the forefront of these actions. Workers rallying in this port city were brutally murdered in the Plaza de Santa María by troops under the command of General Roberto Silva Renard, a spiritual ancestor of General Pinochet. Heredia describes the scene thus:

> Some two thousand workers were mowed down by machine-gun fire, including women and children. They were murdered without putting up a fight, cowardly and treacherously massacred by an army that was fed and clothed by the exhausting and daily labor of its own victims.[13]

For anarchists in Chile and throughout most of Latin America, the Russian Revolution brought a brilliant ray of hope. In it they saw the start of a new socialist and libertarian society, without classes, private property, or the State. But soon enough they, along with many of their Spanish and Latin American comrades, had to rethink their opinions and abandon their hopes upon evidence

---

12   Ibid., 23.
13   Ibid., 25.

of overwhelming centralism, the end of the soviets (i.e., workers' councils), and the emergence of the bureaucracy as the new dominant class. In spite of this, in Chile more than in any other Latin American country, the resistance societies that had gradually taken the place of mutual aid societies enjoyed a relatively peaceful co-existence between anarchists and Marxists, and this made the coordination of resources possible. Nonetheless, some anarchists, with little reflection, did challenge Luis Emilio Recabarren's ideas and political plans.[14] Wishing to erase his youthful libertarian sympathies, Recabarren did not back away from criticizing the position of anarchists, though his arguments were often weak and full of sophistry. Consider the following attempt to show that anarchists are really conservative and dogmatic because they refuse to alter their declaration of principles:

> Some years ago you developed a declaration of principles to guide the organization of workers. Today you bring it forth as if it were virgin fruit, wishing to retain it as is—intact and whole—and with all your strength keep it from change. That is: you are conservatives who wish to conserve tradition, the hereditary property of that declaration, and thereby you show yourselves as conservative as the dogmatic Catholics, and that you oppose even those natural reforms brought about by the passage of time.[15]

Neither anarchists nor anarcho-syndicalists had anything to do with forming the Federación Obrera Chilena (FOCH). That was the work of reformists and moderates. Anarchists and anarcho-syndicalists were equally opposed to channeling the proletarian struggle into a political party. Like Argentinean anarchists, they too confronted the Partido Socialista, founded in Chile in

---

14   See César Jobet, *Luis Emilio Recabarren: los orígenes del movimiento obrero y del socialismo chileno* (Santiago: Editorial Prensa Latinoamericana, 1955).

15   Viñas, *Anarquistas en América Latina*, 168.

1912, and considered their legislative initiatives not just useless but harmful. In 1919, the same year that FOCH convened its Third Congress, anarcho-syndicalists held the First Congress of the IWW, a workers' federation formed in the likeness of the North American IWW, which held great influence among Chilean proletarians through the efforts of sailors and dockworkers. J. Fanny Simon wrote:

> There is no anarcho-syndicalist workers' central of national reach in Chile until 1919. The IWW is the first and took its form from the prototype in the United States. It adopted the very same tactics as the IWW in the U.S. at its First Congress on December 1919—strikes, propaganda, boycott, and sabotage. It took pride in being a revolutionary organization, whose objectives included the struggle against "capital, government, and Church." The IWW was involved in militant work until 1925 and was particularly active among dock and other maritime workers in Iquique, Valparaiso, and Antofagasta. It organized unions among bakers, bricklayers, shoemakers, and municipal employees.[16]

And Luis Heredia notes:

> The IWW was able to harness dispersed movements and to play at all times a combative role against capitalism and the State. It forged a close alliance with Federación de Estudiantes—the dynamic and fighting Federación de Estudiantes of those times—and together they produced important political upheavals and a revolutionary culture.[17]

A similar worker–student alliance had formed in Argentina as a result of the movement of Reforma Universitaria de Córdoba in

---

16   Viñas, *Anarquistas en América Latina*, 163.
17   Heredia, *El anarquismo en Chile*, 31–32; Godio, *Historia del movimiento obrero latinoamericano*, 1, 254.

1918, but it was not as robust as Chile's and was in great part the result of the militancy of a few anarchist students, including Juan Lazarte. Frightened by the libertarian orientation of this worker–student alliance, the Chilean government initiated a severe repression in 1920 and contrived an invasion of Peruvian troops in the north to justify its plan against workers, a typical ploy to arouse nationalistic and militaristic reactions. At the same time, Colonel Varela and his ilk were accusing striking workers in Patagonia of being secret agents of the Chilean government. Heredia writes:

> In plain daylight at one in the afternoon, bands of hot-headed and elegantly dressed patriots raided the headquarters of the Federación de Estudiantes at the center of Santiago and burned its library. Students who defended against the raid as well as some one hundred workers were subjected to a lengthy trial. The poet Gómez Rojas, imprisoned for his participation and guilty if anything of calling on his poetic lyre, lost all reason and died in the mental asylum at Santiago.[18]

The pre-fascist Liga Patriótica carried out similar exploits in Buenos Aires during the Tragic Week of 1919.[19]

The IWW and the Federación de Estudiantes were able to overcome the severe repression that began during the government of Juan Luis Sanfuentes and continued through the succeeding liberal period. Following an accord between socialists in Rancagua on December 25, 1921, in which FOCH joined the Red International of Labor Unions, the Partido Socialista (which then changed its name to the Partido Comunista), and the Third International, the ideological rivalry between these Marxist organizations and the anarcho-syndicalists of the IWW intensified. However, this accord did not impede the syndicalist struggle in achieving concrete common objectives. Anarchists as well as communists had to resist not

---

18   Heredia, *El anarquismo en Chile*, 33.
19   Babini, "La Semana Trágica – Pesadilla de una fiesta de verano," in *Todo es Historia*, No. 5, 1967; Santillán, *La FORA*, 243 *et seq.*

only the attacks by police and army, but also the aggression of the Asociación del Trabajo, organized by pro-fascist entrepreneurs under orders of a Captain Caballero.[20]

All workers' unions and political parties on the Left opposed the civilian-military government that emerged from the reactionary coup of September 5, 1924. When young military officers initiated a conservative restoration movement on January 25, 1925, FOCH (dominated by communists) and the Communist Party quickly joined in hopes of participating in the new government. But anarchist and anarcho-syndicalist organizations, the IWW, and the Centros de Estudiantes Sociales maintained their position towards the government and declared that even if the young officers aimed to overturn the coup of 1924, they were not to be trusted.[21]

In 1925 a tenants' strike in Santiago de Chile erupted that was largely organized by anarchists, like the tenants' strike in Buenos Aires.[22] In response the Chilean government formed a Tribunales de Vivienda, the purpose of which was to resolve disagreements between landlords and renters. The communists accepted this conciliatory gesture; anarcho-syndicalists opposed it, seeing in it a ploy by the government to end the strike. In January 1927 a general strike broke out in Santiago and the port city of Valparaíso. In February, General Ibáñez overthrew President Alessandri Palma and imposed a dictatorship. The already deteriorating economic situation worsened, especially as the economic crisis of 1929 had profoundly negative effects on government and society. In 1930 there were 2,620 *latifundios* (landed estates) covering 78 percent of the country's arable land. In that first year of the Depression, the exportation of minerals dropped to zero. In 1934 the infant mortality rate reached 262 per thousand, the highest in the world. And the average lifespan was barely twenty-three years. This great misery of frightening dimensions sparked a series of syndicalist and political reactions. In 1931 the Confederación de Trabajadores de Chile (CTCH) formed,

---

20   Heredia, *El anarquismo en Chile*, 34–36.
21   Ibid., 38–43.
22   *La Protesta*, No. 1136.

led by socialists and communists. In 1932 Colonel Marmaduke Grove declared Chile a socialist republic and proclaimed as its first objective the "feeding, clothing, [and] housing [of] the people." But his regime would last twelve days.[23]

Anarchists played no role in the formation of CTCH or in the Frente Popular that, along with the Communist Party, it advocated. In 1925 they had founded a Federación Sindical with its strongholds in the north of the country and which was practically destroyed by the dictatorship of Ibáñez.[24] Its most active militants were deported to Más Afuera Island, now called Alejandro Selkirk Island, and to Aysén in Chile's Patagonia region, just as the Argentinean anarchists of FORA would soon be exiled to Usuhaia in Tierra del Fuego. With the end of the dictatorship in 1931, anarcho-syndicalist groups formed the Confederación General de Trabajadores (CGT), which was much closer to the Argentinean FORA than to the old IWW in that it adopted the regional rather than the industrial model as the basic unit of organization. CGT convened five national congresses, beginning in 1933, but its influence gradually waned as reformist unions increased and the Marxist central steadily advanced, assisted by the resources of the Communist Party. The anarcho-syndicalist organizations that did survive the dictatorships of Ibáñez and Uriburu in Chile and Argentina, respectively, weakened, and once deprived of their best militants gradually ceded ground in the 1930s and 1940s to other kinds of organizations inspired by different ideologies. In Argentina anarcho-syndicalism was superseded by the demagogic fascism of Peronism and its corporativist ideal called "the organized community," substituting FORA with the new CGT. In Chile the change was a bit more complex. Suffice it to say that Marxist and democratic Christian organizations replaced the anarcho-syndicalist CGT.[25]

---

23   Carlos Rama, *Historia del movimiento obrero y social latinoamericano* (Barcelona: Laia, 1976), 104.

24   Lagos Valenzuela, *Bosquejo histórico del movimiento obrero en Chile,* cited in Alba, *Historia del movimiento obrero en América Latina,* 60–61.

25   See Jorge Barría Cerón, *Breve historia del sindicalismo chileno* (Santiago:

4. Chile

If anarchism did not thrive in Chile as it did in other Latin American countries at this time, the cause may be attributed to three factors. First is its geographic isolation: it is flanked by sea and mountains, and remote from the great European centers of anarchism, which were able to link, for example, with Mexico, Brazil, Uruguay, and Argentina through the Atlantic. Second is the scale of European immigration, relatively scarce in Chile compared to the major waves experienced in Brazil, Uruguay, and Argentina. And third is Chile's comparatively late industrialization, trailing behind Mexico, Brazil, and Argentina.[26]

In Chile mutual aid societies—already flourishing in the 1870s, as in Uruguay and Mexico—were succeeded in the early twentieth century by a growth of resistance societies founded and directed by anarchists. These societies then encountered serious competition from *mancomunales* or brotherhoods that were organized by territory and trade, and sought better wages and the resolution of other workplace demands. At first they were under the leadership of ideologically moderate individuals, but later they come under control of Marxists. Indeed, under socialist control these brotherhoods joined FOCH, whose Third Congress in 1919 marks the triumph of Marxist ideology in the Chilean workers' movement. One of the secrets of the success of the Socialist Party, founded by Rebacarren in Iquique in 1912, was its ability to capitalize on the nonconformity of many workers and petty bourgeoisie. These moderate democrats were frightened by the revolutionary ideology of the anarcho-syndicalist IWW, which was able to mobilize only ideologists or the most exploited layers of the working class. Nonetheless, anarchist ideology did sufficiently penetrate militant workers. Thanks to anarchists, FOCH's 1919 Congress included in its Declaration of Principles that the "abolition of the capitalist system will be replaced by the Federación Obrera," and not by the workers' State or the dictatorship of the proletariat.

Insora, 1967).

26   See B. Herrick, *Urban Migration and Economic Development in Chile* (Cambridge: MIT Press, 1965).

Anarchist ideology also made inroads among Chilean poets and writers. In his youth, Pablo Neruda was influenced by it, although given his ode to Stalin this might seem implausible. There were also a number of writers who from the 1850s on were influenced by utopian socialism. But unlike what developed in the Río de La Plata region, in Chile utopian socialism attached itself, according to Rama, "to the emerging class struggle and is perhaps the only ideology that recruited from the working classes, especially the artisans and the master workers in Santiago and other cities."[27] At that time, the two main figures of the movement—which made its headquarters in the socialist club Sociedad de la Igualdad, founded in 1850—were Santiago Arcos Arlegui and Francisco Bilbao, translator of Lamennais's *La esclavitud moderna* and author of *Sociabilidad chilena*, which was condemned as immoral and blasphemous, and burned at the hands of the executioner. Arcos Arlegui included radical liberal ideas in his readings of Saint-Simon, Fourier, Considerant, and Enfantin.[28] The most original and brilliant Chilean thinker of the nineteenth century, Bilbao inclined to a kind of Christian socialism that was vehemently anti-ecclesiastic and anti-clerical. He confronted the conservative ideology of the dominant class and its mainstay Catholic dogmatism with a Gospel-based social mysticism.[29]

As in Argentina, so too in Chile some poets of the last decade of the nineteenth century were anarchists at least for a brief period: Víctor Domingo Silva, author of a celebrated battle hymn, "La Nueva Marsellesa," once recited to striking workers in Valparaíso; Antonio Bórquez Solar, author of *Los pobres*, included in the volume *Campo lírico*, and *Los huelguistas* (a eulogy for the Argentinean socialist Miguel Ugarte and published in *Las nuevas tendencias literarias*); Carlos Pezoa Vélis, a kind of trans-Andean Carriego, with

---

27 Rama, *Utopismo socialista*, xxxix.
28 See Jobet, *Santiago Arcos Arlegui y la Sociedad de la Igualdad* (Santiago: Cultura, 1942).
29 See Ricardo Donoso, *Bilbao y su tiempo* (Santiago: n.p., 1923). A recent collection of Bilbao's work may be found in *El Evangelio americano* (Caracas: Biblioteca Ayacucho, 1988).

poems like *El organillo*, *Alma chilena*, and *Pablo y Tomás*; Carlos R. Moncada and Alfredo Guillermo Bravo, both quickly developed a libertarian poetry and just as quickly forgot it; J. Domingo Gómez Rojas, who repudiated his own *Rebeldía líricas* (1913); and Manuel Rojas, born in Buenos Aires of Chilean parents, quickly abandoned the libertarian lyre for a delicate poetry of tasteful forms.[30] At the same time, there were also poets who were natural-born anarchists and never abandoned their ideals. Núñez and Araya, Chilean literary critics, write:

> These men generally wear the proletarian's shirt and work now in the Northern pampas, now in the Southern coal mines, now in the factories, now in the printing presses of the metropolitan dailies or in the offices of some obscure rural newspaper. Some wear disheveled hair and red scarves. They are studious and aware. They stir and draw the popular masses when it concerns the progress of the social-climbing bourgeoisie, the inhuman exploitation of Capital, or the excesses of oligarchic powers. In meetings their aggressive and forceful verses they tend to provoke sordid accusations and stormy eruptions.[31]

Among these, Núñez and Araya include: Magno Esponosa; Luis Olea, one of the promoters of the strike of 1905 and whose *El Cantor del Pueblo* made popular a sonnet "that whips the armed forces"; Alejandro Escobar y Carvallo, who had several poems included in *Poesías Acratas* along with works by Luis Olea, Luis Recabarren, Magno Espinosa and Marcial Cabrera Guerra; Eduardo Gentoso, author of "democratic and combative" prose; and Francisco Penzoa, "the most representative" of his generation of libertarian poets, for many years an active militant in the Chilean social movement,

---

30   Julio Molina Núñez and Juan Agustín Araya, *Selva lírica. Estudios sobre los poetas chilenos* (Santiago: Imprenta y Literatura Universo, 1917), 470–71.
31   Ibid., 471.

a man of broad culture, translator of French, English, and Italian works, an author of more than "three hundred manifestos and proclamations," a tireless lecturer at athenaeums and workers' centers, whose studies addressed topics in anarchism, socialism, and neo-Malthusianism, and from 1895 was a collaborator in *El Rebelde*, *La Protesta*, *El Productor*, *Luz y Vida*, and other Chilean anarchist newspapers.[32]

Again, Núñez and Araya:

> In Iquique someone edited a *Cancionero Revolucionario* with selected verses by Pezoa. In it one can see that red poetry is a feature of popular poetry. Pezoa's verses are adapted and sung to popular music. His best poetic compositions are *El Ladrón*, *Anarkos*, *De vuelta del mítin*, and *Canto de venganza*. The latter has been widely distributed under the title *La Pampa*, and with musical accompaniment as *La Ausencia*. It was popular to the point of being sung by workers not only in Chile but also Argentina and Uruguay. In the Argentinean pampas, in Bolivian mines, and in the building of the Panama Canal the lyrics of *La Ausencia* have been sung by voices that quiver with profound suffering, proving Pezo an ideological poet and songwriter. In the novels and poetry of Pedro Prado—in *La casa abandonada* and *La Reina de Rapa Nui*, among others—one can find a kind of Tosltoyan anarchism.[33]

Acevedo Hernández, libertarian dramatist, is author of agrarian dramas such as *En el rancho*, *La puñalada*, *El inquilino*; ideological plays like *El dueño* and *El salmo de la vida*; suburban theater including *Almas perdidas*, *Carcoma*, *María Luisa*, and others; and the impassioned antiwar work *Por la patria*. We should also mention the refutation of anarchism by positivists, who published a pamphlet by Juan Enrique Lagarrigue titled *Breve observaciónes a*

---

32   Ibid., 471–72.
33   Ibid., 472.

los anarquistas in Santiago on December 15, 1903. Fernando Santiván, whose real surname was Santibañez, is the author of stories like *Palpitaciones de vida* and novels like *La hechizada* and *Confesiones de Enrique Samaniego*. He also wrote *Memorias de un tolstoyano*, relating his personal experiences in an attempt, along with Prado, D'Halmar, and Magallanes Moure, at forming a Tolstoyan community.

5. Bolivia

A number of labor unions and resistance societies assembled in Bolivia in 1908 with the objective of forming the Federación Obrera Local (FOL), and then four years later they formed the Federación Obrera Internacional (FOI). Anarchist ideology was abundant in the latter, as we can infer from the simple fact that it adopted the red-and-black flag as its symbol.

The Federación Obrera Local published the newspaper *Luz y Verdad*, while FOI published *Defensa Obrera*. In the first decades of the twentieth century a number of anarchist or semi-anarchist publications appeared in the interior of the country. By 1906 *La Aurora Social* was available in the streets of Tupiza; *Verbo Rojo* in Potosí; *El Proletario* in Cochabamba; and *La Federación* in Santa Clara de la Sierra.[1]

According to Herbert Klein:

On May 1, 1912 workers' unions and artisans' brotherhoods of La Paz were successful in organizing the first Día del Trabajo parade and a short time later replaced the defunct

---

1   Alberto Pla, *Los orígenes del movimiento obrero en América Latina* (Caracas: 1978, mimeo.), 34. Zulema Lehm and Silvia Rivera, *Los artesanos libertarios y la ética del trabajo* (La Paz: n.p., 1988), 22–23.

Federación Obrera de La Paz with a new kind of modern syndicate that emphasized the perspective of class and avoided party politics. FOI launched the first recognizably workers' newspaper in Bolivia, *Defensa Obrera*, which soon began a campaign for the eight-hour workday and in its editorials challenged the upper-class intellectuals like Franz Tamayo and Tomás Manuel Elío.[2]

Then in 1918 FOI grew into a new organization, the Federación Obrera del Trabajo (FOT). Marxist ideas coming primarily from Chile gradually came to dominate FOT. In 1918 the first of a series of strikes erupted. After sustained struggles against Simón Patiño, called the "Tin Baron," miners from Huanuni achieved the eight-hour workday. They were encouraged in their struggles primarily by anarcho-syndicalists or similar groups. But in 1920 general strikes broke out among railroad workers and telegraphers without anarchist involvement. In 1923, after a demonstration in support of those jailed at a May Day parade, miners from Uncía were massacred by government troops. This massacre was, as Llobet Tavolara put it, the "first link of what would become an impressive chain of sacrifice and death among the mining proletariat."[3] Anarcho-syndicalism proved the weight of its influence on the workers' movement in Bolivia in 1927, when anarchists were able to defeat a proposal by communist members of the Tercer Congreso Nacional de Trabajadoers to join the Third International.

The first specifically anarchist group had formed a few years earlier, in 1923 in La Paz. It took the name La Antorcha and, according to Lehm and Rivera, "was led by Luis Cusicanqui, Jacinto Centellas, and Domingo Pareja. Together with other workers they

---

2   Herbert Klein, *Orígenes de la Revolución nacional Boliviana* (La Paz: n.p., 1968). Quoted in Cayetano Llobet Tavolara, "Apuntes para una historia del movimiento obrero en Bolivia," in Pablo González Casanova, *Historia del movimiento obrero en América Latina* 3, (México: n.p., 1984).

3   Llobet Tavolara, in ibid., 319.

comprised an active nucleus of propagandists that made enormous contributions to the promotion of anarchist thought in the city of La Paz."[4]

In his *Historia del movimiento obrero boliviano*, Guillermo Lora writes:

> After the break-up of the Centro Obrero Libertario in 1923, one faction formed the anarchist group called Despertar, led by Cusicanqui, Desiderio Osuna, the Spaniard Nicolás Mantilla, Carlos Calderón Centellas, Guillermo Palacios, and the always combative Angélica Domitila Pareja, who, according to anarchists, was their equivalent to the Marxist Angélica Ascui. Nicolás Mantilla was doubtless the brain behind La Antorcha. The vast majority of remaining members ended up in opposing trenches. Desiderio Osuna, for example, had no qualms about being chief of the Urban Police during the counter-revolution of July 21, 1946. Others, however, gave their energies to and sacrificed their lives for their ideals. We have known and admired Cusicanqui. He lived in a small apartment and in spite of his advanced age fed his humble family by his work as a mechanic. This honest militant from the high Andean plateau, dark-skinned and short-legged, massive, with a torso like a bull's, kept the faith that had nourished him since his youth. Some Marxists, for example Santiago Osuna, did remain associated with the group Despertar. They were individuals of broad sentiment and tolerance, and sympathetic to anarcho-syndicalism. *La Tea* was being circulated at that time, edited by Desiderio Osuna and printed in Argentina, but did not go beyond a third issue.[5]

And Lehm and Rivera note:

---

4   Lehm and Rivera, *Los artesanos libertarios y la ética del trabajo*, 26.
5   Cited in Viñas, *Anarquistas en América Latina*.

By 1926 the sources for anarchist propaganda had grown in number and geographical reach. Active in La Paz, in addition to Despertar, Redención, and La Antorcha, was the Agrupación Comunista Anárquica, also called Sembrando Ideas, and the group Brazo y Cerebro; in Oruro, the Centro Obrero Internacional; and in Sucre, the Ferrer Guardia school.[6]

Surveying the development of the Federación Obrera Local de La Paz (FOL), Lora observes:

In 1926 anarchists decided to form the Federación Obrera Local de La Paz to oppose FOT, and later rejected the conclusions of the Tercer Congreso de Oruro, which was almost entirely controlled by Marxists. There is no doubt that FOL thought of itself as a national federation. But anarchist ideology was able to control completely only two large organizations, FOL in La Paz and FOT in Oruro. In the rest of the country, anarchism was present only among small circles and its militants were active in different organizations, and in those organizations they represented opposition groups. FOL was structured around thirty-nine groups, including Despertar. La Antorcha never joined. Among the founding groups were: Unión de Trabajadores in Madera, which played an important role in the actions leading to the eight-hour workday; the Sindicato de Albañiles; Sindicato de Sastres; workers at the phosphorous factory; and the group Despertar. Later, unions from the cardboard and textile factories joined. These facts show that FOL was an organization of the highest importance and at one time enjoyed a membership larger than that of the FOL from La Paz. Desiderio Osuna was its first General Secretary, after defeating Fournarakis in the elections held in a small venue on Sajama Street. Fournarakis was an Argentinean anarchist who worked in the phosphorous factory. Later, when membership

---

6   Lehm and Rivera, *Los artesanos libertarios y la ética del trabajo*, 27.

grew, FOL headquarters moved to Pando Avenue. During this period of growth lasting until 1932, FOL attracted the attention of international organizations. In large measure, anarchist organizations were the work of foreigners, and among them the following deserve mention: Fournarakins, FORA militant who arrived as an exile; the Chilean cobbler Armando Treviño, an IWW member; the Peruvians Francisco Gamarra, and Navarro and Paulino Aguilar (the latter was imprisoned and escaped to Brazil); the Spaniard Mantilla, whose *nom de guerre* was Rusiñol; the Mexican Renejel, who was around in 1928; and the Argentinean Huerta.

According to Lora, on July 29, 1929 Cusicanqui was detained, causing an immediate protest that was violently repressed. FOL reported to ACAT, the anarcho-syndicalist Latin American federation to which it was joined, that several comrades who had written the manifesto *La Voz del Campesino* were on the run from authorities, that FOL headquarters was under constant police surveillance, and that the anarchist groups La Antorcha and Luz y Verdad had ceased their activities. Cusicanqui, for a time confined with his partner Ricarda Dalence in Comi, in the province of Murillo, was able to return to La Paz in 1930.

That same year a new Congreso Nacional de Trabajadores formed the Confederación Obrera Regional Boliviana, with the encouragement and support of FORA and the Argentinean anarcho-syndicalist movement. The close relationship is apparent in the choice to name the new organization's official journal after that famous and well-established anarchist newspaper from Buenos Aires, *La Protesta*. But this Bolivian anarcho-syndicalist paper did not last long. It ceased publication in July 1932, perhaps, Nettlau speculates, "due to the war in the Chaco."[7] The year before, Ismael Martí had reported to Nettlau on his project to translate several anarchist works into Quechua and Aymara, the two major indigenous languages of Bolivia, but this too

---

7   Nettlau, "Viaje libertario a través de América Latina," 39.

was frustrated by the outbreak of the war. Other anarchist militants that, like Cusicanqui, were fluent in the various native languages, did write some essays intended for indigenous populations who either were unable or disinclined to read Spanish. In 1940 there was an attempt to reorganize FOL, with Cusicanqui as Secretary General, and in 1946 several peasant organizations and a Núcleo de Capacitación Sindical Libertario were formed.[8]

When the revolution of 1952 led by the Movimiento Nacionalista Revolucionario succeeded, there were still a few anarcho-syndicalist groups left. Two of those groups, La Federación Sindical Local and the Federación Agraria Local de La Paz, resisted forced integration into the Central Obrera Boliviana, as it was very closely allied to the government and the ruling party, but were eventually absorbed.[9] Anarchism since the national revolution has lacked any institutional expression in Bolivia (with the exception of a cultural group in Tupiza); yet it is important to note that among miners, who are the most combative sector of the proletariat, there is a vigorous current, immune to the seduction from any Leftist party, whose strategy and ideology, sometimes referred to as a revolutionary syndicalism, is very close to anarcho-syndicalism (although this term is not used).

Finally, among Bolivian writers who are anarchist or who show some inclination toward libertarian ideas, we include the following: Jorge Moisés, Nicolás Mantilla, Luciano Vértiz Blanco, Rigoberto Rivera, and the collaborators in the weekly *Humanidad*, the official publication of FOL: Salustiano Lafuente, Guillermo Maceda (Rodolfo Mir), Arturo Borda (Calibán), Santiago Osuna (Juan Pueblo), Luis Salvatierra (W. Luiziel), Desiderio Osuna (Rebelde), and Ramón Iturri Jurado (Tomás Katari).[10]

---

8   Lehm and Rivera, *Los artesanos libertarios y la ética del trabajo*, 84.
9   Robert Alexander, *The Bolivian National Revolution* (New Jersey: Rutgers University Press, 1958), 239–41; Lehm and Rivera, *Los artesanos libertarios y la ética del trabajo*, 79–101.
10   Viñas, *Anarquistas en América Latina*, 145. [Names in parentheses are pseudonyms (Trans.).]

6. Peru

In Peru, utopian socialism, Marxism, and anarchism are each associated with one of three major literary figures: Flora Tristán, José Carlos Mariátegui, and Manuel González Prada, respectively. Before addressing the latter, a few general remarks on Tristán and Mariátegui as well as the anarchist movement in Peru are important. Tristan's feminism[1] was greatly influenced by the writings of the proto-anarchist William Godwin and those of his spouse, Mary Wollstonecraft,[2] and her project of forming the Worker's Union

---

1   On Tristán, see J. Bealen, *Flora Tristán: feminismo y socialismo en el siglo XIX* (Madrid: Taurus, 1973); D. Desanti, *Flora Tristán: Vie et oeuvres melées* (Paris: n.p., 1973); J. L. Piech, *La vie et l'oeuvre de Flora Tristán* (Paris: Riviere, 1925); C. Freire de Jaimes, "Flora Tristán," *El Correo de Perú*, July 1875; J. Basadre, "Al margen de un libro olvidado," *Boletín Bibliográfico de la Universidad Mayor de San Marcos*, 2–3, 1932; F. Cossío del Pomar, *El hechizo de Gauguin* (Santiago: n.p., 1939); A. Tamayo Vargas, *Dos rebeldes* (Lima: n.p., 1946). Tristán's most important work, *Peregrinaciones de una patria*, first appeared in French, was translated into Spanish by Emilia Romero, with notes by Jorge Basadre, and published in 1946. The best biography of Tristán is perhaps by Luis Alberto Sánchez, *Una mujer sola contra el mundo*.

2   On William Godwin, the best known work is by H. N. Brailsford, *Shelley, Godwin, y su círculo* (Mexico: F. C. E., 1942). Also see: B. Cano Ruiz, *William Godwin (su vida y su obra)* (Mexico: Editorial Ideas, 1977); J. A. Sabrosky, *From Rationality to Liberation* (Westport: n.p., 1979); and D.

mirrored that of her contemporary, the anarchist Joseph Déjacque.[3]
We should also note the influence of González Prada on Mariátegui.[4] In the latter survives an indigenous agrarianism centered on
the *ayllu*[5] that is quite similar to certain ideas found in González
Prada himself and Flores Magón. Leninist critics did not fail to
point out this similarity and, on that account, classify Mariátegui as
a romantic idealist.[6]

The earliest workers' unions with an anarchist orientation
formed in the last years of the nineteenth century. Several strikes
in 1896 and 1901 led to the organization of the first workers' congresses that "clearly articulated proletarian demands."[7] In 1904
several anarchist militants—Urmachea, Fidel García Gacitúa,
Caracciolo Lévano and his son Delfín—formed the Unión de

A. de Santillán, "William Godwin y su obra acerca de la justicia política," introductory essay to the Spanish translation by Jacobo Prince, *In-
vestigación acerca de la justicia política* (Buenos Aires: Americalee, 1945).
Mary Wollstonecraft wrote *A Vindication of the Rights of Women* (1792),
establishing her as the first modern feminist. This explains the renewed interest today in her life and work. See M. George, *One Woman's Situation*
(1970); E. Flexner, *Mary Wollstonecraft* (1972); and C. Tomalin, *The Life
and Death of Mary Wollstonecraft* (1975).

3   Joseph Déjacque wrote *L'Humanisphere-Utopie Anarchisque*, published
in the New York newspaper *La Libertaire* in 1858 and later, in 1899, in
Bibliotheque de Temps Nouveaux in Brussels, edited by Élisée Reclus. A
Spanish version appeared in the collection *Los Utopistas*, which also published *La Protesta*, with prefaces by Reclus and Nettlau.

4   Mariátegui's basic work, *Siete ensayos de interpretación de la realidad peruana*, was published in 1928 and reissued in 1934 and 1952. On Mariátequi, see G. Rovillón, *Bio-bibliografía de José Carlos Mariátegui* (Lima:
n.p., 1963); M. Wiese, *José Carlos Mariátegui* (Lima: n.p., 1959); G. Car-
nero Checa, *José Carlos Mariátegui, periodista* (Lima: n.p., 1964); M. Pareja Bueno, *José Carlos Mariátegui, símbolo* (Lima: n.p., 1947). A. Tamayo
Vargas, "Actualidad y pasado," *Prometeo*, Lima, June 1930; and A. Bazán,
Mariátegui y su tiempo (Lima: n.p., 1969).

5   See Wilfredo Kapsoli Escudero, *Ayllus del Sol* (Lima: n.p., 1984).

6   See Adam Anderle, "La vanguardia peruana y Amauta," in *Ultimas Noticias*, Caracas, April 5, 1987.

7   Denis Sulmont, "Historia del movimiento obrero peruano, 1890–1980,"
in Pablo González Casanova, *Historia del movimiento obrero en América
Latina*, 3 (Mexico: n.p., 1984), 279.

6. Peru

Trabajadores Panaderos,[8] and that same year the Unión organized the first strike in Lima. On May Day 1905, it held a public tribute to the Chicago martyrs.[9] In 1906 the radical paper *Humanidad* started to publish articles showing anarchist tendencies.[10] The next year anarchists promoted a strike among stevedores in Callao and the "first martyr of the social struggle in Peru fell: the comrade Florencio Aliaga."[11] In 1910 the Centro Racionalista Francisco Ferrer launched the journal *Páginas Libres*, taking its title from a polemical work by González Prada and proclaiming as its mission not only pedagogical analyses but also the organization of workers.[12] Sulmont writes:

> From 1911 to 1926 the newspaper *La Protesta* was published and gathered around it a group of the most active anarchist leaders. That group argued for the necessity of improving methods for organizing workers and promoting the formation of syndicates. Thus was born anarcho-syndicalism, which had its principal nucleus among textile workers.[13]

Anarchist papers also began to show up in the interior of the country: *El Ariete* in Arequipa; and in Trujillo first *La Antorcha* and then *El Rebelde*.[14] In Lima González Prada's *Los Parias* appeared between 1904 and 1906, and in 1905 *El Hambriento* and *Simiente Roja* were published.[15] In 1911 anarcho-syndicalists promoted the first general strike in the textile industry, and in 1912 formed the Federación Obrera Regional Peruana (FORP).[16]

---

8   Federación Anarquista del Perú, *El anarcosyndicalismo en el Perú* (México: Ediciones Tierra y Libertad, 1961), 4; also see Guillermo Sánchez Ortiz, *Delfín Lévano* (Lima: n.p., 1985).
9   Sulmont, "Historia del movimiento obrero peruano," 279.
10   Federación Anarquista del Perú, *El anarcosindicalismo en el Perú*, 4.
11   Alberto Pla, *Los orígenes del movimiento obrero en América Latina* (Caracas: 1978, mimeo.), 32.
12   Federación Anarquista del Perú, *El anarcosindicalismo en el Perú*, 4.
13   Sulmont, "Historia del movimiento obrero peruano, 1890–1980," 279.
14   Alba, *Historia del movimiento obrero en América Latina*, 104.
15   Nettlau, "Viaje libertario," 38.
16   Sulmont, "Historia del movimiento obrero peruano," 279.

The campaign for the eight-hour workday was initiated by the Federación Obrera Regional del Peru (Lima), consisting of the Sociedad de Resistencia of bakery workers and such allied unions as the Federación de Electricistas, Federación de Obreros Panaderos (Estrella del Perú), the Unificación Textil of Vitarte, the Federación Proletaria of Santa Catalina, and other unions in which anarchists played important roles. Anarchist unions also joined the campaign, like Luchadores de la Verdad, publisher of the newspaper *La Protesta*, and Luz y Amor, which published revolutionary propaganda. In late November 1912, meetings were held at the Unión General de Jornaleros local in Callao, and in the Teatro Municipal the first General Assembly was convened to discuss their demands. Among those in attendance were not only members of Federación Obrera Regional del Peru and various libertarian groups, but also representatives of a well-known pro-management entity called the Confederación de Artesanos Unión Universal, which opposed the projected direct action and instead promoted the worn-out path of petitions to those in power. At the second General Assembly on December 15, convened at the Carpa de Moda, anarchists introduced a motion on behalf of the eight-hour workday that was unanimously approved. Then, on the 28th of the same month, during the third Assembly, workers developed a list of specific demands.[17] And with that the campaign for the eight-hour workday was set. The enthusiasm, the solidarity, the awakening of a proletarian consciousness all answered the Chicago martyrs' clarion call to struggle and collective defense. Widespread publication of libertarian and syndicalist propaganda in newspapers and pamphlets completed the work, together with numerous conversations and conferences by the anarchist group of *La Protesta* and the Federación Obrera Regional del Peru.

On January 5, 1913 the Unión de Jornaleros demanded the eight-hour workday, an increase in salaries, and medical benefits for workplace accidents. They gave twenty-four hours for their

---

17   Federación Anarquista del Perú, *El anarcosindicalismo en el Perú*, 5.

demands to be met upon threat of strike. On the next day, the Assembly rejected management's counterproposal, and on January 7 there was a general strike. Typesetters, bakers, steelworkers, millers, and gas fitters from Callao all joined the journeymen in solidarity.[18]

On January 9 the President of the Republic urged striking workers to return to work by appealing to their patriotism, and stressed the damage caused to emerging national industries—whose capital was of course foreign. But the strike committee rejected the President's call and, undeterred by government threats backed by infantry and artillery forces brought in from the capital, stayed its course. This firm attitude brought triumph: all port and dock businesses accepted the reduction of the workday to eight hours, conceded a ten percent wage increase, and organized a medical program for injured workers. The victory encouraged other unions to follow suit and issue their own demands, among them the millers, typesetters, gas fitters, and others. Anarchists, almost the sole promoters of these struggles, used the opportunity to test their method of direct action. On January 12 the Federación Obrera Regional del Peru and the La Protesta group held a meeting to celebrate their triumph and to encourage further action. Fired up by speeches by the most combative militants, the crowd marched through the streets of this port city "with an indescribable enthusiasm, carrying the red flag."[19]

The ideological influence of the vigorous Argentinean anarchists was evident in those strikes—for example, they were initiated by FORP, analogous to the Argentinean FORA, and the newspaper *La Protesta* was named after the anarchist daily in Buenos Aires. Moreover, José Spagnoli and Antonio Gustinelli, two Italian workers who had immigrated to Argentina, were sent to Peru by FORA to give speeches, organize, and generally to agitate. In spite of populist efforts combined with threats and the declaration of a state of siege in Lima, President Billinghurst could not contain the strikes. Anarchists promoted a series of actions focused on the rights of

---

18   Ibid., 6.
19   Ibid., 7.

workers that resonated with the people and proved partially successful in Talara, Negritos, Loritos, and Lagunitas. FORP called for a
boycott of Duncan Fox y Compañia, forcing it to rehire sixty workers it had fired.[20] By 1919 the workers' movement led by anarchists
had achieved the eight-hour workday across the entire country.[21]

The great demand for tropical produce like sugar and cotton
during the First World War significantly increased the wealth of Peruvian landowners. But the wages of both urban and rural workers
remained low, while the cost of living increased as a result of war-
time speculation and lower production of grains like rice and wheat.
In April 1919 anarchists promoted a campaign to reduce the cost
of living, popularly known as the "unemployment of hunger." In
a public gathering at Neptuno Park on April 13, several libertarian activists—D. Lévano, Conde, Céspedes, and others—released a
manifesto demanding a reduction in food prices, public transit fares,
tax rates on basic goods, and rents.[22] On May 1, after Pardo's government rejected these demands, the various unions that signed the
manifesto declared a general strike—weavers, bricklayers, shoemakers, bakers, and other groups in which anarchist ideology exerted an
important influence. In Lima a demonstration protesting the government's intransigence was violently repressed on May 4.[23] No less
stunning was the strike in Callao, where work was suspended in the
docks, beaches, factories, and custom houses; businesses in Playa
del Mercado were looted, leaving many wounded and several dead;
ships scheduled to sail were detained; and army troops joined naval
forces in a clash with workers. The principal organizers were arrested, all of them anarchists, including Gutarra, Fonkén, and Barba.

Workers in Chosica joined in solidarity and were violently
confronted by army troops, with a toll of several dead and many
wounded. Police then kidnapped some of the best-known anarchist

---

20   Ibid., 19–20.
21   Ibid., 11. See also Sulmont, "Historia del movimiento obrero peruano,"
      280.
22   Ibid., 13.
23   Ibid., 14.

militants from their homes. President Pardo, prey to the panic of an angry multitude, declared martial law and appointed Colonel Pedro Pablo Martínez to head the repression. But this was not enough. Both the government and the heads of industry and banking had been warned of troops' increasing reluctance to fire upon workers. Consequently they created a specially trained anti-mob force called Guardia Urbana. The Comité pro Abaratamiento decided to continue the strike until such time as the government met their demands and freed all arrested militants. Meanwhile, President Pardo was deposed on July 8. Large numbers of people hit the streets and renewed their demands. Then on July 12, the libertarians Gutarra, Fonkén, and Barba were released from prison, and a mass assembly gathered at Neptuno Park welcomed them with jubilation.

Several days after these events, the Comité pro Abaratamiento spawned the Federación Obrera Regional Peruana. On July 22 it issued a declaration of principles that was clearly modeled on anarcho-syndicalist ideology. The Federación Anarquista del Peru commented:

> The strike of May 1919 reached epic proportions by the mettle of its dynamic organizers. It directed the destiny of the working class to the straight path of truth and justice, and stressed the indispensable necessity of solidarity as the way to bring the mass of workers together into a single powerful movement.[24]

Anarchist activity was not limited to the urban setting. In 1915 anarchists took part in a sugar workers' strike in the Chicama Valley that, like earlier strikes, was violently repressed by the armed forces. The Reforma Universitaria, initiated in 1918, brought together workers and students, as also happened in Córdoba, Argentina and in Santiago, Chile. Most workers and students who joined this

---

24   Ibid., 20.

association were anarchists.[25] In 1923 an anarcho-syndicalist group attempted to organize a Federación Regional de Obreros Indios, and was immediately and violently repressed by the government, which declared it a special danger.[26]

In 1920 a workers' university was formed under the name of Manuel González Prada (now called Universidad Popular González Prada), with Víctor Haya de la Torre as rector. At least at first, Prada's ideas, in contrast to those of the rector, attracted many anarchist workers. In the same year, a national workers' congress adopted anarchist ideology as its guide to action and published its resolutions in *El Proletariado*.

In his second term as president, Augusto B. Leguía sought to reinvigorate capitalism in Peru and to overturn the old oligarchy. At first he gave the impression of a progressive leader, insofar as he freed political prisoners and left unions undisturbed. Yet he did cause quarrelling in the workers' movement, and the support he received from some of its sectors was short-lived. Soon enough he adopted a series of policies contrary to the interests of the working class and unions, and syndicalist organizations.[27] Anarcho-syndicalists were harshly repressed. Urmachea, editor of *El Proletariado*, was exiled along with a group of militants. When Leguía was overthrown in 1930 by Sánchez Cerro, a new workers' organization was formed called Confederación General de Trabajadores de Perú (CGTP). Marxists and their sympathizers dominated the Confederación. Only remnants of the old anarcho-syndicalist militancy remained.

As we have already noted, anarchist ideology in Peru was intimately associated with one of its great national literary figures, Manuel González Prada. Nettlau observes that in González Prada one sees "an old liberal who gradually assimilates anarchist ideas," and characterized his work, from the point of view of the historian of anarchism, thus:

---

25 Pla, *Los orígenes del movimiento obrero en América Latina*, 33.
26 Alba, *Historia del movimiento obrero en América Latina*, 104.
27 Sulmont, "Historia del movimiento obrero peruano," 280.

He was unequivocal in his rejection of the concept of authority, and, in my opinion, was quite persuasive. His work, like
that of Rafael Barrett, displays the courage of anarchists who
spread their views directly, without pressure from any union
or group. With clear and unrelenting thought such men go
vigorously against the concept of authority.[28]

The comparison to Barrett may be extended to other elements of
his work, without neglecting the distinctive literary styles that
make them two of the most brilliant Latin American writers of this
period.[29]

Manuel González Prada y Ulloa was born in Lima on January 5, 1844 into an aristocratic family.[30] His education, more than
just Catholic, was clerical, and he considered an ecclesiastical career
while a student at the Santo Toribio seminary. Among his class-
mates was Nicolás de Piérola, future president, whom he would
later call in a caustic and witty phrase "the dictator of trickery and
deceit."[31]

His first ideological formation came from his religious education. But his later liberalism was staunchly anti-clerical. His liberal
ideas were notably influenced during youth by his brief but passionate contact with Anglo-Saxon literature in the Colegio Inglés in
Valparaíso. Perhaps his study of Roman Law in the Convictorio de
San Carlos de Lima provided the basis for his unwavering critique
of the State, which he conceived as the guarantor of all social in-
equalities. After leaving the Convictorio and rejecting a legal career
he became, as Luis Alberto Sánchez put it, a "dynastic outlaw."[32]

---

28   Nettlau, "Un viaje libertario," 38.
29   Luis Di Filippo, "Barrett escritor," *Reconstruir*, 101, 5–8.
30   Luis Alberto Sánchez, *Panorama de la literatura del Perú* (Lima: Editorial
      Milla Batres, 1974), 1–3.
31   Augusto Tamato Vargas, *Literatura peruana* (Lima: n.p., n.d.), 734–35. On
      his poetic work, see José Jiménez Boya, "La poesìa de González Parda," in
      Letras, 39, 1948.
32   Luis Alberto Sánchez, "La prosa de Manuel González Prada," Prólogo a
      Páginas libres—Horas de lucha (Caracas: n.p., 1976), x.

The historic catastrophe of the 1879 Peru–Chile war, in which he fought, had a profound change in the life and ideological development of this already radical liberal. Peru suffered complete defeat and saw its capital occupied by troops from a neighboring nation. This was an exceptional, unique event in the history of independent Latin America. González Prada could not help calling to mind the then recent defeat of France by Germany. Consequently, his liberalism became a fierce nationalism; his incipient internationalism turned into hatred of the occupier and, above all, anger at the co-nationals he saw as responsible for this defeat and collective humiliation. But he did not abandon reason or self-criticism. He wrote: "The brutal hand of Chile ripped our flesh and crushed our bones. The real victors were not the enemy's guns, but our ignorance and willing bondage."[33] A decade after the war he still lamented its moral consequences—"the fear, the small-mindedness, the conformity with defeat, and the tedium of living modestly and frugally."[34] Nor could he stop thinking of vengeance—"Let us arm ourselves from head to toe and live in an armed peace or a state of latent war."[35] Such ideas and sentiments have a ready psychological explanation, but a difficult logical justification in the context of a radical liberalism that was fundamentally universal and placed its highest value not in nationality but humanity. González Prada himself confronted this contradiction and sought to resolve it in the following manner:

> There is nothing as beautiful as knocking down borders and destroying the egoistic sentiment of nations so as to make of this Earth one single people and of Humanity one single family. Enlightened and generous people of the world today all are moving towards cosmopolitanism and with Schopenhauer are saying that "patriotism is the passion of fools and the most foolish of passions." But as we wait for the hour of

---

33   Manuel González Prada, *Páginas libres* (Caracas: Biblioteca Ayacucho, 1976).
34   Ibid., 49.
35   González Prada, *Horas de lucha* (Caracas: n.p., 1976), 219.

universal peace and live in a world of wolves and lambs we must be prepared to present ourselves as lambs to lambs and as wolves to wolves.[36]

His texts warned of an interior struggle, a breakdown, a clear tension: on the one hand, he invoked the sanctity of war, and on the other he saw in war "the disgrace and scornful reproach of Humanity."[37]

If for the moment we put aside this "exogenous" nationalism prompted by his emotional reaction to the defeat and humiliation of foreign invasion, we could say that González Prada's social-political ideas developed in a logical and, to some extent, foreseeable manner. Following his initial liberalism, most evident in his anti-clericalism, he turned to a radicalism that was much closer to the Spaniard Ruiz Zorrilla's than to the Argentinean Yrigoyen's.[38] The Partido Unión Nacional that González Prada founded in Lima was very similar to the Partido Radical in Chile.

We can see in him a gradual movement culminating in the complete self-consciousness of his anarchism. Without ever abandoning his anti-clericalism or softening his criticism of the Catholic Church, his attention increasingly turned to what is referred to as the "social question." He denounced the exploitation of indigenous people, was deeply concerned about the misery of rural and urban workers, encouraged the formation of resistance societies in the emerging working class, and with great vigor went beyond a critique of juridical and constitutional nuances to challenge the very basis of political power and especially the State.

---

36 González Prada, *Páginas libres*, 53.

37 González Prada, *Horas de lucha*, 220.

38 In Argentinean radicalism as in Uruguayan Batllism, there were both individuals and groups that either came from or left for anarchism. Recall the political position in Uruguay called anarcho-Batllism. In Argentina, for example, the writer Julio R. Barcos, an anarchist who later joined Yrigoyenist radicalism, never abandoned his earlier ideas, as one can see in his book *Cómo educa el Estado a tu hijo* (Buenos Aires: Editorial Acción, 1928), with a preface by Gabriela Mistral. Also see Rama, *Historia del movimiento obrero y social latinoamericano*, 97–98.

The philosophical flaw in his anarchism, as in his earlier radical liberalism, laid in great part in his seeking a fundamental theoretical basis in positivism, as many other anarchists did. On the one hand, he questioned the value of positivism in the struggle against the Catholic Church, the Hispano-monarchical tradition, Peru's persistent feudalism, and the residues of colonialism. On the other hand, he failed to acknowledge the reactionary dimensions of the positivist thought of Comte and de Taine. Similarly, while he admired the former seminarian Ernest Renan as a historian for his interpretation of the life of Jesus in human terms, he did not see the social and political implications of Renan's racial and scientific elitism, which Nolte considers as one of the historico-ideological roots of fascism. And he appreciated the evolutionary thought of Spencer, but failed to acknowledge its latent, and sometimes explicit, racism. It came as no surprise that Kropotkin stayed away from him.

In any event, González Prada's anti-clericalism was clear. The feudal and absolutist attitudes of Spanish conquistadores persisted within the Catholic Church and had spokespersons, often bold ones, in the majority of bishops, theologians, and pedagogues. Thanks to them the education of children and adolescents, family relations, and literature and culture all developed in accord with the stale norms and outdated values of a colonial power. Through the pulpit and the confessional, Felipe II still reigned.

Circumstances might have been different in other Latin American countries, but Peru, like Ecuador and Columbia, was undoubtedly a monastic republic. González Prada considered this feature of Peruvian society to be the greatest obstacle to its development. Catholic education, the convent school, and Jesuit pedagogy were objects of his hard-hitting critique and of his most ferocious ironies. Like Leibniz, he knew that "one who controls education controls the world," and did not ignore how priests and nuns "work like termites on the wooden structure of a home."[39] So he denounced what any educated and reasonable person knew firsthand about

---

39   González Prada, *Páginas libres*, 72.

girls' schools but dared not criticize: that "the morality of the nuns is nothing but the cultivation of vanity; religion is but the unconscious practice of superstitious rituals; and that science is reduced to nothing of value or at best only as valuable as morality or religion." With the caustic charm of a Mariano de Larra he described the education of Catholic girls:

> A young woman with a third-grade diploma knows enough geography not to know if one gets to Calcutta by land or sea, and knows enough foreign languages to mangle Gascogne nonsense and call it French or mumble a Cajun English. Those most adept in fine arts can pluck cute little songs from the piano, or during their college studies paint copies of Espinal's religious images or virgins from Quito. All the young women educated by the nuns leave school as competent embroiderers: they weave slippers for the father who does not use them, and make clock cases for the brother who has no clock.

González Prada underscored the regressive internationalism of the orders of nuns, their desire for gold, their "kleptomaniac symptoms," and the poor intellectual nutrition they offered girls "during their most critical period of growth."[40]

At the same time, "the education of boys had no fewer vices than that of girls." Generally speaking, González Prada said, Catholic schools served the upper classes, the sons of politicians, generals, ministers and "any of those mulattos or others of mixed heritage enriched by corruption and extortion or exalted by favor and intrigue" who cannot tolerate the thought that their children would come in contact with the "children of artisans and workers" in public schools.[41] On top of the classist character of Catholic education, he railed against the incompetent pedagogy of priests; "the priest lacks the requirements to be a competent teacher," because "living

---

40   Ibid., 73.
41   Ibid., 74.

apart from others he develops a certain rigidity, hardness, and meanness of spirit." Moreover, the absence of biological parenting and lack of feminine love "turns the bad priest into an angry one, and the good one into an unfathomable pool of melancholy." There is nothing more objectionable to González Prada than the "hysterical genius and the groans of priests who posses all the defects of an angry spinster and none of the good feminine qualities: a species of androgyny or a hermaphrodite that collects the vices of both sexes."[42] He noted the aberrant pride of priests who "not content with considering themselves above the human race think of themselves as incarnations of divinity and even imagine that God is eternally grateful for the services they perform in his name on earth."[43]

He also denounced the institution of religious boarding schools in words that very few who suffered them would fail to second:

> The excellence of the boarding school can be commended only by those who did not have to endure the incessant pressure of a puerile and absurd regiment, or who were not driven to despair by the spying of the superior and the betrayal of the classmate, or have one's character questioned by the gossips of a malevolent or stupid crowd, or never known the swinish promiscuity of the rectory, or have breathed the foul atmosphere of a common dormitory.[44]

González Prada did not limit his critique to institutions and their pedagogy, but extended it to the content and goals of religious education. He rejected the subordination of science to dogma, which he took as an attack on all rationalist conceptions and "above everything on all philosophy, especially Greek philosophy, which still resonates throughout the world as the triumphal hymn of reason." His critique was straightforward: Young people were first removed from the world that is ruled by immutable laws and

---

42   Ibid., 78.
43   Ibid., 79.
44   Ibid., 80.

then taken to a phantasmagoric realm in which arbitrary wills prevailed.[45] As his critique ranged from the boarding school to the family, he again denounced the oppressive influence of the clergy, especially on women.

On September 25, 1904, González Prada presented a lecture at the Masonic lodge Stella d'Italia titled "Las esclavas de la Iglesia." While the Church loathes woman, he argued, declaring her a "door to hell, an arrow of Satan, daughter of the devil, a basilisk's venom, a finicky mule, or a scorpion ready to strike," it knows how to manipulate and turn her into its best instrument of domination over the family and society.[46] "Women," he argued, "should reject the religion which oppresses them and keeps them in lasting infancy or indefinite tutelage." And yet this call never fully succeeds. With indignation and astonishment, González Prada showed that "the unredeemed stands against her redeemers, and the victim blesses the weapons and fights on behalf of the victimizer." He knew by experience that women "do not compromise with libertarian thought and reject as their enemy the reformer who aims to spare them both reproach and disgrace, and proclaims the nullification of the matrimonial union not only by mutual dissent but by the will of one party," thereby siding with "the priest who curses free unions and blesses the legal prostitution of marriage."[47]

González Prada's ideas on women and their relation to the clergy can be traced to many Iberian radical works of the period, for example, Benito Pérez Galdós's *Doña Perfecta* and Eça de Queiroz's *O crime do padre Amaro*. For him those works formed part of the struggle for sexual equality and, like Horkheimer in our day,[48] he identified the family as a sphere of oppression that is at least as powerful as the State, if not more so, and maintained that "in a truly human marriage there is no absolute boss but two

---

45   Ibid., 81.
46   González Prada, *Horas de lucha*, 239.
47   Ibid., 240.
48   See Horkheimer, *La familia y el autoritarismo* (Barcelona: n.p., 1970), R. D. Laing, *El cuestionamiento de la familia* (Buenos Aires: n.p., 1972).

partners with equal rights."[49] Moreover, with a liberal if not libertarian audacity he denounced the basic corruption of sex by the bourgeoisie saying that:

[W]ives who surrender themselves to their husband without any love are prostitutes, their children conceived between pendency and a snore are illegitimate. But adulterers who publicly leave their hateful husbands and form a new family blessed by love, noble and legitimate are their offspring conceived in a rapture of passion or in the serene tenderness of a generous love.[50]

In moving from the sphere of the family to the political he made it clear that "the brutal and grotesque dictatorships in Latin America are the product of the Catholic Church and their religious schools." Whenever one can acquire the consciousness of one's own dignity and wherever belief in infallible authorities and passive obedience are rejected, no rulers like Francia, Rosas, García Moreno, or Melgarejo shall emerge.[51]

In those places, like Turkey and England, where the Catholic Church was in the minority, it demanded freedom of worship, González Prada said, yet it rejected that same freedom when it was in the majority. This observation, true since the Patristic period, was reaffirmed in our post-conciliar period—for example, in those countries that were officially Catholic, like Franco's Spain and Videla's Argentina, the Church sought control of education and culture with support from the State, and in countries like China or the U.S.S.R. that were officially atheist it passionately demanded the freedom of worship and thought.

González Prada's polemic was not limited to a critique of the clergy, religious education, and government policies and attitudes that restrict or deny freedoms (of the press, of thought, speech, and

---

49   González Prada, *Horas de lucha*, 243.
50   Ibid., 245.
51   González Prada, *Páginas libres*, 84.

the like). In a lecture he presented on August 28, 1898, later censored by the government, he criticized and lampooned those who reduced freedom of thought to anti-clericalism, and the lay inquisitors who "were stuck in their anti-clerical obsessions and lived totally devoted to hunting cassocks in nuns' cells or catching petticoats in the rectory's bedrooms." Freedom of thought means much more than that and presupposes an inquiry into social questions, he claimed. It is in this concern that we can observe the transition from radical liberalism to anarchism. González Prada wrote:

> While free thinkers are faithful to their doctrine and mean what they say, they do deserve to be censored when they fail to address the social questions and, in a kind of theophobia, limit themselves to an intransigent attack on religion. How can we not laugh at those who act like the inquisitors Torquemadas and Domingo de Guzmán, or the lay inquisitors who are easily disposed to spark a debate and parody acts of faith?[52]

A few years later, in a lecture presented on May 1, 1905 at the Federación de Panaderos that addressed the topic of the relations between the intellectual and the worker, or between mental and manual labor, González Prada advanced a clearly Kropotkian thesis in affirming "that there is no difference between the thinker who labors with his intelligence and the worker who labors with his hands," and moreover that there is no "labor that is purely cerebral [or] another that is exclusively manual." Rather, all wealth is the product of the joined labor of muscle and mind.[53] Sections of this lecture titled "The Intellectual and the Worker" are glosses of Kropotkin's *Conquest of Bread*. For example, González Prada wrote:

> Human labor lives from our muscular and nervous energy. Imagine that in a railroad line each cross tie represents the

---

52   González Prada, *Horas de lucha*, 225.
53   Ibid., 228. See Kropotkin, *Campos, fábricas y talleres* (Madrid: n.p., 1972), 5 *et seq.*

life of a single worker. As we travel our train moves along rails nailed to a series of cadavers. So too when we visit museums or libraries imagine that we are walking through a sort of cemetery in which paintings, statues, and books contain not only the thought but also the life of their authors.[54]

For González Prada the cooperation of mind and muscle in the production of all goods establishes the socioeconomic equality of the intellectual and the worker. "We owe the caste system," he noted, "to the very idea that mind performs a function nobler than muscle."

Instead of Spencer's evolutionary thought, González Prada looked to revolution of the masses and believed it "simplified the issues, the highs and lows, directing them to the practical realm." His chosen method, like Alexander's, would "not untie but cut the Gordian knot." Like Bakunin, he knew that while the revolutionary seeks to awaken the masses and lead them into action, once removed from their lethargy they are not content with following the initial movement and tend to go much beyond the original intention.[55] A few years prior to the Bolshevik revolution, he wrote the following prophetic words: "Every revolution tends to become a government based on force; every triumphant revolutionary degenerates into a conservative." And so, he proposed that "once the initial movement begins, true revolutionaries should follow through with it in all its evolutions," even though this might be objectionable to many and to their self-identity "as revealers of ultimate truth."

It must be stressed that when González Prada spoke of revolution he did not have in mind what is often understood by that term in the history of his country or Latin America, that is, a mere change of government or political party. Nor did he have in mind the establishment of a new socialist State or the control of the means of production by the producers themselves. His was instead the "cry of social demands" to Humanity and "is not moved by secondary

---

54   González Prada, *Horas de lucha*, 229. See Kropotkin, *La conquista del pan* (Madrid: ZYX, 1973), 13.
55   González Prada, *Horas de lucha*, 230.

questions but demands radical change." And if there is any doubt about his anarchist concept of revolution, he added:

> No one expects that the happiness of the unfortunate will be decreed by parliament, or that from a government manna will come as rain from the sky and satisfy the hunger of so many. Parliament enacts laws with loopholes and passes taxes that burden most those who have the least; the governmental apparatus does not function for the benefit of the people, but for the benefit of the dominant classes.[56]

The proletariat will resolve the great social question "by the only efficient means: revolution." But we must be clear that it will not be

> a local revolution that overthrows a president or Czar and turns a republic into a monarchy or an autocracy into a representative government, but a world revolution that erases national borders, suppresses nationalities, and calls humanity to a common and beneficial possession of all the earth.[57]

As we have already observed, revolution is not the conquest of power or government but is the direct control of the means of production and of the earth "because the monopolizers will hardly concede them to us out of good faith or a spontaneous change of heart."

This conception of revolution had its origins in Kropotkin and shares a great deal with Proudhon's idea of property as theft and murder.[58] The latter held that "property, after having been robbed from the worker by usury, murders him by exhaustion," such that "without plundering and crime property is nothing."[59] In a style different from Proudhon's but no less vigorous and combative,

---

56   Ibid., 231.
57   Ibid., 232.
58   See Kropotkin, *La conquista del pan*, 25–26.
59   P.J. Proudhon, *¿Qué es la propiedad?* (Buenos Aires: Proyección, 1970) cap. IV, prop 4.

González Prada expressed the same thesis:

> The ancient Romans chose a most meaningful symbol for property—the lance. We should interpret it thus: Possession of a thing is based not on justice but power; the possessor does not reason or debate, he strikes and wounds; the heart of the proprietor comprises the same two qualities of iron, strength and coldness. According to those knowledgeable of the Hebrew language, Cain is the first property owner. It does not surprise us to see a socialist from the 19th century, in looking at Cain as the first owner of earth and the first fratricide, avail himself of that coincidence and reach a powerful conclusion: *property is murder.*[60]

Although during his lifetime González Prada published only two works of prose, *Páginal libres* and *Horas de lucha*, the courageous and elegant ideas expressed in them can also be found in a number of articles collected in posthumous works: *Nuevas páginas libres* and *Anarquía*, both published in Santiago, Chile in 1936, and *Figuras y figurones,* published in Paris in 1939.

González Prada had a powerful literary and ideological impact on his contemporaries. The writer Enrique López Albújar owed him his radicalism, his concern for the indigenous, his ideas of sexual liberty, and his vehement anti-militarism. In 1898 López Albújar's law school thesis at the Universidad de San Marcos, titled *La injusticia de la propiedad del suelo*, was rejected for being "anarchist."[61] The writers Mercedez Cabello de Carbonera and Clorinda Matto de Turner, who wrote *Aves sin nido*, the first novel with an indigenous theme, were members of the literary group formed by González Prada in 1887. Some of his disciples were poets like Carlos G. Amézaga, Victor G. Matilla, and Germán Leguía y Martínez; novelists like Abelardo Gamarra (also known as "El Tunante"), and

---

60   González Prada, *Horas de lucha*, 233.
61   Tamayo Vargas, *Dos rebeldes*, II, 938–39. See also R. E. Cornejo, *López Albújar, narrador de América* (Madrid: n.p., 1961).

folklorists like Ricardo Rossel.[62]

José Carlos Mariátegui, the principal Marxist theorist in Peru, and Víctor Haya de la Torre, founder of the Alianza Popular Revolucionaria Americana (APRA), were admirers of González Prada and, in spite of their differences, borrowed some of his ideas and endorsed some of his critiques of Peruvian society.[63] It is worth mentioning here that in the struggle against Marxist-Leninism many anarcho-syndicalists collaborated with APRA in its early period, although later they had to confront its party politics. An interesting topic for study would be to look into the ways and the extent to which the ideas of González Prada influenced the Peruvian Revolution of 1969, which one of its main ideologists said was not just anti-capitalist, anti-imperialist, and anti-Stalinist, but also opposed to all chauvinistic nationalism and traditional party politics—indeed, was socialist and anarchist.[64]

---

62   Estuardo Nuñez, *La literatura peruana en el siglo XX* (México: Pormoca, 1965), 17.

63   Although Mariátegui was open to many ideas, he was still an apologist for dogma that González Prada would never have accepted. See Mariátequi's *Defensa del marxismo* (n.p., 1959), Chapter XV.

64   Carlos Delgado, "La revolución peruana: un nuevo camino," *Reconstruir*, 92–94. SINAMOS, "Ocho preguntas a la Revolución Peruana," *Reconstruir*, 89; "Postulados del INDEICOC del Perú," *Reconstruir*, 97; Gerardo Cárdena, "La nueva estructura agraria peruana," *Reconstruir*, 91.

7. Brazil

A. Pre-Anarchist Social Struggles

General Abreu e Lima, born in Recife in 1794, was the first to write a book-length study of socialist thought in Brazil. A warrior with the mettle of Garibaldi, Abreu e Lima fought for the independence of Latin America under Simón Bolívar in Boyacá, Cúcuta, Carabobo, Queseras del Medio, and other places. He published an extensive work titled *O socialismo* in 1855 after his return to Brazil from war. Carlos Rama says, "for many reasons, the book is surprising in the history of Latin American ideas," offering a thorough exposition of the "rigorous development" of its subject matter through 1855, "particularly of the new political, philosophical, and religious French literature."[1] Lima presented the ideas of Saint-Simon, Fourier, Owen, and the communists (e.g., Babeuf) with great clarity, but did not give any attention to Proudhon, though he undoubtedly knew his work.[2]

Several years earlier, in 1840, the French engineer Luis Vauthier had come to Pernambuco under contract to direct the construction

---

1   Rama, *Utopismo socialista*, xlix.
2   Vamireh Chacón, *Abreu e Lima, general de Bolívar* (Caracas: Institutos de Altos Estudios de América Latina, U.S.B., 1985), 177.

of several public works. He supervised the building of railroads and sugar mills, the drawing of regional maps, the development of labor laws, and introduced the ideas of Saint-Simon. He was not a revolutionary and it is known that, like Louis Blanc, he was opposed to the Paris Commune. He later influenced the thought of Antônio Pedro de Figueiredo and collaborated with his journal *O Progreso*.[3]

Antônio Borges de Fonseca, a Brazilian pamphleteer, started promoting a socialism based on Fourier as early as 1844 in Pernambuco.[4] Before him, in 1841, the French Fourierist Juan Benito Mure, a homeopath and close associate of Victor Considerant, had arrived in Santa Catarina. He later formed a utopian community in Palmetara and, beginning in 1845, edited the newspaper *O Socialista da Provincia de Rio de Janeiro*. His compatriot Tandonnet eventually joined him in some of these activities.[5] Ideas promoted by Vauthier and Mure influenced a number of Brazilian writers of this period who were concerned with the social and economic problems of the country, like Nascimento Feitosa, Aprigio Guimurães, and Joaquín Nabuco.

Alongside the ideas brought from Europe, we should look at some events in the history of class struggles in Brazil that may be considered indigenous precedents to the anarchist movement. For example, the struggle of slaves to achieve their emancipation began in the seventeenth century with the formation of the *quilombos,* fugitive slave communities hidden in both jungle and desert areas, which landowners tried to destroy through the colonial government. The most famous of these was the Quilombo dos Palmares, a community that in some sense was socialist and self-managed. Over a period of nearly one hundred years (1602–1694) the Portuguese and Dutch made no less than eighteen attempts to destroy it.[6]

---

3   Gilberto Freire, *Un engenheiro francês no Brasil* (Rio de Janeiro: José Olimpio Editor, 1940).

4   Chacón, *Historia das idéias socialistas no Brasil* (Rio de Janeiro: Civilização Brasiliera, 1965), 208 *et seq.*

5   Rama, *Utopismo socialista*, l–lii.

6   Edson Carneiro, *O Quilombo dos Palmares* (Rio de Janeiro: Campanhia Editora Nacional, 1958).

In the eighteenth and nineteenth centuries, social struggles between classes erupted all over Brazil. In 1798 there was some agitation among tailors (*alfaiates*) in Salvador, Bahía, and an uprising of the poor in Cabanada that Élisée Reclus characterized as a "social war of slaves against their masters." In 1832 in Pernambuco and Alogoas small farmers and fugitive slaves stood up against landowners and sugar mill owners, and in Pará indigenous people and Blacks rebelled. Landless peasants played a leading role in the 1838 Balaiada social revolt in Maranhão. In 1874 the Northeast of the country was the setting for the revolt of the Quebra-Quilos, which led to the liberation of slaves. And while the insurrection known as Insurreição Praieira was primarily motivated by political interests, it also had a social background and a hidden class struggle; so it was no wonder that landowners and the government proclaimed the "great necessity to get rid of the anarchists from Agua Prêta."[7]

In 1893, hardly five years after the abolition of slavery, Antônio Conselheiro and a group of peasants occupied the abandoned Canudos hacienda and there established a community of workers based to some degree on self-management, beyond the exploitation of landowners and the laws of the republican State. The swift arrival of a large number of slaves left without work or means of livelihood by manumission is no surprise, nor is the fact that in a few months the community numbered over 25,000, with all dedicated to agricultural and livestock work. The orientation was undoubtedly communist. The community was founded, as Euclides da Cuhna says, in "the appropriation of homes and their furnishings, and in the absolute community of the land, pastures, flocks and herds, and all farm products."[8] Conselheiro promoted a strain of Christian communism, fought against the consumption of alcohol as much as against clerical influence, did not recognize the State or any constitutional authorities, refused to pay taxes, held no respect for the

---

7 Edson Carneiro, *Insurreição Praieira* (Rio de Janeiro: Edições Conquista, n.d.).
8 Euclides da Cunha, *Os Sertões, Rio de Janeiro, 1903*. For a Spanish translation, see *Los Sertones* (Caracas: Biblioteca Ayacucho, 1980).

military, permitted divorce and free love, and, above all, opposed private property. Years before the founding of Canudos, on May 6, 1887 the conservative *Jornal do Comercio* of Rio de Janeiro wrote: "Antônio Conselheiro was promoting subversive doctrines among the masses, causing great prejudice against religion and the State to the point of distracting people from their occupations." And earlier still, in 1882, the archbishop of Bahía had sent a letter to the parishes of his archdiocese urging that the faithful be absolutely prohibited from listening to Conselheiro.[9]

Neither church nor state can tolerate a community that does not recognize their authority, even one in which crime is rare, and punishment takes the form of expulsion and not imprisonment or death. Rui Facó recalls that in Canudos "burglary and theft were rigorously prohibited and obedience to the prohibitions went to the extreme of not even touching goods that fell from their convoys: meats, flour, wheat, and even money would be left where they fell."[10] It is no surprise that the Baron of Geremoaba referred to a "communist sect" whose high priest was Conselheiro.[11] Four successive military expeditions were sent to suppress Canudos. The first three failed and left behind more than 5,000 dead. The Minister of War himself, Marshall Carlos Machada Bittencourt, went against Canudos until it was beaten and annihilated.

B. The Anarchist Movement Until the First World War

This long history of struggles and popular insurrections is the broad background for anarchism in Brazil, which does not really emerge

---

9   Edgar Rodrigues, *Socialismo e sindicalismo no Brasil* (Rio de Janeiro: Lae-mmert, 1969), 53.
10   Rui Facó, *Cangaceiros e fanáticos*, cited in E. Rodrigues, *Socialismo e sindicalismo.*
11   Afraino Coutinho, *A literatura no Brasil*, Vol. III (Rio de Janeiro: n.p., 1959), 305. See also Macedo Soares, *A Guerra dos Canudos* (Rio de Janeiro: n.p., 1903); Euclides da Cunha, *Canudos* (Rio de Janeiro: n.p., 1903).

until the phenomenon of massive European immigration in the late nineteenth and early twentieth centuries, the period wherein the beginning of industrialization and the development of the workers' movement coincide.

Along with Argentina, Brazil received a large migratory flow. It included small numbers of Germans, Arabs, and Japanese, but the main sources of immigration were Italy, Portugal, and Spain. In those three countries anarchism was the predominant ideology among workers and peasants. That explains why until the 1920s the workers' movement in Brazil was anarchist, as it was in Argentina. Viñas writes: "The ideas of Proudhon, Bakunin, and Kropotkin took root in Brazil, while social democracy was never able to communicate its message to the working masses, thereby restricting itself to small groups mainly of intellectuals and workers of Italian origin."[12]

Just as in Argentina anarcho-syndicalism had been mortally wounded by the direct intervention of Peron's government in workers' organizations, so too in Brazil it suffered under Getúlio Vargas's intrusions. Both presidents shared a corporativist conception of society and believed that the only way to avoid a social revolution in their respective countries was to take over the unions, domesticate them, and use whatever means necessary to exclude all the anarchists and other revolutionaries who had founded and led the workers' movement. But in Brazil, unlike Argentina, the Partido Comunista do Brasil was formed in 1921 as an offshoot of the anarchist movement, under the leadership of a well-known anarchist militant, Astrogildo Pereira.[13] John W. F. Dulles notes that the majority of Brazilian anarchists embraced the Bolshevik revolution with considerable enthusiasm from its beginning. They predicted that with anarchist influence the authoritarian socialism of the Bolsheviks would become a libertarian one, and could in some cases

---

12   Viñas, *Anarquistas en América Latina*, 87.
13   Alba, *Historia del movimiento obrero en América Latina*, 101; Also see João Costa, *Esbozo de una historia de las ideas en el Brasil* (México: n.p., 1957), 137.

tolerate the dictatorship of the proletariat as a necessary, though transitional, instrument to strengthen the revolution.[14]

From the beginning of the nineteenth century, immigrants in Brazil had been forming agricultural colonies. Sometimes these were guided by a social, political, or religious ideology, at other times by the simple quest for a more prosperous life cultivating virgin land. Suffice it to mention the following: Nova Friburgo (founded in 1818), São Leopoldo, São Pedro de Alcântara, Mafra, Corisco do Rio Negro, Vale de Itajai, and Varzea Grande, among others. In São Paulo alone, between 1850 and 1880, fourteen agricultural colonies emerged, and some of them coordinated their relations by the norms of mutual aid. In Mato Grosso, the residents of the city of Miranda, fleeing the army of Paraguayan president Solano López, settled in Maracajú and, in this totally isolated environment, founded a socialist colony with a covenant guaranteeing the equality of all, but without the standard political relations of a legal or parliamentary state.[15] The first experiments in forming an anarchist colony were conducted in the Southern states by Italian immigrants. We must keep in mind that between 1880 and the First World War over one million Italian immigrants arrived in Brazil, and "thousands of them became anarchist or were sympathizers such that anarchism surpassed socialism as the ideology among pre-war Brazilian workers and intellectuals."[16] Dulles writes:

> Between 1884 and 1903, Brazil received more than one million Italians, a number far superior to all other immigrant groups combined for the same period. Eager for agricultural workers, the state of São Paulo subsidized shipping companies for the transatlantic transport of immigrants, while also

---

14   J. W. F. Dulles, *Anarchists and Communists in Brazil, 1910–1935* (Austin, TX: University of Texas Press, 1973), cited in Avrich, *Los anarquistas rusos*.

15   Rodrigues, *Socialismo e sindicalismo no Brasil*, 29–30.

16   Avrich, "Los anarquistas del Brazil," *Reconstruir*, 100. See also Zelia Gattai, *Anarquista, graças a Deus* (Rio de Janeiro: n.p., 1979).

compensating management for persuading Italian peasants to undertake the voyage to "Canaan, the promised land."[17]

In São Paulo alone, between 1883 and 1889, some 300,000 colonials arrived, mostly from Italy.[18] In 1888, Arturo Campagnoli, an Italian sculptor, founded the colony Guararema in São Paulo.[19]

The foundation of the Cecilia colony was the result of the initiative of Dr. Giovanni Rossi. Born in Pisa on January 11, 1855 he received a veterinary degree in Perugia in 1874, founded a libertarian newspaper titled *Il Socialista* in his native hometown in 1883, and in 1886 founded a second newspaper notably titled *Lo Sperimentale*. According to a report in the June 1, 1888 issue of *La Révolte*, in 1887 Rossi began implementing his anarcho-communist ideas in an agricultural cooperative in Citadella, a municipality of Stagno Lombardo in the province of Cremona, Italy, with seventeen families dedicated to cultivating a farm of 120 hectares. In that same year, the Brazilian Emperor Pedro II, whom Victor Hugo called "the grandson of Marcus Aurelius," offered Rossi 300 hectares for an anarchist experiment in Brazilian territory. Two prominent musicians mediated that offer, Carlos Gomes, future author of the opera *O Guarani*, and João Gomes de Araujo. Both were friends of Rossi and his uncle, the musician Lauro Rossi. Even after the Empire fell and Pedro II was dethroned in 1889, a contingency of Italian colonists left Genoa for Brazil on February 20, 1890. Its explicit purpose, as communicated by Rossi in a letter of March 22 to the anarchist Jean Grave, was to "build an anarchist colony in Brazil capable of giving propaganda a practical illustration that our ideas are just and feasible." The Cecilia colony was founded in

---

17   Dulles, *Anarquistas e comunistas no Brasil (1900–1935)* (Rio de Janeiro: Editoria Nova Fronteira, 1977), 17. See also L. Grossi, *Storia della colonizzazione Europe al Brasile e della emigrazione italiana nello stato di São Paulo* (Milan: n.p., 1914); Flávio Venâncio Luizetto, *Presença do anarquismo no Brasil* (São Carlos: Gráfica da U.F.S. Car., 1984).

18   José Maria Bello, *Historia da Republica (1889–1954)* (São Paulo: Companhia Editora Nacional, 1972), 5–51.

19   Viñas, *Anarquistas en América Latina*, 89.

April 1890 near the towns of Palmeiras and Santa Bárbara in the province of Paraná, where a group of Germans from the Volga region had earlier settled. Through ups and downs and vicissitudes of all kinds the colony survived until 1894.[20]

Rossi recounted and reflected upon the experience of the colony in his book *Cecilia, comunitá anarchica sperimentale*, published in Livorno in 1893 and quickly translated into French and German in 1894, and into Spanish in 1896. In 1975 Jean-Louis Comolli produced a beautiful film on this libertarian adventure that does not hide or minimize any of the obstacles or incidents in its story.[21] Rossi always thought his experiment to be a success, as it was able to prove what it proposed: the possibility of a society of producers without private property or government. After some time as a professor at the agricultural institute in Taquari (Rio Grande do Sul), he returned to Italy in late 1905 and died there during the Second World War.

The Cecilia colony came to have as many as three hundred members. Some of them became disillusioned and left for Curitiba, where they waged a slanderous campaign to discredit the colony. Then an alleged comrade made off with funds from the harvest, and, unable to pay the taxes, the colony found itself evicted from the land that authorities of the republic had initially ceded to it.[22] Journalist Lorenzini said the emperor Don Pedro had shown himself to be more liberal than the republican functionaries—although the former did believe, as Afonso Schmidt says, that the earth would eventually swallow the colonists and their ideals, it was the latter who refused to tolerate an agricultural project without the collection of taxes, an enmity ultimately founded not so much

20   Muñoz, "Una cronología de Giovanni Rossi," *Reconstruir*, 83.
21   On the Cecilia colony, see, in addition to Rossi's book, the edited volume *Utopie und Experiment* (Zurich: n.p., 1897); Afonso Schmidt, *Colonia Cecilia: Romance de una experiencia anarquista* (São Paulo: n.p., 1980); Newton Stadler de Souza, *O Anarquismo da Colonia Cecilia* (Rio de Janeiro: Civilização brasileira, 1970).
22   Schmidt, *Colonia Cecilia*, 93 *et seq.*

upon their bourgeois prejudices as fiscal voracity.[23] The dissolution of the Cecilia colony did not stop other similar attempts in Brazil. A North American anarchist founded the Cosmos colony in the province of Santa Catarina. Around 1930, a group of Latvians, partisan to a species of Christian communism and perhaps adherents to Tolstoyan doctrine, founded the Varpa colony in Quatá, in the province of São Paulo.

At the same time, yet independent of the above libertarian experiments in the rural setting, beginning in 1890 small groups of anarchist immigrants in the crafts and the emerging industrial sectors initiated an intense propaganda effort among the urban masses. Some of the earliest propagandists were well-known figures in international anarchism like Felice Vezzani, Gigi Damiani, Giuseppe Consorti, Alfredo Mari, and Oreste Ristori, founder of *La Battaglia* newspaper in 1904.[24] In 1892 Arturo Campagnoli and Galileo Botti began publishing *Gli Schavi Bianchi*, a title alluding to the substitution of slave labor (after the then recent emancipation of Black slaves) with the labor of white immigrant proletarians.[25]

Several Portuguese militants are important to note. Benjamin Mota edited the newspaper *A Lanterna* for a number of years after its first appearance in 1901, and Nero Vasco successively published several newspapers and journals like *O Amigo do Povo*, *Aurora*, and *A Terra Livre*, as well as translating some fundamental works of anarchist literature, such as Élisée Reclus's *Evolution and Revolution*. After his arrival in Brazil, the Frenchman P. Berthelot made contact with some indigenous tribes and attempted to promote libertarian organization among them. He used the pseudonym Marcelo Verema for all his publications in the anarchist press. In 1911, in São Paulo, he published a pamphlet titled *O Evangelho da Hora*, with a prologue by Nero Vasco. It was translated into French and

---

23   Ibid., 105. See also Roselina Gosi, *Il socialismo utopistico: Giovanni Rossi e la Colonia Anarchica Cecilia* (Milano: n.p., 1977).

24   Nettlau, "Viaje libertario," *Reconstruir*, 78, 43–44. Dulles, *Anarchists and Communists*, 20.

25   Viñas, *Anarquistas en América Latina*, 89.

published in *Les Temps Nouveaux*; into Spanish in 1922, first published in Chile, then in Argentina in *Pampa Libre*; and into Esperanto in Amsterdam in 1912.

We should also mention the Icelandic Magnus Soendahl, whose newspaper *O Sociocrata* was published in Sete Lagoas and Minas Gerais. His books *Conhecer para prever a fim de melhorar-União sociocrática-Catecismo Orthologico* (published in 1890), and *Guia sociocrático-Dados praticos e geraes sobre a índole e o plano de propaganda da Razão* (published in 1910), show a mixture of libertarian and authoritarian (positivist) ideas.[26] In 1899 in Rio de Janeiro, the anarchist J. Mota Assunção, a twenty-year-old train conductor, founded *O Protesta* and published eleven issues. And in 1904 the shoemaker Manuel Moscoso and the typesetter Carlos Dias began the publication of *O Libertário*.

Max Nettlau lists the following newspapers for the period 1892 to 1904: in Rio de Janeiro *O Protesto*, *O Golpe*, *A Greve*, *Kultur*, and *O Libertário*; in Curitiba *A Voz do Dever*, *O Despertar*, *Il Diritto*; in São Paulo *Avante*, *O Amigo do Povo*, *Emancipação*, *Gli Schiavi Bianchi*, *L'Asino Umano*, *L'Avenir*, *L'Operaio*, *Il Risveglio*, *La Rivolta*, *La Terza Roma*.[27] Between 1905 and 1914, he lists the following: in Rio de Janeiro *Novo Rumo*, *Liberdade*, *A Guerra Social*, and *Aurora*; in São Paulo *Aurora*, *Terra Livre*, *La Battaglia*, *Il Libertario*, *Il Ribelle*, and *L'Azione Anarchica*; in other localities *A Luta* (Porto Alegre), *O Proletário* (Santos), and *A Nova Era* (Taboleiro Grande-Minas Gerais). The following publications he considers "somewhat libertarian or at least anti-political": in Santos, *União dos Operários*, *A Revolta*, and *Tribuna Operária*; in Campinas, *A Voz Operária*; in Vila Nova de Lima-Minas Gerais, *Luz Social*; in Rio de Janeiro, *Semana Operária*; in Aradas, *O Grito Social*; and in Aveiro, *O Proletário*.[28]

According to José Ingenieros, by 1875 several sections of the International had formed in Brazil, and these were in correspondence

---

26   Nettlau, "Viaje libertario," 46–47.
27   Nettlau, "Contribución a la bibliografía anarquista," 16–17.
28   Ibid., 27–28.

with the sections in Buenos Aires and Montevideo until 1882.[29] On April 15, 1894 anarchists and socialists gathered in São Paulo with the purpose of organizing the first May Day celebration in Brazil. Rodrigues writes: "Informed of this 'criminal' gathering by the Italian consul, São Paulo police raided the meeting and arrested nine, incarcerating Brazilian nationals in state penitentiaries and taking foreigners to Rio de Janeiro, where they were held until December 12."[30] In Rio Grande do Sul, the União Operária, whose ideology fluctuated between anarchism and reformist socialism, was formed in 1896, and the Liga Operária Internacional, definitely more anarchist, formed in 1897. Both organizations promoted the First Workers' Congress of Rio Grande do Sul, convening on January 1 and 2, 1898, and issuing an outstanding position paper titled "Grupo Libertários."[31]

Strikes became more frequent in the last decade of the nineteenth century—for example, in 1890 weavers struck in the Madalena factory in Recife, in 1892 railroad workers in Fortaleza, and in 1898 drivers in Guanabara. Anarchists, as individuals and groups, were always close to the action. In 1899 the *Almanaque de Pernambuco* published the *Decálogo de los anarquistas*, and at about this time Dr. Silva Mendes wrote the following in his doctoral dissertation, *Socialismo Libertario ou Anarquismo*:

> No one is surprised that there are anarchists around. Some of the major intellectuals of our time are anarchist: H. Spencer, Kropotkin, Élisée Reclus, Tolstoy, Ibsen, in other words, the major apostle of liberty, the major geographer, the major Christian thinker, and the major dramatist, such that anarchism is either an awe-inspiring utopia or a social casualty.[32]

29   Ingenieros, *Almanaque socialista de "La Vanguardia" para 1899* (Buenos Aires: n.p., 1988), 26.
30   Edgar Rodrigues, *Socialismo e sindicalismo no Brasil*, 64–65. See also Dulles, *Anarchists and Communists*, 22.
31   Ibid., 73–74.
32   Ibid., 69.

Resistance societies and libertarian groups emerged throughout the country, such as the Sociedade Primero de Maio in Santos in 1900, and in São Paulo in 1901 the Liga dos Artistas Alfaiates. In 1903 the revolutionary syndicalist movement renewed its propaganda efforts and achieved "the founding of hundreds of groups, associations, and unions," including in the state of Rio de Janeiro the Federação das Associações de Classe, later called the Federação Operária do Rio de Janeiro.[33]

The response by this oligarchic republic did not take long. Rodrigues Alves, a conservative from São Paulo, assumed the presidency in 1902.[34] At first Alves ordered the police to repress the growing movement. Abuses in the judicial process were abundantly evident, but one honest judge, Vicente de Carvalho, did raise his voice in protest. The government then decided to bypass constitutional protections and directed the Chamber of Deputies to enact what came to be known as the Adolfo Gordo Law, named after the entrepreneur from São Paulo Adolfo Gordo, a member of the Chamber, whom militant workers considered "the most despicable of the legislators."[35] It was the equivalent of the Law of Residence that Argentina passed in 1902, permitting the imprisonment of Brazilian militants in the remote area of Acre, Brazil's Tierra del Fuego, and the expulsion of foreigners. Edgar Rodrigues notes, "such were the republicans and democrats that succeeded the Emperor Pedro II."

But the proletariat did not retreat. It confronted all dangers, Edgar Rodrigues says, and continued to form more societies of resistance and class-based unions in various regions. Some of them were: in São Paulo, the União dos Trabalhadores Gráficos, União dos Chapeleiros, and União Operária; in Santos, the Sociedad Internacional União Operária, which comprised all unions; in Campinas, the Liga Operária; in Jundiaí, the Liga Operária, Centro Internacional dos Trabalhadores; in Rio Claro, the Liga Operária; and in Rio

---

33   Ibid., 82.
34   See Bello, *Historia da Republica*, 172–84.
35   Dulles, *Anarchists and Communists*, 27.

de Janeiro, the União dos Trabalhadores Gráficos, União dos Trabalhadores em Estivas, União dos Trabalhadores Ferroviária Central do Brasil, União dos Operários em Construção Civil, União dos Artífices em Calçados, Centro Cosmopolita (bars, restaurants, and hotels), União dos Foguistas, Associação dos Trabalhadores da Industria Mobiliária, União dos Operários em Fábrica de Tecidos, Associação dos Marinheiros e Remadores, among others.[36] In 1903 police crushed a strike in Rio de Janeiro by textile workers that, as Dulles puts it, is inscribed in the history of labor struggles as the most important strike carried out in Brazil up to that date.[37]

Many of these resistance societies and labor unions did not limit their activities to agitation and labor struggles, but were also involved in popular education and culture. In the city of Santos the Centro Internacional dos Pintores, founded by anarchists, housed a Universidad Popular in which hundreds of courses were offered. And practices of solidarity and mutual aid, highly recommended by Kropotkin, were familiar to workers; for instance, in 1904 the Centro das Classes Trabalhadoras created a workers' commission to aid peasants from the Northeast hit with a devastating periodic drought to which the bourgeoisie and government were totally indifferent. The Circulo Socialista de França in São Paulo organized the first remembrance of the Chicago martyrs on May Day 1904. In Campinas in 1905 a Liga Operária was founded by several trades, and on December 25 of that year the well-known libertarian writer Everardo Dias presented a lecture titled "Jesus Christ, Social Agitator," causing quite a stir among Catholic circles. In São Paulo the União dos Trabalhadores Gráficos organized a series of weekly lectures with the purpose of promoting ideological clarity. Also in Paratins, in the province of Amazonas, a very active Gremio Operário was founded in 1905.[38] Similarly, protest movements multiplied during this period. The most important was perhaps a demonstration held in 1905 in Santos that was essentially a general strike.

36   Rodrigues, *Socialismo e sindicalismo no Brasil*, 85–86.
37   Dulles, *Anarchists and Communists*, 26.
38   Ibid., 97–98.

On November 11, 1905 in the Rio de Janeiro local of the Federação das Associações de Classe a group of distinguished militants founded the anarchist group Novo Rumo, which eventually put out a newspaper by the same name. Among this group of anarchists were Joel de Oliveira, María de Oliveira, Luiz Magrassi, José Romero, Alfredo Vásquez, Salvador Alacid, Carlos Lobagele, José Rodrigues, Antônio Moutinho, and João Benvenuto.[39]

Attempts to organize a national federation of syndicates and workers' societies began in 1905. The following year, the Federação Sindical Regional do Rio de Janeiro convened a national congress from which the Confederação Operária Brasileira (COB) emerged.[40] In the COB anarchists confronted socialists, mostly Marxists, for the first time. Bobbio and Mateucci write:

> While socialists attempted to transform the movement into one based on a new political party, anarchists opposed such attempts and reclaimed the COB as a syndical, apolitical organization based on the conception of a revolutionary syndicalism sustained by self-sufficient economic resistance societies.[41]

The Congress convened on April 15, 1905 at the Centro Gallego and adjourned a week later at the Teatro Lucinda. COB became active in 1908, inspired by the French Confédération générale du travail, under the leadership of revolutionary anarchists and syndicalists. Ramiro Moreira Lobo served as its first secretary. His newspaper, *A Voz do Trabalhador*, appeared on February 1, 1908 under the editorship of the anarchist Manuel Moscoso.[42] COB's early period, lasting through 1909, is characterized by its campaign against the proposed war between Brazil and Argentina, and its public protest of the execution of Francisco

---

39   Ibid., 39.
40   S. Fanny Simon quoted in Viñas, *Anarquistas en América Latina*, 86.
41   Norberto Bobbio and Nicola Mateucci, *Diccionario de Política* (México: Siglo XXI), I, 59.
42   Dulles, *Anarchists and Communists*, 30.

Ferrer of Spain.[43] In 1906, May Day was publicly celebrated for the first time in Rio de Janeiro, São Paulo, Santos, Jundiaí, Campinas, and other cities. This same year rail workers went on general strike, encouraged in great part by militant anarchists.[44] In December the Primeira Conferência Operária, formed out of the Federação Operária do São Paulo, convened a Congress in 1908.[45] At the same time, President Afonso Pena's administration was busy extending rail lines, organizing the army and navy, and developing a national industrial capacity.[46]

Brazilian anarchists, like their comrades in Argentina, were attentive to the education of children. The Liga Operária in Campinas founded the Escola Livre on February 24, 1907, supervised by Professor Renato Salles and modeled on the Escuela Moderna of Francisco Ferrer.[47] On May Day 1907 a general strike was held in São Paulo and other cities demanding the eight-hour day, which had been planned the previous year at the first Congresso Operária Nacional convened in Rio de Janeiro.[48] São Paulo's chief of police declared that "the strike was provoked by a number of anarchists, professional agitators, paid by foreign governments in order to destroy our industry."[49]

Libertarian propaganda continued to grow, especially with the involvement of militants like Carlos Dias, Oreste Ristori, Edgar Leuenroth and the Federação Operária do Rio de Janeiro, which in 1907 sponsored lectures in different parts of the country on themes like patriotism and militarism, religion and state, education, work, and church.[50] During this period Brazilian anarchists maintained close ties with comrades in Peru and Argentina.[51]

43 Rodrigues, *Socialismo e sindicalismo no Brasil*, 114 *et seq*. Ibid., 27.
44 Ibid, 141–147; Dulles, *Anarchists and Communists*, 28.
45 Rodrigues, *Socialismo e sindicalismo no Brasil*, 173–80.
46 J. Pandía Calógeros, *Formaçao histórico do Brasil* (São Paulo: n.p., 1902), 358–59.
47 Rodrigues, *Socialismo e sindicalismo no Brasil*, 186.
48 Ibid., 196.
49 Dulles, *Anarchists and Communists*, 29.
50 Rodrigues, *Socialismo e sindicalismo no Brasil*, 216.
51 Alba, *Historia del movimiento obrero en América Latina*, 101.

The international solidarity of the Rio de Janeiro anarchists is evident when they learned that the exiled Argentinean militant and former member of the editorial group of *La Protesta* Máximo Suárez was being held aboard a ship anchored in the city's port. With help from stevedores they were able to free him, and soon enough he was active in the workers' and anarchists' struggle in Brazil. In 1907 the Grupo Libertario of Rio Grande do Sul tested a new type of propaganda, mailing postcards containing figures and phrases referring to anarchism. That same year in São Paulo the Grupo Libertario Germinal was founded by the fusion of two unions, and in Santos the Federação Operária showed intense cultural and propagandistic activity in organizing lectures by Eliado César Antunha, Luiz Lascala, Ezequiel Somoni, and Romão Gens, as well as recitals, social theaters, and other performances.

There was no shortage of strikes in 1907. As a result, in Rio de Janeiro coal workers reduced their workday from sixteen to eleven hours, as did painters and electricians of the Teatro Municipal. In Pau Grande weavers went on strike and emerged victorious. But in São Paulo things turned out differently for striking metal workers at the Compañia Fidgerund and for laborers at the Compañia Mecánica, and the Craig y Martins and the F. Amaro foundries in spite of their heroic resistance. In that same city seamstresses also went on strike demanding a more humane workday, and in Bahía two thousand weavers of the Emporio Industrial de Norte struck for better wages. Just as in Buenos Aires, Santiago de Chile, Mexico, and Veracruz, anarchists in Rio de Janeiro began the struggle for lower rents in late 1907, founding the Liga de Inquilinato, and promoting the idea of a "tenant strike."[52]

In the province of Paraná the exploitation of workers—most evident in the meager wages and harsh conditions in the maté mills, analogous to the ones in Paraguay and Argentina, and also in the bakeries—made it perfect territory for organizing the Federação

---

52   Rodrigues, *Socialismo e sindicalismo no Brasil*, 217–19. Also see Heredia, *El anarquismo en Chile*, 45–48; Quesada, *La Protesta*, 1, 87–88.

Operária, promoting anarchism, and distributing the newspaper *O Despertar*.[53] Some convened a Congresso Operária in Curibita. One very prominent militant in the Paraná region was the immigrant Gigi Damiani, of whom Oiticica would say, "he was a great Italian anarchist of the old school worthy of the memory of those who fought along with him." He was a collaborator in *La Battaglia*, and in Curibita founded a Portuguese newspaper titled *O Direito* "in the hope of influencing," Dulles observes, "the local workers, largely Germans and Poles."[54]

But between 1908 and 1910 the movement experienced a period of stagnation and setbacks. On the one hand, repression increased under the presidency of Afonso Pena, whose economic interventionism was based on the model of an armed State.[55] On the other hand, libertarian ideology, the soul and engine of the syndicalist movement at the time, was being diluted as the working class grew and the propagandists' efforts to penetrate it failed to keep pace. Nonetheless, during this period the workers' central and anarchist newspapers did pursue a valiant campaign against the government's plan to impose compulsory military service. But chauvinistic elements organized and agitated public opinion with a trumped-up national border threat. In this instance, the alleged invader was Argentina, the most powerful of Brazil's neighbors.

Curiously enough, because of their anti-nationalist activities, anarchists were often charged with being foreign agents, just as Colonel Varela and the military had accused Argentinean anarchists with being agents of Chile during the strike in Patagonia. With the collaboration of many socialists and some liberals, Brazilian anarchists took the pacifist campaign to all regions of the country, giving speeches and holding meetings and other forums. They founded the Liga Antimilitarista and its newspaper *Não Matarás*, edited by the libertarians Mota Assunção and Eloy Pontes. In 1908 anarchists were active in protests and strikes among many workers—for

---

53   Ibid., 221–25.
54   Dulles, *Anarchists and Communists*, 20.
55   Bello, *Historia da Republica*, 199.

example, hatters, potters at the Conceição dos Garulhos, weavers at Crespy and Company, workers at the Societá Italo Gasparini in Salto de Itu, and, the most significant, dockworkers at Santos, whose strike was cruelly repressed. From April 17 to 19 of that same year the second Congresso Operária Estadual de São Paulo convened.[56] The execution of Francisco Ferrer provoked worldwide protest and condemnation, and was keenly felt in Brazil.[57] Anarchists and socialists, as well as liberals and even conservatives joined demonstrations held in all major cities. In spite of this widespread activity, the Italian militant Edmundo Rossoni was deported from Brazil because he had attempted to establish a rationalist school inspired by Ferrer's teachings.[58]

The anarchist and workers' movement in Brazil showed its solidarity with Argentinean comrades who were persecuted, deported, imprisoned, or killed during their Centennial festivities.[59] Just as in Uruguay, in 1910 Brazilian anarchists formed a Comitê Revolucionário, organizing meetings and conferences, and publishing pamphlets and manifestos—for example, one signed by the editorial staffs of *A Terra Livre* and *La Battaglia*, and by groups like Aurora, Pensamento e Acão, Libertas, Propaganda, Germinal, and the Círculos de Estudos Sociais de Bom Retiro.[60] In 1910, anarchist support was crucial for the rebellion led by the sailor João Cándido among the crews of the Minas and São Paulo, the two main ships of the Brazilian navy, demanding an end to the use of torture in the armed forces. Afranio Peixoto writes about this rebellion, known as the Revolta da chibata (Revolt of the Whip), in his memoirs. In 1911 a fierce struggle led by anarchists broke out between workers at the port in Santo and the company Gaffrée y Guinle for the reduction in the workday, which was then fourteen hours, and an increase in wages,

---

56   Rodrigues, *Socialismo e sindicalismo no Brasil*, 227–45.

57   G. Lapouge and J. Bécarud, *Los anarquistas españoles*, 70.

58   Alba, *Historia del movimiento obrero*, 101.

59   See D. A. de Santillán, *El movimiento anarquista en la Argentina* (Buenos Aires: Argonauta, 1930), 179–86.

60   Rodrigues, *Socialismo e sindicalismo no Brasil*, 279.

which were meager. The newspaper *A Revolta* was then launched, edited by Florentino de Carvalho and Silvio Floreal. Some of their combative essays were translated and published in *Regeneración*, the famous Mexican publication by Flores Magón. Concurrently, in Rio de Janeiro the anarchist group Guerra Social began publishing a newspaper by that same name. Among those who collaborated and wrote for that paper were Gigi Damiani, Carlos Dias, José Martins, and Astrogildo Pereira, as well as several foreign correspondents such as Neno Vasco in Portugal, José Cordeiro in England, Ernesto Herrera in Uruguay, and Manuel Moscoso in Argentina.[61]

Strikes also broke out during this period: in some large farms of rural regions, such as Bragança and Campinas e Ilha Grande in the province of São Paulo, and in the capital among urban masons and locksmiths. The newspaper *A Lanterna* collected the sum of ninety-five reales to assist Mexican anarchists.[62] In Sorocaba masons struggled for the eight-hour and weavers for the ten-hour workday, and in Campinas masons demanded a fifteen percent wage increase. On August 12, 1911 railroad workers in the Northeast declared a strike, the Liga Operária do Bauru was raided by police, with many striking workers banished to the jungles of Mato Grosso. On August 14 railroad workers in Jataí in the province of Goias went on strike, and many of them, according to Everardo Dias, were terribly tortured or executed.[63] On August 16 carpenters in Jau, a province of São Paulo, strike for the eight-hour workday and textile workers in the São Bento province follow them demanding a ten-hour workday, down from fourteen hours. On September 5, shoemakers in Rio de Janeiro achieved a wage increase after a month-long strike. Textile workers in Sorocaba, in the province of São Paulo, were unsuccessful in their strike for better working conditions.

1911 was a hard year. Repression was severe. In spite of this, the workers' movement grew and anarchism exerted a significant

---

61   Ibid., 285–94.
62   Robert J. Alexander, *Labor Parties of Latin America* (New York: n.p., 1942), 29. See also Dulles, *Anarchists and Communists*, 25.
63   Dias, *Historia das lutas sociais no Brasil* (n.p., n.d.).

influence within it.[64] New libertarian publications, books, pamphlets, and groups appeared in 1912, as well as new struggles and strikes, all initiated by anarchists throughout Brazil. In Porto Alegre, the newspaper *A Voz do Trabalhador* was launched; in São Paulo, *O Proletário*; in Rio de Janeiro, *O Progresso*. José Rizal's book *No Pais dos Frades* was released by the publisher of the newspaper *A Lanterna*, and Carlos Dias' pamphlet, *Semeando para colher*, by the publisher of *A Vida*. A number of resistance societies were founded, for example: Liga Operária Internacional in Rio Preto, São Paulo; Liga Operária Machadense in Machado, Minas Gerais; Centro Sindicalista da Classe Trabalhadora do Pará in Belém, Pará; Sindicato dos Pintores in Rio de Janeiro, among others. The shoemakers' strike stands out from the various strikes in São Paulo at this time for its duration and success. It lasted five and a half months and achieved a ten percent wage increase. The July 15th dockworkers' strike in Santos was violently crushed. Many workers were imprisoned and tortured, and several anarchists, like Manuel Gonçalvez, Miguel Garrido, and Florentino de Carvalho were banished from Brazil.[65]

Hermes de Fonseca was elected president in 1910. Bello describes him as embodying "in addition to military imposition, the most irritating form of republican oligarchy and threat to public liberty or, in other words, the crude Latin American petty caesarism of which Carlos Peixoto had spoken."[66]

Several tepid syndicalists led by Pinto Machada and incited by the federal congressman Mario Hermes, son of the president-marshal, convened a congress on November 1912 inexplicably named the Quarto Congresso Operário Brasileiro. The purpose was to put the aggressive workers' movement on a path to reformism and nationalism. "To the annoyance of anarchists," as Dulles puts it, "the socialist congresses of 1892 and 1902 were labeled as 'labor congresses' and making the First Brazilian Labor Congress of 1906 the

---

64   Rodrigues, *Socialismo e sindicalismo no Brasil*, 300–03.
65   Ibid., 308–18; Dulles, *Anarchists and Communists*, 29.
66   Bello, *Historia da Republica*, 214.

third." Anarchists looked on the Conferação Brasileira do Trabalho (CBT) founded at that First Congress as an "evil creature."[67] It sought to reduce anarchist influence on the working class and to inoculate it from any revolutionary inclination by forming a political party. Reformism, nationalism, and populism were the bourgeoisie's formula—welcomed by the military and government—for ridding Brazil of revolutionary anarchism and socialism. The formula failed this time, but eventually Getúlio Vargas achieved a number of victories, which would continue to grow until the present.[68]

The real Second Brazilian Labor Congress convened in the Centro Cosmopolita in Rio de Janeiro between September 8 and 13, 1913, with the participation of two state federations, five local federations, fifty-two syndicates, and four newspapers, all represented by a total of 117 delegates. Even when they refrained from any ideological definition, it is obvious to anyone who analyzes that Congress that anarchism was the dominant position.[69] Astrogildo Pereira, who would become a leading figure of the Communist Party, expressed the following view: "Syndicalism has nothing to do with the Second International, insofar as the latter is concerned with the Party."[70] The Congress recommended that delegates "remove anything 'bureaucratic or coercive' from their statutes and reject any resolution that takes individual autonomy away from the associates or concedes attributes of authority to any one of them."[71]

In 1913 new anarchist papers appeared in various regions of the country, like *A Luta Social*, published in Manaus by the Portuguese Tércio de Miranda; *A Luta* in Porto Alegre published by O Grupo

---

67   Dulles, *Anarchists and Communists*, 32.
68   Bello, *Historia da Republica*, 303–05. Also see Sertório Castro, *A Republica que a Revoluçao distruiu* (Rio de Janeiro: n.p., 1932) and Alejandro Mendible, *El ocaso del autoritarismo en Brasil* (Caracas: n.p., 1986), 26–27.
69   Rodrigues, *Socialismo e sindicalismo no Brasil*, 319–34; Dulles, *Anarchists and Communists*, 33.
70   Rodrigues, *Nacionalismo e Cultura Social* (Rio de Janeiro: Laemmert, 1972), 31.
71   Dulles, *Anarchists and Communists*, 33.

de Homens Livre; and in Rio de Janeiro *Liberdade*, founded by Professor Matera, and *Coluna Operária*. In the main cities there were numerous May Day celebrations and workers' unions. Meanwhile, more resistance societies formed—the Liga Operária Varginhense in southern Minas Geraís, and in Rio do Sul the Federação Operária de Pelotas.[72] José Elías da Silva, a textile worker, sailor, and shoemaker from Pernambuco founded the Federação de Trabalhadores de Pernambuco.[73] Just as in Argentina FORA and other leftist groups—anarchists, syndicalists, and Marxists—maintained a vigorous fight against the famous Law of Residence,[74] so too in Brazil the Confederação Operária, anarchists, and some Marxists stood stalwart against the equally famous Ley Adolfo Gordo. Demonstrations and protest movements were organized in São Paulo, Rio de Janeiro, Campinas, Santos, Ribeirão Preto, and even in Rio Claro, which twenty years later would become a bastion of integralism. Among the orators and journalists who opposed this unjust law were João Gonçalvez, Cecilio Junior, Orlando Xavier, Orlando Corrêa Lopes, Eladio César Antunha, and Manuel Campos, who in 1914 would become a victim of the law.[75]

C. Anarchist Movement Since the First World War

Like their comrades in Latin America and Europe, anarchists in Brazil did not take long to proclaim a firm pacifist position at the outbreak of the Great War. In São Paulo, they printed and distributed postcards with the words "Dad, don't go to war." The poet Ricardo Pinheiro would write:

> *a guerra que arranca inclemente*
> *das choupanas dos pobres plebeus*

---

72 Rodrigues, *Nacionalismo e Cultura Social*, 32–36.
73 Dulles, *Anarchists and Communists*, 34.
74 Quesada, *La Protesta*, 1, 92.
75 Rodrigues, *Nacionalismo e Cultura Social*, 39–40.

a mais forte e mais moça da gente
para dare em tributo ao seu deus.[76]

The war that mercilessly uproots
ordinary poor men from their shanty towns
takes the strongest and youngest of the people
to pay tribute to its god.

The monthly journal *A Vida*, edited by Orlando Corrêa Lopes, began publication and waged an antiwar campaign following the ideas of Sébastien Faure, Errico Malatesta, Élisée Reclus, and other anarchists. Lima Barreto, who subscribed to both *A Vida* and *Na Barricada*, at first supported the Liga pro Aliados, but then came around and adopted the anarchists' antiwar position. Francisco de Assis Barbosa notes that "although Barreto never engaged in direct action he did put his talents as a writer and journalist to work for the growing movement."[77] In Porto Alegre, anarchists founded a Liga Antimilitarista. Later, cadets from the Escola Militar would show their bravado by sacking the Liga's offices, destroying its furniture, and burning its books. As in other Latin American countries that exported agricultural goods, the war caused an increase in food prices. Without a corresponding increase in salaries, the working class was most seriously affected by the price change. At the same time, employers lengthened the workday and reduced the workweek to three days. In response, anarchists began a campaign against the scarcity of goods. On March 8, 1915 the indefatigable Italian anarchist Oreste Ristori spoke at a great rally held in the district of Bom Retiro, São Paulo. As might be expected, strikes for better wages erupted in many places. In February the textile workers in de Juta, São Paulo, had their paychecks held back for two months, and in April a general strike demanding higher wages was declared in Pará.

76   Ibid., 48.
77   De Assis Barbossa, *A Vida de Lima Barreto* (Rio de Janeiro: Civilização brasileira), 250.

Anarchists held a number of May Day public celebrations in the Praça de Se of São Paulo, in Belo Horizonte (with Alexandre Zanella, Donato Donatti, José Torres, and others participating), in Petrópolis (where José Elías da Silva, an anarchist who later would go over to the Communist Party, was arrested), in the Largo de São Francisco of Rio de Janeiro (where they were dispersed by police), in the Largo Monte Alegre, the Praça Telles of Santos, and other places. The antiwar campaign was logically linked to the campaign against scarcity, so anarchists and socialists formed the Comitê de Defensa Proletária to address both issues. On August 15, 1914 in Rio de Janeiro the Comitê organized a mass rally against scarcity that turned into looting of stores and food warehouses. A rally in Santos with Enrique Ramos and Manuel Campos as speakers saw the same unfortunate turn of events.

In July, the Encuentro de Agrupaciones Anarquistas de Brazil was held in São Paulo, and formed a Comissão de Relações with the aim of facilitating communication among the various groups, coordinating activities, and fostering the distribution of anarchist newspapers and literature from Brazil and elsewhere.[78]

Meanwhile new groups were coming together: in Pelotas, in July the Grupo Iconoclasta, in August the Ateneo Sindicalista, and in September the Grupo Teatro Social Primeiro de Maio; in Porto Alegre, the Gremio de Estudos Sociais; in São Paulo, the libertarian Deutschen Graphischen Verbands für Brasilien. Numerous pamphlets were published, like *A sementeira, Onde Esta Deus?*, *Qual é a Religião que Devemos Ensinar aos Nossos Filhos?*, and *A Social Democracia Alemã*, among others. In many cities anarchists vigorously waged an ambitious but unsuccessful campaign to overturn the deportation of Manuel Campos.[79] The recently elected president, Venceslau Brás, was quite "patient and accommodating" toward the bourgeoisie but certainly not the workers.[80] More libertarian newspapers appeared in 1915: *O Debate* in Maceió, *O*

---

78   Rodrigues, *Nacionalismo e Cultura Social*, 57–67.
79   Ibid., 71–76.
80   Bello, *Historia da Republica*, 234.

Combate in São Paulo, *Na Barricada* by Orlando Corrêa Lopes, and *Critica Social e Combate* in Rio de Janeiro.

More strikes broke out, almost always promoted and inspired by anarchists. In March, after not being paid in more than nine months, workers on the construction of the main railroad line in Três Lagoas abandoned the worksite in protest. On May Day 1915, the Comissão de Agitaçao Contra a Guerra, founded by anarchists, held a large antiwar rally in collaboration with the Confederação Operária Brasileira in Largo de São Francisco, Rio de Janeiro. Among the speakers were Orlando Corrêa Lopes, Candido Costa, Labindo Vieira, and other libertarian orators. In São Paulo, anarchist-leaning workers' groups, cultural centers, and newspapers came together to establish the Comissão Internacional Contra a Guerra with an inaugural rally on May Day 1915 in the Praça da Se, featuring several important speakers like José Romero, A. Nalepinsky, Passos Cuhna, and Edgar Leuenroth. Although anarchists throughout Latin America opposed the war, nowhere was the antiwar campaign more vigorous than in Brazil.[81] On October 16 in Rio de Janeiro a Congreso Internacional de Paz was convened. Immediately following, between the 18th and 20th of the same month, a Congreso Anarquista Sudamericano met at the headquarters of the Confederação Operarua Brasileira.[82]

The war's cost in blood, treasure, and unemployment left its scourge on the proletarian classes. The libertarian poet Martins Fontes wrote:

> *O primeiro tem fome. O Segundo tem fome.*
> *O terceiro tem fome. E assim outros, milhares!*
> *Mas en tantas legiões*
> *oes, que e melhor Não contares,*
> *Quantos säo os que a dor da miséria consume!*[83]

---

81 Dulles, *Anarchists and Communists*, 37.
82 Rodrigues, *Nacionalismo e Cultura Social*, 78–118.
83 Martins Fontes, *Vulcão* (Santos: n.p., 1920), cited in Ibid. See also Francisco Root, *Nem patria nem patrão* (São Paulo: n.p., 1983).

The first is hungry. The second is hungry.
The third is hungry. And likewise a thousand more!
But there are so many of them
That it is better not to count them,
So many consumed by the pain of poverty!

The World War brought economic panic to Brazil. International commerce and foreign exchanges came to a near standstill, and exports and imports were substantially reduced. The government found itself in deep trouble. Government revenues drastically decreased and payments fell into arrears, requiring an increase in customs duties and taxes. Lacking essential resources, the Allied Powers were forced to recruit South American countries like Brazil, bringing significant profit to landowners and industrialists.[84] At the same time, European products became unavailable, and workers' and peasants' wages fell terribly short in proportion to the rise in prices and the gains of capitalists. Yet Brazilian industry grew during this period. In the 1920 census, 5,936 of the 13,336 industrial establishments then registered had begun operations between 1915 and 1919.[85] Nonetheless, the condition of workers hardly changed and in some cases worsened. Food became quite scarce, and in 1917 prices increased between 20–150 percent.[86]

In 1917 workers and anarchists combined their antiwar campaign with a fervent support of the Russian Revolution.[87] In it they saw the spontaneous action of working people and their desire for a classless and stateless society. High unemployment, rising cost of living, and low wages naturally led to strikes, of which there were many. A series of conflicts that erupted in the textile mills in the province of São Paulo and culminated in a general strike led to mass layoffs, imprisonments, and assassinations—for example, the

---

84   Bello, *Historia da Republica*, 235–36.
85   Caio Prado Junior, *Historia Economica do Brasil* (São Paulo: n.p., 1956), 257.
86   Dulles, *Anarchists and Communists*, 38–47.
87   Norberto Bobbio and Nicola Matteuci, *Diccionario de Política*, 59–60.

killing of the shoemaker José Martínez—in addition to the deportation of foreigners.[88] Persuaded by Manoel Perdigão, anarchists in Santos struck in solidarity with workers from São Paulo. Consequently Perdigão and Simão Salcedo were imprisoned for one hundred days. The Comitê de Defensa Proletária—with Leuenroth, de Carvalho, and Damiani as members—organized a large funeral procession for José Martínez that turned into an anti-capitalist and anti-government rally. Both in São Paulo and in the interior of the country confrontations broke out between workers and the armed forces brought in to suppress them. In solidarity, anarchists from the Federação Operária de Rio de Janeiro immediately declared a general strike and the poet Sylvio Figueiredo wrote the sonnet *Os Grevistas* (The Strikers):

> *São operarios, andrajosa gente*
> *que a enfermidade inexorável mina*
> *e a miséria acorrenta, impenitente,*
> *aos horrores da vida da oficina.*[89]

> Workers are a ragged bunch
> that sickness inexorably mines
> and misery shackles, unrepentant,
> to the horrors of the workshop.

More anarchist newspapers appeared in 1917, like *A Plebe* in São Paulo, edited by Leuenroth and later by Rodolfo Felipe; *O Debate* in Rio de Janeiro, founded by Adolfo Porto and Astrogildo Pereira; and *A Semana Social* in Alagoas, edited by Antônio Bernando Canelas. Leuenroth was arrested this same year for being a principal ideological promoter of the general strike. At his trial, he was brilliantly defended by Evaristo de Morais, who later wrote *O*

---

88   Dulles, *Anarchists and Communists*, 49–51.
89   Sylvio Figueiredo, *Os Gravitas* in *A Voz do Povo* (Rio de Janeiro: n.p., 1920) cited in Rodrigues, *Nacionalismo e Cultura Social.*

Anarquismo no Tribunal de Júri.[90] When the United States entered the conflict, Brazil also abandoned its neutrality in solidarity with its northern "friend." President Brás, who "seemed the most pacific of men," engaged the country in this war that was totally alien to its interests.[91] But Brazil's official actions did not detain the libertarians' antiwar campaign or diminish its support for the Russian Revolution, which they conceived as the heroic struggle against capitalism and the State, as declared on May 1, 1918 at an assembly held in the Teatro Maison Moderne in Rio de Janeiro. Nor did they stray from a constant denouncement of the scarcity of goods; Comitês Populares were formed to gather statistics on prices in relation to wages. In 1918 half of heads of households earned 80–120 milreis per month. A typical family of two parents and two children could not survive on less than 200 milreis per month, producing a deficit of 100 milreis, as the anarchists Leuenroth and Helio Negro asserted in their work *O que é o maximalismo ou bolchevismo*, published in São Paulo in 1919.[92] Misery and hunger led Manuel Campos, João Perdigão, and anarchists from Santos to plan a revolution in Rio de Janeiro.

On November 18, textile workers in Rio de Janeiro, Niteroi, and Petrópolis went on strike, a pre-arranged signal to begin the occupation of all factories and workshops, just as Italian workers inspired by Malatesta would do a few months later.[93] But in Italy the movement to occupy worksites failed due to the timidity of reformist socialists, and in Brazil it never commenced because an infiltrator had denounced the plan. Again police and army began massive repressions: anarchists' and workers' locals were shuttered, hundreds of workers arrested, and their leaders imprisoned, like Manuel Campos, Astrogildo Pereira, and José Oiticica, the man considered to be the head of the movement and the future Brazilian

---

90   Rodrigues, *Nacionalismo e Cultura Social*, 160–68.
91   Bello, *Historia da Republica*, 237.
92   Rodrigues, *Nacionalismo e Cultura Social*, 215–19.
93   See Luis Fabbri, *Malatesta: Su vida y su pensamiento* (Buenos Aires: Americalee, 1945), 146.

Lenin. Again the wounded and the dead piled up. Metal workers and bricklayers joined the strike, and munitions workers came very close.[94] Several unions (textile, metal workers, and bricklayers) were outlawed and several anarchist newspapers closed; among them was *A Liberdade*, whose editor, Pedro Matera, was detained.

Lima Barreto satirized the military, taking inspiration from French anarchist Agustin Hamon's book *La psychologie du militaire professionnel*, and Oiticica wrote his fellow prisoners a sonnet which begins thus:

> Irmãos, eu vos saúdo! Embora presos,
> Armeaçados, malditos, sem futuro,
> Temos, em nossos braços indefesos,
> Asas de Anjo e tendões de Palinuro.[95]

> Brothers, I salute you! Though imprisoned,
> Threatened, damned, without future,
> We have, in our helpless arms,
> Wings of an angel and tendons of Palinurus.

By this time Epitacio Pessoa was president of Brazil. He had served as chief of the Brazilian delegation to the Treaty of Versailles, yet had a rather keen interest in the developing and increasing the armed forces.[96]

The influence of the Russian Revolution and the prestige of its institutions were so great among Brazilian anarchists that on March 9, 1919 in the nation's capital they founded the Partido Comunista Libertario, and on June 16 in São Paulo the Liga Comunista (which soon enough became the Partido Comunista). By year's end

---

94   Carlos Augusto Addor, *A Insurreição anarquista no Rio de Janeiro* (Rio de Janeiro: n.p., 1986).
95   José Oiticica, "Aos companheiros de prisão," in *A Plebe*, 5, 3, 1919. Cited in Rodrigues, *Nacionalismo e Cultura Social*.
96   J. Pandiá Calógeras, *História dos Partidos Brasileiros* (n.p.: n.p., n.d.), 380–81.

a similar group was formed in Santos. There the battle-hardened militant João Perdigão—an anarchist to the death—was appointed first secretary. In March of the same year the basis of the Partido was drafted, forming the Partido Comunista do Brazil, and in June in Rio de Janeiro and Niteroi its first congress convened. A reading of the basis of the Partido and of its "Principles and Objectives," drafted by Oiticica and published by the anarchist newspaper *Spartacus* on August 16, 1919, leaves no doubt that the basic position of these groups was the libertarian communism of Kropotkin and Malatesta.[97] Something similar had already occurred in Mexico in the 1870s.[98] Brazilian anarchists were convinced that the Bolshevik revolution was of a libertarian character and would open the way for anarchism. They praised Lenin and Trotsky, and on May Day in Rio hailed "the triumph of their brothers in Russia."[99]

The Brazilian libertarian press expanded in 1919 with several new publications: *O Germinal* and *Spartacus* in Rio de Janeiro, *Libertas* in Belo Horizonte, *Libelo Social* in Uberaba, *A Razão* in Baurú, *O Operária* in Taubaté, *Alba Rosa* in São Paulo, and *A Voz Operária* in Campinas. Anarchists in Rio de Janeiro celebrated May Day with a large rally on the Avenida Rio Branco, and those in Santos with a huge crowd in the Plaza Iguatemy Martins, which rolled over into a spontaneous strike the next day at the docks demanding the eight-hour day. The actions lit a spark, and more strikes were held in other parts of the country—in Pelotas by seamstresses, in Porto Alegre by unions demanding the eight-hour day (resulting in several wounded and one dead), in Bahía, Minas Gerais, Vila Izabel, and Laranjerais, among other places.[100]

New libertarian publications emerged in 1920—in São Paulo, *A Patuléia*, and in Rio de Janeiro, *A Voz do Povo*, in which Fábio

---

97   Rodrigues, *Nacionalismo e Cultura Social*, 234–47. See also Dulles, *Anarchists and Communists*, 72.
98   The first association to take the name Partido Comunista Mexicano was formed by Bakuninist groups around 1878 and was short-lived. See Rama, *Historia del movimiento obrero y social latinoamericano contemporáneo*, 64.
99   Dulles, *Anarchists and Communists*, 63.
100   Rodrigues, *Nacionalismo e Cultura Social*, 267–76.

Luz, María Lacerda de Moura, and José Oiticica collaborated. The latter began to publish a series of articles titled *Mau Caminho* that critically evaluated the path of the Bolshevik revolution in light of libertarian ideas.[101] Around this time the distinction between Bolshevism and libertarian communism began to emerge in São Paulo, even though, as in Argentina, anarcho-Bolshevik groups and newspapers continued to be active through the 1920s.[102] But by 1922 "the impossibility of an organic union with Russian communism and its Red International of Labor Unions" had become clear to anarchists in the international workers' movement.[103]

In Brazil the postwar period was one of hunger and misery, and strikes were rampant. Among them the most famous occurred at Leopoldina. It would later receive a published defense by Astrogildo Pereira titled *Greve de Leopoldina*. On March 22 the Federação Operária do Rio de Janeiro called for a general strike through *A Voz do Povo*. The government responded by arresting more than a hundred anarchist militants in Rio, among them were Otávio Brandão and Fábio Luz, and about the same number in São Paulo, including Edgard Leuenroth and Hélio Negro. Many foreigners were deported on the ship *Demerara*.[104]

The Terceiro Congreso Operário convened in Rio de Janeiro between April 23 and 30, 1920, with 150 delegates from throughout the country in attendance. Anarchists like Leuenroth and João Pimenta annexed the Comissão Coordenadora to it. The dominant ideology in that Congress was anarcho-communism, as developed by Otávio Brandão (who would later cross over to Marxist-Leninism). The Liga Operária da Construção Civil of São Paulo, represented by Dioclecio Fagudes and Teófilo Ferreira, proposed

---

101 Ibid., 287–93. See also José T. Lourenço, *Maximalismo ou anarquismo* (São Paulo: n.p., 1920).

102 In Buenos Aires, for example, the newspapers *El Libertario* and *Bandera Roja* had an anarcho-Bolshevik tendency. See López and de Santillán, *El anarquismo en el movimiento obrero*, 44–45.

103 De Santillán, *La FORA*, 282.

104 Rodrigues, *Nacionalismo e Cultura Social*, 296–302; Dulles, *Anarchists and Communists*, 108–11.

joining the Congress to the Third International. But Leuenroth objected, stating that the International was not "a genuinely syndicalist organization." Astrogildo Pereira supported the objection, and then José Elías endorsed Pereira's stance.[105]

Propaganda was disseminated throughout the country by many means: speeches, discussions, and social theater were used, as well as books, pamphlets, and newspapers. Large rallies were held on May Day, 1920 in Rio de Janeiro, São Paulo, Niteroi, Curitiba, Porto Alegre, Aracayú, and other places. On that same day Florentino de Carvalho's paper *A Obra* was launched. And that same year anarchist literature was enriched with several new publications like Afonso Schmidt's *O Evangelho dos Livres*, Oiticica's *Quem os Salva*, Everardo Dias's *Jesus Cristo era Anarquista*, Brandãos' *Despertar*, and the anonymous collection of articles titled *Cancioneiro Vermelho*.[106]

At the core of anarchist groups, an intellectual movement began in 1921 that would lead to the formation of the Brazilian Communist Party, holding a Marxist-Leninist orientation. Everardo Dias, Francisco Alexandre, Alvaro Palmeira, and others formed the Grupo Clarté, fashioned after Henry Barbusse's French group of the same name. It aimed to defend the Bolshevik revolution against its many detractors. The same group of militants also formed the Comitê de Coligação Social that would function as a political party for Brazil much like the Communist Party did in Russia. Needless to say, the majority anarchist view was quite opposed to this. Syndicalist action had not diminished, and in 1921 a number of strikes were held. One by cooks in the merchant marine in Rio de Janeiro left several wounded and dead. Planning for the campaign to free Sacco and Vanzetti also began. Several libertarian newspapers appeared for the first time this year: in Ceará *A Voz do Gráfico*; in São Paulo the daily *A Vanguarda*, under Leuenroth's editorship, and *Remember*; in Rio de Janiero *A Razão* and *Renovação*, edited by Marques da Costa; and in Pernambuco *Diaro do Povo*.

---

105 Dulles, *Anarchists and Communists*, 113.
106 Rodrigues, *Nacionalismo e Cultura Social*, 307–41.

Propaganda in speeches, meetings, and other non-written media was no less rich and prolific. Suffice it to recall, for example, the speeches by Oiticica on propaganda and education at the Centro Gallego, and by Fábio Luz on Russian literature for the Comitê de Socorro aos Flagelados Rusos in Rio de Janeiro. It would be impossible here to review all the activities of 1921 by different libertarian theatrical groups—a few examples are the Grupo 1 de Maio, the Gremio Artístico Renovação, and the "Rationalist" schools. The latter were founded by various workers' associations or anarchist groups and inspired by Francisco Ferrer, like the Escóla Aperária 1 de Maio.[107]

Astrogildo Pereira, whom Dulles refers to as the "intransigent libertarian" of November 1920, the following year became attracted to Bolshevism.[108] During 1922 the core of Brazil's revolutionary left, that is, anarchists and Bolsheviks, defined their ideological positions. In a manifesto published in *A Plebe* in São Paolo on March 18, 1922 a group of militants led by Leuenroth denounced the "communism of State" that Bolsheviks sought to impose in Russia, their authoritarian and centralist politics, and the dictatorship of the proletariat, while lending its endorsement to the International Anarchist Secretariat of Switzerland, formed by the Anarchist Congress in Berlin on September 1921. A large group from Rio de Janeiro headed by Carlos Dias joined Leuenroth's critique and laid even greater stress on the difference between libertarian communism and Marxist communism.[109]

In mid-1921 an emissary from Lenin and the Russian government joined the anarchist daily in São Paulo, *A Vanguarda*, edited by Leuenroth and Ramison Soubiroff. He introduced himself as a representative of a textile mill in Manchester.[110] His purpose was to get Leuenroth to form a Bolshevik party in Brazil and to put him in charge of it. But Leuenroth was not only director of the

107 Ibid., 363–77.
108 Dulles, *Anarchists and Communists*, 137.
109 Rodrigues, *Nacionalismo e Cultura Social*, 382–99.
110 Dulles, *Anarchists and Communists*, 138.

anarchist daily, but also one of the most combative militant workers and revolutionaries in the country. He was an activist journalist, tireless orator, the inspiration behind the general strike of 1917, and, with the publication of his book on maximalism or Bolshevism co-authored with Hélio Negro, did seem to be the person most likely to provide the basis and assume the leadership of a new Leninist party. We should not forget that during this period many militant workers looked on Malatesta as the "Italian Lenin."[111] But Leuenroth had a very sharp critical spirit; he could not accept orders from the Soviet government or the twenty-one principles of the Third International without reservation. And so, in keeping with his long anarchist militancy he rejected the offer. He did support the petition by Soubiroff to appoint Astrogildo Pereira, his friend and collaborator in *A Vanguarda*, as Secretary-Founder of the new party. A short time later Pereira arrived from Rio and was introduced to Soubiroff by Leuenroth.

These men founded the Brazilian Communist Party in 1921 in a room at the Palace Hotel, 418 Florencio Abreu Street in São Paulo. Note that the members of the previous group to employ that name were actually anarchists. In any event, even in this Communist Party—joined as it was to the Soviet government, to Lenin, and to the Third International—the majority of founding members came from anarchism and not the Socialist Party as in Chile and Argentina. They were convinced that Marxist-Leninism and libertarian communism were not contrary, mutually exclusive ideologies, but instead were moments in a single process that included a temporary but necessary dictatorship of the proletariat and would culminate in a classless society without private property or the State. In March 1922 Pereira wrote in his journal *Movimento Comunista* that "Communism and the State repel each other."[112] A

---

111 See E. Malatesta, "La dittadura del Proletariato e l'Anarchia," *Volonta*, 16, 8, 1920; Vernon Richards, *Malatesta* (Buenos Aires: np.p., 1974), 317.

112 Rodrigues, *Nacionalismo e Cultura Social*, 403–420; Moniz Bandeira, Clovis Melo, and A. T. Andrade, *O Ano Vermelho. A Revolução Russa e seus reflexos no Brasil* (Rio de Janeiro: Civilização brasileira, 1967).

similar situation can be observed in the Mexican Communist Party.[113] But it is clear that Pereira and his followers, as rank and file in party discipline, quickly accommodated themselves to the concept of "democratic centralism," and postponed *sine die* the suppression of government and the State.[114] As early as March 1920 Florentino Carvalho reported in *A Plebe* that Russian anarchists were fighting against the dictatorship of the proletariat; in *A Obra* he opined that the Russian regime "is fundamentally opposed to our principles" and that a Bolshevik state in Brazil would be "an absurdity."[115]

According to José Luis Rubio, anarcho-syndicalists in Brazil, as in other Latin American countries, "at first were quite enthusiastic with the Russian Revolution but then felt defrauded by the intransigent position of the Third International, the Red International of Labor Unions, and especially by the annihilation of anarchists in the U.S.S.R."[116] In 1922 delegates from various European and Latin American countries gathered in Berlin and founded the International Workers' Association (IWA), which subsequently saw a long period of decline. At the meeting convened in Turin in 1986 the Spanish CNT, French CNT, Bulgarian CNT, FAU, NSF, USI, Dutch ASF, DAM, and a Chilean group in exile were represented, but no groups from Brazil. The Confederação Operária Brasileira (COB) did participate at the London meeting of the IWA, and a Brazilian delegation with observer status attended its meeting in Amsterdam.[117]

The great public debate between anarchists and communists began in March 1922. Pereira published in *O Movimento Comunista* an article titled "No Nos Assustemos com o Debate." At the same time, Leuenroth published a manifesto in *A Plebe* articulating the position of anarchists from São Paulo.[118] In 1923 anarchists

---

113 Godio, *Historia del movimiento obrero latinoamericano*, 96–97.

114 Pereira, *Formação do P.C.B.* (Rio de Janeiro: Victoria, 1962).

115 Dulles, *Anarchists and Communists*, 132–33.

116 Rubio, *Las internacionales obreras en América* (Madrid: ZYK, 1971), 58.

117 Fidel Gorrón Canoyra, *AIT, la Internacional desconocida* (Madrid: AIT, 1986), 8; Godio, *Historia del movimiento obrero latinoamericano*, 2, 162.

118 Dulles, *Anarchists and Communists*, 144–45.

succeeded in organizing the syndicates of Rio de Janeiro into a single federation, but communists quickly destroyed it. In 1928 anarchist syndicates had a total membership of some three thousand. Brazilian unions formed two great central organizations in 1929, the CGT, primarily communist and attached to the Red International, and the CNT, primarily anarcho-syndicalist and attached to ACAT.[119] In 1930 Getúlio Vargas came to power in Brazil through a *coup d'état*. At that time, illegal communist unions had a membership of some four thousand, and anarcho-syndicalist groups, equally illegal, had some two thousand members.[120] For the next two years Brazil experienced another strike wave, harshly repressed by the new government. Anarcho-syndicalists of the Federação Operária de São Paulo directed several of the strikes, the major one being a lengthy struggle in the textile industry.[121] Numerous anarchist and communist militants were imprisoned.[122] In 1932 the newspaper *A Plebe* once again appeared, for the first time since August 1927. In the interval anarchists in São Paulo continued their propaganda activity through pamphlets and flyers in which they denounced the exploitation of women and children in unhealthy work environments. Admittedly, there were few anarchists. They themselves conceded this point. But as Dulles points out, for anarchists social war is not a matter of mathematics.

In 1934 communists founded the Aliança Nacional Libertaria and attempted a *coup d'état* the following year. After its failure, the government imprisoned Prestes and Gregorio Bezerra in Recife, and carried out a general repression.[123] Vargas ordered that all syndicates register with the Department of Industry, Commerce, and Labor and, in spite of the objections of anarchist and communist leaders, by 1935 almost all of them had done so. According to Alba,

119 Rodrigues, *Nacionalismo e Cultura Social*, 398–99.
120 Alba, *Historia del movimiento obrero en América Latina*, 386.
121 Eduardo Ghitor, *La bancarrota del anarcosindicalismo* (Montevideo: n.p., 1932), 48.
122 Alba, *Historia del movimiento obrero en América Latina*, 387.
123 Pau de Arara, *La violencia militar en Brasil* (México: n.p., 1972), 15–16.

from that moment on it is fair to say that no other Latin American country exercised greater control and regulation of its unions than Brazil, with Argentina after Perón running a close second.[124] Vargas and his generals came close to the integralists, those Brazilian fascists whose motto "God, Nation, Home" would be reproduced by Governor Fresco from Argentina. Led by Plinio Salgado, a mediocre writer from São Paulo, the integralist movement boasted some 180,000 members in 1934 and 4,000 cells in 700 municipalities in 1937.[125] Vargas, just like Perón, was a fascist deep down, and in spite of his alleged pragmatism, held deeply corporativist convictions. And like Perón later on, Vargas was

> aware that workers were somewhat sympathetic to him and he wished to attract them. So he instituted means to secure social well being and restrictions on industry. He was thus able to practice the art of securing money from the wealthy and ensuring support from the poor under the pretense of protecting them both. That political approach led to the organization of a corporativist State, the *Estado Novo*, in accordance with ideas then in vogue while fascism was rising.[126]

Consequently, the Constitution of 1937 denied all workers' rights, and strikes were outlawed as dangerous to the supreme and sole subject of all rights: the State.[127] Nothing could be more contrary to anarcho-syndicalism, which began to decline and ceased to be an autonomous force in the workers' movement, much as in Argentina under Perón. Nonetheless, in the 1940s and up to the present

---

124 Alba, *Historia del movimiento obrero en América Latina*, 389.
125 Rogelio García Lupo, "Resurrección del fascismo favorecida por la crisis," *El Nacional*, Caracas, 7, 2, 1988.
126 Alba, *Historia del movimiento obrero en América Latina*, 387. See also John J. Johnson, *Political Change in Latin America: The Emergence of the Middle Sectors* (Stanford: Stanford University Press, 1959), 167–68.
127 Alejandro Mendible, *El ocaso del autoritarismo en Brasil*, 26–29. See also Pedro Motta Lima and José Barbosa Mello, *O nazismo no Brasil* (São Paulo: n.p., 1938).

specific groups have continued to function whose work has focused on propaganda and the dissemination of anarchist ideas through newspapers, pamphlets, and books, as well as theater and at times the schools. These groups are still located mainly in São Paulo and Rio de Janeiro. Some of the best-known militant workers and propagandists of the golden age of Brazilian anarchism, such as Leuenroth, were active in those groups, and with exemplary perseverance.

D. Literati and Propagandists

Although to a lesser extent than in Argentina and Uruguay, anarchist ideas found a receptive audience in Brazilian writers and poets of the early twentieth century. Euclides da Cunha, the celebrated author of *Os Sertões*, endorsed libertarian ideals for a period and even used the pseudonym "Proudhon." The influence of anarchist ideologues is evident in his materialist explanation of social, historical, and political phenomena.[128] Lima Barreto, as his biographer Barbosa notes, though never a militant or revolutionary, did appeal to anarchist sentiments and ideas in his work. Barbosa also records that in his youth Barreto took part in discussions on positivist philosophy but refuted Comte's ideas, including those of his Brazilian follower Benjamín Constant Botelho, and later railed against Comte's ideological influence on Floriano Peixoto's dictatorship.[129] Barreto declared himself a pacifist during the First World War and endorsed the libertarian position. In *Numa e a Ninfa* he presents an unforgiving political satire; in *Clara dos Anjos* he attacks racism. He edited the magazine *Floreal*, collaborated in *A Voz do Trabalhador* from Rio de Janeiro and also in the anti-clerical newspaper *A Lanterna* from São Paulo, using the pseudonym of Dr. Bogoloff.

---

128 On Cunha, see Eloi Pontes, *A Vida Dramática de Euclides da Cunha* (n.p., n.d.); Silvio Rabelo, *Euclides da Cunha* (n.p., n.d.); Francisco Venâncio Filho, *A Gloria de Euclides da Cunha* (n.p., n.d.).

129 Francisco de Assis Barbosa, *A vida de Lima Barreto*, (n.p., n.p., 1952), 62–64.

In addition to those works of his already mentioned, we should include *Vida e Morte de M. J. Gonzaga de Sá, Os Bruzundangas, Coisas do Reino de Jambon, Bagatelas, Feiras e Mafuás, O Cemiterio dos Vivos*, and, above all, as proof of his libertarian ideas, *Triste Fim de Policarpo Quaresma* and *Recordação do Escrivão Isaias Caminha*. David Viñas considers him a "paradigm of the libertarian intellectual."[130] Even if not strictly speaking an anarchist, Graça Aranha also expressed a number of libertarian ideas and critiques. Some consider his book *Canaã*, published in 1901, to be the first Brazilian social novel. But Graça Aranha's work, like that of Fábio Luz, suffers from an ideological scheme that gives it the appearance of an *avant la lettre* "socialist realism." In any event, Curvelo de Mendonça's narrative approach resembles Tolstoy's, particularly in his novel *Regeneração*.

In considering the anarchist or quasi-anarchist social novel we should include Domingos Ribeiro Filho, who was an active journalist, collaborator in the magazine *A Careta*, and author of *Cravo Vermelho*, published in 1906, and the historian Rocha Pombo, who wrote for *A Plebe* from São Paulo. In his beautiful book *Filhos do Povo*, Tito Batini narrates the story of a group of Italian potters based in the interior of São Paulo province who founded schools, spread libertarian ideals, and were magnificent examples of libertarian solidarity. Ranulpho Prata chronicled the exhausting labor of dockworkers from Santos in his novel *Navíos Iluminados*. It is safe to say that of those who cultivated the social novel in Brazil in the early years of the twentieth century very few escaped the influence of anarchist ideas. Suffice it to recall Aluisio de Azevedo, author of *O Cortiço*, Osvaldo de Andrade, author of *Marco Zero*, and Mario de Andrade, author of *Primeiro de Maio, O Poço, Os Condenados*, and *A Escada*.[131]

Gregorio Nazianzeno Moreira de Queiroz Vasconcelos, known by his pseudonym Neno Vasco, was, Edgar Rodrigues

---

130 Viñas, *Anarquistas en América Latina*, 95.
131 Rodrigues, *Nacionalismo e Cultura Social*, 10–13.

writes, "the great engine of anarchism in Brazil ... [and] gave it an unprecedented dissemination."[132] Vasco was born in Penafiel, Portugal in 1878, and embraced anarchism while a law student at Coimbra. He arrived in Brazil in 1901 and settled in São Paulo. His contact there with Italian anarchists engaged in active propaganda committed him to an impassioned militancy. He wrote two plays with obviously libertarian content, *Pecado de simonia* and *A greve de inquilinos*. He later published the essays "A concepção anarquista do sindicalismo" and "A porta de Europa." Dulles recounts that Vasco, also a linguist and orthographer, proposed a spelling reform of Portuguese "with changes that were later adopted by the Brazilian Academy of Letters."[133] Between 1902 and 1911, he founded the journal *Aurora* and the newspapers *O Amigo do Povo* and *A Terra Livre*. The latter, edited by Manuel Moscoso and Edgard Leuenroth, was launched on December 30, 1905, first as a bi-weekly and then as a weekly. It was one of the best known and most influential libertarian publications. Among its collaborators were Paulo Berthelot, Salvador Alacid, Motta Assunção, and other prominent journalists of the period. Vasco returned to his native land in 1910 and died in São Ramão de Coronada in 1920.

Fábio Lopes dos Santos Luz was born in Valença in the province of Bahía on July 31, 1864, went to secondary schools in Salvador, and pursued medical studies between 1883 and 1887 in the famous local faculty. He practiced medicine in Rio de Janeiro and was also a teacher, school inspector, journalist, and member of the Carioca Academy of Letters. At the same time, he was one of the greatest figures in Brazilian anarchism.[134] He was among the first in Brazil to write social novels, publishing *O Ideólogo* in 1903, *Os Emancipados* in 1906, *Virgem Me* in 1910, and *Elias Barrão-Chica María* in 1915. He also wrote plays such as *Graças a Deus*, historical-literary essays, such as *Estudos de Literatura* and *A Paisagem no Conto, na Novela e no Romance*, and social criticism, like

---

132   Rodrigues, *Socialismo e Sindicalismo no Brasil*, 101.
133   Dulles, *Anarchists and Communists*, 21.
134   Edgar Rodrigues, "El anarquista Fabio Luz," *Orto*, Barcelona, 46, 6–7.

A Internacional Negra and *A Tuberculose do Ponto de vista social*, among others. His journalism appeared in *Jornal do Comercio*, *O Pais*, *Jornal do Brasil*, *A Folha*, *A Manhã*, *Correio do Brasil*, and especially in the anarchist newspapers *A Plebe*, *O Amigo do Povo*, and *A Internacional*. As an educator he promoted the creation of Cajas Escolares and fought furiously against the obsolete teaching methods that lingered from the days of slavery. The style of his novels may be described as the romance-essay, in which sociological theories and political, economic, and religious theses prevail over narrative elements such as trauma and character development. It follows the style of Graça Aranha, which in turn comes from the Russian novelists.[135]

José Oiticica—poet, literary critic, and dramatist—was born in Oliveira, Minas Gerais in 1882 and was an active anarchist militant from 1912 on. In 1913 he joined the workers' movement and took part in meetings and strikes until 1918 when, on account of that participation, he was confined to Alagoas. Dulles writes: "When anarchists met to discuss tactics, propaganda, and doctrine, Oiticica had much to say. An indefatigable scholar, he was inclined to present lengthy expositions on the philosophy of anarchism. Oiticica sought to educate and uplift workers."[136] In 1916 he was named professor of Portuguese in Rio de Janeiro's distinguished Pedro II School. In 1919 he edited the newspaper *Spartacus*, with the assistance of Astrogildo Pereira, who as already noted would be the future founder of the Brazilian Communist Party. In 1924 during the dictatorship of Bernardes he was imprisoned in the island Flores, and while there wrote his work *A Doutrina Anarquista ao Alcance de Todos*. Later he was appointed lecturer of language and literature at the University of Hamburg, and on his return from Germany he and a group of anarchists including María Lacerda de Moura, founded the Liga Anticlerical, soon raided by Gatúlio Varga's police.

---

135   Cedro Pedro Luft, Diccionário de Literatura Portuguesa e Brasileira (Porto Alegre: n.p., 1973), 189. See also Lúcia Miguel Pereira, *Prosa de Ficco (de 1870 a 1920)* (Rio de Janeiro: n.p., 1950).
136   Dulles, *Anarchists and Communists*, 35.

Oiticica has been accused of being paternalistic and anti-Semitic.[137] We should not forget that a certain amount of anti-Semitism is easily detected in the European Left as a whole during the Dreyfus affair, and not even Bakunin and Proudhon, nor Blanqui and Marx, escape the period untainted. Rodrigues writes: "Oiticica was a courageous polemicist. Many felt the power of ideas from the professorate through his voice in newspapers and books."[138] He was editor of the newspaper *Ação Direta*, left behind a series of books and pamphlets, among which we find *Quem nos salva, Pedra que role*, and published no fewer than 1,500 articles in the anarchist press.

Avelino Foscolo, the anarchist from Minas Gerais who was also a pharmacist, dramatist, and journalist, is considered by the critic Fábio Lucas to be the first writer to introduce the social novel in Brazil.[139] His first social novel, *O Mestiço,* published in 1903, was followed by *Vulção* and *A Capital.* In addition he wrote such dramas as *O Semeador.* Also employing the style of the social novel and influenced by anarchist ideas was Lauro Palhano's *O Gororoba,* which recounts the life of a construction worker building railroad lines across the jungle.[140]

Like Argentina and Uruguay, Brazil did not lack for libertarian poets in the early twentieth century. Among them we count the physician and active militant Martins Fontes, who left us several collections of poetry such as *Vulcão Fantásticos*, and the lawyer Ricardo Gonçalves, author of a volume of verse titled *Ipês* and the well-known poem *Rebelião*:

> *Com gemidos agoureiros,*
> *Num pavoroso lamento,*
> *Láfor a perpassa o vento*

---

137 Paul Avrich, "Los anarquistas del Brasil," *Reconstruir*, 100, 56.

138 Rodrigues, *Socialismo e Sindicalismo no Brasil*, 313–14. In 1970, Roberto das Neves edited an anthology of the best articles by Oiticica published in the Brazilian press titled *Ação Direta* (Rio de Janeiro: Editorial Germinal, 1970).

139 Lucas, *O caráter social da literature brasileira* (Rio de Janeiro: Paz e Terra, 1970).

140 Rodrigues, *Nacionalismo e cultura social*, 14.

Chicoteando os pinheiros.
E a morte, caliginosa,
De uma tristeza superna,
É como a boca monstruosa
De uma monstruosa caverna...
E quando comece a luta,
Quando explodir a tormenta,

A Sociedade corrupta,
Execrável e violenta,
Iníqua, vil, criminosa,
Há de cair aos pedaços,
Há de voar em estilhaços
Numa ruina espantosa.

With moans foretelling
In a dreadful lament,
Outside the wind passes by
Whipping the pines.
And the dark death,
Of a supernal sadness,
Is like a monstrous mouth
Of a monstrous cave...
And when the fight begins,
When the storm erupts,

The corrupt society,
Despicable and violent,
Unjust, vile, criminal,
Shall fall to pieces
Shall shatter like fragments
In a frightening ruin.

Gonçalves committed suicide. On that occasion, Monteiro Lobato wrote:

Ricardo killed himself. What can we say about it? The words
that come to me are the same that would come to you, for we
are and forever will be his brothers. The world seems small-
er, Rangel, and I cry and cry. Everything is diminished with
Ricardo's absence. Everything is older, more despicable and
ruinous. I have his portrait before me. That sad expression in
his gaze is so anticipatory of the gunshot. Each time I look at
him I feel my soul rolled into a ball. I feel a great pain inside.
Ricardo, our marvelous Ricardito, dead, covered in dirt, rot-
ting. Dead! Extinct! That light of supernatural goodness and
intelligence is now extinguished. The biggest heart the world
has ever seen has now ceased.[141]

We should briefly mention the journalist and pedagogue Mo-
acir Caminha (1890–1963). From the first decade of the twentieth
century he was attached to anarchist ideas, directed the newspaper
O Regenerador in Fortaleza, promoted Esperanto, and authored a
number of pamphlets, including *Curso Popular de Sociología,* published in 1945.

Among the most active ideologists and propagandists were the
physician Reinaldo F. Greyer (pseudo. Pedro Ferreira da Silva), author of *Cooperativa sem Lucros* and *Eu Creio na Humanidade,* and
Carlos Boscolo, who wrote *Verdades sociais.*

There were a number of women in Brazil whose militancy was
outstanding, as there were in Argentina, Uruguay, Bolivia, and other countries. The best known is perhaps Maria Lacerda de Moura, a
teacher, speaker, and writer from Minas Gerais. She is the author of
Fraternidade da Escola, Serviço Militar Obrigatorio para a Mulher,
and *A Mulher e uma Degenerada,* among other works.[142]

---

141 Rodrigues, *Socialismo e Sindicalismo no Brasil,* 90–94.
142 Antonio Arnoni Prado and Francisco Foot Hardman published in 1985
     an anthology of libertarian prose from Brazil titled *Contos anarquistas,
     1901–1935* (São Paulo: Editora Brasiliense, 1985). It includes works by
     Mota Assunção, Astrogildo Pereira, Avelino Fóscolo, Fabio Luz, José Oi-
     ticica, Neno Vasco, Gigi Damiani, Lucioano Campagnoli, Everardo Dias,
     Florentino de Carvalho, Maria Lacerda de Moura, and others.

Other anarchist writers or those positioned close to anarchism on account of their libertarian socialism are the following: Joaquim Ribeiro, author of *Democracia libertaria*; Héron Pinto, who published an interesting account of police methods during the Vargas dictatorship titled *Nos Subterraneos do Estado Novo*; Ercilio Nogueira, author of a work titled *Virginidade Inútil e Anti-Higienica*; Jacobo Penteado, biographer of Martins Fontes; and Castro Alves, who wrote *Espumas Flutuantes* and *Navio Negreiro*.

Plinio Salgado, leader of the movement for integralism, an admirer of Mussolini and presumed Brazilian duce, wrote a life of Jesus interpreting him as a precursor to fascism. At the other extreme Aníbal Vaz de Melo also published a work on Jesus titled *Cristo, o Maior dos Anarquistas*, and Everardo Diaz published the pamphlet *Jesuscristo era anarquista*, later translated into Spanish. In 1920 the poet Sylvio Figueiredo published a sonnet titled "Jesus Cristo" in *A Voz do Povo*. Here are the opening lines:

> *Grande Anarquista! O pálida figura*
> *de rebelado que, entre gente insana,*
> *ousaste erguer, como una durindana,*
> *o ingente brado contra a escravatura*
> *e que, em contraste á podridão romana*
> *e do opulento á orgia asquerosa e impura*
> *sonhaste um dia a universal ventura,*
> *a libertade e a redençao humana.*[143]

> Great anarchist! Oh pale figure
> of rebellion among insane people,
> you dared to raise, like a Durindana,
> a massive cry against slavery
> and, in contrast to Roman rot

---

143   Rodrigues, *Nacionalismo e cultura social*, 287.

and the opulent, disgusting and impure orgy,
you dreamed of a day of universal happiness,
and the freedom and redemption of humanity.

There were more than a few anarchists, among them some of
the most active and brilliant, that crossed over to the Bolsheviks and
then brutally attacked the very movement they had served. Suffice
it to mention Otávio Brandão and Astrogildo Pereira, author of
Formação do PCB, A Greve de Leopoldina, and editor of several
newspapers like *A Guerra Social, Crónica Subversiva, O Germinal,
Spartacus, Movimiento Comunista*, and others.

Astrogildo Pereira was born in Rio Bonito, a province of São
Paulo. He studied at the Jesuit school Colegio Anchieta de Nova
Friburgo and thought about becoming a monk. Later he studied at
the Colegio Abilio de Niteroi. He was a great admirer of the novelist Machado de Assis and was at the bedside of the dying author.[144]
Unlike Pereira, Edgard Leuenroth remained a lifelong anarchist.
He was editor of *A Lanterna*, the anti-clerical publication, and of *A
Vanguarda*, the anarchist daily from Rio de Janeiro. He compiled
an anthology of writings on anarchism published a few years before
his death, and wrote several popular books and pamphlets of ideological analysis such as *Anarquismo-Roteiro da Libertação Social*
and *O que é Maximalismo ou Bolshevismo* with Hélio Negro. The
gaucho engineer Orlando Corrêa Lopes was school superintendent
of Visconde de Mauá. He was a combative libertarian. In 1913 he
wrote the famous article "Congresso ou Manicomio," published in
A Epoca in Rio de Janeiro, in which he trashed the maneuvers of
Hermes de Fonseca and his deputies' against the rights of the working class.

Among foreigners who promoted anarchist syndicalism were
the Uruguayan Santos Antonio Vidal, the Peruvian Carlos Zebal-
lo, and, above all, the Spaniard Primitivo Raimundo Suárez, better
known by his pseudonym Florentino de Carvalho. The latter was

---

144   Dulles, *Anarchists and Communists*, 34.

7. Brazil

born in Oviedo, Spain in 1871, and migrated with his parents to Brazil as a child. Beginning in 1902 he was active in the International in the port city of Santos; he was exiled to Portugal in 1910. He edited various anarchist newspapers such as *Nova Era*, *A Plebe*, *O Libertario*, and various other publications like *A Obra*, and he published several books, including *Da Escravidão a Liberdade* in 1927 and *A Guerra Civil* in 1932. He died in 1947. Carvalho defended a conception of anarchism that is open and non-dogmatic:

> Anarchism is not a body of definitive and dogmatic doctrines but a libertarian and progressive premise that continually enriches itself with scientific elements and philosophical conceptions. But its essence is immutable.[145]

Another Spaniard by birth was João Perdigão Gutiérrez, originally from the Canary Islands. He was illiterate but came to acquire a solid cultural foundation through union and libertarian circles, and directed *O Sindicalista*, the official journal of the Federação Operária do Rio de Grande do Sul. The Spanish worker José Martins was an active militant in Brazil's anarchist movement and authored an extensive work, with a prologue by Oiticica, called *Historia das Riquezas do Clero Católico e Protestante*. Finally, Everardo Dias, also a Spaniard, arrived in Brazil as a boy in 1887. He collaborated with Oreste Ristori and Benjamin Mota in the anti-clerical struggle, was an editor of the bi-weekly *O Livre Pensador*, and author of several books, including *Perpetuidade do Erro e da Mentira* and *A Luta Socialista Revolucionaria*.[146]

---

145 Quoted in Rodrigues, *Socialismo e Sindicalismo no Brasil*, 267–69. Also see Dulles, *Anarchists and Communists*, 20.

146 Avrich, "Los anarquistas del Brasil," 55. See also *Libertarios no Brasil* (São Paulo: n.p., 1986); *Libertarios e militantes* (Campinas: n.p., 1985); Edgar Rodrigues, *Os Libertarios* (Petrópolis: Vozes, 1988).

8. Ecuador, Colombia, and Venezuela

A. Ecuador

The first attempt to organize workers in Ecuador began after the Liberal Revolution of 1895 and the government of Eloy Alfaro. It coincided with the beginning of industrialization, the rise of the bourgeoisie at the expense of the feudal landowners, and the emergence of lay culture.

The reformist Partido Liberal Obrero was founded in 1906 and it opposed the pro-capitalist politics of the Partido Liberal Radical. At about the same time, on December 31, 1905, the Confederación Obrera del Ecuador was founded in Guayaquil, sharing the ideological orientation of the Partido Liberal Obrero. The Cuban anarchist Miguel Albuquerque became quite prominent in Ecuador at this time. He had gone there seeking assistance for the independence war in his country, but stayed as he became involved in Ecuadorian social and political struggles. He founded the Sociedad de Hijos del Trabajo in 1896.[1] Anarchist groups soon formed, perhaps, as Victor Alba believes, influenced by González Prada. The first strikes, including one by graphic workers in 1919 and the general strike of Guayaquil in 1922, were undoubtedly promoted by anarcho-syndicalists, as Agustín Cuevas writes in his book *Ecuador: 1925–1975*. The Centro de Estudios Sociales, founded in Guayaquil in 1910, held a libertarian orientation.[2]

In 1920 anarchist militants founded the Centro Gremial Sindicalista (CGS). Its stated purpose was to

> liberate all the oppressed of the earth by bringing them into a libertarian syndicate that will replace the present system, and opposing all political and religious doctrines as destructive and prejudicial to the rights and aspirations of workers.[3]

The Centro Gremial published the newspaper *El Proletario*. At the same time, the Sociedad Cosmopolita de Cacahueros "Tómas Briones" put out *El Cacahuero*, the union's official publication promoting libertarian ideas. The newspaper *Bandera Roja* appeared in 1920 and displayed a mixture of anarcho-syndicalist and Spartacist ideas not totally unusual in Latin America.[4]

Max Nettlau identified an undeveloped anarcho-syndicalist propaganda in a 1912 article published in *La Prensa*, a democratic daily in Quito. But the first truly libertarian newspaper, *Redención*, appeared in 1922 in Guayaquil. Several others followed, like *Luz y Acción* in 1929. According to Nettlau, in 1934 an article in the

---

1   E. Muñoz Vicuña and L. Vicuña Izquierdo, "Historia del movimiento obrero del Ecuador (Resumen)," in P. González Casanova, *Historia del movimiento obrero en América Latina* (n.p.: n.p., n.d.), 3, 205.

2   Alba, *Historia del movimiento obrero en América Latina*, 104–05. See also *El anarquismo en el Ecuador* (Quito: n.p., 1986).

3   Alejo Capelo Cabello, *Una jornada sangrienta (15 de noviembre de 1922)* (Guayaquil: n.p., 1973), 36.

4   P. Ycasa Cortes, "Aportes para la historia del movimiento obrero ecuatoriano," *Lombardismo y sindicatos en América Latina* (México: Ediciones Nueva Sociologia, 1982), 332.

Barcelona paper *La Revista Blanca* referred to a new libertarian generation in Ecuador.[5] However, in the 1930s Marxist-Leninism began to gain ground among workers' groups and Ecuadorian intellectuals. Mariátegui held great influence with his journal *Amauta*. At the Primera Conferencia Latinoamericana de los Partidos Comunistas, convened in Buenos Aires on June 12, 1929, it was reported that in Ecuador "the Partido Socialista was gradually becoming the Partido Comunista."[6]

The creation of a unified anti-fascist front and concentration of Leftist political parties served the interests of Marxist-Leninists, who advanced at the expense of reformist socialists and libertarian groups.[7] In spite of that, anarchist action was not altogether annulled. Its influence has extended even into recent years among several workers' organizations, especially Federación de Guayas.

Among writers in the early twentieth century, more than a few identified themselves as anarchists, like Luis A. Martínez, who made clear his ideology in his book *A la Costa*, published in 1904. Viñas mentions Emilio Gallegos del Campo, "with his brother Joaquín, founder of a journal that was among the most representative of Ecuadorian Rubenism, *América Modernista*, published in Guayaquil" and who "from a libertarian viewpoint wrote two plays containing workers, strikes, clenched fists, and multiple allusions to 'auroras and idealist Russian princes': *Crimen social* in 1905 and *Honra de obrero* in 1911."[8]

B. Colombia

Colombia was the only Latin American republic visited by two of the most important figures of nineteenth century anarchism, Élisée

---

5   Nettlau, "Viaje libertario," *Reconstruir*, 77, 39.

6   Muñoz Vicuña, "Historia del movimiento obrero del Ecuador (Resumen)," 216.

7   Ibid., 218–22.

8   Viñas, *Anarquistas en América Latina*, 116.

Reclus and Mikhail Bakunin. But neither travelled there with the aim of agitating or spreading propaganda. One of the most distinguished European geographers of his time, Reclus travelled to Colombia for strictly scientific purposes in 1855.[9] That trip produced the book titled *Voyage à la Sierra-Nevada de Sainte-Marthe*, later published in Spanish as *Mis exploraciones en América*. Additionally, as Muñoz notes, the first volume of Reclus' *Correspondencia*, covering the period from 1850 to 1870, contains much information on Nueva Granada.[10]

Bakunin, for his part, stayed only a few days in the Panamanian isthmus in 1861, when that territory was part of the Republic of Colombia. After his fantastic escape from Siberia through Japan and the Pacific Ocean to the United States, on October 21 of that year he sailed from San Francisco to Panama. Fifteen days later, on November 6, after crossing the isthmus he sailed from Aspinwall-Colón, Panama to New York and in a short time he travelled to London.[11] He did not pursue any conspiratorial or propaganda activity in Panama or New York, nor can we say that he left any seeds of anarchism there, as he was yet not an anarchist, strictly speaking.[12]

In Colombia, as in nearly every Latin American country, there were some expressions of utopian socialism in the mid-nineteenth century and collaborations with "artisans' struggles against the eroding effects of free trade."[13]

---

9   About Reclus, Nettlau has written a biography titled *Eliseo Reclus: La vida de un sabio justo y rebelde* (Buenos Aires: Ediciones La Protesta, 1928).

10   Nettlau, "Viaje libertario," 39; Muñoz Vicuña, "Historia del movimiento obrero del Ecuador," 44.

11   E. H. Carr, *Bakunin* (Barcelona: Grijalbo, 1970), 258–59.

12   On Bakunin see: H. E. Kaminski, *Michel Bakounine: La Vie d'un révolutionaire* (Paris: n.p., 1974); James Guillaume, *L'Internationale: Documents et souvenirs 1864–1878* (Paris: n.p., 1905–1910); Arthur Lehning, *Conversaciones con Bakunin* (Barcelona: Anagrama, 1978); Jean-Marie, *Michel Bakounine. Une vie d'homme* (Genève: Noir, 1976); Max Nattlau, *Miguel Bakunin, la Internacional y la Alianza en España* (Buenos Aires: La Protesta, 1925).

13   Enrique Valencia, "El movimiento obrero columbiano," in P. González

Although there were no resistance societies or syndicates in Colombia prior to 1910, we are aware that beginning in the twentieth
century anarchist ideas had many sympathizers among students, the
literati, artists, and workers. Militant anarcho-syndicalists organized
the first workers' societies. They promoted the mass demonstration of May 15, 1916 that was violently repressed by police. They
encouraged the strike among port workers in Cartagena in 1920.[14]
Along with Marxist socialists they brought a high degree of militancy to many of the activities carried out by Colombian workers
between 1910 and 1930, especially on the Atlantic coast, "which by
virtue of its geographic location was less isolated than the rest of the
country." Militant anarchists took part in the Barranquilla strike of
1910; in the broad movement that developed in 1918 in Cartagena,
Barranquilla, and Santa Marta; in the first strike against the United
Fruit Company in the banana region of Santa Marta in 1918; in the
railroad strike in Girardot and the laborers' and artisans' strike in
Bogotá in 1919; in the strikes of 1924 and 1927 in Barrancabermeja;
in the strike against the Tropical Oil Company, resulting in the firing
of 1,200 workers and a declaration of war against the organizers; in
the second strike in Santa Marta in 1928 that ended in a grand massacre; and in more limited activities as well. [15]

Nettlau's inventory of anarchist publications in Colombia
during the 1920s includes *Organización* in Santa Marta in 1925 and
Vía Libre in Barranquilla in 1926. He also records that after the
great banana strike at the end of 1928 in Magdalena and the massacre in Ciénega "there was no longer any talk of anarchist activities in Colombia nor of any apolitical unionist struggles, whether
because of the harshness of repressions or the presence of Bolsheviks." He also mentions the writer and professor Juan Francisco

Casanova, *Historia del movimiento obrero en América Latina*, 3, 13. In
1913 the Unión Obrera was formed.

14   Alba, *Historia del movimiento obrero en América Latina*, 105.
15   Alvaro Tirado Mejia, *Columbia: siglo y medio de bipartidismo,* cited in
      ibid. In 1925 the Grupo Sindicalista Antorcha Libertaria published *Voz
      popular*. Gerardo Gómez, Carlos F. León, Pedro E. Rojas, and others fre-
      quently wrote for it.

Moncaleano who published the anarchist paper *Pluma Roja* in Los Angeles starting in 1919.

It is doubtful, however, that the writer Vargas Vila can be considered an anarchist. Nettlau opines that his political and social writings present "an important document on domination and victimization in Latin America," although many of his literary characters like Carlyle, Hello, Leon Bloy, and others are not themselves anarchists, strictly speaking. Vargas Vila's tendencies toward anarchism, real or imagined, were the subject of much discussion in *La Revista Blanca* in 1924 and 1925.[16] In fact, his poetic archetype seemed to have been D'Annunzio and his philosophical mentor Nietzsche, although he lacked the richness of the former and the depth of the latter. Rafael Barrett, undoubtedly an anarchist and critic of good taste, referred to some of Vargas Vila's work as there being "nothing more boring, more false, more insignificant." And about his style Barrett says: "Vargas Vila's construction suffers from a hypertrophy of violent and vacuous epithets and of dislocated antithesis. It gives the impression of the maniacal gestures of an alcoholic." He acknowledged, however, that in Vila's work "every once in a while a bit of beauty peeks in."[17] In another essay titled "Sobre Vargas Vila y el decadentismo," after alluding to the emotions the verses of Baudelaire, Verlaine, and Rubén Darío awakened in him, Barrett writes: "Very well, Vargas Vila bores me, bothers me, and afflicts me." He likened the writer's work to an illegitimate transplant, a "mass of plunder brought from afar and spoiled in the transport producing an appalling sight of infection to good taste."[18] In fairness we should say that elevating art to the absolute, to erotic obsession, to a fantasy lying between the desperate and the salacious is not a literary feature common to anarchist writers of that period, even when there is sufficient reason to attract the *odium theologicum* of vernacular critics.[19]

---

16   Nettlau, "Viaje libertario," 40.
17   Barrett, *Obras Completas*, III (Buenos Aires: Americalee, 1954), 171.
18   Ibid., 175–76.
19   See Antonio Curcio Altamar, *Evolución de la novela en Columbia* (Bogotá:

Nor can we seriously say that Guillermo Valencia was an anarchist writer. To be sure, as Viñas writes, "his poem 'Anarkos' (as popular in its time as Campoamor's 'El tren expreso' or Bécquer's 'Las golondrinas' were in different historical periods) by appealing to the series of recourses of the libertarian orator achieved an uncommon popular following."[20] It is true that this famous composition—the profundity and form of which recall Victor Hugo, according to Gómez Restrepo—has verses worthy of Ghiraldo's raucous muse:

> *Son los siervos del pan: fecunda horda*
> *que llena el mundo de vencidos. Llama*
> *ávida de lamer. Tormenta sorda*
> *que sobre el Orbe enloquecido brama.*
>
> *Y son sus hijos pálidas legiones*
> *de espectros que en la noche de sus cuevas*
> *al ritmo de sus tristes corazones,*
> *viven soñando con auroras nuevas*
> *de un sol de amor en mística alborada,*
> *y, sin que llegue la mentida crisis,*
> *en medio de su mísera nidada*
> *¡los degüellan las ráfagas de tisis!*

They are the servants of bread: fruitful horde
that fills the world with the vanquished. A flame
eager to be licked. A deaf storm
that howls over the insane globe.

And their children are pale legions
of ghosts who, in the darkness of their caves
to the rhythm of their sad hearts
live dreaming of fresh auroras

Instituto Caro y Cuervo, 1957), 197–202.

20   Viñas, *Anarquistas en América Latina*, 105.

> of a sun of love in a mystic dawn
> and, without the coming of a false crisis,
> in the midst of their miserable brood
> the rush of sickness beheads them!

But the author of "Anarkos," considered a major Colombian lyrist of the twentieth century, produced many other celebrated works—for example, "Moisés," "Homero," "La tristeza de Goethe," "Alma Mater," "Caballeros teutones"—in which libertarian genealogy made only a fleeting appearance and only as the brilliant guest of a patrician who tolerates its ideological exoticisms.[21] Valencia's poems are dedicated to politicians, landowners, and monsignors. How could it be otherwise from someone who was a diplomat, a functionary, and twice a presidential candidate? "Anarkos" is nothing more than a rhetorical exercise in the fashion of the day.

C. Venezuela

There were never any anarchist organizations, workers' societies, or newspapers in Venezuela. Nonetheless, at the unusually early date of 1810, in the bosom of the Junta Patriótica and speaking against the orators who "combated federalism and pointed to it as a form of anarchist dissent," Coto Paúl declared:

> Anarchy! It is liberty that unties the shackles of tyranny. Anarchy! When the gods of the weak mistrust and curse it dreadfully, I bow to it on my knees. Sirs! May anarchy guide us to Congress with that burning flame of the furies in our hands, and may its smoke intoxicate those partisans of order and lead them to follow it through the streets and plazas yelling "Liberty!"[22]

---

21   José Ortega, *Historia de la literatura columbiana* (Bogotá: n.p., 1935), 809 *et seq.*

22   José Gil Fortoul, *Historia Constitucional de Venezuela* (Caracas: Libreria

Paúl's words should not be interpreted as a mere outpouring of uncritical juvenile sentiment, or as pure rhetoric, as they sometimes have. They bring forth a precise conception of individual liberties against the State as articulated by various Leftist figures of the French Revolution, such as Sylvain Maréchal, who may have inspired Paúl. We cannot say with certainty that because Paúl yelled "Long Live Anarchy!" he was an anarchist. After all, Proudhon would not be around for another couple of decades. But we should place him in tune with Godwin's ideas, at the threshold of anarchism.

Proudhon's ideas were known in Venezuela from the days of Fermín Toro. Rafael María Baralt often cited the French anarchist, especially in the writings from his Spanish period. Moreover, Baralt knew him personally. At the same time, Toro and other writers of the period accepted the ideas of utopian socialists and constructed a mindset in which political federalism was joined to vague socialist aspirations. In 1847 Guillermo Iribarren proposed a kind of reformist socialism, perhaps inspired by Luis Blanc, and commissioned the translation of Wolowski's *De l'organisation du travail*. Fourier's ideas and those of other socialists were certainly present in the writings of Simón Rodríguez, especially in his pedagogical ones. Manuel Díaz Rodríguez says that Simón Rodríguez's contemporaries misunderstood him "because he brought to the America of his time the European socialism of today."[23] The Frenchman Pierre Cerreau, arriving in Venezuela after the failure of the Revolution of 1848 in France, published in La Victoria the *Credo Igualitario*, a newspaper inspired by Babeuf's communism.

Ezequiel Zamora's friendship with José María García, and their discussions inside and outside university classrooms on the "philosophical principles of equality," explains the youthful admiration the future "head of the sovereign people" held for Babeuf, "whose achievements he aspired to emulate."[24] Later, in 1849, Zamora dis-

---

Piñango, 1967), I, 225. Juan Vicente González, *Biografía de José Félix Ribas* (Caracas: n.p., n.d.), 46.

23   Manuel Díaz Rodriguez, *Sangre patricia* (Caracas: Monte Avila, 1972), 71.

24   Federico Díaz Figueroa, *Tiempo de Ezequiel Zamora* (Caracas: Ediciones

cussed with José Brandford and Luciano Requena the Revolution of 1848 in France, the "social republic," and especially Blanqui,[25] the social revolutionary who, in spite of his centrism, had some likeness to Bakunin.[26] Brito Figueroa writes: "After 1851 Zamora broadened his political culture and came close to socialist utopian conceptions due to the relations he had established with the insurrectionists of June 1848 who had taken refuge in Venezuela."[27] Zamora learned of Proudhon's ideas through Brandford and the lawyer Francisco J. Iriate, and the three discussed his theory of property. Brito Figueroa explains:

> Zamora held that in nature *the earth belongs to no one: it is everyone's by use and custom;* and that before the arrival of the Spaniards, the grandfathers of today's Goths, the earth was held in common, like the water, the air, and the sun. Brandford argued that it is certain that someone stole what did not belong to him but belongs to all, and in this way Proudhon was right to declare that property is theft.[28]

In 1852, before Colombia's civil war, known as the Federal War, a volume titled *Análisis del socialismo y exposición clara, metódica e imparcial de los principales socialistas antiguos y modernos y con especialidad los de Saint-Simon, Fourier, Owen, F. Leroux y Proudhon* appeared in Caracas. It aimed to be a didactic and objective synthesis of modern socialist doctrines, and introduced Hispanic American peoples to the social philosophy being discussed in Europe and especially in France during the latter half of the nineteenth century. But forgetting its pedagogical aim, the work concluded, as Carrera Damas writes, with "a fiery argument, almost a manifesto on behalf

---

de la Biblioteca U.C.V., 1982), 32–56.
25   Ibid., 239.
26   See Alan B. Spitzer, *The Revolutionary Theories of Louis Auguste Blanqui* (NY: Columbia University Press, 1957).
27   Brito Figueroa, *Tiempo de Ezequiel Zamora*, 250.
28   Ibid., 346.

of the socialist cause."[29] It is important to underscore the fact that this publication gave the Venezuelan reader access for the first time to a relatively systematic presentation of the social philosophy of Proudhon, who is widely considered the first anarchist. The argument and exposition raised fears and adverse reactions among the propertied classes. Several journalistic versions of the book were produced. Three years later Ramón Ramírez, an apologist for Western and Christian civilization, argued that socialism as presented in Proudhon's work destroys private property (the sacrosanct basis of society and culture) in a work titled *El cristianismo y la libertad: Ensayo sobre la civilización americana*.[30]

The ideas of Bakunin and Kropotkin arrived in Caracas after the Federal War in French and Spanish books that were read by intellectuals and, quite unusually, by workers. The poet and novelist from Caracas Miguel Eduardo Pardo was said by a contemporary critic to belong "to the club of haters, that is, of those nonconformists with society that is their fate either to live or flee."[31] His novel *Todo un pueblo* takes place in Caracas at the end of the nineteenth century and presents a discussion between two young intellectuals in which one affirmed that "Jesus was not only a demagogue but also the first apostle of anarchism," that Ravachol, Vaillant, and Pallás were saints and carried Jesus in their hearts, and that Ravachol was not an ordinary assassin who defiled cadavers, "but an extraordinary being, perhaps greater than Jesus himself."[32] Allusions of this kind were not rare in Venezuelan literature of the period, and they demonstrate that by now cultured audiences had a certain interest in anarchist doctrines. In one turn of his zigzagging ideological trajectory Rufino Blanco stumbled upon Spanish anarchism, but it proved difficult to believe that he ever identified with

---

29   G. Carrera Damas, *Para la historia de los orígenes del socialismo en Venezuela,* "Critica história" (Caracas: n.p., 1960), 125.

30   Carrera Damas, *Temas de historia socal y de las ideas* (Caracas: n.p., 1969), 159.

31   José Antonio Castro, "Miguel Eduardo Pardo y el club de los odiantes," Prologue to *Todo un pueblo* (Caracas: Monte Avila, 1981), i.

32   Pardo, *Todo un pueblo,* 44.

it. Carlos Brandt, for his part, collaborated with *Estudios, Tiempos Modernos,* and other organs of the Spanish libertarian press.[33]

There was never an organized anarchist movement in Venezuela, as already noted, nor workers' societies organized around anarcho-syndicalist ideas. This may be explained, in part, by the lengthy dictatorship between 1899 and 1935. J. Fanny Simon wrote: "The dictatorship of Juan Vicente Gómez was hardly fertile soil for any kind of workers' unions, and certainly not for those controlled by anarchists." European immigration was meager, nothing comparable to what was then happening in the Southern Cone. "Nonetheless," Viñas observes, "if we take into account the activity of anarchists in other countries under dictatorial rule it is not hard to believe that anarcho-syndicalists played a role in the organization of unions that came to form the Unión Obrera Venezolana in 1923."[34]

In 1864 Valentín Espinal founded the first artisanal society in Caracas.[35] In addition to the agricultural peasant, who despite receiving a salary still labored in semi-feudal conditions, in the second half of the nineteenth century there arose a rural proletariat of muleteers and transport workers, a mining proletariat in Guayana, a dockworkers' proletariat and, after 1885, a relatively numerous sector of railroad workers.[36]

Several refugees of the Paris Commune, among whom there were likely a few Proudhonian anarchists, arrived in Caracas and founded an underground Venezuelan section of the International, which continued to function at least until 1893 when it sent a communiqué signed by the workers Bruni Rösner, H. Wilhof, and A. Picehn to the congress in Zurich.[37] In contrast to what occurred in

---

33 Victor García, "El anarquismo en Venezuela" in *Tierra y Libertad,* 459, México, 14.

34 Viñas, *Anarquistas en América Latina,* 111.

35 Pedro Bernardo Salinas, *Retrospección laboral* (Caracas: n.p., 1971), 34.

36 Luis Vitale, *Sobre el movimiento obrero venezolano* (Caracas: n.p., 1968, 1978), 8–9. Domingo Alberto Rangel, *El proceso del capitalismo contemporáneo en Venezuela* (Caracas: n.p., 1968), 58.

37 Brito Figueroa, *Las repercusiones de la Revolución Socialista de octubre de*

the Río de la Plata region, the Venezuelan section was not able to reach the workers of the country, but remained limited to a small circle of French and Swiss workers and died along with them. The communiqué to the 1893 Congress indicates that at that point the section had a reformist character and adhered to the Second International. The Venezuelan Primer Congreso Obrero also seems to have been reformist. It convened on October 28, 1896 in the library Obreros del Provenis in Caracas, and affirmed the necessity of forming a workers' political party. In 1895 there were some ninety-six manufacturing industries in Caracas.[38] The promoters of that Congress, like Dr. Alberto González Briceño and the poet Leopoldo Torres Abandero, were not revolutionaries but freethinkers who were to some extent concerned with the "social question." We can, however, assume that among them there were some anarchist workers of Spanish origin. During the rule of Juan Vicente Gómez Spanish workers who had been militants with the CNT or in anarchist groups undoubtedly arrived in Venezuela, and some of them worked as bricklayers on the numerous construction projects the dictator ordered in Maracay.

Meanwhile, the Asociación de Obreros y Artesanos (with its newspaper, *Unión Obrera*) and the Gremio de Tipógrafos were founded. These are the first manifestations of a unionist movement, although it is severely restricted by regulations and laws imposed by the dictatorship.[39] Several strikes erupted around this time—for example, the telegraphers at the Estación Central de Caracas in March 1919 called a strike that spread to all of Oriente, Valencia, Barquisimeto, Trujillo, and Maracaibo, and led to the imprisonment of the principal organizers.[40] In the next five years, several guilds form syndicates, with the telephone, tram system, and railroad

---

1919 en Venezuela (Caracas: n.p., n.d.), 17.

38 Celestino Mata, *Historia syndical de Venezuela* (Caracas: Urbina y Fuentes, 1985), 22.

39 Hemy Croes, *El movimiento obrero venezolano* (Caracas: Ediciones Movimiento Obrero, 1973), 3.

40 Julio Godio, *El movimiento obrero venezolano 1850–1944* (Caracas: Ildis, 1985), 54–57.

workers among them. But like other syndicates—shoemakers', bakers', bricklayers'—they are cautious not to reveal their purpose or suggest anything like a class struggle, camouflaging themselves as mutual aid societies under the worship of a particular saint, as was the colonial tradition. As Vitale declared, this tactical cover facilitated syndicalist work during the dictatorship, and even made possible the organization of the first Venezuelan workers' central in 1919. But to understand how uneven were the development of workers' struggles and the organization of classes in Latin America, we need only bring to mind the syndicalist and anarchist movements in Mexico, Argentina, or Uruguay.

In any event, strikes increased in Venezuela at this time. Typographers, tram workers, and cobblers organized rallies seeking higher wages. They were sometimes successful, but never without a struggle or violent political repercussions. On July 3, 1918, as Godio notes, "the first industrial strike erupted in Venezuela, affecting not only workshops (mechanics, and iron and foundry workers) in Aroa, but also transit workers (drivers, firefighters, and others) of the British-owned Bolivar Railway Company Limited." Anarchists had an important role in this strike. Godio writes:

> Along with Venezuelan militants, an Italian anarchist named Vincenzo Cusatti appeared, became one of the leaders, and organized, perhaps for the first time in Venezuela, a workers' group to repress strikebreakers. A number of British workers participated in this group along with Venezuelans. The strikers were defeated. But they left their mark on the Venezuelan syndicalist movement.[41]

Pérez Salinas argued that as a result of the repression unleashed in Spain in 1917 a number of Spanish anarchist workers arrived in Venezuela and disseminated their ideology there. And Quintero affirmed that "those 'misguided' but respectable" anarcho-syndicalists

---

41   Ibid., 62.

and their ideas and tactics penetrated the bakers' and railroad workers' guilds, and anarchist ideas were dominant in the underground oil workers' syndicate until 1931.[42] These tendencies were reinforced by the presence of North American workers who were militants in the IWW. We might conjecture that had it not been for the unbending dictatorship of Gómez, so particularly protective of its own, and especially of foreign, interests, anarcho-syndicalism would have led the way to a central workers' organization in Venezuela following the conclusion of the First World War.

The development of the oil industry in the 1920s further altered the composition of the Venezuelan working class in a society with more than a few feudal remnants. From abroad, specialized workers and technicians arrived. Peasants from throughout the country became oil laborers. In 1923 they numbered 5,000 and in 1929 more than 20,000.[43] In 1928 workers were quick to join a university student movement struggling for civil liberties and against the dictatorship, and they ramped up the number of strikes among bakers, dock, and tram workers.

Among the promoters of the university protest was Pío Tamayo, a Venezuelan writer with a long history of social struggle in Guatemala, Panama, Puerto Rico, and the United States, and whose Marxist ideology sprung from an initial inclination toward anarchism. Born in El Tocuyo in 1889, Tamayo came to know a life of exile at an early age. In Costa Rica he directed the publication *Avispa*, celebrated for its attacks against the dictator Gómez.[44] After his return he participated in the student movement of 1928, and during acts of protest held at the Teatro Municipal de Caracas, which included the coronation of a Queen of Students, read his postmodern poem "Homenaje al Indio," and from that day on imprisoned in the

---

42   Vitale, *Sobre el movimiento obrero venezolano*, 18–19.
43   Rodolfo Quintero, "Historia del movimiento obrero en Venezuela," in P. González Cassanova, *Historia del movimiento obrero en América Latina*, 3, 158.
44   Eduardo Gómez Tamayo, "Pío Tamayo, poeta y escritor de envergadura revolucionaria," *La Quincena Literaria*, El Tocuyo, January 15, 1947, 1–2.

Libertador de Puerto Cabello castle he languished until his death on October 15, 1935.

Different political parties began to emerge after the death of Juan Vicente Gómez in 1935, who ruled for nearly three decades. Many of them were wide-ranging in their political orientation, although some pretended to be Leftist and looked for their leaders among intellectuals of the petty bourgeoisie. Workers went directly into a struggle to remove all remnants of the Gómez machinery from the Cabinet. And for a short while, the people came to power in various regions of the country. Workers' and popular committees were formed. Though short-lived, a situation that may be called pre-revolutionary emerged and partly manifested itself in the formation of anti-Gómez "civic guards."[45]

In 1936 various unions formed, as well as the Asociación Nacional de Empleados and the Ligas Campesinas. But a weak class consciousness and the absence of militants representing a revolutionary syndicalism forestalled workers' direct action, and subordinated it to recently formed political parties to such a point that it became confused with the parties themselves. This subordination of unions to political parties, solidified in the 1940s and then again during the dictatorship of Pérez Jiménez in the 1950s, gave the Venezuelan workers' movement its characteristic handicap, and explains why even after 1935 there were no resistance societies of an anarcho-syndicalist or revolutionary syndicalist ideology. Rodolfo Quintero claims they failed to arise because "the unions of an anarcho-syndicalist tendency, preoccupied with maintaining the particularity of the trades, did not make room for a unifying centralization of syndicates, federations, and confederations facilitating the total perception of the production process."[46] But on the contrary, anyone familiar with the history of the international workers' movement—it is enough to be familiar with the Spanish CNT or the Argentinean FORA—knows that at this time

---

45 Domingo Alberto Rangel, *Los andinos en el poder* (Caracas: Vadell, 1980), 308.

46 Quintero, "Historia del movimiento obrero en Venezuela," 159.

anarchists were not preoccupied with "maintaining the particularity of the trades"; indeed, they had accepted a broad representation of industrial trades. If anyone had "a total perception of the production process" and acted in accord with that perception it was the anarcho-syndicalists. The "parceling" of unions explains why those militant workers with a proclivity for anarchist ideology who could not accept the idea of the dictatorship of the proletariat or the vertical organization of the Communist Party were instead active in parties like Acción Democrática, considered democratic socialist. Some of the most important worker-leaders of that party during its early years, like Francisco Olivo, Pedro Bernardo Pérez Salínas, and Salom Mesa, were originally sympathetic to anarcho-syndicalism, nourished in good part by Spanish sources.[47] Their presence in Acción Democrática encouraged the warm reception that the party extended to many Spanish anarchists as they arrived in Venezuela after the triumph of Franco's fascism, and the genuine sympathy of some of the Spaniards for the party.

More recently, some of the many libertarian militants exiled from the Southern Cone arrived in Venezuela, and engaged in various propaganda activities and diffusion of ideas, particularly in the university setting.

---

47   Salom Mesa, *La vida me lo dijo. Elógio de la anarquía* (Caracas: Vadell, 1987), 43–44.

9. Panama and Central America

A. Panama

The construction of the trans-isthmus railroad from 1850 to 1855, the French plan to open a canal connecting the Atlantic and Pacific oceans in 1880, and the canal's eventual construction by North Americans from 1904 to 1914 brought to Panama a mass of workers from Europe, Asia, and the Antilles.[1] From the viewpoint of the history of the workers' movement, those facts differentiate the Isthmus Republic, which gained its independence from Colombia in 1903, from its Central American neighbors. In the first construction phase under French control some 20,000 workers arrived. The majority of them were from Spain, France, and Italy. In the second, North American, phase some 40,000 workers arrived from Central America and especially from Jamaica and the Caribbean. Jorge Turner notes that these workers brought the seeds of class-consciousness and anarcho-syndicalism to Panama.[2]

---

1   Luis Nava, *El movimiento obrero en Panamá* (Panamá: Editorial Universitaria, 1974), 61.

2   Turner, "Raíces históricas y perspectivas del movimiento obrero panameño" in P. González Casanova, *Historia del movimiento obrero en*

Those who distinguished themselves most were libertarian workers from Spain, "because of their organizational and combative capacities."[3] Already during the construction of the trans-isthmus railroad a number of strikes erupted seeking improvement in wages and working conditions, which were extraordinarily deplorable, causing sickness and death among workers. In 1895, during the French phase, strikes again erupted, some of them successful, and mostly led by European anarchists.

The combative spirit anarchists brought to Panama's working class explains the fact that Article 5 of Law 72 (passed on June 11, 1904, regulating immigration) prohibited entry to anarchists.[4] In 1905, during the North American phase, the governor of the Canal Zone, General George W. Davis, made a special effort to hinder all construction work by anarchist workers. Nonetheless in 1907, 2,000 Spanish laborers struck for better wages, undoubtedly encouraged by anarchist co-nationals. There was no lack of violent episodes. At the fringes of the Federación Obrera, formed with the assistance of the liberal president Belisario Porras, anarchists organized among Panamanian workers, making a few converts, and in 1925 promoted a tenants' strike, just as Argentinean, Chilean, Brazilian, and Mexican anarchists had done.

In 1924 a predominantly anarcho-syndicalist group founded the Sindicato General de Trabajadores, eventually gaining thousands of members. It was the first Panamanian workers' central. In the founding group were the Spaniards José María and Martín Blásques de Pedro, the Pole Sara Gratz, and the Peruvian Esteban M. Pavletich, who later joined the Sandino forces. The Panamanians included anarchists and workers with various other ideologies, including the Marxists Eliseo Echevez and Domingo Turner, future founders of the Partido Comunista in 1930. Also participating was Diógenes de la Rosa, who would later be one of the leaders of the

---

América Latina, 2 (México: n.p., 1985), 291.

3   Viñas, *Anarquistas en América Latina*, 99.

4   Turner, "Raíces históricas y perspectivas del movimiento obrero panameño," 294.

Partido Socialista, also founded in 1930.[5]

Among the workers who arrived from Europe in the early twentieth century there were, curiously enough, a number of Stirner individualists influenced by Nietzsche's philosophy who saw in syndicalism a potential enemy of their anarchist ideology. They formed several affinity groups that, according to Nettlau, numbered twenty in 1912. In 1911 the newspaper *El Unico* appeared in Colón, self-identifying as an "individualist publication."[6]

B. Costa Rica

In the first decade of the twentieth century, a number of newspapers appeared in Costa Rica that to one degree or another expressed an anarchist ideology. Vladimir de la Cruz listed the following: *La Aurora Social, Hoja Obrera, Orden Social, El Trabajo, El Amigo del Pueblo, Grito del Pueblo, La Lucha, El Derecho*, and *La Causa del Pueblo*, whose style, de la Cruz writes,

> not only insinuated characteristics of libertarian discourse of the time, but also undeniably made reference to anarchist publications in other regions of Latin America, as well as to journals and weeklies published in Barcelona, and in the Spanish regions of Levante and Andalusia.[7]

De la Cruz also discerned that the anarchist "danger" was already present in Costa Rica in the last few years of the nineteenth century, based on a warning given by Bishop Thiel in his sermon of December 25, 1892.

Anarchist groups organized various demonstrations in San José after the 1909 assassination of Francisco Ferrer, just as they

---

5   Ibid., 296.
6   Nettlau, "Viaje Libertario," *Reconstruir*, 76, 34.
7   Vladimir de la Cruz, *Las luchas sociales en Costa Rica, 1870–1930* (San José: n.p., 1970), cited in Viñas, *Anarquistas en América Latina*.

did in all other Latin American countries. Near the end of the same year, a Centro de Estudios Sociales Germinal was formed and adopted the red and black colors. Active in it were intellectuals like Omar Dengo, Joaquín García Monge, Carmen Lira, and the worker-leader Juan Rafael López.[8] On January 15, 1911 the journal *Renovación* was launched. It had clear anarchist tendencies, and was led by the poet J. M. Zeledón. It published more than seventy issues, an unusual achievement. A while later in Santiago de Puriscal the French-language anarchist newspaper *Le Semeur* appeared. Although not an anarchist paper, *El Sol,* published in Alajuela, frequently welcomed contributions with anarchist tendencies—even until recent days. In San José around 1926 a group formed for the specific purpose of libertarian action.[9]

We should recall that in 1914 Kropotkin wrote two letters to the Costa Rican chemist and anarchist Elías Jiménez Rojas explaining his position on the war that had just begun, a position that was not shared by the majority of anarchists and received the explicit rejection of figures like Malatesta, Rocker, Emma Goldman, Alexander Berkman, Sébastien Faure, Domela Nieuwenhuis, Luigi Bertoni, and others. In those letters, Kropotkin elaborated on his anti-Prussian views: "You understand that in similar circumstances every effort should be made to impede an imperial stranglehold on Europe."[10]

The influence of anarcho-syndicalists on Costa Rican workers in the early twentieth century is unquestionable. Rojas Bolaños writes:

> For example, in the 1905 strike by bakers seeking the eight-hour day several Spanish anarcho-syndicalists played leading roles, among them Juan Vera, who was exiled to Puerto Rico

---

8   Ibid.
9   Nettlau, "Viaje libertario," 42.
10   The two letters remained unpublished until 1960. They appeared in *Revista de Filosofía de la Universidad de Costa Rica*, vol. II, no. 7, translated to Spanish by Alain Vieillard-Baron.

upon the success of anarchist action. And the national leaders of the strike movement were confined in the Alajuela prison.

In 1913, under direction of the Centro de Estudios Sociales Germinal and several workers' unions, May Day was first celebrated in Costa Rica as the Día Internacional del Trabajo. Also, the Confederación General de Trabajadores was formed, exerting significant influence throughout the 1910s.[11]

C. El Salvador

The first Salvadorian syndicates to take up the workers' struggle and organize resistance societies were formed by anarchists, both national and foreign. The influence of Spanish, Mexican, and Panamanian anarcho-syndicalists is undeniable. Anarcho-syndicalist elements were predominant in the Unión Obrera Salvadoreña, founded in 1922, and in the Federación Regional de Trabajadores de El Salvador, founded in 1924 and led by Marxist militants after 1929.[12]

There was a Centro Sindical Libertario operating in the national capital, San Salvador, in 1930; it probably disappeared after the brutal repression of 1932. The very combative French anarchist Anselme Bellagarigue, who published *L'Anarchie-Journal de l'Ordre* in Paris in 1850, may have died in this country. But it is impossible to know whether Bellagarigue penned any articles or otherwise spread his ideas during his stay in El Salvador or his time as a teacher in Honduras. Nettlau mentions the literary journal *Ritos*, first published in San Salvador in 1908, as influenced by anarchist ideas.[13]

---

11   Manuel Rojas Bolaños, "El movimiento obrero en Costa Rica (Reseña historica)," in González Casanova, *Historia del movimiento obrero en América Latina*, 256.

12   Rafael Menjívar Larín, "Notas sobre el movimiento obrero salvadoreño," in ibid., 73–74.

13   Nettlau, "Viaje libertario," 42–43.

D. Guatemala

The publication *Orientación Sindical* began to appear in Guatemala after 1926. It called for direct union action outside political parties and sometimes in opposition to them. Communists promoted the founding of the Federación Regional Obrera de Guatemala and began publication of the newspaper *Vanguardia Proletaria*. But Spanish and Peruvian workers independently chose to join with Guatemalan workers' and student groups to form the Comité Pro Acción Sindical, which embodied the ideas and purposes of anarcho-syndicalists.[14] The military dictatorship ended the Comité and all public manifestations of anarcho-syndicalism and revolutionary syndicalism in the country.[15]

E. Honduras

In the last decade of the nineteenth century mutual aid societies formed in Honduras, such as La Democracia, founded in 1890. During the first decade of the twentieth century workers in mines and banana farms began to organize with the purpose of social struggle and defense. In March 1909 workers at the North American–owned Rosario Mining Company struck and were brutally and bloodily repressed.[16] In July 1916 workers at the Cuyamel Fruit Company also struck, and some four hundred were jailed in the Castillo de Omoa.[17] Foreign anarcho-syndicalists almost certainly participated in these early strikes as well as in the organization of the first resistance societies among miners and banana farm workers, though assigning precise dates is not always easy.

---

14   José Luis Balcárcel, "El movimiento obrero en Guatemala," in González Casanova, *Historia del movimiento obrero en América Latina*, 25–26.
15   Nettlau, "Viaje libertario," 42.
16   Victor Meza, "Historia del movimiento obrero en Honduras," in González Casanova, *Historia del movimiento obrero en América Latina*, 131.
17   Ibid.

F. Nicaragua

The Federación Obrera Nicaragüense was founded in 1918 with the assistance of several workers' mutual societies like Sociedad Central de Obreros, Sociedad Unión Zapateros, Unión de Panaderos, Unión de Sastres in León, and others in Chinandega, Granada, and Managua.[18] Individuals from the traditional political parties, that is, conservative and liberal, had always been in charge of the mutualist and artisanal unions.

Militant workers then formed the Grupo Socialista. In the May 24, 1924 issue of their newspaper *El Socialista*, they denounced manipulation by intellectuals who attempted to use the new Federación to gain political posts. The Grupo was made up of workers like Leonardo Velásquez, Alejandro González Aragón, Victor M. Valladares, and the poet Apolonio Palacio.[19] While they were militant and rebelled against political intrigues, like those by the poet Salomón de la Selva, we cannot infer from their anti-political position an anarchist or revolutionary syndicalist attitude. They were ultimately reformists or social democrats. Although León memorialized the Federación Obrera Nicarangüense on May Day with the battle cries "Long live the martyrs of labor!" and "Long live the social revolution!" it is important to recall that he first sought the approval of employers for their laborers to join in.[20] Salomón de la Selva did all he could to annex the Federación Obrera Nicarangüense to the Confederación Obrera Panamericana, organized by the American Federation of Labor. Professor Sofonías Salvatierra, while critical of a relationship with Yankee unionism, never went beyond mutualist solidarity and liberal nationalism, and opposed all forms of revolutionary internationalism.[21]

---

18 Gustavo Gutiérrez Mayorga, "Historia del movimiento obrero en Nicaragua 1900–1977," in ibid., 200.
19 Ibid., 201.
20 Ibid., 204.
21 Ibid., 205–10.

Thus we cannot say that there were anarcho-syndicalist worker associations in Nicaragua, although it is quite possible that foreign libertarians—Spaniards and Mexicans, among others—were active in the most important stevedore strikes in Corinto in 1919. And we cannot forget Sandino's great sympathy for Latin American anarchism. He felt much closer to it than to Marxist-Leninism, and even chose the anarchists' red and black colors for his own flag.

10. The Antilles and Cuba

A. Puerto Rico

Puerto Rico was a Spanish colony until 1898 and from that year on a colony of the United States. Anarchist ideas did not have as much resonance there as in Cuba. But we may reasonably assume that peninsular militants arrived in Puerto Rico in the 1880s and began the tasks of agitation and propaganda. It is certain that the first artisanal organizations to emerge in the liberal period between 1868 and 1873 were casinos, mutual aid societies, and production cooperatives that counted on the good will of authorities and even the auspices of the propertied class.[1]

The monetary crisis of 1894 to 1895 and the subsequent devaluation that led to price increases triggered a series of strikes and mass protest movements. Spanish anarchists working in the island were quite likely active in these, for in 1898, when the island was already under North American control, they and some socialists founded the Federación Regional de los Trabajadores, modeled on the

---

[1] Gervasio Luis García and A. G. Quintero Rivera, "Historia del movimiento obrero puertorriqueño," in Gozález Casanova, *Historia de movimiento obrero en América Latina*, 1, 358–63.

Federación Regional Española led by anarcho-syndicalist groups. Its program aimed to eliminate the exploitation of men and women, and to achieve the total emancipation of the proletariat.[2] Embracing internationalism, anarchists and socialists in the Federación "condemned the nationalism of the propertied classes and sought an egalitarian society and a world without borders." They refused to get involved in colonial haggling and considered the social question as independent of the national question.[3] Their fight against emerging capitalism led them to adopt an anti-Yankee attitude, and "North American" became synonymous with "capitalist" as well as with governmental, political, and military force. This helps to explain a kind of mixing of libertarian ideas and nationalism found in other parts of the Caribbean as well. On June 18, 1899 the anarchist opposition to political parties, elections, and parliamentarism led many defenders of syndicalist autonomy to leave the Federación Regional—Rosendo Rivera García, as its president, was open to the support of the Partido Republicano—and to form a Federación Libre loyal to the principles of the First International. Yet, in September 1901, this group affiliated itself with the conservative and anti-socialist American Federation of Labor, a contradiction that its leaders, Rámon Romero Sosa and Santiago Iglesias, attempted to explain by alleging a necessity "to survive in a hostile economic environment."[4] Anarchists continued their activities in Puerto Rico in spite of the fact that they were not able to achieve a dominant position in the workers' movement, as they had successfully done in other Latin American countries. Nettlau has mentioned the newspaper *Voz Humana* in Cagües in 1905 and 1906.[5]

Viñas writes the following about anarchist (or proto-anarchist) literary production in Puerto Rico:

If Manuel Zeno Gandía (1855–1930) wanted to use his pen as

---

2   Ibid., 366.
3   Ibid., 367.
4   Ibid., 368.
5   Nettlau, "Viaje libertario," *Reconstruir*, 78, 43.

a social cautery by writing the series of novels titled *Crónicas de un mundo enfermo*—particularly *La charca*, 1894, and *Garduña*, 1896—and if Mariano Abril (1861–1935) sought to survey revolutionary tendencies of his time in *El socialismo moderno*, other writers like José Elías Levis with his *Estercolero* (1900) and Ramón Juliá Marín with *La gleba* (1913) traced the literary space that around 1900 not only surrounded but also sustained a specifically anarchist nucleus. It was a nucleus that was being gradually defined by the permanent influence of Spanish libertarianism. In the course of the Madrid Restoration that nucleus refined its activities by denouncing the conservatives from Cánovas del Castillo and the liberals from Sagasta, and after North American possession of the island it was characterized by the hard questioning of North American imperialism: a constant reality that moved Puerto Rican libertarians close to IWW militants. Luis Bonafoux can be considered one of the most active individuals given his libertarian sympathies (sympathies which provoked Spanish authorities to exile him), his camaraderie with the ideas of Rubén Darío, and his journalistic activities which culminated in the founding of *La Campaña*, launched in 1898 and publishing articles by European collaborators like Malatesta, Tarrida del Mármol, Sébastien Faure, and other anarchists who advanced major theoretical guidelines for that political movement.[6]

B. Dominican Republic

There is no doubt that anarchist propaganda activities were underway in the Dominican Republic in the last two decades of the nineteenth century thanks to Spanish immigrant laborers. Mutualist associations of artisans emerged during that time, among them

---

6   Viñas, *Anarquistas en América Latina*, 81.

La Alianza Cibaeña in 1884 and the Sociedad Artesenal Hijos del Pueblo in 1890. The first union association seems to have been the Unión de Panaderos de Santo Domingo, founded in 1897. The first strikes also erupted during this period, led by bakers, cobblers, and bricklayers protesting in the Colón Park against their respective employers. And railroad workers constructing the Puerto Plata–Santiago line went on strike in 1896.[7] It is very likely that anarchist workers promoted these first strikes, even in the absence of a syndicalist organization. On May 15, 1920 the Primer Congreso de Trabajadores Dominicanos convened in Santo Domingo, and from it emerged the Confederación Dominicana del Trabajo. It sought the eight-hour workday, the right to strike, a salary schedule, and profit-sharing, and demanded an end to North American occupation.[8] The Federación Local del Trabajo de Santo Domingo was founded in the 1920s by thirty-one unions and the Unión Regional de Obreros del Este.[9]

In January 1946 a strike broke out that included all sugar plantations in La Romana and San Pedro de Macorís, with the participation of several Spanish anarchists who had arrived in recent years after the defeat of the Republic. They missed no opportunity to spread their ideas, and many of them would later travel to Mexico and other Latin American countries. Among them was Dr. Pedro Vallina,[10] whom José Viadiu called a "singular anarchist combining Bakunin and St. Francis of Assisi."[11] Ten years earlier, the German physician Dr. Goldberg, founder of an anarchist colony in Berlin, had arrived in the Dominican Republic. Fleeing the barbarities of National Socialism, he travelled first to Córcega and then settled with his family in a rural jungle region of the Republic.[12]

---

7   Rafael Calderón Martínez, "El movimiento obrero dominicano 1870–1978," in González Casanova, *Historia de movimiento obrero en América Latina*, 271–72.
8   Ibid., 273–74.
9   Ibid., 275.
10 Vallina, *Mis memorias* (México: Ediciones Tierra y Libertad, 1971), 34.
11 Viadiu, "Prólogo," in ibid., 9.
12 Nettlau, "Viaje libertario," 43.

C. Martinique, Guadeloupe, and Haiti

A section of the International was already established in Martinique by 1895, with Proudhonians comprising the largest group within it. In a report by the General Counsel of the Lausanne Congress in 1867, we learn that by 1866 a branch of the International was at work on the island of Guadeloupe, though it had stopped paying dues.[13]

Socialism appeared in Haiti in the 1930s "in the midst of a nationalist, ideological, and political struggle against North American domination."[14] The Parti Communiste Haïtien, founded in 1934, broke away from bourgeois nationalism and the old Black nationalism of the nineteenth century, and was able to link anti-imperialism with the struggle between classes.[15] It is difficult to establish whether there were any anarchist groups either before or after that period, although the influence of French culture likely disseminated the ideas of Proudhon and the anarcho-syndicalists of the Confédération générale du travail (CGT). This country—which was the first colony to see the emancipation of slaves, two years after the first Black slave rebellion broke out on August 23, 1791, and the first Latin American country to gain independence, in 1804—had also suffered the longest and most constant dictatorships, culminating in our own time with Duvalierism, nothing short of an "underdeveloped fascism."[16] Under such conditions a libertarian movement could hardly develop, even in a place that sustained among so many individuals strong sentiments of rebellion and hatred of tyranny.

---

13   Nettlau, "Contribución a la bibliografía," 8.
14   Michel Hector, "El movimiento obrero haitiano, 1932–1963," in González Casanova, *Historia de movimiento obrero en América Latina*, 187.
15   Ibid., 190.
16   Leslie Manigat, *De un Duvalier a otro* (Caracas: Monte Avila, 1972).

D. Cuba

The last of Spain's American colonies, Cuba was more closely aligned with the cultural and political life of the peninsula than any other Hispano-American country. The influence of Spanish utopian socialism was felt on the island in the first half of the nineteenth century, and the influence of anarchism in the second half.

Rama writes: "In all of Spanish-speaking America texts circulated during the nineteenth century attacking, criticizing, or excommunicating utopian socialism from the viewpoint of peninsular Catholicism, one of the bastions of clerical orthodoxy."[17] Examples of such writings are the 1844 articles by the philosopher Jaime Balmes published in the newspaper *La Sociedad* in Barcelona, and the famous 1850 *Ensayo sobre el catolicismo, el liberalismo y el socialismo* by Donoso Cortés. Although publications such as these were reprinted and received substantial commentary in all of Latin America and particularly in Cuba, they could not hold back the rising tide of utopian socialism on the island.

Ramón de la Sagra was born in Coruña in 1798 and arrived in Havana in 1823. He was a sociologist, agronomist, economist, geologist, botanist, mathematician, and statistician, whom Manuel Casas called "a living encyclopedia." In Havana he taught mineralogy, served as director of the Jardín Botánico, founded the *Anales de Ciencias, Agricultura, Comercio y Artes* in 1827, and wrote a number of books on diverse subjects. After travelling through the United States and Europe, he was elected several times to the Spanish parliament. He began his study of Proudhon in 1840, and after incessant literary activity put his science to the service of socialism. In his 1919 *Un ideólogo de 1850*, Azorín said of de la Sagra that "he looked to science as an ideal for humanity, as a way of socializing it."[18] His interest in Cuba and Latin America was steadfast throughout his long life. Between 1844 and 1850, he published in

---

17   Rama, *Utopismo socialist*, xliv.
18   See V. Muñoz, "Una cronología de Ramón de la Sagra," *Reconstruir*, 66.

Paris the monumental thirteen-volume work titled *Historia física, política y natural de la isla de Cuba*. He was the most original of Spanish utopian socialists—Manuel Núñez de Arenas opined that it was more apt to call him a "social reformer,"[19] and more recently Antonio Elorza said he was more of a "utopian socialist" than a "socialist utopian."[20] In his work he acknowledged the influence of the Saint-Simonianism of Constantin Pecquer. In 1848 de la Sagra collaborated with Proudhon, and in 1849 published *El Banco del Pueblo*, in which he explained the meaning and origin of that Proudhonian institution. Earlier, in 1845, he had founded a newspaper in Santiago de Compostela presenting certain ideas of Proudhon.[21] Nonetheless, it seems a bit inaccurate to consider him the first Spanish anarchist, as Nettlau does,[22] when one takes into account his rejection of the workers' association as the basis for social struggle, his search for a religious justification for future society,[23] and the fact that little by little, under the influence of Baron Collins, he tended towards neoconservative ideas, to the point that in 1858 he totally condemned Spanish socialism in the pages of the absolutist newspaper *La Esperanza*.[24]

Tobacco workers held Cuba's first significant strike in Havana in 1866, and in that same year Saturnino Martínez launched *La Aurora*, the first proletarian newspaper in Cuba.[25] As early as the crisis of 1857 mutual aid societies had formed, particularly among workers in the tobacco industry and the slaughterhouses. By 1860 they were organized along class lines, and through the efforts of

---

19   Núñez de Arenas, *Don Rámon de la Sagra, reformador social* (Madrid: n.p., 1924).

20   Elorza, *Socialismo utópico español* (Madrid: Alianza, 1970), 15.

21   Muñoz, "Una cronología de Ramón de la Sagra," 63.

22   Ibid., 60.

23   Elorza, *Socialismo utópico español*, 67.

24   Ibid., 10. On de la Sagra, see L. Legaz, "Ramón de la Sagra, sociólogo español, *Revista Internacional de Sociología*, 13, 1946; C. Viñas, "Un gran tratadista español: las doctrinas sociales de Ramón de la Sagra," ibid., 13 and 14, 1946 and 1953; Carlos A. Zubillaga Barrera, "Epistolario Americano de los hermanos Sagra," *Grial*, 22, Vigo.

25   Alberto Pla, *Los orígenes del movimiento obrero en América Latina*, 27.

Saturnino Martínez the Asociación de Tabaqueros was formed in 1866.[26] In a letter dated June 23, 1873, the Mallorcan worker Francisco Tomás wrote that the Federación Regional Española had no information on unions in Cuba—but by 1881 they were common.[27]

Generally speaking, the first workers to organize into resistance societies and syndicates were Spaniards working in the tobacco industry. Their ideology was undoubtedly anarchist or had affinity to some form of revolutionary syndicalism. José Rivero Muñiz notes that at this time "socialist doctrines seemed secondary while priority was given to anarchist doctrines." He adds:

> No one speaks about Marx or Engels, and even less of Owen, Fourier, and other precursors of socialism. Instead, the names of Bakunin, Malatesta, Kropotkin, Reclus, and Anselmo Lorenzo are not unknown among Cuban and Spanish workers in the tobacco factories, where their work is read and interpreted on a daily basis.[28]

Annie Rottenstein says that Saturnino Martínez initiated those readings. Yet after the first anarchist groups formed around 1880, they waged a fight in the pages of the newspaper *El Obrero* against Martínez's reformism, a reformism that, in the words of Enrique Roig San Martín, tied workers "to the feet of capital."[29] Roig San Martín launched the anarchist newspaper *El Productor* in Havana in 1887, at the same time as its namesake in Barcelona was first published, and continued publication after 1890 in Guanabacoa.[30] Like Carlos Cafiero and other anarchists, Roig San Martín read and

---

26   Aleida Plasencia Moro, "Historia del movimiento obrero en Cuba," González Casanova, *Historia de movimiento obrero en América Latina*, 1, 91.

27   Nettlau, "Viaje libertarion," 77, 33.

28   J. Rivero Muñiz, *El primero partido socialista cubano. Apuntes para la historia del proletariado en Cuba* (Las Villas, Cuba: n.p., 1962), 11–12.

29   Plasencia Moro, "Historia del movimiento obrero en Cuba," 93.

30   Nettlau, "Viaje libertario," 76, 41.

commented on Marx's *Capital*, but unlike Favio Grobart he cannot be considered an "anarchist on the way to Marxism."

The Círculo de Trabajadores was founded in 1855, and two years later a Congreso Obrero local convened in Havana with seventy-four delegates in attendance from throughout the island.[31] Anarcho-syndicalist influence is quite clear. Pla writes:

> After lengthy and intense discussions, the Congress agreed to fight for the eight-hour workday through a general strike, to organize workers from each region of the island into sections by trade or profession, to form associations by sections, and to unite them into the Federación de Trabajadores de Cuba. Following anarchist principles, they agreed that each section would have the broadest possible autonomy. There was evidence of the growing maturity of the proletariat in its direct confrontation with racial discrimination, and the adoption of principles against that great evil.[32]

The Catalan typographer Pedro Esteve arrived in Cuba in 1893, and in 1898 the prominent journalist Palmiro de Lidia (Adrián del Valle). The former was one of the best-known Spanish-speaking militant anarchists in the United States, and in 1899 the latter began publishing the newspaper *El Nuevo Ideal*. In February 1900 Malatesta arrived in Cuba from his propaganda tour of the United States, by Lidia's invitation. On May 1, Malatesta gave a lecture in Havana titled "Libertad y civilización," and several days later, harassed by authorities of the Yankee intervention, sailed to New York and then on to London. Plasencia Moro writes:

> On May Day 1890 more than 3,000 workers marched from Campo de Marte to the Skatin Ring in the center of Havana. More than fifteen orators spoke on behalf of the eight-hour

---

31   Pla, *Los orígenes del movimiento obrero en América Latina*, 28.
32   Plasencia Moro, "Historia del movimiento obrero en Cuba," 95.

workday, and denounced the miserable and abusive conditions suffered by workers. The necessity of unity and solidarity among workers was repeatedly emphasized. Anarchist ideas were not lacking, particularly among the principal organizers. It is important to note that in the speeches racism was condemned and equality of rights for blacks and whites was declared.[33]

Strikes proliferated in the 1890s, repression increased, *El Productor* was shuttered and its anarchist editors jailed. In 1892 police raided the Círculo de Trabajadores and closed the Junta Central de Trabajadores. In 1893 anarchists founded the Sociedad General de Trabajadores, and in 1896 led a great strike in the port of Havana. During the second war for independence, anarchist workers supported Máximo Gómez "with more enthusiasm than any other group," as Victor Alba notes. Enrique Messonier, an anarchist with a long history of activism in Cuba, collected funds for the war. José Martí himself more than once showed his sympathy with anarchists and his affinity for the ideas they represented.

Numerous anarchist newspapers were published in Cuba between 1890 and 1905, like *El Socialismo, El Trabajo, Hijos del Mundo, La Alarma, Germinal,* and more in Havana; *El Productor* in Guanabacoa; and *El Trabajo* in Puerto Príncipe. *Archivo Social* was also founded in Havana in 1894, publishing a number of short literary and sociological pieces of a libertarian bent, along with *La Defensa,* a publication by tobacco rollers, most of whom were anarchists.[34] Later, between 1905 and 1914, *El Libertario, La Batalla,* and *Vía Libre* were launched in Havana, and in Regla *Rebelión* was first published, taking the place of *Seminario anarquista.*[35]

It is important at this point to be clear about the contribution of various anarchists to the struggle for Cuban independence. In *Guángara Libertaria,* Frank Fernández writes:

---

33   Ibid., 96.
34   Nettlau, "Contribución a la bibliografía anarquista," 15.
35   Ibid., 26.

[A]narchists in exile joined Martí in forming leagues and clubs, and after the accords of 1892 Martí himself made them the base for founding the Partido Revolucionario Cubano (PRC). This was not a political party in the sense of traditional electoral politics, but a revolutionary party, as its name declares, that would assemble the largest number of combatants to wage war in Cuba.... Martí also formed another type of party influenced by close collaborators or as a concession to anarchists, who were humble men and workers. His vision was clear: organize active and honest elements to wage a courageous and brief war. Those elements did not represent the class or economic interests of any group, as had been the case in the Guerra de los Diez Años. Instead, they represented the poorest and most popular elements, the dispossessed, racially and socially marginalized and discriminated: blacks, laborers, peasants, and others.[36]

Leaders in Martí's party were not the ones to provide necessary funds; it was rather the base itself that did so. Moreover, it was a decentralized party formed by diverse interests with a common goal, namely, the creation of a republic in which "the colonial authoritarian spirit and bureaucratic structure were absent."

Martí sought the participation of a wide range of groups of Cubans in exile, and among them were the anarchists. "Relations between Martí and the anarchists were cordial, and anarchists joined the cause with great enthusiasm." On August 1892 Martí wrote to Serafín Bello that "the letter from Messonier is quite worthy and he wishes to say some words about it." Messonier, a prominent Cuban anarchist, informed Martí in this letter about events in the Congress of 1892. Later, in May 1894, Martí again referred to the anarchist Messonier in the pages of *Patria*, published in exile. He said: "Cuba has orators and men for this period who are robust and vibrant like a

---

36   Frank Fernández, "Los anarquistas cubanos, 1865–1898," *Guángara Libertaria*, 1983, 4–7. The following quoted passages are from the cited text

stone, and like the sun, justice shines through them; they are cautious and deliberate as they edify. Enrique Messonier is one of them." Later in a letter to him, Martí wrote: "My friend Messonier…nothing confuses or distracts me, we shall establish a house of love."

Martí referred to José Joaquín Izaguirre, founder of the anarchist club Enrique Roig San Martín, as "one with the evangelist's fire" who "enthuses everyone." And in speaking about that anarchist club, he said, "in the Club Enrique Roig the Cuban soul vibrates and groans in pain for man." Martí considered the anarchist Ramón Rivero y Rivero, among the founders of the PRC, as a friend and referred to him as having "a pure heart, rich and fervent, and cautious reason." In 1894 exiled Cuban anarchists founded the Club Fermín Salvochea, named after the Andalusian anarchist sympathetic to Martí's cause of independence, and the newspapers *El Esclavo* in Tampa and *El Despertar* in Brooklyn.

A fact maliciously hidden by historians is that Pedro Esteve and Malatesta would often speak on behalf of independence in their oratory to Cuban workers in the United States. Other Cuban anarchists who participated in the PRC were: Ramón Santana, Teodoro Pérez, Juan de Dios Barrios, Francisco María González, Angel Peláez, Gualterio García, José Dolores Poyo, Pablo Rousseau, Pastor Segada, Luis M. Ruíz, García Purón, González Acosta, and Ambrosio Borges. Carlos Benigno Baliño, an anarchist at the time but later a Marxist, was also part of the independence party aligned with and friends of Martí. In 1889 he founded *La Tribuna del Trabajo*, whose articles were sometimes reprinted in Roig San Martín's *El Productor*. In a speech he gave on October 10, 1892 he tried to show how anarchism is compatible with the ideal of national independence, citing Dyer D. Lum, an "anarchist, friend, and confidant of Parsons,'" the German anarchist Justus H. Schwab, and Esteve. Moreover, he appealed to the activities of Bakunin and de Fanelli, both of whom fought for Polish independence. A few days later, on November 7, Martí reprinted the speech in *Patria*. In August 1893, when owners of tobacco industries in Tampa and Key West tried to lower wages, workers went on strike, led by anarchists. In collaboration with Spanish colonial authorities, owners brought scabs from Cuba. The PRC then hired Horatio Rubens, a friend of Martí, who successfully defended the strikers from the illegal actions of the owners.

In August and September 1899 bricklayers waged the first general strike for the eight-hour workday, inspired and promoted mostly by anarchists. It was unsuccessful, and met with violent repression from the Yankee military government. Apprentices led another important strike, seeking to end discrimination against young Cuban men wishing to work in the tobacco industry. During the second North American intervention, between 1906 and 1909, there were twenty-eight strikes. All of them were repressed and nearly all were unsuccessful.[37]

In 1902 Abelardo Saavedra and Francisco Sola launched the newspaper *Tierra*, which in 1904 promoted a boycott of imported meat from Argentina, calling it a "South American Russia" where anarchists are persecuted and exiled.[38] Adrián del Valle[39] founded the newspaper *El Nuevo Ideal* in 1899, and also wrote an essay on Kropotkin, later published in Buenos Aires in 1925, which offered "many important insights," according to Nettlau.[40] Although living in Europe, the Cuban Tarrida del Mármol was at this time one of the most prominent libertarian thinkers and proposed an "anarchism without adjectives," above the disagreements among communists, collectivists, and individualists that divided the international movement. In French he published *Les Inquisiteurs d'Espagne* in 1897.[41]

Tobacco workers from Tampa and Key West—whose intellectual guides were Rámon Rivero y Rivero, Ambrosio Borges, José Rivas, and Enrique Messonier—formed the Liga General de

---

37   Plasencia Moro, "Historia del movimiento obrero en Cuba," 100–01.

38   Manuel González Prada, *Anarquía* (n.p.: n.p., n.d.), 49 (cited by Alba, *Historia del movimiento obrero en América Latina*).

39   On del Valle see L. Dulzaides Noda, *Adrián del Valle, hombre y señal* (México: n.p., n.d.).

40   Nettlau, "Viaje libertario," 76, 33.

41   Pere Gabriel, "El anarquismo en España," in Woodcock, *El anarquismo* (n.p.: n.p., n.d.), 351–55.

Trabajadores Cubanos in 1899 during the bricklayers' strike. They began to publish *Alerta* and issued a Declaration of Principles proposing, among other things, the complete equality of Cuban and foreign workers on the island.[42]

An anarchist with significant political influence in Cuba during the early twentieth century was the Italian Orestes Ferrara. Named to the post of secretary of the civil government in Santa Clara by General José Miguel Gómez, a position that led to a number of conflicts with North Americans and personally challenged many of their functionaries, from Lieutenant Cordell Hull to Proconsul Wood. In 1901 he served as interim Governor of Santa Clara province and, moved by the misery of the peasants and the abysmal inequality between laborers and landowners, workers and capitalists, he proposed a solution, albeit a provisional and partial one. "We must redeem Cuba by increasing wages, whatever the costs," he wrote in his *Memorias*. "Consequently, I led a movement to do so." Landowners in Cienfuegos went along, while those from Sagua la Grande did not, and Ferrara then decided to turn to agitation. Fernández writes:

> Thus, Ferrara the anarchist, interim Governor of the province, Colonel in the Liberating Army, backed by troops and the people, armed with ideas and rifles, becomes an agitator in the best of Bakunin's style in defense of oppressed workers and hungry peasants, and against the wealthy Spanish storeowners and industrialists, and foreign-owned railroads. Workers declared a strike and Ferrara joined them in solidarity. It created an abstract impressionistic portrait with profound contradictions and complications that is typical of an unjust society bequeathed by colonialism and maintained by an interventionist government. It displayed for us the social situation of the period.[43]

---

42 Fernández, "Los anarquistas cubanos II, 1899–1930," *Guángara Libertaria*, 1984, 5–6.

43 Ibid., 6.

Naturally, Proconsul Wood could not tolerate this situation and Ferrara, accused by the North Americans of being a "professional agitator and anarchist" (which was true), perhaps should have left Cuba.[44]

Anarchists were among the very few with the courage to protest the Platt Amendment imposed on Cuba in 1901, speaking out through their newspapers *Tierra* and *Alerta*. But Estrada Palma and the functionaries of the nascent Republic did not hesitate to violently repress strikes, workers' movements, and libertarian propaganda activities. In the above-mentioned strike by apprentices on November 24 and 25, 1902 rural guards left two dead and dozens wounded among the striking workers. At the same time, and for the first time in the history of Cuba, anarchists succeeded in organizing rural workers into the Federación Obrera Local de Villa Clara. In no time they organized strikes in the sugar industries, and soon enough they had their first martyrs, Casañas and Amado Montero in 1903, but not without shutting down the Caracas sugar central, the largest in the country. Three strikers were killed a month later in the tobacco pickers' strike in Yaguajay, and the Cuban Hipólito Rojas and the Spaniard Antonio Cendán were strangled to death in the strike at the Narcisa central.[45]

Tobacco workers stayed on strike from February 20 to July 20, 1907 and demanded that their wages be paid in United States dollars, given the devaluation of the Spanish peseta.[46] That year and the next saw strikes by railroad workers, organized by anarchists of the Comité Federativo, and again by tobacco workers, among others. During the presidency of José Miguel Gómez between 1909 and 1913, strikes proliferated as the weight of North American capitalism was increasingly felt. Anarchists led the majority of those strikes, seeking higher wages, the eight-hour workday, and

---

44   See Orestes Ferrara, *Una mirada sobre tres siglos–Memorias* (Madrid: n.p., 1976).
45   Antonio Penichet, "El proceso social, 1902–1933," in *Curso de introducción a la historia de Cuba* (La Habana, Cuba: n.p., 1937), 450 (cited by Fernández).
46   Plasencia Moro, "Historia del movimiento obrero en Cuba," 101.

improved work conditions. In 1911 sewage workers went on strike and in 1912 sugar mill workers in Oriente, and both were brutally repressed by Gerardo Machado, then Secretary of Government and future president. According to Plasencia Moro:

> The escalation in strike activity, the spread of struggles in the sugar industry, the development of a spirit of solidarity among workers, and the growing experience of the proletariat led to the strengthening of government repression and the use of anti-labor methods. Among the latter, the most outstanding were the expulsion of foreign workers and the use of scabs.[47]

It was the same anti-labor methods employed in Argentina and Brazil (Ley de Residencia, Ley Adolfo Gordo).

The conservative government of General Mario García Menocal, like many other Latin American governments, took a demagogic form and aimed to break the combative spirit of workers, creating the Asociación Cubana para la Protección Legal del Trabajo, naming to its vice-presidential spot the reformist leader Pedro Roca, and convening a Congreso Obrero. Plasencia Moro wrote: "This Congress was opposed by anarcho-syndicalists, due to its official character."[48]

When the First World War broke out, tobacco factories were shuttered, thousands of workers were left unemployed, and a committee formed by anarchists organized a hunger strike. At the same time, inflation hit one hundred percent, wages barely rose in relation (merely some thirty percent), basic goods became scarce, and on the pretext of a state of war the working class was more closely watched and severely repressed than before.[49]

Strikes were waged in all parts of the country, with anarchists among the leaders. They were struggling for wages, for lower prices on basic goods, to stop the importation of workers receiving

---

47   Ibid., 102.
48   Ibid., 104.
49   Ibid., 105.

hunger wages from the neighboring Antilles, and against military conscription. Between 1917 and 1920 more than 220 strikes broke out. Again, Plasencia Moro:

> In 1917 anarcho-syndicalists predominated in workers' organizations, whose leaders supported that ideology. Alfredo López, an anarchist leader of typographical workers, stood out as a fighter for the organization and unity of workers, and played an important role in the constitution of the Sindicato General de Obreros de la Industria Fabril. The Sindicato had broken away from the old and ineffective union structure that prevented close ties among workers in the same union and weakened them *vis-à-vis* management. Anarchists dominated the workers' movement during this period. But Alejandro Barreiro, leader of cigar rollers and an active militant with Carlos Baliño in 1918, and José Peña Vilaboa, leader of the painters' union, gradually rose to prominence in the Agrupación Socialista de la Habana.[50]

In February 1915 Fernando Iglesias organized sugar workers in Cruces to strike for the eight-hour workday and a twenty-five percent wage increase. It was unsuccessful due to Iglesias's incarceration. But soon enough other strikes erupted in sugar mills. In particular, one at the Soledad central owned by the North American company Guantánamo Sugar demanded an end to vouchers as a form of pay; it was violently repressed by the Yankee consul employing bands of gangsters. Plasencia Moro again provides valuable commentary:

> Menocal sought to justify the repression through a campaign in the bourgeois press denouncing the presence of an anarchist conspiracy against public peace. Thus he was able to explain in 1915 the imprisonment and deportation of Spanish

---

50   Ibid., 106.

workers accused of being anarchists. At the same time, the anarchist press was outlawed, and police and army intensified the persecution and repression of workers' activities.[51]

Alfredo López, previously mentioned, was a member of the Asociación de Tipógrafos de la Habana, one of the most active unions. Frank Fernández says the following about him:

> He was a man of proletarian extraction, born in the early 1890s in Camagüey. From his youth he was an organizer and militant for the anarcho-syndicalist cause, a true leader of the Cuban working class, remembered today as a precursor of the libertarian syndicalism of the twentieth century.... In 1919 he was persecuted by Menocal's repression when labor unrest in Havana reached a crisis.[52]

López and other Cuban anarchists supported the October Revolution,[53] as did many Latin American anarchists. But after the suppression of workers' councils and the installation of "democratic centralism," after Kronstadt and the killing of Makhno's Ukrainian guerrillas, they came to recognize that that Revolution had nothing to do with libertarian socialism. Tobacco rollers from Havana and Pinar del Río convened a Congreso Obrero Nacional with 120 delegates in attendance between April 14 and 16, 1920. Among other accomplishments, this Congress resolved to hold a meeting for the purpose of forming a national workers' federation. That meeting took place on November 26, 1920 with eighteen syndicates participating. A preliminary draft of regulations presented by the Federación Obrera Local was approved and sent to all syndicates in the country for discussion and eventual approval. On April 29, 1922 the Federación Obrera de la Habana (FOH) was formed,

---

51 Ibid., 107.
52 Fernández, "El 60 aniversario de la Confederación Nacional Obrera de Cuba" in *Guángara libertaria*, 1985, 4.
53 Plasencia Moro, "Historia del movimiento obrero en Cuba," 108.

comprising twenty-one unions. Its first Secretary-General was the anarchist Alfredo López, and its first secretary of finances the anarchist Alejandro Barreiro. In December of 1924, Alfredo López convened a meeting to promote the efforts to found the Confederación Nacional Obrera de Cuba. Later a successor assembly met in Cienfuegos in February 1925, with 105 delegates representing 75 unions.

Among these delegates were Alfredo López, Barreiro, Penichet, Antes, García, V. Rodríguez, Rafael Serra, Manuel Deza, Emilio Rodríguez, J. Villasuso, M. Landrove, and José Rivero Muñiz, all or most of them anarchists. It was agreed that in accordance with the principles of anarcho-syndicalism the future Confederación would not be a political party or participate in electoral contests.[54] Alba claims that anarcho-syndicalists controlled the Confederación Nacional Obrera de Cuba from 1929 to 1935.[55] By 1930, however, near the end of Machado's government, communists were already in control of the Confederación, though not of the FOH. At the preliminary assembly in Cienfuegos there were a number of syndicates that were influenced by anarcho-syndicalism but were really reformist, like the Hermandad Ferroviaria, and a few that tended towards Marxism. Still, anarcho-syndicalists were in the majority among the representatives from all trades in Cuba that convened between August 2 and 7, 1925 at the Victoria de Camagüey Club to determine the definitive constitution of the Confederación Nacional Obrera. There were 160 delegates representing 82 unions. Later 46 more would be added for a total of 128 organizations. Among the anarchists whose militancy stood out, in addition to Alfredo López, the following deserve mention: Pascual Núñez, Bienvenido Rego, Nicanor Tómas, José M. Govín, Domingo Rosado Rojas, Florentino Pascual, Luis Trujeda, Paulino Diez, Venancio Rodríguez, Rafael Serra, Enrique Varona (who was imprisoned on charges of terrorism in Camagüey), and a delegate representing anarchist working women, Juana

---

54   Fernández, "El 60 aniversario," 5.
55   Alba, *Historia del movimiento obrero en América Latina*, 106.

María Acosta. This Third Congress with delegates representing more than 200,000 workers from throughout the island approved a series of accords, adopted a declaration of principles, rejected electoral and political struggle, and confirmed Alfredo López as Secretary-General of the Confederación Nacional Obrera de Cuba, officially established in Camagüey on August 6, 1925.[56] The maturity of the Cuban working class movement was reflected in the anti-political positions adopted by this Congress.

Ten days after the founding of the Confederación Nacional Obrera de Cuba, a shaky assembly comprising seventeen delegates convened to found the Partido Comunista de Cuba. Its founding members were, as Fabio Grobart put it, "Marxists at heart." But because they had shared an anarchist ideology for many years, they still manifested that critical nonconformity that distinguishes anarchists from Marxists, and which Marx himself had considered the most valuable quality in a socialist. Thus it was not until 1936 that the Partido Comunista was able to adopt a program.[57]

The government of Gerardo Machado took office in 1925. Like many other governments in Latin America, Machado's was characterized by repression of workers and defense of North American interests. The Confederación Nacional, the Federación Obrera de la Habana, and their anarcho-syndicalist leaders were fiercely persecuted. Enrique Varona and Alfredo López, two of the most active and combative militants, were assassinated; many others were imprisoned or fled the island. Marxists exploited this situation by grabbing up various posts in the Confederación, and some five years later, through the efforts of Rubén Martínez Villena and others, they exerted a significant influence on workers' organizations, but without totally displacing the anarcho-syndicalists.

As a consequence of the economic crisis, in 1931 Cuba experienced very high unemployment and significant social stress affecting all social classes, particularly the working class. Strikes

---

56   Fernández, "El 60 aniversario," 6.
57   Plasencia Moro, "Historia del movimiento obrero en Cuba," 117.

broke out. On January 29, 1931 one of the bastions of anarcho-syndicalism, the Sindicato de Viveristas (fishermen who conserve their catch in perforated hulls) declared a strike protesting the exhausting workday imposed by their bosses and resorted to direct action as the unique weapon of proletarian struggle.[58] The strike, supported by FOH, "lasted more than seven months, and was the first one to challenge Machado's threat that no strike would last more than twenty-four hours."[59]

On March 5, 1930, in Santiago de Cuba, a fistfight broke out between students and young anarchists, ending with the torture and death of one of them, Alfredo Rodríguez, a young Spaniard. Fidel Miró, a member of the libertarian group that met at the cafe La Nuviola and later active in the Juventudes Libertarias de Barcelona, was able to escape to Jamaica.[60] An important strike was declared on July 30, 1931 by the Gremio de Conductores y Motoristas de la Havana Electric when the company sought to reduce salaries. The struggle paralyzed urban transportation for one and a half months. Anarcho-syndicalists led the strike, and many of them were imprisoned, including Rámon Pérez Anglada, Manuel Fonteboa, and Graciano Lipis.[61] A "spontaneous and leaderless" local strike at the end of July 1933 that turned into a general strike marked the beginning of the end of Machado's dictatorship. Allying with the dictator, communists tried to end the strike on August 7, while anarchists encouraged and participated in it from the start. In collaboration with Colonel Caballero, the military governor, communists put up flyers throughout the city appealing to workers to return to their jobs. Fortunately the appeal failed, and so too did the meeting they convened on August 9 at the Artística Gallega for the purpose of explaining their counterrevolutionary position.

---

58   *El movimiento obrero cubano. Documentos y articulos* (La Habana: n.p., 1977) II, 229–31.
59   Fernández, "Los anarquistas cubanos, revolución y constitución (1931)," *Guángara libertaria,* 4.
60   Ibid., 5–6.
61   Ibid., 7.

Working underground, anarchists of the Federaciones Habaneras denounced these efforts by communists in a *Primer Manifiesto*. By August 12 communist efforts had totally failed. The editorial collective of Guángara Libertaria wrote:

> Rewriting this history years later and charging them with "adventurism," communists excommunicated César Vilar and his gang. But it is doubtful that at this dramatic moment Vilar and his gang could have acted on their own without the consent of the Central Committee, as was and is the communists' sacred rule.

Even if most historians ignore or try to silence it, the valor and resolve of the anarchists was "one of the most important factors of that revolutionary day of August 12, 1933."[62]

Confronted by opposition from political parties, from students, workers, and the people, Machado found himself obliged to resign. Sumner Wells, the North American envoy and personal representative of President Roosevelt, assumed the power of Grand Elector and appointed Carlos Manuel Céspedes president of Cuba. His presidency lasted twenty-one days. The Directorio Estudiantil, the radicals of the ABC, army sergeants headed by Fulgencio Batista, and Sergio Carbó's newspaper *La Semana* all rejected the decision by the Yankee arbitrator. On September 4, Céspedes found himself forced to leave. In his place a government referred to as the Pentarquía was installed, comprising five members, including Dr. Grau San Martín. One of the first actions by that government was to denounce the Platt Amendment.[63]

On August 28, 1933 the Federación de Grupos Anarquistas de Cuba published a manifesto addressed to all workers in the country, reaffirming its radical opposition to Machado, and condemning the attitude of communists in recent events, especially in the general

---

62   Colectivo Guángara Libertaria, "La revolución del 33. Introducción," *Guángara Libertaria*, 9.
63   M. Velezcaviedes, "El 4 de septiembre," *Guángara Libertaria*, 12–13.

strike against the dictatorship. It accused leaders of the Partido Comunista and the Congreso Nacional de Obreros Cubanos of complicity with the Butcher of Las Villas, as Machado was known. They had committed themselves to the dictator in exchange for concessions—e.g., recognition of the Partido Comunista and the Defensa Obrera Internacional—and encouraged strikers to return to work, reestablishing mass transportation. César Vilar, Vicente Alvarez Rubio, Joaquin Fau, Francisco González, Jesús Vázquez, and Pedro Berges y Ordoqui were singled out. In spite of the fact that the Comité Central "with some vested interest nervously harangued the mass of striking workers to return to work," the "authoritarian and repulsive" speeches "by Vilar, Ordoqui, and other workers were rejected" and happily disregarded.[64] At the December 1933 Fourth Congress of the Confederación Nacional Obrera, communists prevailed over anarcho-syndicalists and a Trotskyist minority. They also appointed César Vilar Secretary-General and affiliated with the Internacional Sindical and the Confederación Sindical Latinoamericana (CSLA).

On March 1935 Cuban anarchists participated in the general strike held against the new dictatorship of Batista and Mendieta. The Partido Comunista and the Confederación Nacional Obrera, under the former's control, opposed the action. The strike was crushed by armed forces, a state of war was declared, unions were shuttered, university autonomy was cancelled, and thousands of educators and workers were jailed.

When fascist militants rose up in Spain against the Republic, many Cuban anarchists joined the fighting ranks of the CNT-FAI, together with comrades from Argentina, Uruguay, and Mexico.

In January 1939 the Partido Comunista founded the Confederación de Trabajadores de Cuba and assigned its presidency to Lázaro Peña. Undoubtedly there were anarcho-syndicalists in it. Even though communists were in control from its inception,

---

64 Federación de Grupos anarquistas de Cuba, "Manifiesto," *Guángara Libertaria*, 14–15.

anarcho-syndicalists were still in the majority in several unions, such as the food workers' union from Santiago.

Anarchists organized in the Movimiento Libertario Cubano fought alongside other socialists and democrats against the dictatorship of Fulgencio Batista,[65] and elaborated a program of self-managed agrarian reform, total municipal autonomy, and industrialization through workers' associations. In June 1960, under the new Castro regime, the Agrupación Sindicalista Libertaria warned of the danger that the revolution would head in the wrong direction, and affirmed that it "belonged to no one in particular but to the people in general." Moreover, giving clear articulation to the anarchist position against the Marxist-Leninism of the new government, it declared: "We shall support, as we have until now, all revolutionary means that resolve the ancient evils that we face, but we shall also fight tirelessly against the authoritarian tendencies present at the very core of the Revolution."[66]

---

65   Justo Muriel, "Los cubanos y la libertad," *Reconstruir*, 41.
66   Alba, *Historia del movimiento obrero en América Latina*, 106. On anarchists and the Castro regime, see Alfredo Gómez, "Los anarquistas cubanos y el régimen castrista," *Guángara Libertaria*, Summer 1981, 5–9; Abelardo Iglesias, *Revolución y dictadura en Cuba* (Buenos Aires: n.p., 1963).

11. Mexico

A. The Nineteenth Century

Utopias were already known in Mexico during the colonial period. Suffice it to mention Vasco de Quiroga's two utopian communities founded in the 1530s outside of Mexico City and Michoacán in his attempts to realize Thomas More's *Utopia*.[1] In an unpublished manuscript "Constitución Orgánica para el Régimen de Mexico," Dr. Francisco Severo Maldonado (1775–1832), a priest from the Tepic region, conceived of a utopia that "aspired to economic equality, suppressed all monopoly, and guaranteed all families a plot of land and employment."[2] The priest and senator José María Alpudre tried to start a socialist-style community of Freemasons in 1825.[3] Juan Nepomuceno Adorno, a Leibnitzian philosopher and author of *Los males de México y sus remedios practicables*, in 1858, and *La armonía del Universo y la ciencia de la Teodicea*, in 1862, combined an optimistic metaphysics with conceptions of utopian socialism.[4]

---

1   Silvio Zabala, *La "Utopía" de Tomás Moro en la Nueva España* (México: n.p., 1937) and *Ideario de Vasco Quiroga* (México: n.p., 1941).

2   José Bravo Ugarte, *Historia de México* (México: n.p., n.d.), 402.

3   Gastón García Cantú, *Utopías americanas* (México: n.p., 1963).

4   Pablo González Casanova, *Una utopía en América* (México: n.p., 1963).

We can also look to the priest Miguel Hidalgo, who proposed to abolish, even if by "gentle and gradual means," what he called in almost Proudhonian terms "the horrible right of territorial property—perpetual, hereditary, and exclusive."[5] Even Benito Juárez, who later would not hesitate to harshly reprimand anarchist agrarian movements, may be said to have had the "mark of Saint-Simon."[6] In 1828 Robert Owen, the famous English socialist,[7] approached Vicente Rocafuerte, a Mexican diplomat in England, and requested approval from the Mexican government to start a socialist colony in Texas. According to García Cantú:

> His petition consisted of a compendium of his *Essays on the Formation of Human Character*, published in 1813. It is not a repetition of that work, strictly speaking, but a fresh presentation of the same argument. His materialism and some ideas he derives from Godwin and the French Enlightenment are the immediate antecedents for his theory of the character of man, and together they present the possibility a new human being in a rational and just society.[8]

Melchor Ocampo, whose influence on Juárez led him to "a complete evolution and an emancipation from received ideas,"[9] during his exile in New Orleans read not only Fourier but also Proudhon, and translated a chapter from his *Philosophy of Poverty* in 1860 (though this does not make him a Proudhonian).[10]

Plotino C. Rhodakanaty, a Proudhonian and Fourierist, was a little-known figure who was mistakenly believed to have disguised

---

5   García Cantú, *El socialismo en México. Siglo XIX* (México: ERA, 1986), 112–13.

6   Ibid., 142.

7   See E. Dólleans, *Robert Owen* (Paris: n.p., 1907).

8   García Cantú, *El socialismo en México. Siglo XIX*, 141.

9   Justo Sierra, *Juárez, su obra y su tiempo* (México: n.p., 1970) 52 (cited by Rama).

10   García Cantú, *El socialismo en México. Siglo XIX*, 148. See also José C. Valadés, *Don Melchor Ocampo, reformador de México* (México: n.p., 1954).

himself as a Mexican physician and "had the silly idea to change his name, to present himself as Greek, and to spread Spinozian ideas."[11] He was indeed born in Athens on October 14, 1828 into an aristocratic family. After his father was killed in the war for national independence against Turkey, his mother, an Austrian, took him with her to Vienna. There he began medical studies during a boom period of romantic idealism and homeopathy. In 1848 he travelled to Budapest to join Hungary's war of independence. With the rebellion suppressed, he went on to Berlin where he took an interest in philosophy. Like so many other university students of that time he admired Hegel, and might have followed lectures by Schelling.

Some similarities in the lives of Bakunin and Rhodakanaty are worth noting. Both were of aristocratic backgrounds, were interested in philosophy and admired Hegel, and committed themselves to the struggles for independence by people subjected to an imperial yoke. Also, both travelled to Paris and were profoundly influenced by the thought of Proudhon. But there is no indication that they were at all personally acquainted with each other. In 1848 Rhodakanaty was in Budapest, and Bakunin was in Leipzig and then Prague, conspiring with the Czech patriots against the Austrian empire. Bakunin was arrested in May 1849 in Saxony for his involvement in the Dresden Uprising and sent to the Saints Peter and Paul fortress in St. Petersburg, then to Schlüsselburg and Siberia, finally escaping to North America in 1861; Rhodakanaty on the other hand resided in Paris for several years and then a few months in Spain.[12] He had heard from some friends in Paris that Mexican President Ignacio Comonfort sought to encourage the establishment of foreign agricultural colonies in Mexico. Consequently, Rhodakanaty planned to travel there with the hope of putting the ideas of Fourier and Proudhon into practice. But Comonfort was toppled and the young Rhodakanaty had to delay his trip, finally arriving in Mexico in February 1861.[13]

---

11   Emeterio Téllez, *Tres escritores excéntricos. Bibliografía filosófica mexicana*, libro V, cap. XV, 91 (cited by Ignacio Ortiz).

12   Jeanne-Marie, no title, 132–72.

13   Valadés, "Precursores del socialismo antiautoritario en México,"

A few months after his arrival, Rhodakanaty published a pamphlet titled *Cartilla socialista o sea el catecismo eleméntal de la escuala de Carlos Fourier, el falansterio*, marking the beginning of a quarter-century of intense theoretical and practical activity on behalf of libertarian socialism in Mexico, where there is no doubt that he was the first anarchist ideologist. In 1877 an anonymous biographer wrote in *El Socialista*:

> By conviction a philosopher, he adopted the profession of medicine. But as a partisan to progress, he joined the homeopathic school, for wherever a new truth or discovery was made, he was there. He was fluent in seven languages and in philosophy as well, and he sought an honorable livelihood: without fee and with all his effort he healed the sick, and taught those who retained him as educator. He harmed no one, did good for others, and those who knew him recognized his high moral standards.[14]

In 1886 he left the terrain of social struggles in Mexico. His name was never again mentioned; it is very likely that he returned to Europe—either to Greece, his homeland, or France, his intellectual home—and died there.

Rhodakanaty's thought may be grouped into three areas: philosophical, religious, and social, sharing as their foundation a metaphysical conception based on Spinoza's pantheism that Rhodakanaty preferred to call "panteosophy." Spinoza was one of principal figures of German idealism between Fichte and Hegel. It is not surprising that Rhodakanaty would be deeply influenced by his thought, given the philosophical environment in German universities during the period when he studied in Vienna. Spinoza's

---

Supplement to *La Protesta*, 1928.

14   Ignacio Ortiz, *Pensamiento y obra de Plotino C. Rhodakanaty*, Tesis de licenciatura, Facultad de Filosofía y Letras, UNAM (inédita), 16–17. See also Juan Hernández Luna, "Movimiento anarco-fourerista entre el imperio y la Reforma," in *Cuadernos de orientación política*, April 1956.

rationalist, if not geometric, method guarantees a break with traditional theology and all positivist religion, and his conception of *Deus sive natura* as the sole infinite substance integrated into infinite attributes frees the imagination, giving it wings for a romantic flight without limits or borders.

Rhodakanaty does argue for the necessity of religion and the superiority of Christianity over all other religions. For him the essence of Christianity is charity, that is, love for all, as it is taught in the Gospels. And that essence is the moral foundation of socialism and revolution as well. "Pure Christianity," he wrote, "is the religion that will regenerate the world when people finally come to understand the power of its basic principles: liberty, equality, and fraternity."[15] But it is Christianity without dogma, like Saint-Simon's, and without priesthood, liturgy, or hierarchical organization, the model for which he finds in the life of Jesus and his earliest followers. Primitive Christianity is authentic Christianity. But it has been entirely degraded by the Catholic and Protestant churches, and has nothing to do with so many sects that call themselves Christian. For Rhodakanaty, the Christian religion is not only compatible with the rationalist and monist metaphysics of Spinoza and the libertarian socialism of Proudhon, but is indeed the hinge between them. He is, in short, a libertarian socialist basically influenced by Fourier and Proudhon.

Victor Considérant, a French Fourierist, tried to aid the liberation of Mexican peasants during Maximilian's imperial government in 1865.[16] He was the author of *La destinée social*, published in 1834, and *Le socialisme devant la vieux monde*, published in 1848, and was a member of the National Assembly, editor of several Fourierist newspapers like *La Phalange* and *La Democratie Pacifique*, and the founder of a colony called La Reunión in Texas. It had as

---

15   Rhodakanaty, "De la influencia del cristianismo sobre la organización social de las naciones," *La Democracía*, No. 15, 1 (Col. 3. Enero 30, 1873), cited by Ortiz.

16   See Maurice Dommangent, *Victor Cosidérant. Sa vie, son oeuvre.* (Paris: Editions Sociales, 1929).

little success as those of Owen or Cabet. During the French military occupation of Mexico he wrote four letters to marshal Bazaine, head of the military. Without trying to sell him on the advantages of Fourierism, he did attempt to persuade the marshal to eliminate the system of servitude in rural Mexico, something that the latter did, in fact, seriously try.[17]

But Rhodakanaty went further than Considérant, who dedicated himself to parliamentary politics in his last years. He combined the idea of an agricultural community with Proudhon's critique of private property and the State. When in contact with the reality of rural peasants and the problematic of the working classes in Mexico, he incorporated a number of ideas from Bakunin. From the point of view of his social ideas he can be classified as a libertarian socialist or an anarcho-socialist, with Christianity as the moral base of the doctrine, as religion, for him, is reducible to a humanistic ethics. In any event, García Cantú's reference to him as a Christian socialist fits him no better than it does Saint-Simon. Like Kropotkin and other anarchist theoreticians, Rhodakanaty thinks of socialism as the logical conclusion of the French Revolution, the fullest expression of the motto "Liberty, equality, fraternity." For Rhodakanaty, "the French Revolution is the formula for today's socialism—Liberty, Equality, Fraternity, to which we now add Unity."[18] That is why he said, "after the French Revolution all revolutions in the world are French."[19]

Property is the origin of all evil and the great enemy of the unity of mankind. The immediate objective of socialism is the "extinction of poverty, the distribution and increase of the common wealth, the abolition of prostitution, and the conservation of all of our faculties, including the intellectual, physical, and moral

17 Rama, *Utopismo socialista* (1830–1893), LVII–LVIII.
18 Rhodakanaty, "Programa social-último sacrificio. Determinación del nivel histórico," *El socialista*, No. 178, 1 (Col. 2, May 28, 1976), cited by Ortiz.
19 Rhodakanaty, "Refutación de la imputación que el Sr. D. Roberto A. Esteva hace al Manifiesto de Congreso de Obreros," *El Socialista*, No. 175, 1 (Col. 2, May 7, 1876), cited by Ortiz.

ones"; and its ultimate objective is "the transformation of humanity through science, beauty, and virtue."[20]

Cosmopolitanism was one of the essential elements of Rhodakanaty's thought:

> We are cosmopolitans by nature, citizens of all nations, and contemporaries to all the ages. The greatest and most heroic human actions belong equally to all. Wherever the regenerative idea emerges, the greatest problems of democracy are examined, and freedom is established: there we immediately attach ourselves, and recognize as our adopted nation any country in which the sacred rights of humanity are preserved.[21]

Ubi libertas ibi patria: where there is liberty, there is homeland. "Our country is the entire world and all men are our brothers."[22] Proudhon's critique of the state and of government is present in Rhodakanaty's conception of socialism. "In a people renewed by socialism," he wrote, "all government is synonymous with slavery and with the most monstrous inequality because free men do not need tutors or guardians, but friends and collaborators in their future happiness."[23]

For Rhodakanaty, the abolition of the state—which some consider impossible and others a dangerous source of evil and disorder—opens new doors. "The abolition of all government in the nations, which frightens you and you consider impossible and absurd, though you have never tried it, will usher in a totally new world of institutions ... in which the peoples of the world will live

---

20 Rhodakanaty, "¡Pueblo soberano!" in *El hijo del Trabajo*, No. 4, 2–3, May 9, 1876; cited by Ortiz.

21 Rhodakanaty, "El 5 de mayo. Discurso pronunciado por el C. Plotino Rhodakanaty, como secretatio ques es de una sociedad progresista de esta capital, el día 5 de mayo de 1874," in *El Craneoscopo*, No. 4, supl. 2 (Col. 1), cited by Ortiz.

22 Rhodakanaty, "¡Pueblo soberano!" 3.

23 Rhodakanaty, "La revolución social," in *El Combate*, No. 432, 1 (Col. 3, June 8, 1877), cited by Ortiz.

in happiness."[24] Like Bakunin, Rhodakanaty insisted that socialism will emerge from a class struggle, a struggle between the poor and the rich. At first his Fourierist background kept him away from the idea of a violent revolution. Bit by bit, however, he seemed to accept it, following the path of his young Mexican Bakuninist friends, and came to acknowledge the necessity of a "social revolution in which many heroic victims will be sacrificed on the sacred altar to restore the justice denied to the people."[25]

After his attempt to start a socialist agricultural colony and the publication of his *Cartilla Socialista*, Rhodakanaty dedicated himself to intense journalistic and organizational efforts for the dissemination of socialist ideas. In 1863 he initiated the first Grupo de Estudiantes Socialistas, in which the influence of Bakunin's ideas was clear. In the 1860s and 70s the first ideologists and leaders of Mexican libertarian socialism emerged from that group—Santiago Villanueva, who tried to organize the workers' movement, Hermenegildo Villavicencio, and, above all, Francisco Zalacosta, leader of rural masses.[26] This nucleus served as a base for a more important anarchist group, La Social, which was at once dedicated to propaganda and action, and also a free school. Its members not only created the first mutual aid society and reestablished the inactive Sociedad mutual del Ramo de Sastrería, but also took workers associated with both groups beyond mutual aid to an active systematic defense of their class interests against entrepreneurs and bosses. Thus the mutual aid societies became resistance societies.

In June 1865 anarchists from La Social promoted the first industrial strike in Mexico against two textile mills.[27] Emperor Maxi-

---

24   Rhodakanaty, "Garantismo humanitario," in *El Socialista*, No. 21, 1 (Col. 4, November 1877), cited by Ortiz.

25   Rhodakanaty, "La revolución social," 1.

26   John M. Hart, *Los anarquistas mexicanos, 1860–1900* (México: Sep'setentas, 1974), 34.

27   Jacinto Huitrón remembers that on "August 13, 1766 the first strike began by ditch diggers against Don Pedro Romero de Terreros, conde de Regla" in *Orígenes e historia del movimiento obrero mexicano* (México: Editores Mexicanos Unidos, 1980), 40.

milian's soldiers quickly repressed it. The occupation of the country by a foreign power, governance by a sovereign totally alien to the people, the country burdened by a fatuous and extravagant court, and, most of all, the harsh economic conditions imposed on workers and artisans encouraged the spread of anarchist ideas in Mexico City. Also in 1865 Rhodakanaty established the Escuela del Rayo y del Socialismo in Chalco, and in November he met with his disciple, Zalacosta. Julio Chávez would later emerge from the Escuela as an important leader of the peasant rebellion prior to Emiliano Zapata and a strong anarcho-communist. "I am a socialist," he is reported to have said, "because I am an enemy of all governments, and a communist because my brothers want to work the fields together."[28] Followed by a group of friends who shared his ideals, he began a process of land expropriation. Many peasants who saw in this a return to the ancient indigenous regime of common property, the *calpulli*, soon joined him. His activities ranged from the Chalco-Texcoco region, where he began, to all the states of Puebla and Morelia. The federal army finally moved against him. Defeated and imprisoned, he was executed in 1869 by order of President Juárez. Dying, he cried out, "Long live socialism!"

A few months earlier he had released a manifesto calling for armed struggle. According to Hart:

> The importance of the manifesto in the development of agrarian ideology is not only to have introduced the European socialist concept of the class struggle to the Mexican movement, but also to have situated the injustices suffered by peasants in a historical context, and to have identified those responsible. He proposed to replace the sovereignty of the national government, which he looked on as the corrupt collaborator of the landowning class, with the venerated principle of communal autonomy, an ideal common to many agrarian revolutions.[29]

---

28 M. Díaz Ramírez, *Apuntes históricos del movimiento obrero y campesino en México, 1844–1880* (México: n.p., 1938), 77.

29 Hart, *Los anarquistas mexicanos, 1860–1900*, 64.

It is the classic anarchist thesis of a free commune in a confederation with other communes, without government or state. Other disciples of Rhodakanaty, like Villavicencio and Villanueva, undertook the work of organizing artisans and workers in the urban context. Their initial Proudhonian character soon enough turned Bakuninist. And immediately after the fall of the Empire they had to fight not only against employers and the old conservative politicians, but also reformers, like Romero and Cano, who supported Juárez's liberal government. In July 1868 they promoted an industrial strike in the textile mills in Tlalpan. It was the first one to achieve its objective. In 1869 they established the Círculo Proletario, in 1870 the Gran Círculo de Obreros de México, and in 1871 the newspaper *El Socialista*, which sometimes expressed ideas that were clearly anarchist. This activity soon spread to the interior of the country, influenced by libertarian ideology. "It was at that time," Hart writes, "that the red-and-black was adopted as the official symbol of the Mexican workers' movement."[30]

During the 1870s Mexican anarchists encouraged cooperativism and collectivism, supported a struggle in the workers' and artisans' organizations against moderate elements that counted on support from the government, and promoted the syndicalist struggle through the proletarian press—for example, *El Socialista*, *El Hijo del Trabajo*, *El Obrero Internacional*, and others. They disseminated libertarian ideology and began the organization of workers at the national level.[31] The Congreso General Obrero de la República Mexicana convened in March 1876. Its manifesto revealed "an expansion of libertarian ideology in Mexico," according to Hart, in which anarchists were successful in having women accepted as delegates for the first time. Valadés reported on two opposing groups in that Congress—first the socialists, like Mata Rivera, Larrea, and then the anarchists, like Rhodakanaty and members of La Social—along with those who, though not

---

30   Ibid., 80.
31   B. Cano Ruiz, *Ricardo Flores Magón. Su vida. Su obra.* (México: Ediciones Tierra y Libertad, 1976), 24.

anarchists, were opposed to government intervention in working class issues, like Ricardo V. Vellatti, Rivera Cambas, Serralde, and others.[32]

Unfortunately the Mexican workers' movement soon found itself torn apart by partisan and electoral politics. Some groups supported the presidential campaign of Lerdo de Tejada, while others went for José María Iglesias or Porfirio Díaz. Needless to say, anarchists rejected any involvement in the electoral process and saw in the various candidates nothing but greed and desire for power. Meanwhile, the increasingly harsh conditions of the working class in the city and the growing proletarianization heightened the prestige of anarchist socialism. Through his newspaper *La Internacional*, Zalacosta was busy promoting a twelve-point program, including the idea of a "universal social republic, autonomous municipal government, women's rights, worker's associations, abolition of wages, and equality in property."[33]

While José María González, a disciple of Villanueva, proposed the creation of agricultural communities, based on free association and a plan partly influenced by Prouhonian ideas,[34] Zalacosta, a Bakuninist, was convinced that socialism could not be realized in either the city or country without direct action. Consequently, in 1877 he led a peasant insurrection in Sierra Gorda and Planes de la Barranca. His followers fought the federal troops until 1880. And even though he was defeated and imprisoned in Querétaro in 1881, the peasant rebellion did not die with him. In the meantime, his friend, Colonel Alberto Santa Fe, proposed the Ley del Pueblo, a document showing clear influence of Bakunin's ideas, though not an anarchist manifesto as such.

---

32 García Cantú, *El Socialismo en México. Siglo XIX*, 200. Nettlau remembers that between 1873 and 1880 the Spanish anarchist Carlos Sanz, who had been influenced by R. Farga Pellicer, worked intensely in Mexico. See Valadés, "Sobre los orígenes del movimiento obrero en México," in *Certamen internacional de La Protesta*, (Buenos Aires), 1927, 72–85.

33 Hart, *Los anarquistas mexicanos, 1860–1900*, 97; García Cantú, *El Socialismo en México*, 235–41.

34 Ibid., 209–10.

The Ley del Pueblo's four fundamental points, as summarized in *El Hijo del Trabajo*, were: distribution of lands, promotion of national industry, suppression of the army, and free and compulsory education. According to Colonel Santa Fe only the distribution of lands would bring the independence of Mexico. "In those days," García Cantú writes, "the peasants in Coahuila, State of Mexico, Michoacán, and Hidalgo forcibly recovered the lands that had been robbed by landowners.... The daily newspaper *La libertad* called it an *unconscionable communism*."[35]

General Negrete supplied arms to Santa Fe's revolutionary program. He had already supported Chávez López in 1869 and Zalacosta in 1879. Santa Fe's exemplary resistance to Porfirio Díaz's dictatorial government went beyond democratic opposition and electoral politics. He sought nothing less than the transfer of political sovereignty to the autonomous municipality, and of land to peasant collectives. The resistance lasted until the 1890s. Nonetheless, using first bribery and then repression, Díaz was able to control or suppress almost the entire workers' movement in both urban and rural contexts in the last two decades of the nineteenth century. During that period the great mass of peasants saw meager wages, while industrial workers and miners were better paid (which is not to say they were paid well— and by 1898 they too began to feel the effects of the crisis). According to Cardoso and Hermosillo, after 1898 "labor wages began to decline steadily, and even when there was some improvement, in 1910 wages were at their lowest levels ever seen."[36]

B. The Liberal Party and Magonism

The start of the twentieth century witnessed a rebirth of the

---

35   Ibid., 222.
36   Ciro F. S. Cardoso and Francisco G. Hermosillo, "Las clases sociales durante el Estado liberal de transición y la dictadura porfirista (1867–1910)," in *La clase obrera en la historia de México, Vol. 3, De la dictadura porfirista a los tiempos libertarios* (México: n.p., 1985), 70.

workers' movement and anarchism in Mexico. The arrival of new groups of Spanish immigrants is partly to thank, as well as contact with North American anarcho-syndicalists. But the decisive factor was the ideological evolution of the great Partido Liberal Mexicano [PLM]. Initially this was an anti-clerical and anti-dictatorial party, but its programmatic basis did not exclude a concern with agrarian reform. At some point, it ceased being liberal and became libertarian. This qualitative change accompanied the ideological evolution of Ricardo Flores Magón, and marks the triumph of his radical position over the moderate one of Camilo Arriaga.

In Peru, Manuel González Prada was experiencing a similar evolution from radical liberalism to libertarian socialism. But when he declared himself an anarchist, he also abandoned the Unión Nacional he had founded, and its members proved unable to follow him. By contrast Magón stayed with the Partido Liberal, and tried to retain its original name even when it became clear to him that he was no longer a liberal but had become a libertarian, and the organization could no longer really call itself a "party" but was more properly a "revolutionary organization." On February 5, 1901 the first Congreso Liberal convened in San Luis Potosí. Among the resolutions adopted, it is important to note those that refer to the "means to combat the influence of the clergy" (Resolutions 33 and 37), and the "guarantees that ensure the rights of all citizens" (Resolutions 44 and 52).[37] At this time, the socialist and libertarian viewpoints seemed far off in the distance. But it will be a matter of only a few years. During the Congress, Magón, the main promoter of these viewpoints, was already attacking Díaz's dictatorship and denouncing the exploitation of Mexican workers.

Magón was born in San Antonio Eloxochitlán, state of Oaxaca, on September 16, 1873. On his father's side, he was a descendant of Indians, and on his mother's side of mestizos. A Spanish great-grandfather from Cartagena perhaps explains his less than

---

37   Jacinto Huitrón, *Orígenes e historia del movimiento obrero en México*, 93, 95–96.

indigenous features.[38] He began the study of law in Mexico City during hard economic times, but did not complete his degree. As early as his student years at the Escuela Nacional Preparatoria he was involved in political struggles, took part in anti-government rallies, and in 1892, before his twentieth birthday, became acquainted with the prisons of the dictatorship. In 1893 he joined the editorial staff of *El Demócrata*, an anti-Díaz publication that was soon shut down. On August 7, 1900 he founded *Regeneración*. It would become the most important publication of the Mexican Left in the twentieth century. Santillán says that its language "frightened both Díaz and the scientists."[39] From May 1901 to April 1902, Magón was imprisoned in Belén, but publication of *Regeneración* continued. Again, Santillán:

> It appears that during this time Ricardo read the works of Kropotkin, Malatesta, and Gorki, and those readings helped to clarify several uncertain points and to strengthen his faith. There are a number of testimonies of an early adoption of libertarian ideas. But for several years the struggle against the dictatorship left the anarchist tendency simply to incubate in his heart.[40]

Magón had secured those anarchist readings from the personal library of the wealthy liberal landowner Camilo Arriaga,[41] who on January 29, 1902 was also incarcerated for an entire year along with the leaders of the Club Liberal de San Luis Potosí. In the meantime, Magón was publishing *El Hijo del Ahuizote* in the capital, a satirical anti-Díaz publication for which he was again imprisoned in April 1903. When he gained his liberty in 1904 he moved on to

---

38   G. Aguirre Beltrán, *Introducción a Ricardo Flores Magón: Antología* (México: CEHSMO, 1972), VII.

39   Santillán, *Ricardo Flores Magón. El Apóstol de la Revolución Social Mexicana* (México: n.p., 1978), 24.

40   Ibid., 27.

41   James D. Cockroft, *Precursores intelectuales de la Revolución Mexicana* (México: Siglo XXI, 1976), 81.

Texas, and in San Antonio renewed publication of his famous paper *Regeneración*, bringing together all sectors of the radical opposition to Díaz's dictatorship. Proof of this is the fact that the Partido Liberal Mexicano was founded in 1905, after the reissue of *Regeneración*. That year the paper had a circulation of twenty thousand and by the next year it had grown to thirty thousand. The Junta Organizadora of the Partido appointed Magón as president, Juan Sarabia as vice-president, and Antonio Villareal as secretary. Even when the newspaper was being introduced in Mexico and had as its objective "the struggle by any means against the dictatorship of Porfirio Díaz,"[42] being internationalists they did not fail to engage themselves with the North American Left, and particularly with the IWW. According to James Cockroft, the "support the North American Left extended to the Partido Liberal Mexicano became even stronger in subsequent years. They were natural allies."[43]

Persecution by Yankee police and Pinkerton thugs (paid and encouraged by agents of Porfirio Díaz) forced Magón to move even further north to St. Louis. There he renewed publication of his newspaper in February 1906. The PLM platform drafted in June of the same year was not limited to demanding a single-term presidency; abolition of compulsory military service and military tribunals during peacetime; free, secular, and mandatory education; and limitations on clerical privileges. It also included the eight-hour workday, minimum wage, holidays and weekends, prohibition of child labor, and the appropriation of nonproductive lands.[44] Cockroft notes:

> If the program of the PLM was the first one to present publicly and nationally the main ideas of the Mexican Revolution, it was also the only public document that went beyond the Constitution of 1917 in some of its progressive aspects. In

---

42 Santillán, *Ricardo Flores Magón*, 32–33.
43 Cockfort, *Precursores intelectuales de la Revolución Mexicana*, 120.
44 Chantal López and Omar Cortés, *El programa del Partido Liberal Mexicano de 1906 y sus antecedents* (México: Ediciones Antorcha, 1985).

spite of the fact that the authors of the program deliberately softened their declaration so as not to alienate certain elements of the upper class that, though conservative, were sympathetic to the cause, the framers of the Constitution, by way of its Jacobin majority, intentionally radicalized their propositions to satisfy the demands of the peasantry and the working class, which, having waged armed rebellion, were still in a posture of war. As a pioneering document, the program of the PLM has no equal.[45]

Meanwhile in Mexico, Francisco I. Madero began organizing the Partido Demócrata with the aim, according to Magón, of weakening support for the PLM. Its program was entirely political and lacked any explicit concern with social problems, particularly agrarian reform.[46] Madero was an upper-class intellectual, a free marketeer and democrat, generally indifferent to the problems of the Mexican masses, an enthusiast of Allan Kardec, and an assiduous reader of the *Revue Spirite*. He sought to replace Porfirio Díaz's administration with a democratic regime elected through free and fair elections, with laws prohibiting all presidential reelection.[47] But it would be very difficult to consider him a revolutionary.[48]

On October 12, 1905 Magón, his brother Enrique, and Juan Sarabia were detained and charged with defaming the Mexican government. Consequently, the offices of *Regeneración* were raided, its printing press and furniture confiscated, and its postal permit suspended. Publication was renewed a few months later when they

---

45 Cockroft, *Precursores intelectuales de la Revolución Mexicana*, 123–24.

46 Salvador Hernández Padilla, *El magonismo: historia de una pasión libertaria 1900–1922* (México: Ediciones Era, 1984).

47 Cockroft, *Precursores intelectuales de la Revolución Mexicana*, 62.

48 The diplomat Victoriano Salado Alvarez, said: "To me it is unfair to credit Madero and his friends with the Revolution. The real revolutionaries were the Magonists. Not only did they maintain a consistent position, but also were able to involve the entire frontier, provoking a deep hatred for the tyrant Díaz." Cited in A. Cué Cánovas, *Ricardo Flores Magón, la Baja California y los Estados Unidos* (México: Libro Mex Editores, 1957), 22–24.

were released. In February 1906, it was again published from St. Louis. But Magón was forced to flee to Canada. The United States government was complicit in the Díaz dictatorship, which it saw as a "guarantee" against the revolutionary tide, and it thus became increasingly hostile to exiled liberals.[49]

Between 1906 and 1908 the PLM either directly or indirectly promoted a series of strikes and popular uprisings in different regions of the country. The first strike took place on June 1, 1906 in Cananea in the copper company of William C. Greene, a subsidiary of the sadly celebrated Anaconda. A group of readers of *Regeneración* and sympathizers of Magón's ideas—Esteban Baca Calderón, Francisco M. Ibarra, Manuel M. Diéguez, and others—started the Unión Liberal Humanidad in Cananea, which grew to have some one hundred members. The lawyer Lázaro Gutiérrez de Lara, for his part, organized the Club Liberal de Cananea. Like the Unión Liberal Humanidad, it soon joined the PLM in St. Louis.[50]

Mexican miners from Cananea were being paid barely subsistence wages, and faced shameless discrimination in their own land, while foreign workers received twice their wages in U.S. dollars. Led by Calderón, liberals organized a miners' union for the first time. In May 31 a strike unexpectedly erupted in the Oversight mine. Miners demanded higher wages, the eight-hour workday, dismissal of various foremen, a workforce comprising seventy-five percent Mexican workers, and equality of treatment and opportunity for them. William C. Greene, president of the company, rejected all demands, and tried to convince the miners that his treatment was fair and the wages he paid them excellent. Meantime, Porfirio Díaz thought it reckless to raise wages for Mexican workers.[51]

Later, a peaceful miners' demonstration was attacked by gunshots from several Yankee employees. The miners then set against

49 Santillán, *Ricardo Flores Magón*, 36–37.

50 León Díaz Cárdenas, *Cananea. Primer brote del sindicalismo en México* (México: CEHSMO, n.d.), 26–28.

51 Daniel Cosío Villegas, *Historia moderna de México* (México: Ediciones Hermes, 1965), 316 *et seq.*

the company's employees and a spontaneous rebellion broke out. Police and thugs massacred a multitude of demonstrators using dum-dum bullets, prohibited even in war by all international agreements.[52] The rebellion spread, and the workers, supported by the people of Cananea, appeared to triumph for a moment. But rural Mexican forces under orders of Colonel Kosterlisky together with more than five hundred North American Rangers and police officers under the command of Captain Thomas Rynning drowned the rebellion in blood. The massacre left more than two hundred dead, twenty thousand jailed, and an indeterminate number wounded. Diéguez, Calderón, and Ibarra avoided execution but were condemned to fifteen years in the San Juan de Ullúa prison.[53] Porfirio Díaz was cognizant of the revolutionary character of the strike in Cananea and he knew very well that Magón and the "liberals" of St. Louis had provided the inspiration.[54]

Strikes of crucial importance by textile workers of Río Blanco in Veracruz were held in 1906 and 1907. The main leader was the worker José Neira, a worthy successor to Villanueva and Zalacosta, a friend of Camilo Arriga, and a follower of Magón's ideas since 1903. It is important to keep in mind that "after mining, the textile industry was the most important economic activity in Mexico in the twentieth century."[55] French capitalists owned the textile mills in Orizaba and Río Blanco, and British workers held the most important administrative and technical positions. An engineer was paid forty-one pesos and seventy-five cents weekly, while a worker received a meager thirty-five cents per day, a female worker twenty-five cents, and a child ten cents for a workday varying from twelve to fourteen hours. Neira and a group of Magonists like Porfirio Meneses and José Olivares responded to the urgent need to organize workers to defend their rights. These men sought to

---

52   Díaz Cárdenas, *Cananea*, 53–64.

53   Ibid., 65–84.

54   Hernández Padilla, *El magonismo: historia de una pasión libertaria 1900–1922*, 47–49.

55   Ibid., 50.

start a true resistance society, but others like the Protestant pastor José Rumbia were more moderate in that they did not want to go beyond a mutual aid society. Ultimately the moderates prevailed. Once the Gran Círculo de Obreros Líbres de Río Blanco was founded its presidency went to Rumbia and Neira was elected vice-president. But Rumbia and Manuel Avila's moderation "did not serve for much." Management began to harass the leadership and some of them were forced to leave the Río Blanco region.[56]

At a meeting held in Nogales on May 5, workers decided to start a newspaper that would be the voice for the rights and aspirations of the working class. In spite of objections by some moderates, the name of the paper would be *Revolución Social*, with Neira at the editorial helm. Avila died suspiciously and in the days following his death, Neira assumed the presidency of the Gran Círculo. His acceptance speech ended with the following words: "When we run into difficulties with management, we shall strike. And if the strike is not successful, we shall turn to dynamite and revolution." He was able to have a resolution passed that the Gran Círculo would maintain "secret relations with the Junta Revolucionaria residing in St. Louis, of which Magón is president," and act on behalf of all workers in the country "by any means necessary against the abuses of capitalism and the Díaz dictatorship."[57]

Díaz and his government could not tolerate the few victories won by Neira and his Magonist comrades against entrepreneurs. So orders were given to apprehend them, but they evaded arrest by fleeing to Puebla. An intense repression against Magonist leaders then followed, and it was not long before the workers' movement in the Río Blanco region decayed under the schemes of the collaborator Morales. However, Morales was not able to accept the decision Díaz offered him in January 1907 without open protest from workers. To all accounts the settlement favored the interests of bosses and ordered workers to be better team-players.

---

56   Ibid., 52.
57   Ibid., 54.

On Monday, January 7 as the whistle sounded in Río Blanco "a group of workers walked towards the mill not with the intention of resuming their labor but of setting the mill ablaze with bosses and scabs in it." They threw rocks through windows and were met with an armed response by Lieutenant Arroyo and his troops. But workers were not intimidated. "They initiated," Hernández Padilla says, "not a strike but the *workers' rebellion in Río Blanco*, as it is still called today."[58] Workers raided and set the company store on fire, freed prisoners at the local jail, and cut electrical wires. Then they set out for Nogales. In Orizaba they armed themselves by breaking into pawnshops and took command of the railroad station. General Rosalino Martínez arrived at midnight in Santa Rosa with orders to execute the rebels without trial, and the next day, Governor Colonel Próspero Cahuantzi, arrived with the 24th Infantry Regiment from Puebla "to help landowners and subdue the bandits."[59] A systematic search of workers' homes began on January 8. Hernández Padilla writes:

> Men, women, and children were pulled from their homes and executed in the barracks. Those able to flee were later captured and killed. Meanwhile, management at the Río Blanco mill raised their champagne-filled glasses and in unison honored General Martínez with a toast. They celebrated the massacre.[60]

On the January 9, as workers entered the mill at Santa Rosa, Colonel Francisco Ruiz pulled three individuals from their work: Rafael Moreno Alvarado, president of the Gran Círculo, Manuel Juárez, vice president, and Ceferino Navarro, secretary. All three were executed: the first in front of his store which had already been looted and burnt; the second on the corner of the ruins of *El Modelo*; and the third among the rubble of *El Fénix* in

---

58   Ibid., 75–76.
59   Huitrón, *Orígenes e historia del movimiento obrero en México*, 116.
60   Hernández Padilla, *El magonismo: historia de una pasión libertaria 1900–1922*, 77–78.

Nogales.[61] Herzog writes, "*El Imparcial* of Mexico City, a daily paper underwritten by the dictatorship, published an editorial on the bloody events that was filled with praises for General Díaz. The title of the editorial was 'That's How to Govern.'"[62]

The uprisings in Cananea and Río Blanco, undoubtedly inspired by Magón's anarcho-syndicalist ideas, were not the only ones during this period. A peasant rebellion broke out in Acayucán in 1906, promoted by Hilario C. Salas. Mancisidor observes: "The armed uprising led by the Partido Liberal Mexicano spread to the municipalities of Tuxtlas, Minatitlán, and the state of Tabasco. But once again cruelties and defeats put down the peasant insurgency."[63] Magonists led other peasant uprisings in 1908. A highly dedicated group rebelled in Viescas the night of June 24, even when they knew their revolutionary plans had been reported to government officials. The libertarian poet and journalist Práxedis G. Guerrero,[64] whom his friend Magón called the "landowning peasant" and the "capitalist worker," recounts the following events:

> The comrades met at midnight, each was assigned a post, and they got to work. Police tried to resist and gunfire was exchanged, wounding one person on each side, and leaving one gendarme dead. The jail was then emptied, the liberal program proclaimed, and the dictatorship declared null. There was a request for horses and they took the few funds they found in the public offices. The revolution had taken control of the entire town without a single violent act against neutral families or individuals.[65]

---

61 Huitrón, *Orígenes e historia del movimiento obrero en México,*117.
62 Jesús Silva Herzog, *Breve historia de la revolución Mexicana*, I (México: F.C.E. 1960), 57.
63 José Mancisidor, *Historia de la revolución Mexicana* (México: n.p., 1976), 81.
64 Huitrón, *Orígenes e historia del movimiento obrero en México,* 127. See also Pietro Ferrúa, *Gli anarchici nella Rivoluzione messicana, Práxedis G. Guerrero* (Ragusa: n.p., n.d.).
65 Guerrero, *Artículos de combate* (México: Editorial Antorcha, 1977), 161.

Another Magonist revolutionary group under the leadership of José M. Rangel and Basilio Ramírez attacked the town of Las Vacas on June 26, 1908. The fight lasted over five hours. Guerrero describes it thus:

> Everywhere one looked there were acts of heroism among the volunteers for liberty. Each man was a hero; each hero a portrait animated by the spirit of a great epic.... A young man, blonde like the Scandinavians, ran from one to another danger, his clothes tattered and bloodstained. He had been shot in the shoulder, the leg under the knee, the thigh, and his bag. The shock knocked him down. But the bullet encountered the strength of a libertarian in its path and jumped, leaving intact the life of this valiant young man who returned to his feet and resumed the fight.

Mancisidor, commenting on this passage, adds, "acts of heroism like the one described were abundant."[66]

On July 1 another anarchist group exiled in El Paso raided the town of Palomas near the border, with the goal of facilitating a later invasion and the movement of revolutionary troops into the interior of Mexico. Guerrero writes: "with a fistful of bullets and a few bombs that were quickly assembled with less than effective materials, this small group was formed during a period of violent repression, and set itself against an enemy equipped with more than sufficient elements to resist it." The raid failed. Francisco Manrique, a friend of Guerrero, was killed. Magón and Guerrero were just able to cross the border.[67] Another Magonist insurrection broke out in Valladolid, Yucatán, and was also defeated by the government's

---

See also, Mancisidor, *Historia de la revolución Mexicana*, 82.

66   Ibid., 157. See also Mancisidor, *Historia de la revolución Mexicana*, 83; Pietro Ferrúa, "Ricardo Flores Magón en la Revolución Mexicana," *Reconstruir*, 72, 45.

67   Huitrón, *Orígenes e historia del movimiento obrero en México*, 138–39; Santillán, *Ricardo Flores Magón*, 66.

enormous numerical superiority in men and guns. Ramírez Bonilla, Albertos, and Kankum were summarily executed there. "There justice was not," Guerrero says, "a devious and underhanded lawyer, but a uniformed beast."[68]

In 1906, while in Canada, Magón planned a general rebellion throughout Mexican territory, under the leadership of the PLM. Díaz's government, informed of the revolutionary plan through its network of spies, was able to abort it without great effort. One of the spies from the infamous Pinkerton agency described Magón, leader of the movement at the time, in a report to Enrique C. Creel, Governor of Chihuahua:

> He is a very intelligent journalist, a hard worker, active, and disciplined. He is never drunk. He is also a good typist, well-respected by all who know him, a resolute and energetic character fascinated by the cause he pursues, and possessing all the brutal and dangerous fanaticism of the anarchists.[69]

With their revolutionary plan defeated, but encouraged by North American anarchists and socialists, Magón and his followers planned another rebellion for 1908. But it was frustrated for the same reasons. Cockroft writes: "In 1906 as well as in 1908 the Mexican government learned of the planned insurrection by the PLM, and with the assistance of the United States was able to crush it."[70]

On August 23, 1907 Magón, Sarabia, and Villareal were again jailed for a period of three years. All the resources available for their defense were in vain as the "powerful of Mexico and the United States were determined to imprison them and keep them from agitating and promoting uprisings against Díaz."[71] Their appeal

---

68   Ibid., 139.

69   Santillán, *Ricardo Flores Magón*, 39.

70   James D. Cockroft, *Precursores intelectuales de la Revolución Mexicana*, 142. See also Hernández Padilla, *El magonismo: historia de una pasión libertaria 1900–1922*, 80–135.

71   Manuel González Ramírez, *La revolución social en México*, I (México: F.C.E., 1960), 100. See also J. Muñoz Cota, *Ricardo Flores Magón, El sueño*

to President Theodore Roosevelt went unanswered; the Supreme Court denied their request for conditional liberty. Meanwhile, the North American journalist John K. Turner, a friend of PLM, published individual chapters of his book *México bárbaro* in a magazine. It was a passionate but accurate testimony of the social and political situation that the Magonists were fighting, and not, as Cosío Villegas recklessly says, "a demagogic exaggeration."[72]

After serving their sentence, Magón and his followers left prison in August 1910. They immediately went to Los Angeles and there were received by a large rally organized by the Partido Socialista. Publication of *Regeneración* was renewed. The old German anarchist Alfred Sanftleben, Turner's spouse, and later W. C. Owen edited its English-language section. Years later, Owen wrote the following in *Freedom*:

> The English-language section of *Regeneración* had a circulation of some 27,000 papers when I took the place of John Kenneth Turner as editor, and the paper should have been making money. But all the money was spent on propaganda. We had between 600 and 700 newspapers in our exchange list. Our hope was a unified opinion in Mexico, Central and South America against the invasion by plutocrats, and a sentiment sufficiently strong in North America to undo the constant threat of intervention.[73]

Such objectives required the constant vigilance of the Latin American Left.[74] To get a sense of the direction of propaganda by *Regeneración* it is crucial to keep in mind that in the United States there was then a robust socialist movement, numerous European anarchists, and a workers' central, the IWW, whose revolutionary syndicalism was close or identical to anarcho-syndicalism. At the same

---

de una palabra (México: Ediciones Doctrimez, n.d.), 29.

72   González Ramírez, ibid., 107–08.
73   Santillán, *Ricardo Flores Magón*, 67–68.
74   Cano Ruiz, *Ricardo Flores Magón. Su vida. Su obra*, 33.

time, Mexican workers in the Southern United States were taking part in the revolution that was developing in their native country with assistance from the IWW and other organizations attached to the PLM.[75]

By this time there was no doubt about the anarchist ideology of Ricardo Flores Magón and his followers. So it was no surprise when he failed to join the anti-dictatorial campaign of 1910 led by Madero. The goals of representative democracy, anti-reelectionism, and political liberty could not begin to satisfy his aspirations. For him these were all lies, for the working masses achieved nothing by being able to elect their legislators. The true goal of the revolution was to achieve the social and economic emancipation of the proletariat, and to put both land and the means of production in the hands of workers' communities. In the January 28, 1911 issue of *Regeneración*, Magón wrote:

> Governments are the representatives of capital and therefore have to oppress the proletariat. For once and for all, know this: No Congress will approve the program of the PLM because we, the dispossessed, are not the ones who will be seated in Congress, but our masters, and our masters will be careful not even to let us breath. Our masters will angrily reject the liberal program of July 1, 1906 because it proposes to expropriate their lands, and they will mock proletarian aspirations. Anarchists do not take seats in Congress, only the bourgeoisie.[76]

It is obvious that such openly anarchist ideas (in spite of what Jean Grave in France or others said) were incompatible with Madero's moderate program. But as Cockroft rightly notes, "Madero's revolution, later renewed and guided slightly left by Carranza, is the

---

75   J. Torres Parés, "El movimiento obrero de los Estados Unidos y la revolución Mexicana," *Latinoamérica*, 18, 185.

76   *Regeneración 1990–1918*, Prólogo, selección y notas de Armando Bartra, (México: ERA, 1982), 268.

one writers seem to have in mind when they refer to the Mexican Revolution as a bourgeois revolution. For the PLM, however, and to a lesser degree for Zapata and his peasant army, who had adopted the PLM's motto 'Tierra y libertad,' the Mexican Revolution was a revolution of urban and rural workers *against* the bourgeoisie."[77]

Hence it was a social and not purely political revolution; it was moreover, a libertarian revolution.[78]

Magón persistently rejected offers from President Madero, made via the ex-Magonist Sarabia, just as he had rejected earlier offers from Porfirio Díaz. The manifesto published by the Junta of the PLM on September 23, 1911 reaffirmed Magón's anarchist ideology.[79] Already in February 25 he had written an article for *Regeneración* titled "Francisco I. Madero es un traidor a la causa de la libertad" that provoked a deep chasm between the two wings of the anti-Díaz movement.[80] When the PLM troops that rebelled with Madero's—but without making common cause with them—lost strategic positions in Chihuahua (with Pascual Orozco and the middle class siding with Madero) and had to retreat, they turned their attention to Baja California. This sparsely populated territory of the Mexican Republic was the property of North American, British, and French businesses. Magonists decided to seize control of it and establish a libertarian society there, serving as a model for America and the world. On January 29, 1911, a small contingency under the command of José María Leyva and Simón Berthold took control of Mexicali, on February 21 of Los Algodones, on March 12 of Tecate, and finally, on May 9 of Tijuana. North American landowners and newspaper owners in California (who were frequently the same individuals, e.g., Chandler, Otis, and Hearst) with good

---

77 Cockroft, *Precursores intelectuales de la Revolución Mexicana*, 161; Eduardo Blanquel, "El anarco-magonismo," in *Historia Mexicana*, 51, vol. XIII, 407.

78 Santillán, Ricard Flores Magón, 72–76; Hernández Padilla, *El magonismo: historia de una pasión libertaria 1900–1922*, 139.

79 *Regeneración 1900–1918*, 306–12; Cano Ruiz, *Ricardo Flores Magón. Su vida. Su obra*, 34.

80 Ibid., 271–276; Santillán, *Ricardo Flores Magón*, 78–79.

reason took alarm and in no time trumped up the absurd legend of Magonist military adventurism.

Some conservative Mexicans and more than a few supporters of Madero (to say nothing of Díaz's friends like Salado Alvarez) accused Flores Magón of seeking Baja California's secession in order to incorporate it to the United States, something the Californian magnates surely would have liked. In a *Regeneración* article of June 16, 1911 addressing himself to "patriots," Magón asked:

> Does Baja California belong to Mexico? It does not belong to it but to the United States, England, and France. It is under the control of Cudahy, Otis, and other North American millionaires. The entire western coast of Baja belongs to a powerful British pearling company, and the region in which the town of Santa Rosalía is located belongs to a wealthy French company. And what do Mexicans own of Baja? Nothing! And what will the Partido Liberal Mexicano give them? Everything! So, dear patriots, what are you doing when you say that we are selling our country to the United States? Respond. We have no country because all of Mexico is owned by foreign millionaires who enslave our brothers. You have no country, and simply put you do not have even a place to die. And when the Partido Liberal Mexicano wants to establish for you a true country without tyrants or exploiters, you object, bluster, and insult. When you hinder the work of the PLM you impede our own people from throwing all bourgeoisie out of the country and taking possession of their properties.[81]

His invasion of Baja California had nothing to do with Madero's maneuvers in Chihuahua. His goal was not political change, as Madero's followers pretended, even less to incorporate the territory into the United States, as proclaimed by so many misinformed journalists and politicians of bad faith. On the contrary, Magón's

81   Ibid., 296–97.

goal was nothing other than a classless and stateless libertarian society that would provide the archetype and point of departure for the Mexican and world revolution. "The Magón brothers," Silva Herzog observes, "waged an armed struggle in accord with the principle of international anarchism, with the aim of establishing an ideological base for Mexico's economic, social, and political reorganization."[82] North American capitalists then began an aggressive propaganda campaign against Magonists through their newspapers, like the *Los Angeles Times*, *Los Angeles Examiner*, and *San Francisco Chronicle*, and developed a plan to annex Baja California by first separating it from Mexico, as had been done in Texas. Leftist groups, above all the IWW, so far as they were able, assisted Magón's movement and invasion.

In a manifesto that appeared in all the North American socialist press and was addressed to the "dear and valiant comrades of the Mexican Revolution," the great novelist Jack London wrote:

> We Socialists, anarchists, hobos, chicken thieves, outlaws and undesirable citizens of the United States are with you heart and soul in your efforts to overthrow slavery and autocracy in Mexico. You will notice that we are not respectable. Neither are you. No revolutionary can possibly be respectable in these days of the reign of property. All the names you are being called, we have been called. And when graft and greed begin to call names, honest men, brave men, patriotic men and martyrs can expect nothing else than to be called chicken thieves and outlaws. So be it. But I for one wish there were more chicken thieves and outlaws of the sort that formed the gallant band that took Mexicali. ... I subscribe myself a chicken thief and revolutionist. [83]

---

82   Silva Herzog, *Breve historia de la revolución Mexicana*, I, 180.

83   Drewey Wayne Gunn, *American and British Writers in México 1556–1973* (Austin and London: n.p., 1974), 56, cited by Hernández Padilla, *El magonismo: historia de una pasión libertaria 1900–1922*, 147–48.

A group of Italian anarchists from Chicago as well as several IWW militants joined the ranks of the Magonists. One of them, the proletarian songwriter Joe Hill, wrote:

> While the red flag fluttered in Baja California, hard as I tried I could not find any "important people" in the rebel ranks. I only found common and everyday working people, and in great number .... It's about time that each rebel comes to realize that "important people" and the working class have nothing in common. Let us then sing the song that says: "the workers' flag is a deep red, and to hell with the 'important people.'"[84]

The revolutionary project in Baja California failed not as a result of adventurers and gangsters like Dick Ferris, motivated by the interest of North American magnates, but because of its defeat in the field of battle to Madero, the leader of the bourgeois democracy, who was supported by the North American government and eager capitalists from Los Angeles. What remained of the Magonist army was defeated by Celso Vegas in a long, hard fight under the command of Jack Mosby.[85] Moreover, as Ricardo Flores Magón himself declared then, "Madero has joined his forces to Díaz's federal army and executed a number of Magonists on the pretext that they were bandits. Madero has begun a war of extermination against our combatants."[86] By mid-1911 the Magonist movement in Baja California was finished. But that was not the end. Detained along with three of his associates on June 14, 1911 and accused of violating U.S. neutrality laws, Magón was tried in Los Angeles and condemned

---

84 Gibbs M. Smith *Labor Martyr: Joe Hill* (New York: n.p., 1969), 54–55, cited by Hernández Padilla, *El magonismo: historia de una pasión libertaria 1900–1922*, 158.

85 Hernández Padilla, *El magonismo: historia de una pasión libertaria 1900–1922*, 161.

86 Ethel Duffy Turner, *La revolución en Baja Californis,* 78–79, cited by Hernández Padilla, *El magonismo: historia de una pasión libertaria 1900–1922*, 161.

to McNeil Island Prison, in the State of Washington, where he remained until 1914.

The Manifesto of the PLM identifies private property as the root of all social injustice. It reads: "Abolishing the principle of private property annihilates all political, economic, social, religious, and moral institutions comprising the environment in which the free initiative and association of human beings are choked." Without that principle there is no reason for government, which itself is necessary to repress the dispossessed from their rebellion against the rich, or for the Church, which pursues the same goal by preaching humility and submission, and promising the poor a reward in the afterlife. The Manifesto continues:

> Capital, authority, clergy. That's the bleak trinity that turns this beautiful earth into a paradise for those who through the power of their claws, cunning, violence, and crime have monopolized the products of the sweat, blood, tears, and sacrifice of thousands of generations of workers, making a living hell for those who with their arms and intelligence toil the earth, run the machines, build the homes, transport the goods, and in this way leaving humanity divided into two classes of diametrically opposed interests—the capitalist class and the working class, the class that possesses the earth, the production machine, and the means of transporting wealth; and the class that counts on nothing more than its arms and intelligence to secure a living.

It goes on to say that between one and the other class there can be no friendship or harmony, their interests are mutually exclusive and necessarily in conflict—one aims to retain the present state of affairs, and the other to destroy this iniquitous system. The PLM recognizes that all men have equal right to the enjoyment of all advantages of civilization, that work is indispensible for subsistence, that no one but children, the aged, and infirm are exempt from it, and that government and clergy are the pillars of capital.

"Expropriation must be carried out by blood and fire during this great movement." With a language that is undoubtedly Kropotkin's and mirrors the programs of revolutionary action from the Federación Obrera Regional Argentina, the Confederación Nacional del Trabajo, or the Federación Anarquista Ibérica, the PLM described in detail the process that will follow the expropriation of lands:

> The inhabitants of every region in which such an act of supreme justice is carried out have only to agree to a place of easy access for storing all the goods found in stores, warehouses, and granaries, where women and men of good will may then conduct a detailed inventory of all that has been gathered and calculate their shelf life, taking into account the needs and the number of inhabitants who have to make use of them from the moment of expropriation until the first harvest of the new system, and in the other industries until the first goods are produced. Once the inventory is complete, workers from different industries will come to a brotherly understanding to regulate production so that during this movement no one will lack essential goods, and only those who do not wish to work will die of hunger, with the exemption of the children, the handicapped, and the elderly, who will have the right to full enjoyment of goods. Everything that is produced will be sent to the general warehouses of the community, and everyone will have the right to take everything *according to their needs* with no other requirements than to provide the password showing employment at one or another industry.[87]

In February 1916 Flores Magón was again deprived of his liberty. This time he was jailed under the Espionage Act for writing several articles against Carranza. The government of the "liberal" Woodrow Wilson kept him in jail until July, when a group of exiled

---

87 *Regeneración, 1900–1918*, 306–12.

anarchists led by Emma Goldman and Alexander Berkman joined in solidarity to pay for his bond. These and many other Europeans taking refuge in the United States showed an understanding of and sympathy for Flores Magón and the Magonist movement that was totally lacking in Jean Grave and certain other collaborators of *Les Temps Nouveaux*, who instead attacked them and even went so far as to claim that the Mexican Revolution exists only in the imagination of the editors of *Regeneración*. Kropotkin refuted such attacks on April 27, 1912.[88] Emma Goldman, the Russian revolutionary and editor of the anarchist publication *Mother Earth*, always supported *Regeneración* and the PLM, offering them her moral and material support, and without any of the prejudice that often carried racial overtones.[89] The same can be said of another anarchist, Voltairine de Cleyre,[90] daughter of a Belgian and born in the U.S., who made the following observation about the Magonists:

> They are involved in a struggle to the death, precisely what anarchists claim to believe. Compared to our publications the pages of every issue of *Regeneración* are impregnated with a genuine anarchism, a combative anarchism that takes measures to destroy the basis of this damned system.[91]

Meanwhile, Flores Magón did not cease from his campaign against those whom he saw as departing from the Mexican revolutionary process. He attacked Carranza and his government while calling on Zapata to move the agrarian revolution forward and

---

88   Santillán, *Ricardo Flores Magón*, 92–96.

89   On Goldman, see Richard Drinnon, *Rebelde en el paraíso yanqui* (Buenos Aires: Proyección, 1965); on Berkman, see Paul Avrich, "Vida y lucha de Alejandro Berkman," *Reconstruir*, 95.

90   On Voltairine de Cleyre, see Paul Avrich, *An American Anarchist: The Life of Voltairine de Cleyre* (Princeton: Princeton University Press, 1978); Vladimiro Muñoz, "Una cronología de Voltairine de Cleyre," *Reconstruir*, 60, 51–58.

91   Avrich, *An American Anarchist*, 227, cited by Hernández Padilla, *El magonismo: historia de una pasión libertaria 1900–1922*, 155.

return land to peasant communities. On June 13, 1914 he wrote the following for *Regeneración*:

> No, we do not have to be content with the distributions of land. We have to take it all so that we can make it common, not individual property, and to achieve that goal members of the Partido Liberal Mexicano not only fight in libertarian groups organized for this war, but also spread throughout the entire country promoting in both rural and urban settings the salvific principles contained in the manifesto of September 23, 1911, principles that advocate for the permanent removal of authority, capital, and clergy.[92]

From his internationalist perspective, Flores Magón criticized the entry of the United States into the First World War, and more strongly than Kropotkin and other famous European anarchists. For him that war had no other cause than protecting the supremacy of North American plutocracy in the world. On September 19, 1915 he gave a speech titled "La patria burguesa y la patria universal," later included in the book *Tribuna roja*, in which he wrote:

> The capitalist system will die from self-inflicted wounds, and a shocked humanity will witness a formidable suicide. It was not workers who dragged nations into a conflict against each other, but the German bourgeoisie, motivated by its desire to dominate markets. The German bourgeoisie has achieved tremendous progress in industry and commerce, making its rival the British bourgeoisie quite jealous. That is what is at the bottom of this conflict that is called a European war: jealousies between merchants, hostilities among traffickers, and the quarrels of adventurers. The honor of a people, a race, or country is not litigated in the fields of Europe, instead it is the pocketbook of each that is in dispute in this fight

---

92   *Regeneración, 1900–1918*, 329–30.

between wild beasts. It is not the wounded national honor or an outraged flag that has brought on this war, but the control of money—money that was first produced by the sweat of the people in fields, in factories, in mines, in all the different places of exploitation and that now wants this same exploited people to protect it and keep it safe in the pockets of those who robbed it.

And:

The poor are killing each other in the European fields for the benefit of the rich, who want you to believe it is a war for the benefit of the nation. Tell me, what nation do the poor have? What nation do those who labor for mere subsistence with their arms have? A nation should be like a loving mother who equally protects all her children. What protection do the poor have in their respective countries? None! The poor person is a slave in all nations, is equally wretched in all of them, and is a martyr under all governments.[93]

Several months later Wilson, whom Flores Magón had called a "political dwarf," an "amusing farce," and a "little toy of the bourgeoisie," declared the United States at war. Flores Magón responded by publishing a manifesto that called people to rebel against this war by oppressors, and to turn it into a war against the oppressors themselves, that is, into a social revolution.[94] The predictable result of this revolutionary proposal was once again imprisonment. He was sentenced to twenty years and sent to McNeil Island Prison once more; later he was transferred to Fort Leavenworth in Kansas where his precarious health continued to deteriorate. On March 22 he wrote the following to Ellen White, a North American friend:

---

93   Flores Magón, *Discursos* (México: Ediciones Antorcha, n.d.), 88, 89.
94   Santillán, *Ricardo Flores Magón*, 106–08; also see Flores Magón, *La primera Guerra mundial y la revolución rusa* (México: Ediciones Antorcha, 1983).

Any doctor will tell you that diabetes is an incurable illness. Sugar can temporarily disappear from one's urine in this strange disease, but the condition will persist. Is it true that low blood pressure, my current anemic condition, cannot be attributed to my diabetes, as my present physician informed me on September 13, 1920? And what about the rheumatism that continually makes me suffer, and this eternal freeze in which healing cannot occur? As you can tell, not only am I losing my sight, I am also afflicted by a number of other conditions.[95]

Flores Magón was firmly opposed to the constitutionalist government of Venustiano Carranza and accused him of being a strike-breaker, an assassin, and a wolf in sheep's clothing in the August 26, 1916 issue of *Regeneración*.[96] In spite of all this, the Chamber of Deputies offered him a pension that, as one would expect, Flores Magón rejected. In a letter to Nicolás T. Bernal on September 20, 1920, after expressing his happiness for the "fraternal breath of Mexican workers" he conveyed gratitude "for the generous sentiment that moved the Chamber of Deputies to provide a pension to me," and then added:

I do not believe in the State; I support the abolition of international borders; I fight for the universal brotherhood of man; I consider the State an institution created by capitalism to ensure the exploitation and subjugation of the masses. Consequently, all money obtained by the State represents the sweat, the anguish, and sacrifice of workers. If this money came directly from workers, I would gladly and even proudly accept it because they are my brothers. But when it comes through the intervention of the State after being compelled from the

---

95   Flores Magón, *42 cartas, escritas en inglés durante los dos últimos años de su prisión y de su vida*. Trans. by Proudhon Cárbo. (México: Ediciones Tierra y Libertad, 1976), 11.

96   *Regeneración 1900–1918*, 389–96.

people, the money would only burn my hands and fill my heart with remorse.[97]

Kropotkin adopted a very similar attitude towards Lenin and the Bolshevik government when they offered him an academic position.[98] During this same period, the North American government made it clear to Flores Magón that it would consider his release from prison if he publicly repented and petitioned for a pardon. But it goes without saying that this incorruptible fighter could not accept such conditions.[99] In another letter to Bernal dated August 3, 1921, he remarked on the required repentance, saying that "sarcasm touches the limits of tragedy." With the indignation of the just against agents of a State so often corrupted and corrupting, he exclaimed:

> Repentance? I have not exploited the sweat, anguish, fatigue, and labor of others; I have not oppressed a single soul; I have nothing to repent for. My life has been lived without my having acquired any wealth, power, or glory, when I could have gotten these three things very easily. But I do not regret it. Wealth, power, and glory are only won by trampling others' rights. My conscience is at peace, for it knows that under my convict's garb beats an honest heart. I could be released if only I sign a petition for pardon repenting of what I have done, as the Department of Justice suggests I do. I could then join my poor, abandoned family; I could then attend to my failing eyesight that casts shadows around me and brings bitterness into my heart. But I think that the joy of being out of this hell that seems to have swallowed me forever would ruthlessly be stifled by the remonstrance of and indignant conscience that would shout to me: shame! shame! shame! For it is my honor as a fighter for freedom, my honor as a champion of the poor

---

97   Flores Magón, *Epistolario revolucionario e íntimo* (México: Ediciones Antorcha, 1983), 43–45.

98   Avrich, *Los anarquistas rusos* (Madrid: n.p., 1967), 230–32.

99   González Ramírez, *La revolución social en México, I*, 445–46.

and dispossessed, invigorated in a thirty-year struggle for justice for all that is in danger here. Thus, I do not surrender the ideal, come what may.[100]

Ricardo Flores Magón was found dead in his cell at Fort Leavenworth on November 20, 1922. A few hours earlier he had spoken with his comrade and friend Librado Rivera. Suspicions that he was assassinated are very likely true.[101] But even if he was not assassinated, the North American government was certainly responsible for his premature death.[102] Mexican workers were later able to repatriate his remains which today rest in the Rotunda de Hombres Ilustres.[103]

In the course of the anti-Díaz Revolution, alongside the Partido Liberal—or better yet, alongside the left wing of that party and its undoubtedly anarcho-communist ideology which with good reason we have called Magonist—there emerged a second popular movement: a movement of landless peasants centered in the State of Morales and led by Emiliano Zapata. From the strategic and ideological viewpoints, this movement may be considered an extension of the rural revolutionary movements of the 1870s. As these were inspired by ideas from Bakunin and other anarchists of the time, it is important that we mention them here. A spontaneous and almost intuitive revolutionary, Zapata had no real ideology at first other than that of the *calpulli*, which runs deep in the collective unconscious of the indigenous population. Later, nonetheless, he raised the anarchist motto "Tierra y Libertad" on his flag, which was originally Magonist and first used by Práxedis Guerrero. Soto y Gama, Secretary of the Zapatista army, served as a conduit for the libertarian ideas of Flores Magón, and may have been the author of the famous Plan de Ayala.

---

100 Flores Magón, *Epistolario revolucionario e íntimo*, 111–12.
101 "Salvajismo inconcebible," in *Revista CROM*, May 1, 1923, in Flores Magón, *La primera guerra mundial y la revolución rusa* (México: n.p., 1983), 11–15.
102 Santillán, *Ricardo Flores Magón*, 120.
103 Cano Ruiz, *Ricardo Flores Magón. Su vida. Su obra*, 39.

According to Blaisdell, even if Zapata never considered himself an anarchist he did popularize Flores Magón's revolutionary plan and fought to bring it into practice.[104] John Womack underscores the initial moderation of Zapata's program, but does not fail to recognize that the intransigence of landowners forced him to embrace the revolutionary agrarianism of Soto y Gama and Flores Magón.[105] Based on information from Nicolás Bernal, José Muñoz Cota reports that Zapata received a messenger from Flores Magón, who sent the suggestion to use the motto "Tierra y Libertad."[106] Pietro Ferrúa cites a letter from Flores Magón in which the latter explains that "the only group akin to ours is Zapata's," and concludes that between both revolutionaries "with or without messenger, there was real communication."[107] George Woodcock compares Zapata to Makhno and adds:

> The philosophy of the Zapatista movement—with its egalitarianism and desire to recreate a natural order, with its insistence that the people should control the land in village communities, with its mistrust of the police and its contempt for personal gain—looks very much like the rural anarchism that emerged in Andalucía under quite similar circumstances.[108]

And in Latin America Zapata can be compared with the Venezuelan Ezequiel Zamora, whose frustrated revolutionary career is analogous to Zapata's in a number of important points.

In any event, Flores Magón could see a clear difference between Zapata and other revolutionary *caudillos* like Pancho Villa. In the July 11, 1914 issue of *Regeneración*, he wrote the following:

---

104 Lowell L. Blaisdell, *The Desert Revolution. Baja California 1911* (Madison: University of Wisonsin Press, 1962), 198.

105 John Womack, *Zapata y la revolución Mexicana* (México: Siglo XXI, 1974), 190.

106 Muñoz Cota, *Tierra y Libertad*, No. 45, 18.

107 Ferrúa, "Ricardo Flores Magón en la Revolución Mexicana," *Reconstruir*, 73, 35.

108 Woodcock, *El anarquismo*, 425.

We all know the sincerity of Emiliano Zapata as a revolutionary. He practices expropriation for the benefit of all, while Villa is a dog for the bourgeoisie, and executes the proletarian who takes a piece of bread to ease his hunger. Zapata understands that worker control of lands is the firm basis on which the liberty of the proletariat rests, and consequent on his ideas he is not opposed to inhabitants of those regions in which his army operates taking control of the lands and working them for themselves, while in that region under control of Villa workers cannot count even on enough dirt to cover their bodies when dead. It is absurd to speak of a union between Villa and Zapata. The latter is an honorable and sincere revolutionary who wrests riches from the hands of the bourgeoisie and delivers them to their true owners: the poor.[109]

Indeed, other than in some conditional alliance against Carranza, Zapata and Villa had nothing in common, and in a letter dated August 21, 1914 Zapata stated that "national peace depends on observance of all the clauses of the proposed Plan de Ayala."[110]

It is worth mentioning the effect the Mexican Revolution had in other Latin American countries, for example, in the Río de la Plata region. In September 1911, Dr. Juan Creaghe, then editor of *La Protesta* in Buenos Aires, travelled to Los Angeles for the sole purpose of joining the Magonists.[111] The anarchist poet Alberto Ghiraldo dedicated almost the entire July 11, 1912 issue of his publication *Ideas y Figuras* to discussing and celebrating the revolutionary accomplishments in Mexico.[112] In Montevideo libertarian publications, particularly *Idea Libre*, *Tiempos Nuevos*, and *El Anarquista*, provided extensive coverage of those accomplishments. Rafael

---

109 *Regeneración 1900–1918*, 349. See also A. Díaz Soto y Gama, *La revolución agraria del sur y Emiliano Zapata su caudillo* (México: n.p., 1976).
110 Zapata, *Cartas* (México: Ediciones Antorcha, 1987), 49. See also Huitrón, *Orígenes e historia del movimiento obrero en México*, 185 *et seq.*
111 See E. Carulla, S. Locascio, E. G. Gilimón, no title.
112 See Héctor Adolfo Cordero, *Alberto Ghilardo, precursor the nuevos tiempos*, 180–82.

Barrett wrote an article titled "Mexico" in which he denounced: "Not only have Yankees positioned large capital in Mexico, but they have also imported Mexican manual labor at an infamously low wage to the southern States."[113] For their part, Marxists like the Uruguayan Evaristo Bouzas Urrutia, following the lead of Juan B. Justo, founder of the Partido Socialista Argentino, attacked the extreme anarchism of Mexican liberals.[114]

C. The Workers' Movement and Anarcho-Syndicalism

While Flores Magón was fighting in the north and Zapata in the south, a workers' movement was reemerging in Mexico City. It was in large part the result of Spanish immigrants who, having arrived in the early twentieth century, set out to promote and spread anarchist ideals. One of the most outstanding of them was the Catalan Amadeo Ferrés. He was an educated man and a good orator, who, Hart writes,

> during the last months of the Díaz regime, began the seemingly hopeless task of organizing an independent anarcho-syndicalist Mexican labor movement, free of all government influence, by arranging small secret meetings of workers from the typographic industry in Mexico City.[115]

Ferrés was more of a firm believer in education and organizational solidarity than in violence. He was insistent on the value of frugality, of work and mutual aid, and on the necessity of a rational education that would make the worker and the anarchist a "responsible being" and a "Titan of good will."[116] A few days before the

---

113   Barrett, *Obras Completas*, III, 201.
114   Rama, *Historia del movimiento obrero social*, 113 *et seq.*
115   Hart, *El anarquismo y la clase obrera Mexicana, 1860–1931*, 113 *et seq.*
116   Ibid., 141–43.

resignation of Porfirio Díaz, with the collaboration of Díaz Soto y Gama, Ferrés and several anarchist workers started the Confederación Tipográfica de México, destined to become the point of departure for the organization of Mexico's working class. Two important anarchist leaders emerged from it, José López Dónez and Rafael Quintero. They were joined by other "intellectual workers" who would later play important roles in the activities of La Casa del Obrero Mundial: Federico de la Colina, Enrique H. Arce, Fernando Rodarte, Lorenzo Macías, Pedro Ortega, and Alfredo Pérez.[117]

On October 8, 1911 Ferrés began publication of *El Tipógrafo Mexicano*, an organ of the Confederación with an anarcho-syndicalist focus. In its objective of mobilizing the urban working class it was, Hart writes, the predecessor to newspapers of the 1970s like *El Socialista*, *El Hijo del Trabajo*, and *El Obrero Internacional*.[118] Anarchist typographers contributed to the formation of numerous unions like the Unión de Canteras Mexicanos, which published *La Voz del Oprimido*. Many of these unions' leadership joined the anarchist society Luz, and were among the founders of La Casa del Obrero. Spontaneous strikes erupted during the interim administration of De la Barra, such as one by tramway workers in July 1911.[119] Subsequently, typographers promoted several strikes in the capital and the interior of the country, in spite of the moderation of Ferrés, López Dónez, and other leaders who considered them "tactically harmful." In 1914 the Confederación, now called Artes Gráficas, joined La Casa.[120]

On June 22, 1912 the Columbian teacher and journalist Juan Francisco Moncaleano arrived in Mexico from Cuba. There he

117 Ibid., 143–145. For a bibliography, see Valadés, "Noticia para la bibliografía anarquista en México," *Certamen de La Protesta*, (Buenos Aires, 1927), 133–41.

118 Ibid., 146.

119 Jorge Alfredo Robles Gómez, *Huelga tranviaria y motín popular* (México: UNAM, 1981).

120 Hart, *El anarquismo y la clase obrera Mexicana, 1860–1931*, 147–50. See also Huitrón, *Orígenes e historia del movimiento obrero en México*, 193–97.

founded a workers' group in which we find Jacinto Huitrón, Luis Méndez, Ciro Z. Esquivel, Pioquinto Roldán, and Eloy Armenta. He also founded Grupo Luz and its newspaper by the same name (starting on July 15), and sought to start a rationalist school following the model of Francisco Ferrer.[121] The unions of graphic workers and stonemasons, along with those of tailors and train conductors, and the Grupo Luz made up, as Huitrón says, "the keystone of La Casa del Obrero, which later would become a powerful national syndicalist movement."[122] Those four unions and the Grupo Luz had met on September 22, 1912 and founded La Casa del Obrero, giving it an anarcho-syndicalist orientation. By 1913, La Casa had to reject proposals by Junco Rojo and Alberto Frisson that it direct its activities towards electoral politics. According to Huitrón, syndicalism was understood then as "the working class movement that sought to achieve complete rights in the factory and workshop, and to show that the emancipation of work is based on the personal and direct effort of workers."[123] Marxist socialism, having proposed a reformist and legalist approach and excluded anarchists from the Second International, was rejected in accordance with the principles of anarchist syndicalism, as was all collaboration with political parties, bourgeois or proletariat.[124]

La Casa del Obrero offered courses and lectures, organized a popular library in which classical anarchist texts were abundant, and in place of the defunct newspaper *Luz* began to publish a biweekly titled *Lucha* on January 11, 1913. It also continued to participate in worker-owner conflicts and to support all strikes that erupted in Mexico City, including the boycott of the Café Inglés called by the Unión de Dependientes de Restaurantes on January 27, 1913. May Day was observed for the first time in Mexico that year with assistance from many workers' unions and mutual aid

---

121 Huitrón, *Orígenes e historia del movimiento obrero en México*, 198–99.
122 Ibid., 209.
123 Ibid., 213–15.
124 Rosendo Salazar, *La Casa del Obrero Mundial. La CMT* (México: n.p., 1972), 11.

societies, bringing together some 20,000 workers in the old Palacio Municipal to hear a speech by Soto y Gama. It was then that the word "Mundial" was added to the banner of La Casa del Obrero, and the red flag changed to the red-and-black.[125] The martyrdom of the Chicago anarchists was also remembered on that day in Mérida, Monterrey, and Río Blanco. Other unions joined La Casa.

Direct action took several forms: tailors organized a boycott of the Palacio de Hierro, and textile workers called strikes in factories in Colmena, Miraflores, and other places. The Huerta dictatorship did not ignore the activities of La Casa, particularly when its members began to criticize it for usurpation and militarism: it deported several foreign activists, jailed many Mexicans, some of whom were then kidnapped and murdered, and closed the headquarters of the vigorous proletarian association.

On August 1913, the Confederación de Artes Gráficas joined La Casa del Obrero Mundial and began to publish *El Sindicalista*, under the editorship of Rosendo Salazar and José López Dónez. Anarcho-syndicalism was firmly established in La Casa's organizational structure, while at the same time its members set out to clarify their goals and purposes. Partial strikes had limited purposes—wage increases, the eight-hour workday—but each one of them served as a rehearsal for the general strike that would end capitalism and the State, and bring about the industrial republic. Nonetheless, there was no lack of philosophical differences. Some adopted a positivist attitude and maintained, like Agustín Aragón, the inevitability of a new libertarian order emerging out of the natural law of human progress. Others, however, like the tireless fighter Díaz Soto y Gama, professed a kind of Christian but firmly anticlerical anarchism analogous to Rhodakanaty's.[126] The difficult situation in which La Casa del Obrero Mundial found itself made impossible the continued publication of *El Sindicalista*, but did open the way for another kind of propaganda tactic: a popular group of orators

---

125   Huitrón, *Orígenes e historia del movimiento obrero en México*, 213–34.
126   Hart, *El anarquismo y la clase obrera Mexicana, 1860–1931*, 164–66; Huitrón, *Orígenes e historia del movimiento obrero en México*, 252.

known as the *tribuna roja*. Beginning in late 1913, these speakers reached masses of illiterate workers and yielded large numbers of new members. In May 1914, publication of *Emancipación Obrera* began. But in no time Huerta's brutal dictatorship violently repressed the paper, raided La Casa, and destroyed its library.[127]

Huerta's government represented an attempt to return to Díaz's regime. General Venustiano Carranza, who defeated Huerta, wanted to continue the work of Madero. His greatest concern was to modernize the institutions of the country, end the *caudillo* system, and show the world an organized and democratic Mexico. Although he had no real sympathies for anarchism, he found himself having to seek the support of La Casa and its affiliated unions, not only because opposing them would have made the consolidation of his government and development of his plans difficult, but also because, besieged by Villa in the north and Zapata in the south, he needed to recruit as many workers as possible into the ranks of the constitutional army. Alvaro Obregón, Carranza's minister, showed an attitude favorable to many of La Casas's hopes and received the welcome of its members. He followed up that welcome by offering the Jesuit college Santa Brígida for use as their headquarters. This understanding between anarchists and the new government seemed contradictory in the light of libertarian doctrine, but old and proven militants justified it on grounds of special historical circumstances, and contested the claim that acceptance of certain gifts from the government entailed some compromise with it.

La Casa del Obrero began an intense proselytizing campaign in the interior of the country. Other Casas were founded in Guadalajara and Monterrey. Hart writes:

> La Casa moved toward a more refined and elaborate national structure composed of affiliated groups. Throughout the country a local Casa del Obrero operated independently of,

---

127 Hart, ibid., 167–68; Edgar Rodrigues, "La revolución Mexicana," *Reconstruir*, 84, 53.

and affiliated with, the Mexico City Casa at the national. At both the national and the local level they remained "self-governing." Any action taken in concert with the national Casa occurred at the local and regional Casas' discretion. They also affiliated with the national Casa for armed defense through local workers' militias and armories.[128]

By the end of 1914, while La Casa was making every effort to raise class consciousness among its affiliates and to spread anarcho-syndicalist ideals, founding the paper *Tinta Roja* under the editorship of Arce, Salazar, and la Colina, discussions began about the necessity of giving the Constitutionalists military support against Villa and Zapata. There was some ideological confusion among anarchists; also, non-anarchist leaders like the electrical worker Luis N. Morones had some influence in this conversation. While an anarchist syndicate may find itself forced by historical circumstances to provide military support to a democratic government—as would happen twenty years later in Spain—it can do so only against a more reactionary power. Even assuming that such was the case with Villa, who had more in common with the clergy and the banks than the anarchists, it was certainly not so with Zapata. Nonetheless, the numerous measures favorable to workers that the Carranza government had taken since 1914, as well as a certain aversion to peasant guerrillas who often carried banners of the Virgin of Guadalupe, encouraged many Casa members to take a collaborationist position. They saw the workerist, lay government of Carranza, with its labor law proposals and seemingly sophisticated agrarian reform plan, as the lesser of two evils.

Zapatistas entered the capital city on November 24, 1914 and withdrew in January 1915. Zapata thus showed that he was not interested in the presidency, as Villa would have wanted him to be. Nonetheless, in La Casa there was much talk that both *caudillos* were enemies. So, when Obregón's troops returned to the capital, the way was already prepared for La Casa to accept a pact with the

---

128   Ibid., 171.

government, and even to offer its collaboration in military activities. The pact was signed in Veracruz on February 17, 1915. In it members of La Casa del Obrero Mundial committed themselves to engage "in active propaganda to win the sympathies of all workers of the Republic for the Constitutionalist Revolution," and to form "red" battalions in Carranza's army.[129]

Recent investigations, however, have determined that the majority of anarcho-syndicalist militants were never in agreement with this pact and, moreover, "because of its nature or historical determination, the working class was never really allied to the Constitutionalist project."[130] In any event, those who signed the pact should have defended themselves from the challenges issued by representatives of anarcho-syndicalist orthodoxy: "We are also accused of meddling in politics and misrepresenting our syndicalist creed. To show that this assertion is false it suffices to say that in a short time we have been able to establish syndicalism from one end of the Republic to the other."[131] What is certain is that among many members of La Casa, starting from about 1914, anarcho-syndicalist ideology seems to have been contaminated with a "radical" nationalism.[132] Such contamination later made possible the direct or indirect subordination of the majority of syndicalist organizations to a "workerist" State, and to the realization of a populist politics that, since Carranza and Obregón and then through Calles and Cárdenas, persists to the present day.[133]

The pact between La Casa and the Constitutionalists produced results that were favorable to both sides. With government

129 Huitrón, *Orígenes e historia del movimiento obrero en México*, 263.

130 J. Fernández, J. Jáber, J. A. Robles, *Alrededor de febrero de 1915 (La COM, los batallones rojos, Atl y las huelgas, 2do Coloquio Regional de Historia Obrera, I. El movimiento obrero y la revolución mexicana* (México: n.p., 1979), 460.

131 Rosendo Salazar and José G. Escobedo, *La pugnas de la gleba* (México: Ediciones Avante, 1972), 115.

132 Rocío Guadarrama, *Los sindicatos y la política en México: La CROM (1918–1928)* (México: Era, n.d.), 26.

133 Jean Meyer, "Los obreros en la revolución Mexicana: Los batallones rojos," *Historia Mexicana*, No. 81, 1971, 12.

support, the organization was able to increase its proselytizing activities among workers in Oaxaca and Orizaba, and to start affiliates in Jalapa, San Luis Potosí, Zacatecas, Pachuca, Tampico, Tabasco, Morelia, Uruapan, Zamora, Mérida, and other places.[134] The Constitutionalists substantially reinforced their army with the incorporation of some 10,000 workers, the Red Battalions, and cornered Villa in Chihuahua. La Casa kept growing in 1915 with the addition of numerous unions, published a new and combative newspaper, *Ariete*, and finally realized Moncaleano's project of a rationalist school. But inflation and high unemployment in 1915 led to great discontent among workers, who responded by demanding higher wages and price controls. In the summer teachers and drivers affiliated with La Casa declared a strike; so too did bakers in late July, oil workers at the British company El Aguila in October, followed by textile workers, and in December carpenters, button makers, and barbers. Battles broke out between workers and scabs at the foreign-owned El Oro mines. Hart writes:

> The anarcho-syndicalist leaders of La Casa openly challenged both capitalists and government and were confident in their course of action. No era in the history of Mexican labor has witnessed the militancy and belligerence that La Casa demonstrated in the last six months of 1915 and the first eight months of 1916. The pressure and turbulence were building up towards the general strike of 1916.[135]

In January 1916 the Red Battalions were decommissioned. But after leaving the barracks workers found themselves jobless, joining an already high number of unemployed in the capital.

---

134   Raúl Trejo Delarbre, "Historia del movimiento obrero en México 1860–1982," in González Casanova, *Historia del movimiento obrero en América Latina*, 21.

135   Hart, *El anarquismo y la clase obrera Mexicana, 1860–1931*, 185–86. See also Huitrón, *Orígenes e historia del movimiento obrero en México*, 266 *et seq.*

Unemployment, high prices, low wages, and the devaluation of the peso forced La Casa into a combative posture. A number of strikes and protests erupted in the first months of 1916. On February 4, the government shut down La Casa's offices and jailed a number of militants, among them Jacinto Huitrón. General Pablo González referred to syndicalist actions as the "dictatorship" of the proletariat.[136] A Congreso Obrero Nacional convened in Veracruz between March 6 and 17, 1916, with delegates from 73 unions. That congress created the Confederación del Trabajo de la Región Mexicana, ideologically defined by the principles of anarcho-syndicalism, including the class struggle, socialization of the means of production, and rejection of all political activity, its goal was not to conquer power but to abolish it as a force independent of the will of workers.[137]

In May 22 a general strike was called in Mexico City to protest the imprisonment of La Casa's leadership and to achieve a number of emergency economic measures to ease the very difficult situation confronting the working class. The strike was an immediate success but set a nefarious precedent for the revolutionary spirit of anarcho-syndicalists. Due to its ease, many young militants from La Casa came to believe that improvements could be achieved through a popular and benevolent State. Among those who signed the agreements with the Carranza government was Luis Morones, future leader of the Confederación Regional Obrera Mexicana (CROM), and of the Partido Obrero Socialista, which "changed the recognized mode of struggle from direct to multiple action."[138] A second general strike erupted on July 31. Workers had been driven to a state of profound pauperization by an agreement between government and capitalists that fixed the value of the peso, used to pay wages, at two cents. Carranza ordered mounted police to attack workers' assemblies, closed the local Casas, arrested the leaders who came to meet with him, accusing them of being traitors to the nation,

---

136 Huitrón, ibid., 293.
137 Ibid., 294; Hart, *El anarquismo y la clase obrera Mexicana, 1860–1931*, 186.
138 Huitrón, ibid., 299; Hart, ibid., 188–89.

and declared martial law. The government was thus able to break the strike, and even Obregón, the minister most sympathetic to the workers, distanced himself from the conflict. The Strike Committee, headed by Barragán Hernández, decided to suspend all action and the defeat was definitive. One of the committee's leaders, the electrician Velasco, was condemned to death, although the sentence would be later commuted and he was freed in February 1918.[139]

The closure of La Casa del Obrero Mundial and the failure of the general strike of August 1916 were heavy but not mortal blows to the Mexican anarchist movement. In mid-1917 the group Luz and its newspaper were renewed. Other groups emerged in the capital— Jóvenes Socialistas Rojos, Los Autónomos, Solidaridad—and in the interior of the country: Casas del Obrero Mundial in Guadalajara, Tampico, and Saltillo; Cultura Racional y Rebeldía in Aguascalientes; Germinal, Vida Libre, and Fuerza y Cerebro in Tampico; Hermanos Rojos in Villa Cecilia; Alba Roja in Ciudad Victoria; Francisco Ferrer Guardia in Nuevo Laredo; Acción Consciente in Monterrey; Acracia and Ni Dios ni Amo in Ciudad Juárez; Acción Cultural Sindicalista in Zacatecas; Ciencia y Libertad and Luz y Fuerza in Toluca; Emancipación in Saltillo; Hermandad Acrata in Orizaba; and Grupo Cultural Libertario in León.[140] In October 1917 anarchists were defeated at the Segundo Congreso Obrero Nacional by the reformist and pro-government group of Luis Morones. Later at the Tercer Congreso Obrero, Moreno founded CROM. It retained at best only a few anarchist symbols, and quickly aligned itself with Samuel Gompers' famous pro-management American Federation of Labor (AFL).[141] The anarchist López Dónez referred to a group called Acción, formed by Morones and his "carrancistas" friends, as the Cowhide Apostolate (*Apostolado de la Vaqueta*).[142] Another Mexican worker,

---

139 Huitrón, ibid., 295–96; Hart, ibid., 190–94.

140 Hart, ibid., 195–96.

141 Ibid., 197–98; Huitrón, *Orígenes e historia del movimiento obrero en México*, 300; Miguel Rodríguez, *Los tranviarios y el anarquismo en Mexico* (Puebla: Editorial Uniersidad Autónoma de Puebla, 1980), 31–32.

142 Huitrón, *Orígenes e historia del movimiento obrero en México*, 301.

speaking of the pact between the new CROM and the AFL, asked: "Is it the American Federation of Labor that sends us its delegates or the government of the White House?"[143]

In September 1919 a Congreso Socialista convened in Mexico City and founded the Partido Nacional Socialista, which quickly changed its name to the Partido Comunista and joined the Third International.[144] Among its founders were several foreigners like the Hindu Manabendra Nath Roy and the North American Lynn A. Gale, as well as a Mexican, José Allen, who turned out to be an agent of the Yankee government.[145] On December 21, the group Acción started the Partido Laborista Mexicano, which quickly offered its support to the presidential candidacy of Alvaro Obregón.

The Russian Revolution had a certain influence on anarcho-syndicalist groups. On March 1, 1918 the worker Vicente de Paula Cano celebrated it in the pages of the anarchist publication *Bandera Roja*:

> *¡Obrero mirad hacia el oriente.*
> *Ved cómo el pasado se derrumbe.*
> *Oíd cómo suena lentamente.*
> *La hora de redención onmipotente.*
> *En que los muertos se alzan de la tumba!*

> Workers look to the east.
> See how the past crumbles.
> Listen slowly to how it sounds.
> The hour of omnipotent redemption.
> When the dead rise from their tombs![146]

---

143   Ibid., 302. See also Jorge Basurto, *El proletariado industrial en México 1850–1930* (Mexico: n.p., 1975), 203.
144   Trejo Delarbre, "Historia del movimiento obrero en México 1860–1982," 24.
145   Paco Ignacio Taibo II, Rogelio Vizcaino, *Memoria roja* (México: n.p., 1984), 7–25.
146   Ibid., 29.

The impact, however, was not as great as it was in other Latin American countries and the information available perhaps was more confused.

On May 21, 1920 President Carranza died in the highlands of Puebla, while fleeing to Veracruz. Obregón, who succeeded him, while he supported the CROM reformists, did not adopt a hostile attitude towards anarcho-syndicalists, as Carranza had since 1916. During the interim administration of Adolfo de la Huerta, a number of strikes erupted, beginning in June 1920 and mobilizing more than 22,000 workers. Textile workers in La Hormiga and San Antonio Abad, Federal District; miners in Velardeña, Mina Vieja, and Dolores in Chihuahua; foundry workers in Monterrey; rural peons in La Laguna; oil workers in El Aguila; and others staged conflicts with their bosses for a variety of reasons.[147] The fact that de la Huerta, and after him Oregón, Calles, and other Mexican presidents, thought of themselves as "socialists" and intervened in strikes and other labor conflicts between workers and bosses, generally deciding on behalf of workers, was not a good thing for anarcho-syndicalists. In July 1920 the number of strikes increased to affect some 65,000 workers—metallurgists in Torreón, miners in Chihuahua and Durango, textile workers in Valle de México, oil workers in Tamaulipas, railroad workers in Yucatán, dockworkers in Veracruz, and still more—in spite of CROM's reformist attempts to stop them.

The Federación Comunista del Proletariado Mexicano (FCPM) was founded on August 11, 1920, with both Marxist-Leninist and anarchist members. But its ideology advocating a "free communism" or libertarianism and its evidently federalist organization came more easily to the anarchists.[148] Between February 15 and 22, FCPM sponsored a congress in the capital city with the aim of creating a workers' revolutionary regional that would oppose CROM, already joined to the AFL and supported by the Mexican

---

147 Ibid., 74.
148 Ibid., 80–83.

government. To do so they founded the Confederación General de Trabajadores (CGT), with the participation of some fifty unions. In its constitution the CGT accepted a "libertarian communism," the "rationalist system for the instruction of workers," "the class struggle," and "direct action, which implies the exclusion of all political activity" as fundamental principles necessary for the "complete emancipation of workers and peasants."[149] Julio Godio considered the weakening of political action proof of CGT's "ultra-Leftist sectarianism."[150] The truth is, as Fernando Córdova says, that the anarcho-syndicalist founders of the CGT were "the first to criticize the Constitution of 1917, the social institutions, Gompers' imperialist tactics, the recruitment of workers to fill parliamentary seats, and, in a simple word, the failure of the Mexican Revolution."[151]

In the tradition of the anarchism of the first decade of the century, CGT vigorously denounced North American imperialism, attacked Morones, whom anarchists considered as "Mexico's Mussolini,"[152] and repudiated the alliance with Gompers and the AFL. It was also openly critical of recent deportations of foreign anarchists and socialists like José Rubio, Natalia Michaelova, Michael Paley, and Sebastián San Vicente, a Basque anarchist from Guernica, founding member of the CGT, and a victim of the "socialist" Obregón.[153] Proclamations by CGT, whose formation was assisted with an Iberian push from Buenaventura Durruti, were signed with the motto "Health and Libertarian Communism," and even when it came to accept the issue of the dictatorship of the proletariat it never endorsed the Leninist interpretation of this concept (as democratic centralism) but rather that of Rosa Luxemberg and of those called "councilists" (Pannekoek, and others). But a confrontation between the Partido Comunista Mexicano and the

---

149   Hart, *El anarquismo y la clase obrera Mexicana, 1860–1931*, 200.
150   Godio, *Historia del movimiento obrero latinoamericano*, 2, 99.
151   Córdova, *El movimiento anarquista en México 1911–1921* (México: n.p., 1975), 183.
152   Jean Meyer, "Los obreros en la Revolución Mexicana: Los batallones rojos," *Historia Mexicana*, No. 81, 1971, 30.
153   Taibo and Vizcaino, *Memoria roja*, 185–90.

majority of anarcho-syndicalists could not be avoided. Anarchists could not feel at ease in the Third International, promoted by the same Russian government that persecuted and exterminated anarchists.[154] At its First Congress in September 1921 CGT withdrew from the Third International, while communists loyal to Moscow walked out. A specifically anarcho-syndicalist group, called Centro Sindicalista Libertario (CSL), was then formed at that Congress in the hopes of serving this CGT the same role played by FAI for the Spanish CGT.[155] Luiz Araiza, who had left CROM for the CGT, served as editor of *Verbo Rojo*, organ of the new anarcho-syndicalist central.[156]

Since that First Congress, the CGT showed its concern for workers throughout the American continent. And in spite of ignoring and denying all representative legitimacy to the so-called Confederación Pan-Americana del Trabajo, the CGT worked energetically for the Confederación Obrera Revolucionaria de toda América, for which a meeting would be called with "representatives from communists, syndicalists, and anarchists from the entire American continent." At the same time, it declared that "the Mexican proletariat recognizes its brothers in the world proletariat and their struggles."[157]

In March 1921 the CGT supported the great strike called by the Confederación de Sociedades Gremiales Ferrocarrileras against North American companies. Obregón and his minister Calles were at first opposed to the strike, but in the end they recognized the CGT, conceded to their demands, and gave priority to their

---

154   See Jacques Baynac, *El terror bajo Lenin* (Barcelona: n.p., 1978), 155–65. The first documentation of persecution of anarchists in the U.S.S.R. is a pamphlet by G. P. Maximoff, *Por qué y cómo los bolcheviques deportaron a los anarquistas de Rusia*. (Not translated).

155   Hart, *El anarquismo y la clase obrera Mexicana, 1860–1931*, 201.

156   L. Araiza, *Historia del movimiento obrero mexicano* (México: Casa del obrero mundial, 1965), 72–73. Guillermina Baena, "La CGT 1921–1931," *Revista Mexicana de Ciencia Política*, No. 83, 142.

157   Florence Rosenberg and Margarita Zárate, "Informe CGT 1921–1924," *Historia y crónica de la clase obrera en México* (México: n.p., 1981), 105.

members over scabs.[158] In 1922 the anti-political position of the CGT leadership was once more put to the test. On January 14 the CGT's Consejo Confederal challenged attempts by the Partido Comunista to control CGT's functions and reiterated its position that it could not have any commitments or relations of any kind with any political party. Four months later, on May 13, the Consejo Local of Mexico City, convened by Huitrón and Montoya, after a long discussion into the night, expelled Salazar and Escobedo, members of the Consejo Confederal, for having aligned themselves with the presidential candidacy of Adolfo de la Huerta.[159] In a telegraph to President Obregón in October of the same year, CGT clarified its position on government and the State:

> Of course we are convinced of the fundamental truth that there is not today, nor can there ever be good governments. The very word "government" means "abuse." Without going far into proletarian protests and without having to repeat on this occasion what the most cultured and disinterested men have written through the ages concerning the organic and sociological foundation of governments, can you tell us sincerely, Mr. Obregón, what good the Executive under your command has done for us? We do not seek help, Citizen Obregón. Leave us at peace to continue our struggle, without compromises or humiliations.

And a little later, it added: "The CGT is not a political organization: it is rebellious, anti-statist, and libertarian."[160]

On May Day 1922 the commemoration of the Chicago martyrs turned into an act of protest in front of the North American consulate demanding the release of Librado Rivera and Ricardo Flores Magón, both being held at Fort Leavenworth. But this peaceful act was broken by street violence provoked by the reactionary Caballeros de

---

158   Taibo and Vizcaino, *Memoria roja*, 118–21.
159   Huitrón, *Orígenes e historia del movimiento obrero en México*, 307–08.
160   Salazar, *Las pugnas de la gleba*, 207.

Colón, who murdered a marcher's son as the CGT crowds passed by its headquarters.[161] And the bourgeoisie knew how to use other weapons against the CGT, like misinformation and calumny. In August the newspaper *El Universal Gráfico* announced the dissolution of the workers' central, the embezzlement of funds by its directors, the demoralization of its members, and expressed the desire to see CGT disappear because it was an anarchist organization.[162]

As in Buenos Aires and Santiago de Chile, in Mexico City anarchists promoted a tenants' strike on March 17, 1922, giving way to the organization of the Sindicato Inquilinario. While the Partido Comunista Mexicano took the initiative, several anarchists affiliated with the CGT, like Valadés, were its soul.[163] Veracruz anarchists organized a tenants' strike as early as January; among them was the tailor Herón Proal, an old militant from the Partido Liberal Mexicano.[164] In September a strike was called at the textile mill in San Ildefonso, after the failure of management to make good on an agreement to increase wages. In October workers at the same mill joined CGT and gave the bosses seven days to settle the matter. When they failed to do so, the anarcho-syndicalist CGT called a general strike. It proved successful. But on October 20 a rally to protest the kidnapping of the Secretary of the Federación de Hilanderos de Santa Teresa was battered in San Angel by mounted gendarmerie, and two workers were killed. The CGT blamed Celestino Gasca, who had once been a Casa member and was then Military Governor of the Federal District.[165]

The Second Congress of the CGT convened between November 4 and 12, 1922 and decided to concentrate its organizational

---

161   Hart, *El anarquismo y la clase obrera Mexicana, 1860–1931*, 202–03.

162   Rosenberg and Zárate, "Informe CGT 1921–1924," 123.

163   Taibo and Vizcaino, *Memoria roja*, 147–83.

164   Hart, *El anarquismo y la clase obrera Mexicana, 1860–1931*, 208–11; Octavio García Mundo, *El movimiento inquilinario de Veracruz, 1922* (México: n.p., 1976), 31; Huitrón, *Orígenes e historia del movimiento obrero en México*, 308–09.

165   Rosenberg and Zárate, "Informe CGT 1921–1924," 124–26; Hart, *El anarquismo y la clase obrera Mexicana, 1860–1931*, 203–04.

efforts in the industrial setting, as it offered "the best chance for successful strikes."[166] In addition to *Verbo Rojo*, other anarcho-syndicalist publications appeared: *Tierra Libre* and *Sagitario* in Villa Cecilia; *El Rebelde* in Jalapa; and *La Humanidad* and *Nuestros Ideales*. In January 1923 a strike broke out among transit workers in response to a threat of termination *en masse*. In February CGT militants confronted mounted riot police in the streets of Mexico City. Thirteen militants were wounded and more than one hundred detained at the Inspección General de Policía.[167] In March anarchists from Mexico City marched in protest of the assassination of the Spanish CNT member Salvador Seguí (pseud., Noy del Sucre), who was shot by gangsters hired by his employers, and in April they protested the prison sentences of Sacco and Vanzetti in Boston.[168]

A series of letters and telegrams were exchanged during this period between Obregón and CGT's leaders. Even if this exchange cannot be classified as always cordial, it is nonetheless true that Obregón was the only head of a Latin American country who directly dialogued with anarcho-syndicalists, with the exception of Batlle in Uruguay. In June 1923, CGT resisted a lockout called by employers in Orizaba and Veracruz.[169] That same month during a strike at the textile mills twenty-one unions from Puebla joined the CGT, and within a few weeks the CGT led the new members to occupy all textile mills as the only means to resolve the issue of unemployment. Meanwhile, a number of groups, like Luz y Vida, Esfuerzo Libertario, Juventud Comnnista Anárquica, Tierra Libre, and others, were busy forming the Alianza Local Mexicana Anarquista (ALMA) in Mexico City. In September CGT joined the then recently formed International Workingmen's Association in Berlin, and in December convened its Third Congress.[170]

---

166   Rosenberg and Zárate, ibid., 126–27.

167   Ibid., 129–31; Hart, *El anarquismo y la clase obrera Mexicana, 1860–1931*, 204–06.

168   Rosenberg and Zárate, ibid., 132; Hart, *El anarquismo y la clase obrera Mexicana, 1860–1931*, 206.

169   Huitrón, *Orígenes e historia del movimiento obrero en México*, 309.

170   Rosenberg and Zárate, "Informe CGT 1921–1924," 132–34; Araiza,

New libertarian newspapers appeared in 1923: *El Sindicalista*, *Alma Obrera*, and *Nuestra Palabra* (organ of the CGT) in Zacatecas; and *Germinal* and *Tribuna Roja* in San Luis Potosí.[171] In 1924 the CGT celebrated Labor Day at its headquarters in the Plaza Vizcaínas and continued to receive new members from the interior, like the Grupo Libertario de Mujeres de Nuevo León (in January), the feminist group Emancipación of Margaritas, from Villa Acuñas (in June), the Agricultores Unidos del Bravo and the Organizaciones Libertarias de Tampico (also in June), the Federación Anarquista of San Juan Potosí, and the Sindicato de Obreros Molineros (in September). In August and September the CGT participated in the strike waged by the Federación del Ramo Textil and mobilized some 15,000 workers. In October CGT members organized a meeting in solidarity with striking teachers and oil workers, while the Federación Textil held a rally in front of the factory in San Antonio Abad demanding liberty for the militant anarchist Enrique Rangel, imprisoned in Tuxpan, Veracruz. More anarchist publications appeared that year: *Alba Anárquica* in Monterrey; *Humanidad* (a continuation of *La Humanidad*) and *Verbo Rojo* in Guadalajara; and *Nueva Solidaridad Obrera*.[172]

General Plutarco Elías Calles assumed the presidency at the end of 1924. His support for CROM was in direct proportion to his aversion to the CGT. He was at once less anti-imperialist and more anti-anarchist than Obregón was. It is safe to say that only the Catholic clergy aroused his ire more than militant libertarians.[173] On November 19, 1924 CROM held its Sixth Congress in Ciudad Juárez, determined to defend "the interests of the Mexican proletariat" and "its relations with the Socialist government over which comrade Calles presides."[174] In December Calles appointed

---

Historia del movimiento obrero mexicano, 123–24.

171 Rosenberg and Zárate, ibid., 134.

172 Ibid., 135–37.

173 See José Rivera Castro, "En la presidencia de Plutarco Elías Calles (1924–1928)," in González Casanova, *La clase obrera en la historia de México* (México: n.p., 1980).

174 Huitrón, *Orígenes e historia del movimiento obrero en México*, 313.

Morones Secretary of Industry, Commerce, and Labor and enacted important labor legislation that openly favored CROM and undermined CGT. In 1925 CGT "had to confront a combined CROM/ government attack in the Federal District that threatened its very existence."[175]

Between May 4 and 10, 1925 a Fourth Congress was convened that decided to fight for the eight-hour workday as a temporary remedy for unemployment (FORA pursued the same tactic in Buenos Aires), and to support the peasant movement and the Zapatista deputy Díaz Soto y Gama in his radical agrarian reform project.[176] But 1925 was above all,

> The year of the great oil strike in El Aguila; of conflict between CROM and Calles's government over control of the workers' movement in Chihuahua, Jalisco, and Tamaulipas; of miners' strikes in El Boleo and Nueva Rosita; of the CROM offensive against "red" bakers in the Federal District; of confrontations between CROM leadership and its peasant base, which carried out a general strike on its own; and of the great institutional offensive against the "red" textile workers of the Valle de México.[177]

In these workers' struggles—persistent, violent, sometimes paramilitary—the anarcho-syndicalist CGT showed its very best. "It was between 1922 and 1925," Rodríguez says, "that CGT achieved its greatest strength and dissemination, concentrating its energies on social conflicts."[178] In 1926 CGT comprised 108 syndicates, 23 unions, 13 groups, 9 federations, and 4 agrarian communities for total of 157 affiliated societies.[179]

---

175 Hart, *El anarquismo y la clase obrera Mexicana, 1860–1931*, 213.

176 Salazar, *Las pugnas de la gleba*, 191–210.

177 Guadalupe Ferrer and Paco Ignacio Taibo II, "Los hilanderos rojos," in *2° Coloquio Regional de la Historia Obrera I* (México: n.p., 1979), 671.

178 Rodríguez, *Los tranviarios y el anarquismo en Mexico*, 49.

179 Guadarrama, *Los sindicatos y la política en México: La CROM (1918–1928)*, 123.

In July 1926 CGT held its Fifth Congress and, echoing FORA V two decades earlier, made a clear profession of its anarcho-syndicalist ideology. From that moment on it demonstrated a special interest in the problems of the countryside, joining the agrarian leagues, and later that year convening a peasant's congress in Guadalajara.[180] In 1927 CGT supported a general strike in Mexico City in solidarity with the railroad workers, and through the oil workers' syndicate in Tampico promoted another one that—for no reason other than its leaders were anarcho-syndicalists—Calles tried to put down with guns.[181] In 1928 CGT supported a large strike by the textile workers of Río Blanco and one by telephone workers from Ericsson.

CROM began a rapid decline due to the conflict between Obregón and Morones, whose presidential ambitions forced the latter to resign his position as Secretary of Industry, Commerce, and Labor, and kept his supporters Gasco and Moneda from high government office. Contrary to what one might imagine, CROM's decline did not mean CGT's revitalization. It was instead the beginning of its own demise. With CROM's loss of official favor, CGT found itself increasingly ignored by the government and its functionaries. A new conflict with President Calles ended by destroying both Morones and CROM. In 1929 some CROM syndicates joined CGT, pushing its membership from sixty thousand to eighty thousand.[182] But at the same time many in its leadership began to take a CROM-style attitude and to think that "direct action, anarchism, and revolutionary syndicalism were unrealistic."[183] When in 1931 the government of the engineer and general Pascual Ortíz Rubio introduced a new labor code, many CGT leaders, like Luis Araiza and Ciro Mendoza, welcomed it, while others, like

---

180 Baena, "La CGT 1921–1931," 170; Rodríguez, *Los tranviarios y el anarquismo en Mexico*, 49.

181 Salazar, *Las pugnas de la gleba*, 261; Marjorie Ruth Clark, *Organized Labor in México* (Chapel Hill: The North Carolina University Press, 1934), 115–19.

182 Salazar, *Las pugnas de la gleba*, 261.

183 Hart, *El anarquismo y la clase obrera Mexicana, 1860–1931*, 218.

Jacinto Huitrón and Enrique Rangel, refused any relation with the State. In 1934, Marjorie Ruth Clark wrote: "In a few years CGT became more conservative. It has continued to call itself anarchist, but in truth it is nothing more than trade unionism, lightly nuanced syndicalism."[184]

Something quite similar had occurred in Argentina with the FORA IX and the Unión Sindical Americana. Nonetheless, as in Argentina anarchism did not totally disappear in Mexico, even though its influence declined in both countries after the 1930s. The Federación Anarco-Comunista Argentina (FACA) had its complement in the Federación Anarquista Mexicana (FAM), and Jacinto Huitrón was among its most active organizers and leaders until his death. Just as FACA published *Acción Libertaria*, so too FAM published a second run of *Regeneración*. The arrival of many Spanish members of CNT and FAI after 1939 led to the formation of new groups that published the newspaper *Tierra y Libertad*, and to a series of libertarian works, including the outstanding *Enciclopedia Anarquista*. Other small nuclei worked, and continue to work, in the syndicalist terrain or in active propaganda, among them the Grupo Cultural Ricardo Flores Magón.

---

184   Clark, *Organized Labor in México*, 83, cited by Rodríguez, *Los tranviarios y el anarquismo en Mexico*.

Appendix A: Chronology

1861   Plotino C. Rhodakanaty arrives in Mexico and publishes his *Cartilla Socialista*. Bakunin spends two weeks in Panama. José Antonio Páez becomes president of Venezuela, Benito Juárez of Mexico, and Gabriel García Moreno of Ecuador. Buenos Aires defeats the Confederación Argentina in the Battle of Pavón. Spain again occupies the Dominican Republic. F. Varela publishes *Nocturnas*; and Bernabé Demaria *La América Libre*.

1862   Rhodakanaty begins organizing workers and students in Mexico City.

Bartolomé Mitre becomes president of Argentina, Miguel de San Román of Peru, and Francisco Solano López of Paraguay. Alberto Blest Gana publishes *Martín Rivas*; and Antonio Díaz *Los treinta y tres orientales libertadores*.

1863   Rhodakanaty founds the Grupo de Estudiantes Socialistas in Mexico City. Maximilian I is proclaimed Emperor of Mexico. Triumph of federal armies in Venezuelan civil war: the Treaty of Coche is signed and Juan Crisóstomo Falcón becomes president. A Spanish fleet blockades the Peruvian port city of Callao. José Hernández publishes *Vida del Chaco*; and Juan de Arona *Ruinas*.

1864   Rhodakanaty publishes his *Neopanteísmo* and continues organizational and propaganda efforts. Mariano Melgarejo proclaims himself president of Bolivia. A Spanish fleet captures the Chincha Islands of Peru. A Congress of American States convenes in Lima, Peru. Venezuela adopts a new federal constitution and the name Estados Unidos de Venezuela. In Mexico republicans fight Maximilian I and the French occupying forces. Uruguayan city of Paysandú is under siege by Brazilian forces. Joaquim Machado de Assis publishes *Crisálidas*.

1865   La Social is founded in Mexico and a Section of the International Workingmen's Association in Martinique. Rhodakanaty founds Escuela del Rayo y del Socialismo in Chalco, where Francisco Zalacosta and Julio Chávez are students. The War of the Triple Alliance (Brazil, Uruguay, and Argentina) is fought against Paraguay. Peru signs treaty with Spain recognizing Peruvian independence. Jerónimo Carrión becomes president of Ecuador and José María Cabral of the Dominican Republic. Juana Manuela Corriti publishes *Sueños y realidades*.

1866   A Section of the International is functioning in Guadeloupe. The Spanish-Peruvian War is fought. Francisco Solano López is defeated in Tuyutí. In Havana, Saturnino Martínez founds the newspaper *La Aurora*, showing a Proudhonian influence. Estanislao del Campo publishes his satirical poem *Fausto*; and Francisco X. Acha *La union se va a las nubes*.

1867   Rhodakanaty leaves Chalco and returns to Mexico City. Maximilian I is executed in Querétaro. Juárez enters the Mexican capital. Santos Acosta becomes president of Columbia and Mariano Prado of Peru. In Haiti, Sylvain Salvane overthrows Fabre Geffrad. Jorge Isaacs publishes *María*; and José H. Uriarte *El angel de los pobres*.

1868   Anarchists promote a strike at the textile mills of Tlalpan. Juárez again becomes president of Mexico, Fernando Guzmán of Nicaragua, Domingo Sarmiento of Argentina, and

José Balta of Peru. Blue Revolution is fought in Venezuela. In Cuba, the Ten Years War begins. The city of Asunción, Paraguay falls to the armies of the Triple Alliance. In Puerto Rico, the rebellion known as the Grito de Lares breaks out and the government of Francisco Ramírez assumes power. Pedro Achagüe publishes *Amor y virtud*; and Juan María Gutiérrez *Noticias históricas sobre el orígen y desarrolo de la enseñansa pública y superior en Buenos Aires*.

1869   Mexican anarchists found the Círculo Proletario. García Moreno again assumes the office of president of Ecuador. Juárez confronts an insurrection. I. M. Altamirano publishes *Clemencia*. Publication of *La Prensa* begins in Buenos Aires. Julio Chávez publishes *Manifiesto a todos los oprimidos y pobres de México y del Universo*, and four month later is executed.

1870   In Mexico anarchists found the Gran Círculo de Obreros. Francisco Solano López dies. The War of the Triple Alliance concludes. Nissage Saget becomes president of Haiti and Antonio Guzmán Blanco of Venezuela. Free and compulsory education begins in Venezuela. Dictatorship of Melgarejo in Bolivia ends. The Partido Republicano forms in Brazil. Lucio V. Mansilla publishes *Una excursion a los indios ranqueles*. In Buenos Aires the daily *La Nación* begins publication, and in Rio de Janeiro *La Republica*.

1871   In Buenos Aires, refugees from the Paris Commune begin to arrive, among them Gobley. The Mexican workers' movement adopts the red-and-black flag. In Montevideo, the Asociación Rural is founded. In Chile, church privileges are eliminated. Yellow fever breaks out in Buenos Aires. In Brazil, the *Lei do Ventro Livre* is established, granting freedom to the children of slaves. Federico Errázuriz Zañartu becomes president of Chile, José Vicente Cuadra of Nicaragua, and, once again, Juárez of Mexico. Andrés Lamas, Vicente Fidel López, and Juan María Gutiérrez's *Revista del Río de la Plata* begins publication. The latter publishes *Juan Cruz Varela*. In Mexico, anarchists of La Social begin publication of the newspaper *El Socialista*.

1872 An Uruguayan section of the International Workingmen's Association is founded, with anarchists the largest group. An Argentinian section is also founded. In it a French group is mainly Marxist, and Italian and Spanish groups anarchist. José Pardo becomes president of Peru and Sebastián Lerdo de Tejada of Mexico. Honduras, El Salvador, Guatemala, and Costa Rica form the Unión Centroamericana. José Hernández publishes *Martín Fierro*; Hilario Ascásubi *Santos Vega*; Ricardo Palma *Tradiciones peruanas*; and José María Estrada *La política liberal bajo la tiranía de Rosas*.

1873 The Spanish worker Francisco Tomás reports that the Federación Regional Española has received no news from the Cuban Sections. The Proudhonian botanist José Ernesto Gebert publishes *Ennumeratio pantarum sponte nascentium agro montevidensi*. The Jacobin dictatorship of Justo Rufino Barrios ends. Slavery is abolished in Puerto Rico. José Martí publishes *Revista Universal* and his book *La República española ante la Revolición cubana* in Mexico.

1874 Nicolás Avellaneda becomes president of Argentina and Michel Domingue of Haiti. A new constitution is adopted in Venezuela. *El craneoscopio–Periódico frenológico y científico* is published in Mexico. J. P. Varela publishes *La educación del pueblo*. In Mexico, the anarchist newspapers *El Obrero Internacional* and *La Comuna* appear.

1875 The Uruguayan Section of the International Workingmen's Association convenes its first meeting, and under the leadership of Francisco Galcerán some members publish an anarchist manifesto. Tomás Estrada Palma becomes president of the provisional government of Cuba and Pedro J. Chamorro of Guatemala. Nicolás de Piérola fails to oust Peruvian President Pardo. Tobías Barreto publishes *Estudios de filosofía e crítica*; and Antonio Díaz *El franc y el chiripa*.

Appendix A: Chronology

1876   The Federación Regional de la República Oriental del Uruguay (later called Federación Obrera Regional Uruguaya) is founded. In Mexico, the Congreso General Obrero convenes. Many anarchists participate. Bakuninists make up the largest group in the Argentinian section of the International Workingmen's Association. In Mexico, the newspapers *El Hijo del Trabajo* and *La Internacional* appear. Civil war ends in Mexico and Porfirio Díaz assumes power. Lorenzo Latorre, Uruguayan Minister of War, takes control of the country. Hilarión Daza becomes president of Bolivia, Aníbal Pinto of Chile, and Pierre Boisrond-Canal of Haiti. Bartolomé Mitre publishes *Historia del Belgrado*; J. C. Bustamante *El veterano oriental*; Juan Montalvo *El Regenerador*; and J. P. Varela *De la legislación escolar*.

1877   In Mexico, Zalacosta begins a peasants' rebellion inspired by libertarian ideas. Again anarchists promote strikes in the textile mills of Tlalpan. Rhodakanaty's translation of Proudhon's *Idea general de la revolución en el siglo XIX* appears. Francisco Linares Alcántara becomes president of Venezuela. Uruguay adopts the *Ley de educación laica y obligatoria* (Law of Secular and Fee Education). In Paraguay, Colegio Nacional is founded. Olegario Andrade publishes *Nido de cóndores*; Martín Coronado *La rosa blanca*; Orosmán Moratorio *Una mujer con pantalones*; and Rui Barbosa *O Papa e o Concilio*.

1878   In Mexico, Zalacosta presents a plan to expropriate large estates and to suppress the central government. The Uruguayan Section of the International Workingmen's Association begins publication of the newspaper *El Internacional*. Alberto Santa Fe's *La Ley del Pueblo* is published. In Puebla, *La Revolución Social* appears. In Cuba, the Ten Years War ends. Julián Trujillo becomes president of Colombia, Ignacio de Veintemilla of Ecuador, and Cándido Barreiro of Paraguay. Eduardo Wilde publishes *Tiempo Perdido*; Ricardo Gutiérrez, *Poesía*; J. B. Alberdi *Peregrinación del Luz* *del Día*; E. Gordon *El hijo de la miseria*; and Manuel de Jesús Galván *Enriquillo*.

1879   Colonel Alberto Santa Fe is arrested after the failure of an uprising in the Valle de San Martin, Peru. Antonio Guzmán Blanco initiates the first of his five-year plans in Venezuela. General Julio Roca launches a military campaign to establish Argentine dominance over Patagonia called Conquista del Desierto. La Guerra Chiquita, the Small or Little War, is fought in Cuba. War of the Pacific is fought by Chile against Bolivia and Peru. Nicolás Piérola becomes president of Peru, Joaquín Zabala of Nicaragua, and Lysius Salomon of Haiti. *El Descamisado*, the first anarchist newspaper in Argentina, appears in Buenos Aires. Eduardo Gutiérrez publishes *Juan Moreira*; Fermín Ferreira y Artigas *Donde las dan las toman*; José Hernández *La vuelta de Martín Fierro*; Juan Zorilla de San Martín *La leyenda patria*; and J. L. Mera *Cumandá*.

1880   Héctor Mattei, Italian libertarian journalist, arrives in Buenos Aires. Julio Roca becomes president of Argentina, Justo Rufino Barrios of Guatemala, Bernardino Caballero of Paraguay, and Rafael Núñez of Colombia. The Ley de Instruction pública (Public Education Law) is adopted in Colombia. The popular revolt known as the Revolta do Vintén breaks out in Rio de Janeiro. Buenos Aires is declared the federal capital of the República Argentina. Rhodakanaty publishes *Garantismo social*. *El Obrero*, a newspaper with anarchist bent, begins publication in Cuba. Florentino Ameghino publishes *La antigüedad del hombre en el Plata*; Enrique José Varona *Conferencias filosóficas*; and Juan Montalvo *Las Catilinarias*.

1881   Zalacoasta is defeated by federal troops in Querétaro. The Swiss-inspired Helvetic Constitution is adopted in Venezuela. Chile occupies Lima and President Calderón is imprisoned and removed to Chile. Domingo Santa María becomes president of Chile. Aluísio Azavedo publishes *O*

Mulato; Joaquim Machado de Assis *Memorias póstumas de Brás Cubas*; W. Bermúdez *Una broma de César*; Prudencio Vázquez y Vega, *Críticas de la moral evolucionista*; and Eugenio Cambaceres *Potpouri*.

1882   Máximo Santos becomes president of Uruguay, Ulises Heureaux of the Dominican Republic, and Próspero Fernández Oreamuno of Costa Rica. La Plata becomes capital of the Province of Buenos Aires. The weekly publication *La Revolución Social* appears in Montevideo. Juan Montalvo publishes *Siete tratados*; José Martí *Ismaelillo*; José Medina *Los aborígenes de Chile*; and Paul Groussac *Ensayo histórico sobre Tucumán*.

1883   In Montevideo, on March 18 a group of anarchists celebrate the anniversary of the Paris Commune. José Otalora becomes president of Colombia. Uruguay adopts the Ley de matrimonio civil (civil marriage). Chile annexes Tacna, Arica, and Tarapacá through the Treaty of Ancón. João Capistrano de Abreu publishes *O Descobrimento do Brasil*; D. F. Sarmiento *Conflicto y armonía de las razas en América*; R. Silva *Artículos de costumbres*; Manuel Gutiérrez Nájera *Cuentos frágiles*; Julio Calcaño *Cuentos fantásticos*; and Enrique José Varona *Estudios literarios y filosóficos*.

1884   Joaquín Crespo becomes president of Venezuela, Porfírio Díaz, again, of Mexico, and Rafael Núñez, again, of Colombia. Chile annexes Atacama and its coast. *La Lucha Obrera* appears, organ of the Federación Internacional de Trabajadores del Uruguay. C. M. Ramírez publishes *Artígas*; Francisco Gavidia *Versos*; Diego Barros Arana *Historia general de Chile*; Olavo Bilac *Poesías*; Lucio V. López *La gran aldea*; A. de Oliveira *Meriodales*; Paul Groussac *Fruto vedado*; Samuel Blixen *Los dos primores*; Miguel Cané *Juvenilia*; and Antonio Argerich *Inocentes o culpables?*

1885   Errico Malatesta arrives in Buenos Aires and begins publication of *La Cuestión Social* (in Spanish and Italian). In Havana, the Círculo de Trabajadores is founded. Yankee troops occupy the city of Colón, Panama. Uruguay returns spoils of war to Paraguay. In Peru, Miguel Iglesias renounces the presidency. War in Central America: El Salvador, Nicaragua, and Costa Rica against Guatemala. Fiscal crisis in Venezuela: budget reductions. In Montevideo, the anarcho-collectivist weekly *La Federación de Trabajadores* appears. Rubén Darío publishes *Epístolas y poemas*; José Martí *Amistad funesta*; Eugenio Cambaceres *Sin rumbo*; Diógenes Decoud *La Atlántida*; Miguel Cané *Charlas literarias*; Calixto Oyuela *Teoría literaria*; Rafael Obligado *Poesías*; Juan de Arona *Sonetos y chispazos*; José Lastarria *Antaño y hogaño*; and W. D. Hudson *La tierra purpúrea*.

1886 Malatesta searches for gold in Patagonia to finance the social revolution. Guzmán Blanco again becomes president of Venezuela: the period known as the Gobierno de la Aclamación begins. Patricio Escobar becomes president of Paraguay, José Manuel Balmaceda of Chile, Miguel Juárez Celman of Argentina, Andrés Cáceres of Peru, and Rafael Núñez, again, of Colombia. The latter promotes the Constitution of 1886 forming a single, unified state. Salvador Díaz Mirón publishes *Poesías escogidas*; Juan Montalvo *El espectador*; and José Podesta debuts *Juan Moreira* in Buenos Aires. In Montevideo, the daily *El Día* is launched.

1887 The Partido Colorado is founded in Paraguay and the Partido Demócrata in Chile. Free and compulsory education initiated in Mexico. In Havana, Roig San Martín begins publication of *El Producto* and the first Congreso Obrero Local convenes. Héctor Mattei publishes the anarcho-communist weekly *El Socialista* and Malatesta organizes the Sociedad Cosmopolita de Obreros Panaderos. Emilio Rabasa publishes *La bola*, Rubén Darío *Abrojos*; Isidoro de María *Montevideo antiguo*; Bartolomé Mitre *Historia de San Martín*; and Ricardo Palma *Poesía*.

1888 The Círculo Socialista Internacional, founded by Spanish and Italian anarchists, operates in Buenos Aires. Slavery is abolished in Brazil. J. P. Rojas Paúl becomes president of Venezuela, Juan Bautista Sacasa of Nicaragua, and François Denys Légitime of Haiti. Rubén Darío publishes *Azul*; Zorilla de San Martín *Tabaré*; Eugenio María Hostos *Moral social*; Silvio Romero *História de la literature brasileira*; Acevedo Díaz *Ismael*; Belmiro de Almeida *Arrufos*; Sanín Cano *Colombia hace sesenta años*; Ignacio Manuel Altamirano *El Zarco*; and Leopoldo *Díaz Sonetos*.

1889   Malatesta returns to Europe. In Brazil, Pedro II is overthrown. In Paraguay, the Universidad de Asunción is founded. Honduras, El Salvador, and Guatemala unite. Florvil Hyppolite becomes president of Haiti. Ricardo Jaime Freyre publishes *Castalia bárbara*; Vicente F. López *Historia de la República Argentina*; Manuel T. Podestá *Irresponsable*; C. Matto de Turner *Aves sin nido*; Picón Febres *El sargento Felipe*; Justo Sierra *México social y político*; J. S. Decoud *Sobre la literature en el Paraguay*; José Martí *La edad the oro*; José Veríssimo *Estudios brasileiros*.

1890   In the province of Paraná, Brazil Giovanni Rossi founds the anarchist colony Cecilia. In Iquique, Chilean anarchists promote a strike among maritime workers that ends in slaughter. Adueza Palacios becomes president of Venezuela, Juan G. González of Paraguay, Morales Bermúdez of Peru, Herrera y Obes of Uruguay, C. Pellegrini of Argentina. In Venezuela, universities are founded in Zulia and Carabobo. In Argentina, the Unión Cívica Radical is founded. In Montevideo, P. Amilcare publishes *La Voz del Trabajador*. In Buenos Aires, *El Perseguido*, anarcho-communist paper, begins publication. R. V. Romerogarcía publishes *Peonía*; A. Azevedo *O Cortiço*; L. López Méndez *Mosaico de politica y literatura*; Acevedo *Díaz Nativa*; J. Calcaño *El héroe de Turbaco*; Carlos Roxlo *En la sombra*; and Lucio V. Mansilla *Entre nos*.

1891   In Chile, José Manuel Balmaceda commits suicide and Pedro Montt becomes president. In Caracas, *El Cojo Ilustra-*

do is published. Republican constitution adopted in Brazil. Liberal revolt aborted in Paraguay. In Havana, the libertarian newspaper *El Trabajo* is published. J. Muñoz Tébar publishes *El personalismo y el legalismo*; M. García Merou *Recuerdos literarios*; Carlos María Ocantos *Quilito*; Julián Martell *La bolsa*; Machado de Assis *Quincas Borba*; José Martí *Versos sencillos*; and A. Rojas *Orígenes venezolanos*.

1892 Federalist revolution in the Rio Grande do Sul region. Legalist revolution in Venezuela: Joaquín Crespo becomes president of Venezuela. Liberal revolution in Honduras: Bonilla becomes president. In Rio de Janeiro, the first workers' congress in Brazil convenes, and anarchists form a majority among delegates. In Paraguay, the group Los hijos del Chaco publishes a libertarian manifesto. José Martí founds the newspaper *Patria*. In São Paulo, *Gli Schiavi Bianchi* begins publication. E. Blanco publishes *José Félix Ribas*; Adolfo Saldías *Historia de la Confederación Argentina*; Julián del Casal *Nieve*; and J. Gil Fortoul *Idilio?*

1893 In Cuba, Pedro Esteve arrives, a prominent anarchist and Catalan typesetter, and Cuban anarchists found the Sociedad General de Trabajadores.

The Partido Reformista is formed in Cuba. Admiral Custódio de Melo, allied to federalists from the Rio Grande do Sul, orders ships under his command to attack Rio de Janeiro. In Nicaragua, Liberal Party General José Santos Zelaya deposes Juan Bautista Sacasa and becomes president. José Yves Limantour becomes Minister of Finance in Mexico. Venezuela adopts a new constitution. The utopian communist settlement La Nueva Australia is founded in Paraguay.

Giovanni Rossi publishes his book *Cecilia, comunitá anarchica sperimentale*. In Buenos Aires, the anarchist newspapers *La Liberté* (in French) and *La Riscossa* (in Italian) are published; in Santiago de Chile, *El Oprimido*; in Montevideo, *El Derecho de la Vida*; and in São Paulo,

L'Asino Umano (in Italian). R. J. Cuervo publishes *Diccionario de construcción y régimen de la lengua castellana*; Joaquín V. González *Mis montañas*; L. Level de Goda *Historia contemporánea de Venezuela política y militar*; Julián del Casal *Bustos y rimas*; J. L. Flores *Horas*; Elías Regules *Las vivezas de Juancito*; J. da Cruz e Sousa *Broqueles*; G. Picón Febres *Fidelia*; Alejandro Audibert *Los límites de la Antigua provincial del Paraguay*.

1894   José Prudente de Morais becomes president of Brazil, Manuel Bonilla of Honduras, Joaquín Crespo of Venezuela, Juan Bautista Eguzquiza of Paraguay, Juan Idiarte Bora of Uruguay, and Remigio Morales Bermúdez of Peru. Tacna and Arica are incorporated into Chile. Border problems between Venezuela and British Guiana.

El *Oprimido* is published in Luján, Argentina, in São Paulo *L'avvenire* (in Italian), in Havana, *Archivo Social*, and in Puerto Príncipe, Cuba, *El Trabajo*. Manuel González Prada's *Páginas Libres* is puiblished in Paris. Lucio V. Mansilla publishes *Retratos y recuerdos*; J. A. Silva *Nocturno*; Carlos Reyles *Beba*; and Orosmán Moratorio *La flor del pago*.

1895   Eloy Alfaro becomes president of Ecuador, Nicolás Piérola of Peru. The second war for independence is fought in Cuba and José Martí dies. J. E. Uriburu succeeds Sáez Peña as president of Argentina. Peace treaty signed between Rio Grande do Sul and the federal government.

In Buenos Aires, the libertarian journal *Le Cyclone* (in French) is published and in Rosario *La Libre Iniciativa*. C. Guido Spano publishes *Eco lejanos*; Leopoldo Díaz *Bajo-relieves*; Enrique Bernardo Núñez *Sol Interior*; J. M. Núñez Ponte *Estudios acerca de la esclavitud en Venezuela*; Juan Montalvo *Capítulos que se olvidaron a Cervantes*; J. S. Chocano *Iras santas*; Manuel Zeno Gandía *La charca*; and José María Vargas Vila *Flor de fango*.

1896   In Lima, the first workers' congress convenes, with anarchists in attendance. Vilbrun Guillaume Sam becomes president of Haiti, Federico Errázuriz of Chile, and Manuel Vitorino is provisional head of Brazil. Yaqui rebellion erupts in Sonora, Mexico. Leandro Alem, leader of the Unión Cívica Radical, commits suicide. In Cuba, Antonio Maceo dies in battle. The Instituto Paraguayo is founded. In Buenos Aires, the Partido Socialista begins operations.

In Buenos Aires, the anarchist paper *Ni Dios ni Amo* is published. In Rosario, *La Verdad* and *La Federación Obrera* appear, and in Montevideo *Il Socialista* (in Italian). Francisco G. de Cosmes publishes *La dominación española y la patria Mexicana*; Rubén Darío *Prosas Profanas* and *Los raros*; Ricardo Palma *Neologismos y americanismos*; and Rui Barbosa *Cartas da Inglaterra*.

1897 In Rio do Sul, the Liga Operária Internacional is founded. The Cuban anarchist Tárrida del Mármol publishes his book *Les inquisiteurs d'Espagne* in Paris. José Manuel Hernández, known as El Mocho Hernández, and Aparicio Saravia, both nationalists, lead insurrections in Venezuela and Uruguay, respectively. Spain cedes autonomy to Puerto Rico. Iriate Borda is assassinated in Uruguay. An Italian fleet threatens Colombia demanding payment of a debt.

In Buenos Aires, *La Protesta Humana*, the most important Latin American anarchist publication, as well as *Germinal*, *Ciencia Social*, *La Revolución Social*, and, in Montevideo, *La Verdad* appear. Joaquim Nabuco publishes *Un estadista del Imperio*; Fray Mocho *Memorias de un vigilante*; Emeterio Valverde y Téllez *Apuntaciones históricas de la filosofía en México*; Paul Groussac *Del Plata al Niágara*; Martín Coronado *Justicias de antaño*; Leopoldo Lugones *Las montañas de oro*; José Enrique Rodó *La vida nueva*; Jaimes Freyre *Castalia bárbara*.

1898 Manuel Ferraz Campos Sales becomes president of Brazil, Ignacio Andrade of Venezuela, General Julio Argentino Roca of Argentina, and Manuel Antonio Sanclemente of

Colombia. Spanish American War ends. Palmiro de Lidia (Adrián del Valle's pseudonym) arrives in Cuba.

Pietro Gori, the Italian criminologist, arrives in Buenos Aires and founds the journal *Criminología Moderna* at the same time that he begins his intense anarchist propaganda. In Rio de Janeiro, *O Despertar* appears and in São Paulo *Il Risveglio*. In Buenos Aires, Alberto Ghiraldo publishes *El Sol*. Iglan Lafarga translates August Hamon's *Psicología del socialista anarquista*. Ernesto Quesada publishes *La época de Rosas*; Alfredo Duhau *El hijo legítimo*; Amando Nervo *Perlas Negras*; J. O'Leary *El alma de la raza*; Manuel Díaz Rodríguez *De mis romerías*.

1899   In Havana, bricklayers hold a general strike demanding the eight-hour day and the Liga general de trabajadores cubanos is founded. In Venezuela the civil war known as the Revolución Restauradora is fought and Cipriano Castro becomes president. Yankees rule Cuba. In Colombia, the civil war known as Guerra de los Mil Dias begins. In the Dominican Republic, Ulises Heureaux is killed and is succeeded by Juan Isidro Jiménez. Tomás Regalado becomes president of El Salvador, Juan Lindolfo Cuestas of Uruguay, Eduardo López de Romaña of Peru.

In Montevideo, *La Aurora Anarquista* and *El Amigo del Pueblo* appear, in Havana *El Nuevo Ideal*, in Rio de Janeiro *O Protesta*, in Curibita *Il Diritto*, and in Buenos Aires *El Ideal Anarquista*. *El Almanaque de Pernambuco* publishes a *Decálogo dos anarquistas*. Silva Mendes presents a doctoral dissertation titled *Socialismo libertario ou anarquismo*. Francisco Bulnes publishes *El porvenir de las naciones latinoamericanas ante las conquistas recientes de Europe y los Estados Unidos*; Guillermo Valencia *Anarkos*; César Zumeta *El continente enfermo*; and Joaquim Machado de Assis *Dom Casmurro*.

1900   Malatesta visits Cuba. José Manuel Marroquin becomes president of Colombia. A French fleet pressures the Dominican Republic. In Venezuela, a new insurrection by Mocho Hernández strikes. In Mexico, Porfirio Díaz becomes president again. Chile and Argentina sign a border treaty. President McKinley of the United States signs the Foraker Act establishing a civil government in and granting autonomy to Puerto Rico.

Florencio Sánchez publishes in *El Sol* his *Cartas de un flojo*. In Santiago de Chile a student group founds *La revuelta* and the Centro de estudiantes sociales obreros. In Valparaíso, the group La Libertad is founded. In Montevideo, *Tribuna Libertaria* appears, in São Paulo *Palestra Social*, in Buenos Aires *Los Tiempos Nuevos* and *El Alba del Siglo XX*. In Santos, the group Sociedadé Primero de Maio is founded. In Mexico, Ricardo Flores Magón begins publication of *Regeneración*. The physician Dr. Emilio Z. Aranta publishes *Los males sociales: Su único remedio,* and Mariano Cortés *Fundamentos y lenguaje de la doctrina anarquista.* Juan Augustín García publishes *La ciudad indiana,* José Enrique Rodó *Ariel;* F. Bareiro *El Paraguay en la Argentina;* Ricardo Palma *Cachivaches;* Joaquim Nabuco *Mi formación;* José María Vargas Vila *Ibis;* and Justo Sierra *Evolución política del pueblo mexicano.*

1901 In Cuba, Platt amendment and first constitution, Estrada Palma becomes president. Battle of the Río Hacha fought between Columbian and Venezuelan troops. Mayan insurrection erupts in Yucatan. In Argentina, the Ley Richeri establishes compulsory military service. Flores Magón steeps himself in anarchist literature and is imprisoned in Belén. The Federación Obrera Argentina (FOA) is founded. In Rosario, anarchists promote a general strike.

In Buenos Aires, publication of *La Nueva Era* and *La Nuova Cività* begins, in Santiago de Chile, *La Campaña, La Agitación, La Rebelión,* and in São Paulo *La Terza Roma.* Benjamín Mota begins publication of *A Lanterna,* Alberto Ghiraldo directs *La Organización Obrera.* Graça

Aranha publishes *Canaã*. V. Pérez Petit publishes *Tribulaciones de un criollo*; M. Díaz Rodríguez *Idolos rotos*; F. Lazo Martí *La Silva criolla*; Díaz Mirón, *Lascas*; L. A. Herrera *La tierra charrúa*; J. de Viana *Gurí*; A. Cernevalli *Bolivita*; P. E. Coll *El Castillo de Elsinor*; H. Quiroga *Los arrecifes de coral*.

1902   Second Congress of FOA convenes and Marxists are removed. In Buenos Aires, FOA declares a general strike. Argentinian legislature adopts the Ley de Residencia (no. 4144). Anarchists in Chile and Argentina declare themselves opposed to the war both countries are about to enter. In Cuba, opposition arises against Platt Amendment and North American administration. Rodrigo Alves becomes president of Brazil. In Venezuela, the libertarian revolution fails, Germany and Great Britain bomb Puerto Cabello. Argentina adopts Drago doctrine. A new Venezuelan constitution extends presidential term to six years. Peru and Bolivia sign a border treaty. Central American contries accept binding arbitration to settle mutual differences. Zelaya is again president of Nicaragua and Nord Alexis becomes president of Haiti.

The Chilean anarchist D'Halmar, sympathizer of Tolstoyan anarchism, publishes *Juana Lucero*. Ricardo Flores Magón publishes the satirical newspaper *El Hijo del Ahuizote*. In Santiago de Chile, *La Luz* begins publication, in Havana *Tierra!* and *La Defensa*, and in São Paulo, *O Amigo do Povo*, *Germinal*, and in Italian *La Gogna*. Otto Miguel Cione publishes *Maula*; Martín Coronado *La piedra del escándalo*; A Nin Frías *Ensayos de critica e historia*; and Nicolás Granada *¡Al Campo!*

1903   In Argentina, socialists found the Unión General de Trabajadores (UGT). José Batlle y Ordóñez becomes president of Uruguay, Manuel González de Candamo of Peru, Pedro José Escalón of El Salvador. In Nicaragua, the Revolución del Lago erupts. Brazil annexes the Acre territory. Panama breaks away from Columbia, declares independence, cedes the Canal Zone to the United States, and Manuel A. Guerrero becomes president. Cuba allows U.S. bases in Guantánamo. In Brazil, revolutionary syndicalists promote hundreds of unions. In Buenos Aires, FOA convenes its Third Congress with forty-two affiliated societies and over fifteen thousand members.

In Buenos Aires, the newspaper *Vida Nueva* is published, in Montevideo *La Verdad*, in Santiago de Chile *Los Nuevos Horizontes*, in Rio de Janeiro *A Greve*, in Curitiba *A Voz do Dever*, in São Paulo *La Rivolta* in Italian and *La Voz del Destierro* in Spanish. Félix Basterra publishes his book *El crepúsculo de los gauchos*; Fábio Luz *O Ideólogo*; Avelino Foscolo *O Mestiço*; and Florencio Sánchez debuts his play *M' hijo el doctor* and publishes the essay *El caudillaje criminal en Sud América*. Euclides Da Cunha publishes *Os sertões*; D. Jímenez Espinosa *Pancha Garmendia*; Porfírio Parra *Nuevo sistema de lógica inductiva y deductiva*; M. Cané *Prosa ligera*; L. Lugones *El imperio jesuítico*; Martiniano Leguizamón *Cuentos de la pampa*; O. Bunge *Nuestra América*; and M. E. Pardo *Villabrava*.

1904   In Brazil, the Chamber of Deputies passes the Ley Gordo, equivalent to Argentina's Ley de Residencia (no. 4144). In La Plata, FOA convenes its Fourth Congress and adopts a new name, Federación Obrera Regional Argentina (FORA). It comprises 66 societies and 32,893 members. On May Day, Buenos Aires police attack anarchists. The anarchists Urmachea, Lévano, and others found the Unión de Trabajadores Panaderos. Cuban anarchists Saavedra and Sola organize a boycott of Argentinian beef to protest persecution of Argentinian anarchists. José Pardo becomes president of Peru, Rafael Reyes of Colombia, Juan Bautista Gaona of Paraguay, and Manuel Quintana of Argentina. Aparicio Saravia leads a new uprising in Uruguay. Venezuela adopts the Ley del divorcio. In Argentina, Alfredo

Palacios becomes the first socialist elected to national office, and in Bolivia Ismael Montes begins a period of liberal governments. In Paraguay, the Revolución de los Azules is fought in Paraguay. Bolivia, Peru, and Chile sign a peace treaty.

In San Antonio, Texas Flores Magón restarts publication of his newspaper *Regeneración*. In Montevideo, *Futuro* is published, in Concepción, Chile *Luz*, in Buenos Aires *Martín Fierro*, and in Curitiba *O Despertar*. Florencio Sánchez debuts *Canillita*, *Las cédulas de San Juan*, *La gente pobre*, and *La gringa*. Ghiraldo publishes *Música prohibida*; Alberto Weisbach *Blancos y colorados*; G. Delgado Palacios *Orígenes de la vida*; Ricardo Rojas *El país de la selva*; I. Pane *Poesías paraguayas*; F. García Calderón *De Litteris*; P. C. Dominici *Dionysos*; and G. de Laferrére *¡Jettatore!*

1905 In Buenos Aires, FORA convenes its Fifth Congress and declares itself anarcho-communist. In Santiago de Chile, the Semana Roja breaks out. In Rio de Janeiro, the libertarian group Novo Rumo is founded. Flores Magón is arrested in the Unites States and offices of *Regeneración* are raided. The Federación Obrera Regional Uruguaya (FORU) is founded. Cecilio Báez becomes president of Paraguay and Estrada Cabrera of Guatemala. Reyes' dictatorship is prolonged in Colombia and C. Castro's in Venezuela. In Cuba, Estrada Palma is reelected. In Argentina, the Universidad de la Plata is founded. In Buenos Aires, a radical revolution fails.

In Lima, *El Hambriento* and *Simiente Roja* are published, in Montevideo *El Libertario*, in Rosario *Nuevas Brisas*, in São Paulo *A Tierra Libre*, the monthly *Aurora*, in Italian, *La Battaglia*, and in Havana, *El Libertario*. Ghiraldo publishes *La tiranía del franc*; Pellicer Paraire *Conferencias populares de Sociología*; César Duyan *Stella*; Leopoldo Lugones *La guerra gaucha* and *Los crepúsculos del jardín*; A. Chirveches *Celeste*; T. Febres Cordero *Don Quixote en América*; Juansilvano Gondai *La muerte del mariscal*

López; R. Darío *Cantos de vida y esperanza*; J. Clausel
Paisajes mexicanos; A. Nervo *Jardínes interiors*; and J. Ribeiro *Páginas de Estética*.

1906   Afonso Pena becomes president of Brazil, Benigno Ferreira
of Paraguay, Figueroa Alcorta of Argentina, Pedro Montt
of Chile, and Zelaya, again, of Nicaragua. In Ecuador, E.
Alfaro defeats L. García and a liberal constitution is adopted. Liberal rebellion erupts in Cuba and United States
intervenes. In São Paulo a general strike breaks out among
railroad workers. In Mexico, anarchists promote a miners'
strike at the Cananea mines, two hundred are killed, and
another one in Río Blanco in Mexico among textile workers, which continues until the following year. A peasant's
insurrection erupts in Acuyacán. In Rosario, FORA's Sixth
Congress convenes. In Rio de Janeiro, the Confederação
Operária Brasileira (COB) is founded, and in Asunción the
Federación Obrera Regional Paraguaya.

    Ribeiro Filho publishes *Cravo Vermelho*; Angel Falco
Cantos Rojos; Roberto J. Payró *El casamiento de Laucha*;
Martiniano Leguizamón *Alma native*; Almafuerte *Lamen-
taciones*; R. Blanco Fombona *Camino de imperfección*; O.
Cione *Paja brava*; A. Arvelo Larriva *Enjambre de rimas*; J.
E. Rodó *Liberalismo y jacobonismo*; G. Picón Febres *La lit-
eratura venezolana en el siglo XIX*; and F. Sánchez debuts
El Conventillo and *El desalojo*.

    In St. Louis, Missouri *Regeneración* reappears. In Bue-
nos Aires, *El Trabajo*, *Rumbo Nuevo*, *Fulgor* are published,
in Rosario *El Rebelde*, in Montevideo *En Marcha* and *La
Giustizia*, in Salto (Uruguay) *Germinal*, in Asunción *El
Despertar*, in Santiago de Chile *El Oprimido*, in Lima *Hu-
manidad*, in Río Blanco, Mexico *La Revolución Social*, in
Rio de Janeiro *Novo Rumo*, in Porto Alegre *A Luta*, and in
Taboleiro, Brazil *A Nova Era*.

1907   Flores Magón is sentenced to three years in prison in the
United States. A tenants' strike erupts in Buenos Aires.

FORA's Seventh Congress convenes in La Plata. Strike by miners in Iquique leaves massive casualties. General strike organized in São Paulo, and the Grupo libertario Germinal is founded. The Liga Operária from Campinas founds a free school under the supervision of Renato Salles. Claudio Williman becomes president of Uruguay, Fernando Figeroa of El Salvador, E. Alfaro, again, of Ecuador. Nicaragua is at war with El Salvador and Honduras, and occupies Tegucigalpa. Manuel Bonilla president of Honduras resigns. A Central American conference convenes in Washington, D.C. The United States administers customs and import taxes in the Dominican Republic. Uruguay abolishes the death penalty and adopts a law of secular divorce.

Florencio Sánchez debuts *Moneda falsa*, *Los Curdas*, *Nuestros hijos*, and *Los derechos de la salud*. In Córdoba, Argentina *El proletario* is published, in Buenos Aires *Los Nuevos Caminos* and *Nosotros*, in Montevideo *La Linterna* and *La Emacipación*, in Rio de Janeiro *Semana Operária* and *Novo Aurora*. Luis Razetti publishes *Qué es la vida*; Loepoldo Lugones *Lunario Sentimental*; E. Banchs *Las barcas*; Delmira Agustini *El libro blanco*; J. Rodríguez Alcalá *El Paraguay en marcha*; M. Azuela *María Luisa*; Vaz Ferreira *Los problemas de la libertad*; F. García Calderón *Le Pérou contemporain*; R. Blanco Fombona *El hombre de hierro*; Ramos Mejías *Rosas y su tiempo*.

1908   Anarchists promote a peasants' uprising in Viescas, Las Vacas, Palomas, and Valladolid, Mexico. FORA organizes a general strike in Buenos Aires protesting the Ley de Residencia.

The Federación Obrera Local is founded in La Paz and publishes *Luz y Verdad*. COB begins to publish its newspaper *A Voz do Trabalhadores*. In Asunción *La Rebelión* is published, in Santiago de Chile *La Protesta*, and in Regla, Havana the weekly *Rebelión*. In Buenos Aires, *La Batalla*, a new anarchist daily appears, in Mendoza *Pensamiento*

Nuevo, and in Paraná *La Ráfaga*. *Vanidades* is published in Peru. Evaristo Carriego publishes his collection *Misas herejes* and *El alma del suburbio*; Alejandro Sux *Seis dias en la cárcel de Mendoza*; Herrera y Reissig *Tertulia Lunática*; González Prada *Horas de Lucha*; H. Quiroga *Historia de un amor turbio, Bohemia*, and *Los perseguidos*; Roberto Payró, *Pago chico*; G. de Laferrere, *Las de Barranco*; E. Larreta *La Gloria de Don Ramiro*; Vaz Ferreira *Moral para intelectuales*; M. Díaz Rogríguez *Camino de perfección*; J. Cortinas *El Credo*; R. Blanco Fombona *Más allá de los horizontes*; D. Mayer *Estudios sociológicos*; O. Luco *Casa grande*; J. S. Chocano *El Dorado*; V. A. Belaúnde *El Perú antiguo y los modernos sociólogos*.

1909 The execution of Francisco Ferrer in Barcelona sparks demonstrations in Buenos Aires, Rosario, Montevideo, Santiago de Chile, Rio de Janeiro, São Paulo, Havana, and other Latin American cities. Simón Radowitzky assassinates Colonel Falcón, chief of Police in Buenos Aires. In San José, Costa Rica the Centro de Estudios Sociales Germinal is founded. In Brazil, Vice President Nilo Peçanha assumes the presidency after Pena's death, and in Columbia Vice President Holguín after Reyes' resignation. Constitutional reforms held in Venezuela. Secular education adopted in Uruguay. Civil war breaks out in Honduras, and in Nicaragua a rebellion erupts against Zelaya with Yankee intervention. Porfirio Díaz meets Taft at the border. Colombia recognizes Panama's independence.

In Caracas, the daily *El Universal* appears, in Buenos Aires *Boletín de la Federación Regional Argentina* and the antimilitarist paper *El Cuartel*, in La Plata *Ideas and Reverbaciones*, in Montevideo *Adelante*, *El Surco*, and *La Nueva Senda*, in Asunción *La Tribuna*, in Rio de Janeiro *Libertade*, and in São Paulo *Il Ribelle* (in Italian). In Buenos Aires the offices of *La Protesta* are sacked and shuttered. Benito Lynch publishes *Plata dorada*; A. Arvelo Larriva *Sones*

y canciones; A. Chirveches *La candidatura de Rojas*; Vaz
Ferreira *Pragmatismo*; A. Arguedas *Pueblo enfermo*; Blest
Gana *El loco Estore*; J. Gil Fortoul *Historia constitucional de Venezuela*; Pío Gil *El cabito*; J. E. Rodó *Motivos de
Proteo*; Herrera y Reissig publishes *Las Clepsidras*; R. de
las Carreras *La Venus Celeste*; F. Santiván *Palpitaciones de
vida*; and A. Ghiraldo *Alma gaucha* and begins publication
of his journal *Ideas y Figuras*.

1910   Many anarchist militants are deported from Argentina and
others sent to Usuhaia during the Centennial festivities.
Again offices of *La Protesta* are raided and shuttered. Uruguayan and Brazilian comrades show their solidarity, and
the latter form a Comité Revolucionario de Apoyo. Brazilian anarchists support the Revuelta del látigo in the navy.
FORA convenes its Eighth Congress. Flores Magón is released from prison and restarts publication of *Regeneración*
with a subscription of 27,000. In Guayaquil the anarchist
leaning Centro de Estudios Sociales is founded. Hermes
Rodrigues da Fonseca, former Minister of War, becomes
president of Brazil, Manuel Gronda of Paraguay, R. Sáenz
Peña of Argentina, C. Restrepo of Colombia, J. J. Estrada
of Nicaragua, and Estrada Cabrera, again, of Guatemala.
The Trans-Andean railroad Mendoza-Valparaiso begins
operations. The Conferencia Panamericana convenes in
Buenos Aires. Justo Sierra reopens the Universidad de
México. Centenary of the first national government celebrated in Argentina. Mexican Revolution commences, with
insurrections in several states.

   In Montevideo, *Tiempos Nuevos* is published and the
sociological journal *Ideas*, in Rio de Janeiro *Novo Rumo*,
and in Caracas *Alma Venezolana*. R. Barrett publishes
Moralidades actuales and *Lo que son los yerbales*; Fábio
Luz, *Virgem Mãe*; Javier de Viana *El estanque*; Roberto
Payró *Divertidas adventuras del nieto de Juan Moreira*;
José Gálvez *Bajo la luna*; P. Henríquez Ureña *Horas de*

studio; Vaz Ferreira *Lógica viva*; Gerchunoff *Los gauchos judíos*; M. Ugarte *El porvenir de América Latina*; Celio Báez *Ensayo sobre el dictador Francia*; C. Torres *Idola foir*; C. Reyles *La muerte del cine*.

1911   In Uruguay, out of a total of 117, 000 workers in the country 90,000 are affiliated with FORU. In Peru, anarchists promote the first general strike in the country. *El Manifiesto* published by the Partido Liberal Mexicano is clearly anarchist in orientation. Zapata's Plan de Ayala is inspired by libertarian ideas. Magonists invade Baja California with the objective of starting a libertarian social revolution. Flores Magón is again imprisoned. Francisco A. Madero becomes president of Mexico, C. Leconte of Haiti, and Batlle y Ordóñez, again, of Uruguay. Adolfo Díaz, employee of Yankee industries, is installed in the presidency of Nicaragua by a military junta. The Academia Militar is founded in Venezuela. War breaks out between Peru and Colombia. The ruins in Macchu Pichu in Peru are discovered.

In Buenos Aires *El Trabajo*, *La Cultura*, and *Francisco Ferrer* are published, in Montevideo *Guerra Social*, in Valparaíso *Luz al Obrero*, in Lima *La Protesta*, in Colón *El Unico*, in San José *Renovación*, in Havana *La Batalla* and *Vía Libre*, in Rio de Janeiro *A Guerra Social*, *Atlántida* in Nicaragua, and in Santos, *O Proletario*. Santiago Locascio publishes *Orientaciones*; E. Gilimón *Hechos y comentarios*; Ernesto Herrera *El León Ciego*; Pedro Manuel Arcaya *Estudios sobre personajes y hechos de la historia venezolana*; L. Lugones *Historia de Sarmiento*; Alberto J. Ureta *Rumor de almas*; E. Banchs *La urna*; A. Valdelomar *La ciudad de los tísicos*; Eguren *Simbólicas*; A. Reyes *Cuestiones estéticas*; J. T. Arreaza Calatrava *Canto a Venezuela*; and Pío Gil *Los felicitadores*. R. Barrett's *El dolor paraguayo* and *Cuentos breves* are published.

1912   In Bolivia the Federación Obrera Internacional is founded, and its symbol is the red and black flag. Anarchist groups like Luchadores de la Verdad and Luz y Amor organize a general strike in El Callao, Peru. The Federación Obrera Regional Peruana is founded. The strike in the port city of Santos is violently repressed. In Panama some twenty affinity groups are operating, in general they are anarcho-individualist. Kropotkin defends Flores Magón from attacks by Jean Grave. In Mexico, La Casa del Obrero is founded; it will later be called La Casa del Obrero Mundial. In Chile, the Partido Socialista is founded. Guillermo Billinghurst becomes president of Peru and Mario García Menocal of Cuba. Eloy Alfaro is assassinated in Ecuador. In Argentina, the Ley Sáenz Peña establishes secret and mandatory vote. In Puerto Rico, the Partido Independentista is founded. United States armed forces land in Cuba to repress rebellion by blacks, also in Honduras and in Nicaragua, where occupation lasts until 1925.

In Mexico *Luz* is published, in Lima the daily *La Crónica*, in Buenos Aires *El Manifiesto* and *La Anarquía*, in Montevideo *Crónicas Subversivas, Solidaridad, Ideas*, in Santiago de Chile *El Productor*, in Rio de Janeiro *A Revolta*, and in Paris by R. Darío *Revista Mundial*. José de Maturana publishes *Canción de Primavera*; Pierre Quiroule *Sobre la ruta de la Anarquía*; Rafael Barrett, posthumously, *Mirando vivir, Al margen, Ideas y Críticas, Diálogos y conversaciones y otros escritos*; Pedro Pardo *La casa abandonada*; Rafael Villavicencio *La evolución*; J. Sánchez Gardel *La montaña de las brujas*; F. García Calderón *La creación de un continente*; A. Ortiz *El parnaso nicaragüense*; R. Uribe Uribe *De cómo el liberalismo no es pecado*; J. Capello *Los menguados*; Ortega Arancibia *40 años*; Luis Alberto de Herrera *El Uruguay internacional*.

1913 In Rio de Janeiro the second Congreso Operário Brasileiro convenes. José Bordas becomes president of the Dominican Republic, Gil Frotoul of Venezuela, M. Orested of Haiti. In El Salvador, Araujo is assassinated and the dictatorship of Meléndez begins. In Mexico, Madero is assassinated and dictatorship of Huerta begins. He is challenged by Carranza, Obregón, Villa, and Zapata.

In Buenos Aires, *El Obrero* is published, in Rosario *La Rebelión*, in Chacabuco *El Combate*, in Diamante (Chile) *Prometeo*, in Asunción *Hacia el Futuro*, in Santiago de Chile *La Batalla*, in Havana *Cultura Obrera*, in Aradas, Brazil *O Grito Social* and in Aveiro, Brazil *O Proletario*, and in Mexico *Lucha*. *La Protesta* resumes publication in Buenos Aires. José Ingenieros publishes *El hombre mediocre*; Udón Pérez *Anfora Criolla*; J. R. Pocaterra *Política feminista*; J. E. Rodó *El mirador de Próspero*; Delmira Agustini *Los cálidos vacíos*; R. Sierra *La dama de San Juan*; Dávalos y Lisson *Leguía*; R. Blanco Fombona *Dramas mínimos*; E. Crosa *La razón social*; and Leoncio Lasso de la Vega *El morral de un bohemio*. Edmundo Bianchi debuts his *Perdidos en la luz* and Alberto Ghiraldo *La columna de fuego*.

1914   In all Latin American countries anarchists declare themselves opposed to the war. In Buenos Aires, a workers' congress joins CORA, a syndicalist organization, and FORA, anarchist. In Porto Alegre, anarchists found the Liga Antimilitarista. In São Paulo a meeting of anarchist groups convenes. Flores Magón released from imprisonment seeks to give the Mexican Revolution a socialist and libertarian orientation.

Venceslau Brás becomes president of Brazil, Óscar Benavidez of Peru, Venustiano Carranza of Mexico, Oreste Zamor of Haiti, Márquez Bustillos of Venezuela. Panama Canal opens. U.S. Marines land in Veracruz and Port au Prince. Villa and Zapata fight Carranza.

La Casa del Obrero Mundial publishes *Emancipación Obrera* and is raided by police. *Tinta Roja* is published. In Lima, the newspaper *La Lucha* is published, in Puno *La Voz del Obrero*. Corrêa Lopes's libertarian publication *A Vida* begins its antiwar campaign. Pedro Prado publishes

La reina de Rapa Nui; Manuel Gálvez *La maestra normal*; J. Rosales *Bajo el cielo dorado*; A. Díaz Guerra *Lucas Guevara*; Vargas Vila *La muerte del condor*; A. Aquirre Morales *Flor de enseño*; R. Darío *Canto a la Argentina*; E. Arroyo Lameda *Momentos*; V. Huidobro *Manifiesto*; R. Arévalo Martínez *El hombre que parecía un caballo* and *El trovador colombiano*; and M.H. Escuder *El diablito del amor*.

1915   FORA's Ninth Congress convenes and a schism between anarchists and syndicalists follows. A Congreso Anarquista Sudamericano convenes in Rio de Janeiro. In Cuba, the anarchist press is outlawed and several Spanish militants are expelled. In Veracruz, anarchists sign a pact with Carranza's government and the Red Battalions are formed to provide him assistance. La Casa del Obrero Mundial extends into the interior and publishes the paper *Ariete*.

J. Pardo becomes president of Peru, Viera of Uruguay, S. Dartiguenave of Haiti, and Arévalo Cedeño moves against J. V. Gómez in Venezuela. ABC Treaty signed by Argentina, Brazil, and Chile. United States troops in Haiti and the Dominican Republic. In Peru, law adopted allowing religious liberty. In Cuba, the Unión Antillana is founded.

In Montevideo, *La Batalla* begins publication, later a voice of anarcho-Bolshevism. In Rosario, *Estudios* is published, in Paraná *Ideas*, in Campana *Voces Proletarias*. Alberto Ghiraldo publishes his book *La Ley Baldón*. Almafuerte publishes *Evangélicas*; R. Güiraldes *El cencerro de cristal*; B. Fernández Moreno *Las iniciales del misal*; C. González Peña *La fuga de la quimera*; Max Henriquez Ureña *Episodios dominicanos*; J. Braschi *La úlcera*; E. Barrios *El niño que enloqueció de amor*; R. Blanco Fombona *El hombre de oro*; A. Marasso *La canción olvidada*; and Ernesto Herrera *El caballo del comisario*.

1916   In Mexico, the Red Batallions are decommissioned, a Congreso Obrero Nacional is convened in Veracruz and from it emerges the anarcho-syndicalist Federación del

Trabajo de la Región Mexicana. La Casa del Obrero Mundial closes. Flores Magón is sentenced to 20 years in the United States for his anti-war position. In Argentina the anarchist FORA V confronts the syndicalist FORA IX.

Hipólito Yrigoyen becomes president of Argentina, José Luis Sanfuentes of Chile, R. Bentín of Peru, and Menocal, again, of Cuba. United States invades Dominican Republic. Pope Benedict XV issues a strong condemnation of Venezuelan dictator Juan Vicente Gómez.

In Santa Fe, *La Verdad* is published, in Mar de la Plata *El Grito del Pueblo*, in Bahía Blanca *Brazo y Cerebro*. Fernando Santiván publishes his novel *La hechizada*; R. López Velarde *La sangre devota*; R. Cardona *Oro de la mañana*; Benito Lynch *Los caranchos de la Florida*; Belisario Roldán *El rosal de las ruinas*; Manuel Gálvez *El mal metafísico*; Alfonsina Storni *La inquietud del rosal*; M. Brull *La casa del silencio*; P. Henriquez Ureña *El nacimiento de Dionisos*; L. M. Urbaneja Achelpohl *En este país*; Azuela *Los de abajo*; and Eguren *La canción de las figuras*.

1917   In Mexico, the group Luz is founded and a number of libertarian groups, like Solidaridad, Los Autónomous, Jóvenes socialistas rojos, and others. Luis Morones and pro-government reformists defeat anarchists at the second Congreso Obrero Nacional. General strike breaks out in São Paulo and Santos. Leuenroth jailed for his participation in those strikes, and is defended by Evaristo de Morais, who writes *O Anarquismo no Tribunal do Júri*.

Brazil enters the First World War. F. Tinoco is dictator of Costa Rica, and Venustiano Carranza, again, becomes president of Mexico. Peru and Uruguay sever relations with Germany. Puerto Rico becomes territory of the United States (Jones Act), and several thousand Puerto Ricans join European war.

In São Paulo, *A Plebe* is published, in Rio de Janeiro *O Debate*, in Alagoas *A Semana Social*. In Buenos Aires,

La Rivolta is published (in Italian), in San Juan *Humanidad*, in Junín *Nubes Rojas*, and in Bahía Blanca *Alba Roja*. Antillí and González Pacheco publish the weekly *La Obra* in Buenos Aires. Carlos Díaz releases *A Luta Socialista Revolucionaria*. José Vasconcelos publishes *El monismo estético*; Ricardo Rojas *Historia de la literatura argentina*; E. Berisso *Con las alas rotas*; Rafael Alberto Arrieta *Las noches de oro*; R. López Velarde *Zozobra*; C. Sabat Ercasty *Pantheos*; J. Torri *Ensayos y poemas*; J. M. Pichardo *Tierra adentro*; Alfonso Reyes *Visión de Anáhuac*; and Ureta *El dolor pensativo*.

1918   Mexican anarchists are in the minority in the Tercer Congreso Obrero Nacional de Saltillo, and Morones founds la Confederación Obrera Regional Mexicana (CROM). Brazilian anarchists form the Comitês Populares against scarcities. Oreste Ristori publishes the anticlerical newspaper El *Burro* in Buenos Aires, Del Intento publishes *Ideas* in La Plata.

Marco Fidel Suárez becomes president of Colombia. Students rail against the dictatorship in Venezuela. Rodrigues Alves becomes president of Brazil for a second time. University reform in Córdoba, Argentina. New constitution in Haiti. In Peru, law is adopted providing free and compulsory education. Horacio Quiroga publishes *Cuentos de la selva*; Vicente Huibdobro *Ecuatorial, Poemas árticos*; J. González Castillo *La mujer de Ulises*; F. Defilippis Novoa *El diputado de mi pueblo* Alfonsina Storni *El dulce daño*; Pedro M. Obligado *Gris*; J. M. Poveda *Versos precursores*; César Vallejo *Los heraldos negros*; J. R. Pocaterra *Tierra del sol amada*; J. E. Lossada *Madréporas*; Valdelomar *El caballero Belmonte*; and Azuela, *Las moscas*.

1919   La Semana Trágica occurs in Buenos Aires, after a strike promoted by FORA anarchist among metal workers. In Chile, anarcho-syndicalists found the IWW. Miners from Huanuni, Bolivia achieve the eight-hour day. Peruvian anarchists organize the hunger strike called Paro del hambre, as well as work stoppages in El Callao, Chosica, and other places. A reorganized FORP issues a declaration of principles and declares itself anarcho-syndicalist. FORU convenes 49 syndicates and federations. The Partido Communista Libertario is founded in Brazil.

Epitácio Pessoa becomes president of Brazil, J. Gutiérrez Guerra of Bolivia. Leguía is dictator in Peru. Zapata is killed in an ambush. Founding of the Partido Socialista in Colombia. General Peñaloza invades Venezuela and moves against the dictatorship of J. V. Gómez. Ch. Perlate rises in Haiti.

FORA publishes *Tribuna Proletaria*. The anarcho-Bolshevik daily *Bandera Roja* is published. *La Protesta* has some 15,000 subscribers. In Rio *Spartacus* and *O Germinal* are published, in Santa Fe *La Campaña*. González Pacheco publishes his book *Carteles*, and Edgard Leuenroth *O que é o maximalismo ou bolshevismo*. C. Iglésias Paz publishes *El Nuevo nupcial*; Julio Escobar *El hombre que sonríe*; Manuel Gálvez *Nacha Regules*; L. Vallenilla Lanz *Cesarismo democrático*; A. Zum Felde *Proceso histórico del Uruguay*; A. Nervo *La amada inmóvil*; Luis A. Sánchez *Los poetas de la revolución*; A. Hidalgo *Jardín zoológico*; and E. Crosa *El sagrado delito*.

1920   The anarchist FORA convenes an extraordinary congress with assistance of 200 workers' societies. In Santiago, Chilean "patriots" attack headquarters of the anarchist leaning Federación Estudiantil. A national workers' congress meeting in Lima adopts anarchist ideology. In Peru, popular universities Manuel González Prada are founded and are widely attended by libertarian workers. In Rio, the Third Brazilian Workers' Congress convenes with 150 delegates in attendance.

In Mexico, Carranza dies in Tlaxcalantongo, De la Huerta is interim president, and Alvaro Obregón is elected. Arturo Allesandri becomes president of Chile, J. L. Tamayo of Ecuador. A new constitution is adopted in Peru.

In Uruguay, a coup by followers of Fructuoso Rivera fails. In Venezuela, first petroleum law is adopted. A gradual and partial agrarian reform begins in Mexico.

In Ecuador, a group of anarchists found the Centro Gremial Sindicalista, and publishes *El Proletario*. In Rio, Oiticica and Fábio Luz publish *A Voz de Povo*, and the former publishes his critique of the Bolshevik revolution in a series of articles titled *Mau Caminho*. In Buenos Aires two newspapers favorable to the Bolshevik revolution are published, *Frente Proletario* and *Frente Unico*. González Pacheco publishes *El Libertario*, Astrologildo Pareira *A Greve de Leopoldina*, and Neno Vasco *Concepção Anarquista do Sindicalismo*. The antimilitarist *El Soldado* is published. In Asunción, Paraguay the libertarian newspaper *Renovación* appears and in São Paulo *A Patuieia*. Emilio Rabasa publishes *La evolución histórica de México*; González Castillo and Martínez Cuitiño *La santa madre*; Juana de Ibarbourou *Raíz salvaje*; Carmen Lyra *Los cuentos de mi tia Panchita*; J. Stefanich *Aurora*; A. L. Moock *La serpiente*; R. Gallegos *El último Solar*; F. Paz Castillo *La huerta de Doñana*; and A. Korn *La libertad creadora*.

1921 FORA supports the great strike at La Forestal in the Argentinian Chaco. Workers organized by anarchists in Patagonia are massacred by Argentinian army. In Mexico, anarchists and Marxists found the Confederación General de Trabajadores (CGT), with fifty syndicates, and within it the Centro Sindicalista Libertario (CSL) emerges.

J. Holguín becomes president of Colombia, A. Zayas of Cuba. An indigenous congress convenes in Peru. In Mexico Vasconcelos is appointed Minister of Education. Panamerican conference convenes in Havana. The Communist Party is founded in Argentina and Bolivia. In Uruguay the Socialist Party becomes the Communist Party.

In Rio de Janeiro the daily *A Vanguarda*, edited by Leuenroth, and Marques de Costa's journal *Renovação* are published. González Pacheco begins publication of the weekly *La Antorcha* and debuts his play *Hijos del Pueblo*. In the Argentinean city of General Pico *Pampa Libre* is published, in Buenos Aires *El Sol*, in Montevideo *Trabajo*, *La Ruta*, *Tribuna Libertaria* and *Ideas y Estudios*. José Martí publishes *Historia das Riquezas do Clero Católico e Protestante*.

D. Moreno Jiménes publishes *Psalmos*, J. L. Bengoa, *Los sacrificados*; Andrés Eloy Blanco *Tierras que me oyeron*; F. Silva Valdés *Agua del tiempo*; C. Wyld Ospina *Las dádivas simple*; R. Hurtado *La hora de ámbar*; A. Fernández García *Bucares en flor*; Valdelomar *Los hijos del sol*; and De la Riva Agüero *El Perú histórico y artístico*.

1922 Flores Magón dies in a North American prison. The Mexican CGT declares itself antipolitical and confronts the Partido Communista. Anarchists organize a tenants's strike in Mexico City and Veracruz. The Second Congress of the CGT convenes. FORA IX and some unions of FORA V form the Unión Sindical Argentina. The Unión Obrera Salvadoreña is founded and anarcho-syndicalists are in the majority. Also founded is the Federación Obrera de La Habana, predominantly anarcho-syndicalist.

A. Benardes becomes president of Brazil, Marcelo T. de Alvear of Argentina, P. Ospina of Colombia, L. Borno of Haiti, J. B. Vicini of the Dominican Republic. First oil well is drilled in Zulia. Venezuela must cede a large portion of the Goajira peninsula to Colombia, pursuant to Swiss arbitration.

In São Paulo's *A Plebe*, a manifesto rejecting "el communism de Estado" is published. In Guayaquil the libertarian publication *Redención* is published, in Tandil *La Verdad*, in Ingeniero White *Mar y tierra*, in Necochea *Nuestra Tribuna*. Ghiraldo publishes *La Argentina: Estado social de un pueblo*; Oliverio Girondo *Veinte poemas para ser leidos en el tranvía*; Salomón de la Selva *El Soldado desconocido*;

César Vallejo *Trilce*; R. Heliodoro Valle *Anfora sedienta*; Antonio Caso; *Discursos a la nación Mexicana*; A. Cancela *Tres relatos porteños*; J. C. Dávados *El viento blanco*; E. Rivera Chevremont *La copa de Hebe*; A. Martínez Mutis *Mármol*; Gabriela Mistral *Desolación*; A. Cruchaga Santa María *Job*; E. Fariña Núñez *Cármenes*; and J. R. Pocaterra *Cuentos Grotescos*.

1923   CGT confronts police, debates Obregón, and resists a lock out in Veracruz. The Alianza Local Mexicana Anarquista (ALMA) is founded. CGT joins IWA recently founded in Berlin and convenes its Third Congress. The anarchist Kurt Wilckens executes Colonel Varela, who was responsible for the massacre of workers in Patagonia. In Bolivia, the anarchist groups Despertar and La Antorcha are founded. A group of anarcho-syndicalists in Peru organizes the Federación Regional de Obreros Indios.

A Conferencia Panamericana is convened in Chile. Haya de la Torre begins his political activities and is deported from Peru. The centenary of national independence is celebrated in Brazil.

Flores Magón's collection of stories *Sembrando ideas* is published. In Buenos Aires the anarcho-Bolshevik paper *El Libertario* in published, in Montevideo *El Hacha*, and in Caracas *Fantoches*. José Valdés publishes *Poesía pura*; A. Hidalgo *Química del espiritu*; Armando Discépolo *Mateo*; Horacio Rega Molina *El árbol fragante*; José Pedroni *Gotas de Agua*; Luis Felípe Rodríguez *La Pascua de la tierra natal*; J. L. Borges *Fervor de Buenos Aires*; Honorario Delgado *Rehumanización de la cultura científica por la psicología*; Andrés Eloy Blanco *Canto a España*; and E. Barrios *Páginas de un pobre diablo*.

1924   In Panama, a group of anarcho-syndicalists promotes the founding of the Sindicato General de Trabajo. In Mexico, the CGT organizes a textile strike. Calles becomes president of Mexico, Ayala of Paraguay, G. Córdova of Ecuador, Chiari of Panama, R. Jímenez of Costa Rica, and H. Vásquez of the Dominican Republic. In Venezuela, concessions are made to U.S. oil companies.

In Mexico *Nueva Solidaridad Obrera* is published, in Monterrey *Alba Anárquica*, in Guadalajara *Verbo Rojo*, in Avellaneda *Renovación*, in Santa Fe *Orientación*, in Montevideo *El Sembrador* and *Ahora*. In Buenos Aires *Martín Fierro* is published. González Pacheco debuts his drama *Herrmano Lobo*. In prison, Oiticica writes *A Doutrina Anarquista ao Alcance de Todos*. Two social dramas, *Tierra y Libertad* and *Verdugos y Víctimas*, and a collection of stories, *Rayos de luz,* by Flores Magón are published.

Pablo Neruda publishes *Veinte poemas de amor y una canción desesperada*; Ricardo Rojas *Eurindia*; Benito Lynch *El ingles de los güesos*; Conronado Nalé Roxlo *El Grillo*; Fermín Estrella Gutiérrez *En cántaro de plata*; Teresa de la Parra *Ifigenia*; Eustacio Rivera *La vorágine*; V. García Calderón *La venganza del condor*; Tristán Maroff *Suetonio Pimienta*; and A. Arráiz *Aspero*, González Lanuza *Prismas*.

1925 In Santiago, Chile anarchists promote a tenants' strike, and found the Federación Sindical, centered in the northern part of the country. In Cuba, the Partido Communista and the Confederación Nacional Obrera are founded, in the latter anarchists are in the majority. The Mexican CGT supports the great oil strike in El Aguila, the textile strikes in Valle de Mexico, and the "red" bakers in the national capital.

H. Síles becomes president of Bolivia, G. Machado of Cuba. In Venezuela, the national constitution is once again reformed and the trans-Andean highway is inaugurated.

In Santa Marta, Colombia the anarchist newspaper *Organización* is published, and in Tucumán *Tierra Libre*. The anarchism of Vargas Vila is discussed in the *Revista Blanca* from Barcelona. Raúl Contreras publishes *La princesa está triste*; Elías Castelnuovo *Entre los muertos*; J. A. Ramos Sucre *La torre de Timón*; Jorge Luis Borges *Inquisiciones*;

R. Mariani *Cuentos de oficina*; R. Jijena Sánchez *Achalay*; L. de Greiff *Tergiversaciones*; A. Hidalgo *Simplismo*; Alfonsina Storni *Ocre*; R. Gallegos *La Trepadora*; Natalicio González *Baladas Guaraníes*; Norah Lange *La calle de la tarde*; Felisberto Hernández *Fulano de Tal*; and J. Vasconcelos *La raza cósmica*.

1926   Anarchists in Bolivia found the Federación Obrera Local (FOL) in La Paz. In Guatemala City the Comité Pro Acción Sindical, led by anarcho-syndicalists, begins operations. The Mexican CGT comprising 108 syndicates, 23 unios, 13 groups, 9 federations, and 4 agrarian communities convenes its Fifth Congress and adopts anarcho-syndicalism.

Washington Luís becomes president of Brazil, M. Abadía Méndez of Colombia, Isidro Ayora of Ecuador, Adolfo Díaz of Nicaragua. Sandino rises against the U.S. occupation. In Mexico, Catholic fanatics begin the Guerra Cristera.

In Barranquilla, Colombia *Vía Libre* is published, in Guatemala City *Orientación Sindicalista,* in Rosario *Libre Acuerdo*, in Buenos Aires *La Piqueta* and *Bezviastie* (in Hungarian), in Montevideo *El Esfuerzo*, and in Mexico *Horizontes*. In Lima, Peru Mariátegui publishes the journal *Amauta*.

Elías Castelnuovo publishes his play *Almas benditas*; Alvaro Yunque his stories *Barcos de papel* and *Zancadillas*. Agustín Acosta publishes *La Zafra*; G. Estrada *Pero Galín*; Ricardo Güiraldes *Don Segundo Sombra*; V. Martínez Cuitiño *Café con leche*; A. Spelucín *El libro de la nave dorada*; M. Rojas *Hombres del sur*; L. Cardoza y Aragón *Maelstrom*; R. González Tuñón *El violin del Diablo*; C. Mastronardi *Tierra amanecida*; M. Briceño Iragorri, *Lecturas venezolanas*.

1927   The Mexican CGT holds a general strike in solidarity with railroad workers. Demonstrations are held throughout Latin America in opposition to the execution of Sacco and Vanzetti.

C. I. Ibáñez becomes president of Chile, P. Romero Bosque of El Salvador. In Guatemala the Liga Antiimperialista is founded. In Mexico, Guerra Cristera continues.

In Santa Fe *La Obra* is published, in Colón, Argentina *Abriendo Cancha*, in Cerro, Uruguay *Luz y Vida*, in Montevideo the bilingual *Voluntad-Volontá*.

Fernando del Intento publishes *Libro del Hombre*; Florentino de Carvalho *Da Escravidão a Liberdade*; and González Pacheco debuts *A contramano*. L. Barletta publishes *Royal Circo*; R. Arévalo Martínez *Las rosas de Engaddi*; J. Germendía *La tiendo de muñecos*; J. Torres Bodet *Margarita de Niebla*; R. Molinari *El imaginero*; and J. R. Pocaterra *Memorias de un venezolano de la decadencia*.

1928   The Mexican CGT supports strikes by textiles workers in Río Blanca and Ericsson telephone workers. In Buenos Aires FORA convenes its Tenth Congress with attendance by one hundred syndicates. In Colombia, anarchists lead the great banana strike in Magdalena and are violently repressed in the Ciénaga massacre.

Obregón is reelected president of Mexico, Machado of Cuba, and in Argentina Yrigoyen assumes the presidency for a second time. In Caracas, students rise against the dictatorship, and many of them are jailed. A new constitution is adopted in Venezuela.

In Buenos Aires the publication *Palote* appears, and in Punta Alta, Argentina the monthly journal *Impulso*. González Pacheco debuts his play *El hombre de la plaza pública*. Alías Castelnuovo publishes *En nombre de Cristo*; Macedonio Fernández *No toda es vigília de los ojos abierto*; M. L. Gúzman *El águila y la serpiente*; Jenaro Prieto *El socio*; J. Edwards Bello *El chileno en Madrid*; R. Blanco Fombona *Tragedias grotescas*; R. G. González Tuñón *Miercoles de ceniza*; and J. C. Mariátegui *7 ensayos de interpretación de la realidad peruana*.

1929   Some of the syndicates aligned to CROM go over to the

CGT, which increases to some 80,000 members. In Brazil, anarcho-syndicalists join CNT, affiliated with ACAT, which had just been established in Buenos Aires. Ortiz Rubio becomes president of Mexico, Moncada of Nicaragua, Mejía Colindres of Honduras, Leguía, again, of Peru. Delgado Chalbaud invades Venezuela through Cumaná and Urbina through Coro. Unsuccessfully Gabaldón rises in Portuguesa and Borges in Miranda.

In Buenos Aires, the journal *Elevación* is published. Ghiraldo publishes his *Yanquilandia bárbara*; Armando Discépolo *Stéfano*; Ricardo Miró *Caminos silenciosos*; J. A. Ramos *Sucre: El cielo de esmalte* and *Las formas del fuego*; R. Gallegos *Doña Bárbara*; Teresa de la Parra, *Memorias de la Mamá Blanca*; R. Arlt *Los siete locos*; A. Orrego *El monólogo eterno*; and Pereda Valdés *Raza negra*.

1930　In San Salvador, the Centro Sindical Libertario is operating. FORA membership rises to over 100,000 members. The Uriburu dictatorship unleashes a brutal persecution of anarchists in Argentina and, in Rosario, executes Joaquín Penina. Hundreds of militants are exiled or imprisoned in Ushuaia. In Argentina, a military coup by Uriburu topples Yrigoyen. Getúlio Vargas becomes president of Brazil, J. Guaggiari of Panama, E. Olaya Herrera of Columbia, Stenio Vincent of Haiti, R. L. Trujillo of the Dominican Republic, and Siles resigns as president of Bolivia. Sánchez Cerro defeats Leguía in Peru, and APRA is founded there.

The Confederación Obrera Regional Boliviana is founded and publishes its newspaper *La Protesta*. Federação Operária de São Paulo anarcho-syndicalists organize a major textile strike and many are jailed. In Santa Fe the newspaper *Verbo Prohibido* is published clandestinely. Elías Castenuovo publishes his novel *Carne de cañón*; and D. A. de Santillán publishes *El movimiento anarquista en la Argentina*. Justo P. Sáenz publishes *Baguales*; Ricardo Molinari *Panegírico*; H. Robleto *Sangre en el tropic*; A. Alvarez Lleras *Ayer, nada más*; M. A. Asturias *Leyendas de Guatemala*; G. Casaccia *Hombres, mujeres y fantoches*; and Drummond de Andrade *Alguma poesía*.

1931 The anarchist Federación Obrera de La Habana promotes a strike among agricultural workers that lasts seven months, and supports another strike by transportation workers lasting one and a half months. Some of the leadership of the CGT accepts the new Código de Trabajo promoted by Ortíz Rubio, but others are opposed, like Huitrón. In Buenos Aires, the dictatorship executes Severino Di Giovanni and Paulino Scarfó. An anarcho-syndicalist group in Chile founds the Conferación General de Trabajadores (CGT). In Venezuela, anarchist tendencies dominate the clandestine oil workers' syndicate SAMOP. Jorge Ubico rises as dictator of Guatemala, and in Venezuela the Gómez government pursues the seventh constitutional reform.

Arturo Capdevila publishes *Las vísperas de Caseros*; Scalabrini Ortíz *El hombre que está solo y espera*; H. Rega Molina *Azul de mapa*; A. Hernández Catá *Manicomio*; N. Guillén *Sóngoro Cosongo*; J. Marín Cañas *Memorias de un hombre triste*; A. Uslar Pietri *Las lanzas coloradas*; R. Arcíniega *Engranajes*; R. Arlt *Los lanzallamas*; and A. Carpentier *¡Ecué-Yamba-O!*

1932 Agustín P. Justo becomes president of Argentina, Juan E. Montero of Chile, Eusebio Ayala of Paraguay, Abelardo Rodríguez of Mexico. Chaco War is fought between Paraguay and Bolivia. In Rosario, a Congreso Anarquista Nacional convenes and from it emerges the Comité Regional de Relaciones Anarquistas (CORA). FORA renews its activities.

Under the direction of Santillán, *La Protesta* begins a new period, and with Juan Lazarte publishes the book *Reconstrucción social – Bases para una nueva edificación económica argentina*. E. Acedevo Díaz publishes *Ramón Hazaña*; E. Larreta *El linyera*; R. Artl *El amor brujo*; and G. Arciniegas *El estudiante de la mesa redonda*.

Appendix A: Chronology

1933   Dictatorship of Tiburcio Carías begins in Honduras. Batista leads the Sergeants Revolt in Cuba. Argentina and United Kingdom enter into the Roca-Runciman Pact. US troops withdraw from Haiti. Dictatorship of Gabriel Terra begins in Uruguay. While opposed by communists, La Federación Obrera de La Habana lends its support for a general strike against Machado. La Federación de Grupos Anarquistas de Cuba publishes a manifesto against the dictatorship. In Buenos Aires *Acción Libertaria* begins publication. Diego Abad de Santillán publishes *La FORA*; Fernando Santiván *Confesiones de Enrique Samaniego*; Ricardo Rojas *El santo de la espada*; Arturo Capdevila *La santa furia del padre Castañeda*; E. Martínez Estrada *Radiografía de la pampa*; C. Uribe Piedrahita *Toá*; Salarrué *Cuentos de barro*; A. Pareja Diez-Canseco *El muelle*; F. Espínola *Sombras sobre la tierra*; and R. Alt *El jorobadito*.

1934   Lázaro Cárdenas elected president of Mexico and Velasco Ibarra of Ecuador. Luís Carlos Prestes leads an uprising in Rio de Janeiro. In Uruguay a new constitution gives the executive branch broad powers. In Buenos Aires the journal *Nervio* begins publication. Elías Castelnuovo publishes *Vidas proletarias*; María Lacerda de Moura *Fraternidade na Escola*; A. Malfatti and N. de las Llanderas *Así es la vida*; G. Meneses *La balandra Isabel llegó esta tarde*; J. Fabbiani Ruiz *Valle hondo*; J. de la Cuadra *Los Sangurimas*; J. Icaza *Huasipungo*; and E. Amorim *El paisano Aguilar*.

1935   Cuban anarchists struggle against the new dictatorship of Batista. The second Congreso Anarquista Nacional convenes in secret in La Plata and forms the Federación Anarco-Comunista Argentina (FACA). J. V. Gómez dies and E. López Contreras succeeds him as president of Venezuela. Chaco War ends in great part due to Saavedra Lamas, foreign minister of Argentina.

José Portogalio publishes *Tregua*; E. Maella, *Historia de una pasion argentina*; J. L. Borges *Historia universal de la infamia* and *Ficciones*; R. Gallegos *Canaima*; F. Henao Toro *Eugeni la pelotari*; J. A. Ramos *La leyenda de las estrellas*; Juan Bosch *Indios*; B. Arias Trujillo *Risaralda*; Ciro Alegría *La serpiente de oro*; and José María Arguedas *Agua.*

1936 Argentinian, Mexican, Uruguayan, and other Latin American anarchists collaborate with CNT-FAI and fight against fascism in Spain. In Buenos Aires Solidaridad Internacional Antifascista and Comisión de Ayuda al Pueblo Español are founded. David Toro becomes president of Bolivia. February Revolution in Paraguay and R. Franco becomes president. Somoza dictatorship begins in Nicaragua. The Conferencia Interamericana convenes in Buenos Aires. In Caracas ORVE and PRP are founded.

The second series of González Pacheco's *Carteles* is published and his play *Compañeros* is debuted. Alvaro Yunque writes *España 1936*. D. A. de Santillán publishes *El organismo económico de la revolución*. Articles on social themes by González Prada are published in a volume title *Anarquía*. J. José Morosoli publishes *Los albañiles de "Los Tapes"*; José Rubén Romero publishes *Mi caballo, mi perro y mi rifle*; Agustín Acosta *Los camellos distantes*; Alcides Greca *La pampa gringa*; Samuel Eichelbaum *El gato y su selva*; R. Alt *El fabricante de fantasmas*; J. L. Borges *Historia de la eternidad*; R. Díaz Sánchez *Mene*; and A. Céspedes *Sangre de mestizos.*

1937 In Brazil there is a new constitution, and start of the dictatorial period Estado Novo. Dictatorship of G. Bush begins in Bolivia. In Peru the Ley de Defensa Social is enacted.

FACA publishes *Documentos Históricos de España*. González Pacheco starts the Compañia de teatro del pueblo in Barcelona. César Tiempo publishes *Pan criollo*; M. Latorre *Hombres y zorros*; J. Lezama Lima *Muerte de Narciso*; Max Jiménez *El jaul*; Octavio Paz *Raíz del hombre*; A. Guzmán *Prisionero de Guerra.*

1938 FACA's first congress convenes. Roberto M. Ortiz is elected president of Argentina and Pedro Aquirre Cerda of Chile.

Ghiraldo publishes *Cancionero libertario*; Arturo Capdevila *Las invasions inglesas*; L. Marechal *Cinco poemas australes*; L. Lugones Romances del *Río Seco*; F. L. Bernárdez *La ciudad sin Laura*; Gabriela Mistral *Tala*; and E. Aguiar *Eusebio Sapote*.

1939 Latin American anarchists condemn Nazi aggression and all forms of totalitarianism. J. F. Estigarribia elected president of Paraguay and M. Prad Ugarte of Peru.

In Buenos Aires FACA publishes Juan Lazarte and José Maguid's *Definición de la guerra*. Ricardo Rojas publishes *Ollantay*; S. Nolasco *Cuentos del sur*; X. Villaurutia *Nostalgia de la muerte*; and M. Otero Silva *Fiebre*.

1940 FACA's second congress convenes. Enrique Peñaranda is elected president of Bolivia, H. Morinigo of Paraguay, Avila Camacho of Mexico, C. A. Arroyo del Río of Ecuador, and Fulgencio Batista of Cuva.

In Buenos Aires the publication *Hombre de América* appears, it has an obvious libertarian orientation but is open to all antifascist writers. José Gaos publishes *Dos ideas de la filosofía*; E. Martínez Estrada *La cabeza de Goliath*; T. Carella *Don Basilio mal casado*; E. Mallea *La bahía del silencio*; L. Marechal *Sonetos a Sofía*; and A Bioy Casares *La invención de Morel*.

Appendix B: Texts

The following titles comprise the entirety of the Spanish edition of *El Anarquismo en America Latina*. They are arranged by country, from south to north.

Diego Abad de Santillán
The State and Liberty
The Economic Organism of the Revolution, Chapters 1–7.
Notes on a Dilemma in Anarchism
Reason and Revolution
On Justice and Liberty

Emilio López Aragón
DOCTRINE, TACTICS, AND AIMS OF THE WORKERS' MOVEMENT
    Resistance to Capitalism
    Ideas and Systems
    The Innovative Mania
    Means of Struggle
    The Miraculous Virtue of Syndicalism
    Revolutionary Syndicalism
    Syndicalism and Anarchism
    The Workers' Movement and Doctrinal Differences

Appendix B: Texts

Appendix B: Texts

Francisco Pezoa
SONG OF THE PAMPA

Manuel González Prada
ANARCHY

    Anarchy
    Universal Holiday
    The Anarchist's Duty
    The State
    Authority
    The Beginning
    The Sword
    Change in Tactics
    Reaping Rewards
    In Barcelona
    The Intellectual and the Worker
    Teutonic Ferocity
    The First of May
    Follies
    In Free England (Alien's Act of 1905)
    Socialism and Anarchy
    Strikes
    Soldier's Rebellion
    The First of May (1907)
    The Usefulness of Rebels
    Antipolitics
    Revolution
    José Nackens
    The First of May (1908)
    Individual Action
    In Spain
    Chicago's Crime
    Police
    Luisa Michel
    The Two Nations

Appendix B: Texts

Index

Index

Index

Index

O

Index

AK Press is small, in terms of staff and resources, but we also manage to be one of the world's most productive anarchist publishing houses. We publish close to twenty books every year, and distribute thousands of other titles published by like-minded independent presses and projects from around the globe. We're entirely worker-run and democratically managed. We operate without a corporate structure—no boss, no managers, no bullshit.

The Friends of AK program is a way you can directly contribute to the continued existence of AK Press, and ensure that we're able to keep publishing books like this one! Friends pay $25 a month directly into our publishing account ($30 for Canada, $35 for international), and receive a copy of every book AK Press publishes for the duration of their membership! Friends also receive a discount on anything they order from our website or buy at a table: 50% on AK titles, and 20% on everything else. We have a Friends of AK ebook program as well: $15 a month gets you an electronic copy of every book we publish for the duration of your membership. You can even sponsor a very discounted membership for someone in prison.

Email friendsofak@akpress.org for more info, or visit the Friends of AK Press website: https://www.akpress.org/friends.html

There are always great book projects in the works—so sign up now to become a Friend of AK Press, and let the presses roll!